To those who, at the most difficult of times, find and create
ways to talk, to cooperate, to keep talking, to resolve differences,
to honor agreement—peacemakers all.

M. Arden Hauer

ACKNOWLEDGMENTS

This 8th edition of the *Friendly Divorce Guidebook* has benefited immeasurably from the dedicated and expert work of its editor Candace Boyle. Her wise questioning and tireless assistance have contributed immeasurably to the quality of this project. Thank you, Candace for your insightful editorial comments and encouragement, and for being available for discussion of everything from the big picture concept of the book to the smallest detail, making our work together enjoyable and always interesting.

Thank you to Christine Chambers for your work in typography and graphics, and for your dedication to making every page appear attractive and balanced for ease of reading.

M. Arden Hauer

The concept for this Guidebook began as a small procedural booklet written by Wendy Whicher, one of the original co-authors of this *Friendly Divorce Guidebook for Colorado.* This Guidebook is the result of two talented authors, Arden Hauer and Wendy Whicher, who spent three years pouring helpful words onto the pages of this book. They shared their many, many years of experience and knowledge so that each reader could find their way through a difficult time, and build a better future for themselves and their children.

Although Wendy no longer participates in the authorship of this book, we wish her the very best as she moves on to other things that she loves.

We would like to express our heartfelt thanks to Arden Hauer, who continues to dedicate many hours to updating this book and for keeping it in the non-adversarial sprit that it is written. We are very grateful for the substantial part she has always played and for accepting the role of sole author.

CONTENTS

INTRODUCTION

Welcome to the *Friendly Divorce Guidebook: How to Do Your Own Divorce in Colorado*, which is in fact the eighth edition of the *Friendly Divorce Guidebook for Colorado.* We changed the name slightly to make it easier to find for those who seek the assistance it provides. The ever-changing terrain of divorce law and procedure, and now the emergence of another domestic relationship, the Designated Beneficiary, are behind the need for what now totals eight editions in sixteen years. Again we revise in order to keep our commitment to you to provide accurate and current information for doing your own divorce or legal separation in our beautiful state.

"From pro's and con's they fell to a warmer way of disputing." Miguel de Cervantes, *Don Quixote*.

This edition is updated for changes in forms and procedures since 2007 through the 2012 Legislature, and federal tax changes through 2012. Instead of a CD in the back of the book, purchasers will find instructions and a code that allows free online access to the forms you will need to file for divorce in Colorado. These fillable forms are available in both PDF and Word template format. We've adjusted the number of days for deadlines to conform with statutory changes and Supreme Court directives. The decades old 90-day waiting period is now 91 days. We have expanded the sample wording for your separation agreement and parenting plan in Chapter 12 to illustrate a greater variety of options. We've added information about the Colorado Designated Beneficiary Agreement Act, effective July 1, 2009 (chapters 1 and 2 and Appendix E), which creates a new form of domestic relationship that is not only available to some who may not marry, but also offers an alternative for those considering marriage. Information that we added starting in the 5th edition about the ending of a living together relationship, regardless of sexual orientation, where a couple ceases to be partners, and where the law and procedure is sometimes the same as, and in many places significantly different from that for dissolution of marriage, continues in this edition.

Same Sex Marriage

Voters amended the Constitution of the State of Colorado in 2006 to bar marriage and common law marriage between same sex partners, and also to bar the recognition of such marriages from other jurisdictions. There is currently no legal remedy in Colorado for such spouses who need to divorce or legally separate.

Colorado voters rejected a proposed domestic partnership law in 2006, which would have provided the equivalent of marriage and divorce for same sex couples. The Legislature rejected civil unions legislation in 2012.

The main body of this work continues to be about legal marriage, divorce, and legal separation in Colorado. Information for "partners" is set apart with the partners icon, as explained below.

This Guidebook is particularly useful in conjunction with mediation. You and your mediator can work through this book together. It also provides useful information for people whose attorneys are negotiating for them, and who want to better understand and participate in their own settlement process. It can also be used by the spouse who is alone, where the other spouse cannot participate in the process because he or she has disappeared, is ill or otherwise unavailable.

You can read the Guidebook chapter by chapter, in order, going through every step in the contemporary, amicable Colorado divorce. You can also begin anywhere in it. Each chapter contains a complete topic. Look up specific questions as they occur to you. You can use the index and treat this book like an encyclopedia.

This Guidebook can also be used for specific stages on the long road to being single. Pick it up as needed over time as your situation changes. For example, when you are just starting out and everything is too raw and confusing to even contemplate an entire divorce, just read the beginning chapters, especially Chapter 3 Taking Care of Yourself, and Chapter 4 Moving From One Household to Two. If you are ready to divorce or legally separate and eager to begin, read Chapters 5 through 12 if you have children or Chapters 5 through 7 and 10 through 12 if you do not have children. If you are concerned about whether your final agreement will be kept or how changes in your life will be affected, read Chapters 2 and 13.

"There is truly a magical quality about conflict which can call out the best in us, that which is not summoned under ordinary circumstances." Thomas F. Crum, *The Magic of Conflict.*

As a practical matter, it takes two to have a marriage, and only one to have a divorce. Either spouse, or both, may opt out of the marriage, and there is no legal penalty for being the one who makes this choice. Regardless of who is making the choice to end the marriage, you each continue to have options about how to carry it out. The choice to end the marriage does not control the manner in which you go about it. This Guidebook shows you how to end your marriage in a cooperative way—which can be a sound foundation for the next part of your life.

"When they [people] no longer trust themselves, they begin to depend upon authority." Lao-Tzu, *Tao Te Ching.*

This Guidebook is not likely to be useful in litigation—a trial in court. Cooperation and the adversarial process have very different consequences, although the results may be the same. The terms of a privately developed or a mediated agreement may be virtually identical to those a court would order, or lawyers would negotiate for you. It is possible that these methods might arrive at the same outcome for property division, parental responsibilities, child support and maintenance as a mediated agreement, but each method has very different emotional consequences. In the court-ordered divorce, the terms are dictated to the parties by the judge, based on law and precedent. In the lawyer-negotiated settlement, the provisions are likely to be given to the parties as law or legally-acceptable compromise. The parties may not fully understand the terms—they may feel ambivalent about them and each other, and they are statistically less likely to carry them out as written. Privately developed and mediated agreements which come from the parties themselves are more likely to be honored because the parties understand, endorse and are committed to, each provision.

This book contains

- Discussion of divorce and its alternatives (Chapter 1).
- A list of all the facts and figures you must collect in order to undertake and conclude a fair and complete settlement (Chapter 6).
- A helpful outline of how to plan your separation, and make other temporary arrangements and agreements (Chapter 4).
- An overview of divorce and the legal system, and the role of law in your divorce agreement (Chapter 2).
- Information about some of the indirect results of divorce in areas such as taxes and credit (Chapters 7, 11 and 13).
- Information about Case Management procedures necessary to obtain a dissolution of marriage (a divorce) or legal separation in Colorado (Chapters 2, 5, 6, and 12).
- Copies of the court forms and instructions for filling them out (Chapters 5, 6, and 12).
- Instructions on obtaining your final Decree (Chapter 12).
- Instructions on how to transfer title to property between you, and how to put into effect other aspects of your agreement (Chapters 7 and 13).
- Occasional information about partners in similar or parallel situations (throughout).

The Guidebook format combines a complete discussion of each topic with illustrative examples, charts, checklists, questionnaires, resources and full-size sample forms. There is a bibliography at the end, and the major technical, legal, and tax terms used in the divorce process are defined in sidebars throughout the book.

We have incorporated certain icons in the text to set apart categories of information.

IR$ Indicates tax information

CAUTION is a caution, or something of particular importance not to be overlooked;

"My spouse won't give me a divorce."

You don't need each other's permission to get a legal divorce. If either of you declares to the court in a written petition that the marriage is irretrievably broken, you have established sufficient legal grounds for the divorce process to begin. This does not prevent you from working together to complete it.

"This Guidebook is the only help you will need with your divorce."

This is not true. In addition to the information provided in this Guidebook, you may need to consult with an attorney, a counselor or therapist, accountant, appraiser, pastor, family and friends in order to be able to make clear and wise choices yourself.

is a warning about something with dire consequences;

indicates the definition of a legal term;

indicates information for partners, those in relationships without marriage; including those in same sex marriages, civil unions, or domestic partnerships from others states, and designated beneficiaries in matters not covered by the Revocation of Designated Beneficiary Agreement.

Lastly, we introduce Bunky:

A Bunky is an opinion or belief that is, in whole or part, not quite accurate. Some are more fiction than fact. Bunkies abound in the area of marital difficulty and divorce. We discuss many of these widespread views in order to "debunk" the inaccuracies that can really cause harm, as well as to clarify what is true.

Our purpose is to provide the information you will need as you go through the divorce process. This Guidebook is not a substitute for a lawyer's advice to you about your particular situation. Remember, you are legally responsible for whatever assumptions and agreements you make in your divorce, so be sure you obtain all the information and advice you need in order to be secure in your choices. Do not rely on your spouse to do this for you.

This Guidebook is designed to give you a broad and detailed sweep of the cooperative divorce process. It will help you gather all the data you will need to consider, and organize it so that you can make informed decisions. It will assist you in developing an agreement that makes optimal sense of your situation now and into the future.

CHAPTER 1

THE INITIAL DECISION

How Do You Know if You Should Get a Divorce?

THE INITIAL DECISION

How Do You Know if You Should Get a Divorce?

Every marriage ends in either death or divorce.

Most of us said "Till death us do part" when we married, and meant it. The prospect of divorce is unsettling and threatening as an earthquake for some of us; the welcome end of an intolerable situation for others; somewhere between these two extremes for most. Throughout this critical time, both what you do and especially how you do it are important to the present and future well-being of you and everyone in your family.

Violence and Abuse

If your marriage is experiencing physical or serious emotional abuse it is important to get physically separated as soon as possible—regardless of what you are deciding about legal separation or divorce.

If you need help with this, you can call your local police or sheriff's office and ask for Victim's Assistance or the Domestic Violence Unit. Most communities have a domestic violence victim's assistance organization that will help every step of the way, from providing a Safehouse, to reporting, investigation, and trial. Many will help you terminate an abusive marriage or relationship with free or low-cost legal advice.

Options for the Marriage in Difficulty

When a marriage begins to experience significant difficulty, it sometimes seems impossible to step back and take a serious and rational look at the possible alternatives. Some of the available options are marriage counseling and the possibility of reconciling (staying together and working on the relationship); marital mediation; physical separation (often called trial separation); legal separation; dissolution of marriage (divorce); or annulment. Following is a short discussion of each of these.

Marriage Counseling

Every spouse thinks about separation and divorce once in awhile. Is the cause of your current marital discord a single incident or an acknowledged problem? Do you both want to stay married if you can resolve the difficulty? If so, you might want to hold off on any legal filing and seek marriage counseling.

How to Find a Marriage Counselor

- Get a referral from a friend you trust who can make a recommendation based on personal experience.
- Ask your therapist, mediator, lawyer, social worker, or pastor to make a recommendation.
- Search the Internet for the following:
  Marriage and Family Counseling
  Psychotherapists
  Psychologists
  Divorce Services
- Inquire at your local mental health center.

Some common marital problems which can be helped through marriage counseling are:

- Situation stress: loss of job, death of a loved one, major illness or injury of a family member, new child, disabled child, or elderly relative in the home, child at difficult age or sudden major expenses.
- Ongoing quarrels over money, or difficulty in budgeting.
- Addictions, such as alcohol, gambling, drugs.
- Sexual dissatisfaction or dysfunction: this is often a specialty within the field of marriage counseling. If this is the type of problem you are experiencing, ask specifically about expertise in this area during your first contact with any professional you are considering.

If you are thinking of divorce, it is a good idea to explore all reasonable possibilities for continuing the marriage—so you're not plagued with guilt later. Marriage counseling can be of help with this, regardless of whether you decide to continue your marriage.

Marital Mediation

Mediation is a process for resolving conflict and coming to agreement. A mediator helps you reach your own agreement. Mediation can be appropriate for clearing things up so that the marriage can continue, or for reaching an agreement for separation or divorce. If you are looking at staying married and doing some problem solving, mediation can be particularly helpful. In marital mediation, it is not unusual for couples to enter into marital agreements which contain understandings about money management and house rules similar to those in pre-marital agreements.

Marital mediation will help you reach your own agreement based on your unique needs. You can use marital mediation as much or as little as you need. You may only need help in clarifying an understanding you already have. You may need help in learning how to bargain collaboratively, or in understanding a complex financial situation.

Some common marital problems which are especially appropriate for marital mediation are:

- Ongoing money problems.
- Major changes in fortune, such as finishing school and getting the first big job, significant inheritance, losing one's job.
- Addictions, such as alcohol, gambling, drugs.
- Changes in family structure: new baby, in-law moving in, children leaving home, illness or injury requiring long term attention, retirement.

Be sure you look for a mediator who specializes in family matters. See Chapter 2 for information about mediation for divorce.

Physical Separation (Trial Separation)

Most people use this term to mean getting physically—especially sexually—away from each other. In most cases, one spouse moves out. Some people separate within the same house by one of them moving to the finished basement, to another bedroom, or to the

How to Find a Marital Mediator

- Ask friends or professionals whom you trust for a personal recommendation or referral.
- Search the Internet for "Mediation Service" in your area.

P PARTNERS

Relationship counseling and relationship mediation are both available for the partnership in difficulty.

D DEFINITION

Marital Agreement

A written agreement between spouses made in contemplation of continuing the marriage, although it may also contain agreements for "in the event of" divorce, or death.

D DEFINITION

Mediation

A process in which a neutral third person helps people develop their own agreement.

D DEFINITION

ADR: Alternative Dispute Resolution. This is the title the legal profession has given to cover all methods of resolving conflicts outside of court. It includes mediation, arbitration, a hybrid called med-arb, negotiation, shuttle diplomacy, even flipping a coin.

BUNKY

"Once a married couple is physically separated they are legally separated"

This assumption is incorrect, and can be very costly. You are legally separated only if and when you receive a signed decree of legal separation from a court. **Physical separation is not legal separation.**

P PARTNERS

Living Together Agreements

Partners may create a written a living together agreement that sets out the terms of their arrangement, and make it an enforceable contract.

mother-in-law apartment. Working out a schedule of different kitchen and laundry room times can help create a feeling of separateness, and is a way to avoid difficult surprises. Many people need to be further apart.

The question of whether to physically separate ultimately comes down to whether one or both of you is so uncomfortable being around the other that he or she cannot function well. Sometimes physical separation brings with it the insight needed to work on resolving serious differences and prompts a renewed commitment to the marriage. Other times, however, it awakens the realization that you really want the marital relationship to end.

"If you leave the family home, your spouse can 'get' you for desertion or abandonment."

Not any more. It is not a crime to leave a marriage. 1972 saw the end of fault grounds for divorce in Colorado, but leaving the family home may impact your discussion of parenting.

PHYSICAL SEPARATION HAS BOTH LEGAL AND TAX CONSEQUENCES

Unless you agree otherwise, the legal consequences of your marriage continue after you separate. The law presumes that any property or debts either of you accumulates are marital – joint. For example, during a long separation the husband continues to contribute to his retirement account, and the wife incurs substantial credit card debt. The increase in the retirement amount is marital property and the increase in credit card debt is marital debt, i.e. joint property and joint debt even if only one name appears on the account.

Your tax filing status may be affected by the date of your physical separation, as may the tax status of your home as your personal residence. See Chapter 7.

It is often a very good idea to write out in detail the agreements you make with each other about your physical separation. This is what makes a physical separation into a trial separation—it is a time to try out your ideas about parenting, support, and meeting marital obligations. See Chapters 2 and 4 for how to plan your separation.

Legal Separation

Legal Separation: The legal process which declares marriage partners to be separate persons not responsible for each other.

Legal separation is the same as dissolution of marriage except that neither party is free to re-marry, and the right to inherit is not terminated except by written agreement.

A decree of legal separation declares that you and your spouse, as well as your financial assets and obligations, are legally separate. The decree requires everyone, including creditors, financial and other institutions, to treat the two of you as separate persons. You can no longer file your income taxes as married taxpayers, either jointly or separately. After the decree of legal separation is entered, you are no longer responsible for each other's debts or actions, no longer entitled to each other's earnings or property. You are also no longer obligated to support each other except as provided in your separation agreement. (A decree of dissolution of marriage does all this too.)

Before the court can enter a decree of legal separation, you or the court must divide your marital property and debts, determine your parenting plan, and set child support and/or maintenance (alimony/spousal support), just as you must do for a divorce. In practice, the procedure and timing in court for a legal separation is generally the same as for a dissolution. **This Guidebook is about how to reach these decisions yourselves.**

"Possession is nine-tenths of the law."
Not true. You do not give up your rights to ownership in your home or other property by moving out. Marital property is presumed to be anything you acquired during your marriage, except by gift or bequest. You don't lose it by letting the other spouse use or occupy it.

WHY WOULD YOU WANT A LEGAL SEPARATION?

Some couples aren't sure they want to divorce. A legal separation is a way to separate, to divide property, to end mutual responsibility for each other's support and debts except as agreed, and to take a good look at the relationship—while making divorce one easy step away.

Some religions forbid or frown on divorce. Legal separation permits you to lead separate lives without divorcing.

Many kinds of health insurance, and some survivor benefits or life insurance connected with retirement plans, will still cover or benefit legally-separated persons while they cut off people who are divorced.

Separation Agreement
A written agreement between spouses made in contemplation of divorce or legal separation.

Social Security benefits can be figured on the basis of a former spouse's earnings if those benefits are higher. To qualify, the marriage must have lasted 10 years or longer, you are unmarried when you request the benefits, and you are 62 or older. If you are close to meeting these requirements, it might be good planning to do a legal separation until you qualify, then convert to a divorce.

If you are unsure of whether to do a legal separation or a divorce, one place to start to ask questions is the benefits and/or personnel office where each of you works. Find out which benefits, if any, apply to the non-employee spouse after either a legal separation or a divorce. Find out what your respective Social Security benefits are now, and are projected to be. Some careful research now may save you thousands of dollars in benefits later.

CHANGING FROM LEGAL SEPARATION TO DIVORCE

After you begin a court action for legal separation, (but before the decree for legal separation is signed), either or both of you may change your request to one for dissolution of marriage.

If you have already received a Decree of Legal Separation it may not be converted to a divorce until at least one hundred eighty-two days (approximately 6 months) has passed since the Decree was signed. After that time period, the motion to convert will be granted whether requested by both of you, or only one. You only need to sign and file the motion, and prove to the court that you gave notice to your spouse that you want the conversion to happen. The terms of your agreement—about property, debts, parenting, support, maintenance—stay the same unless you specifically change them at this time. If neither of you ever asks to have your legal separation converted to a divorce, you can remain legally separated for life. To end your legal separation and resume your full marriage, you may request that your legal separation case be dismissed.

Annulment

If your marriage was prohibited—not valid right from the start—then you may ask the court to annul your marriage, called a Declaration of Invalidity in Colorado. In this procedure you are asking the court to "declare" that your marriage never happened. A marriage may be annulled because one of you was already married, you are siblings or close relatives, you are underage, or the marriage was never consummated or was based on fraud or "gross misrepresentation."

Annulment is a legal action that requires "grounds" which must be proven—unlike a dissolution of marriage. Consult with a lawyer if you think this is what you need.

Dissolution of Marriage (Divorce)

Dissolution of marriage, more commonly known as divorce, can only be obtained through a court action.

The marriage is dissolved—ended—when the judge signs the decree of dissolution of marriage. The decree ends the mutual obligation spouses have to support each other—to provide the necessities of food, shelter, and clothing—and ends conjugal rights, although you may continue a sexual relationship if you wish. The divorce also ends a person's right to any part of his or her spouse's estate at death. The moment a divorce decree is signed by the court, the spouses are each free to marry again.

Before the court can sign the decree ending your marriage, you or the court must establish that the marriage is irretrievably broken, divide the property and debts, determine a parenting plan, and

D DEFINITION **Annulment:** The legal process which declares that a marriage never existed.

D DEFINITION **Declaration of Invalidity:** The Colorado term for an annulment.

D DEFINITION **Dissolution of Marriage:** The Colorado term for divorce.

D DEFINITION **Divorce:** The legal process which ends a marriage; dissolution of marriage; not available in Colorado for same sex marriages, civil unions, or domestic partnerships.

D DEFINITION **Civil Unions and Same Sex Marriages:** Neither of these exist in Colorado law, and cannot be dissolved under current Colorado law.

BUNKY **"You're automatically divorced if your spouse has been gone for 7 years."** This is not true. There is no "automatic" divorce, even if your spouse has disappeared.

set child support and/or maintenance (alimony, spousal support). **This Guidebook is about how to reach these decisions yourselves.**

COMMON LAW MARRIAGE IN COLORADO

"Common law" refers to laws of conduct which evolved from custom and usage, as well as opinions of the Colorado Court of Appeals and the Colorado Supreme Court rather than laws written by a legislature. Common law marriage and a marriage with a license and a ceremony are legally equal and equally legal. They are both marriages.

You have a common law marriage in Colorado only if:

1. You have lived together ("cohabited") in Colorado (or in another state that recognizes common law marriage) while "holding yourselves out" as being married, meaning that you acted as though you were married. Typical proof of this is that you introduce each other as wife and husband, have the same last name, hold joint accounts, put the other on your health insurance, or file married/joint income tax returns; *and*
2. Neither of you was still married to someone else, either by a marriage license and a ceremony (called a statutory marriage), or by common law; *and*
3. Both of you were at least 18 years of age if the marriage was entered into on or after September 1, 2006. A common law marriage entered into before that date has no age requirement.

If you introduced each other as fiancees or some other term besides husband, wife, or spouse, and talked about getting married some day later, then you are not common law married, no matter how long you have been living together.

AN ALTERNATIVE TO MARRIAGE IN COLORADO

In 2009, the Colorado Legislature passed, and Governor Ritter signed, the Colorado Designated Beneficiary Agreement Act, effective July 1, 2009. This statute provides that two parties, regardless of sexual orientation, may sign a prescribed form to designate each other as the other's "designated beneficiary" in up to sixteen different categories, including health and life insurance, retirements, priority in one's estate at death, hospital visitation, inheritance rights, and the like. Not only does this offer some specific marriage-like rights to some who may not marry (same sex couples, close relatives), but it also offers an alternative to those considering marriage.

D DEFINITION

Common Law Marriage: A marriage in which the parties did not obtain a license or go through a recognized ceremony, but lived together as married, openly manifesting your intention that your relationship is that of husband and wife.

BUNKY

"We don't need to go through court for our divorce, we're just common law married."

There is no such thing as common law divorce. If you are common law married and you want a divorce or legal separation, you can only obtain it from the court.

Constitutional Amendment

In 2006 the people of the State of Colorado amended the Colorado Constitution to add the following Section 31 to Article II Bill of Rights: "Only a union of one man and one woman shall be valid or recognized as a marriage in this state." Therefore same sex marriages are neither valid nor recognized, and such couples may not be divorced here. Such residents of Colorado are, at this writing, without remedy, i.e., in legal limbo.

Signing the Designated Beneficiary Agreement is done privately, in front of a notary, and then the agreement is recorded with the county clerk and recorder. Should the relationship end, one or both parties simply sign a prescribed form of Revocation of Designated Beneficiary Agreement, record it, the Clerk sends a copy to the other party, and it's done. (Samples of these prescribed documents starting are shown at Appendix A.) There is no court involvement unless one or both parties seek assistance with an unresolved dispute. While this statute extends many rights of married persons to designated beneficiaries, it does not change the existing law of implied contract for property division for partners, or provide for maintenance, alimony, or anything comparable to legal separation.

P PARTNERS The ending of a long term, or even not so long term, living together partnership, like a divorce, can involve a profound emotional upheaval, even when done with understanding and cooperation. Be sure to take care of yourself during this difficult time to help ensure a peaceful conclusion and the ability to move on. See Chapter 3.

Your Other Divorces

The ending of a marriage is much more than a legal event. It is the letting go of dreams. It is the dissolution of a financial partnership. It is the forming of a new relationship with the other parent of your children. It usually involves profound emotional upheaval.

The legal divorce, no matter how final that process may be, may do little or nothing toward taking care of your "other divorces." Some people wake up the morning after the final decree has been signed to find they don't feel divorced at all, and equally legal.

Working through this Guidebook from the first to the last page is a good way to ensure that all your divorces happen together.

CHAPTER 2

DIVORCE AND THE LEGAL SYSTEM

DIVORCE AND THE LEGAL SYSTEM

The Court Aspect of Divorce – An Overview

"The court will automatically grant our divorce on day 92."

Nothing occurs automatically at the end of 91 days. You have to take action to request that the court finalize your divorce.

Divorce is a legal matter. It can only be obtained through court.

You begin the legal process by filing a petition with the clerk of the district court. The present costs of filing a Petition of Dissolution or Legal Separation are $195; Petition for Parental Responsibilities, $187; Response, $95. Fees are subject to change.

The waiting period of 91 days, required by law, begins once you have filed the petition and have obtained jurisdiction over your spouse, by either filing jointly as co-petitioners or completing service of process, both of which are explained in Chapter 5. The reasoning behind the 91-day wait is that a marriage should not be ended without serious thought. The law therefore imposes this "cooling off" time for the couple before the judge has the power to grant a divorce. During this period, couples have information to gather and exchange, things to do that are required by law, as well as many decisions to make. The court has developed a process to monitor all of this called *case management.*

How long will it take for my divorce?

The Court Case Management Procedure is designed, in part, to keep cases moving efficiently through the court process. While this will vary some from one court to another, and from one part of the state to another, there is one overall factor that determines how long it will take, and that is how friendly is it. The more contested your divorce, the more you require the court to decide things for you (particularly if you require multiple hearings), the longer it will take. Hotly contested complex situations can take months or even years.

The quickest way through the court process is for the two of you to come to complete acceptable agreement so that the court's only involvement is to read and approve your agreement (a non-contested hearing), usually a ten to fifteen minute process. This is what this book is about.

COURT CASE MANAGEMENT PROCEDURE

Once you have filed your petition, the court will assign a judge, magistrate, or family court facilitator to manage and facilitate your divorce through the court system, to help you understand your process in court, and to encourage you to reach agreement yourselves, thereby maintaining decision-making in the family, rather than in the court.

At the time you file your petition, or shortly after, the court will issue a *case management order* that gives you important information about the court process, the things you are REQUIRED to do, and your deadlines. In most cases, the court will order both of you to attend an *initial status conference* within 42 days of filing your Petition. This is an informal meeting where you both, along with your lawyers if any, meet with the family court facilitator, or other designated person (sometimes a magistrate or judge, sometimes in a large gathering with other couples awaiting their turn) to discuss how you are progressing toward your divorce agreement, which matters you have resolved and which ones remain, and your timing to resolve them. Usually before the end of your initial status conference, they will set the time and date for your next status conference or court appearance.

P PARTNERS

Partners don't need a statement or decree from a court to end their partnership.

The case management order also lists *mandatory disclosures* that you must exchange, either before or at the initial status conference, such as tax returns, completed sworn financial statements that detail your incomes, assets, and debts, and much more. The order usually includes a requirement for parents to take a parenting-after-divorce class. It may also tell you the date of your final hearing, or that court's procedure for setting it, the procedure for setting any contested hearings, and how to provide notice about your witnesses and their testimony.

TEMPORARY AGREEMENTS AND ORDERS

Couples usually make a temporary separation agreement about who lives where, uses what property, and pays which bills while their divorce or legal separation is pending. This may be an informal, unwritten understanding between them. It may be written and signed. It may be submitted to the court for approval by the judge – something you can do at a status conference or at any other time – in which case it becomes a temporary order. You decide how formal you must make your temporary arrangements. A discussion of temporary agreements and orders is found in Chapter 4.

SEPARATION AGREEMENT

Before the court may sign a decree of divorce or legal separation, you must work out your complete divorce plan. The written document that details these terms, and is given to the court, is called a separation agreement. Chapters 7 through 11 discuss all the necessary elements for writing your own separation agreement.

Your separation agreement must cover all the following: property division (real estate, cars, houschold goods, art, sporting equipment and other personal property, investments, businesses, retirement plans and pensions, and the like), payment of debts, maintenance (spousal support, alimony), allocation of parental responsibilities, parenting time and support of children, taxes, and medical and life insurance.

Your separation agreement may also include: a detailed plan for sharing the children, payments agreed to now but to be paid later, future higher education costs for each other or for your children, career plans or goals for each or either of you, and financial planning for the future. Your separation agreement may also anticipate the "Oh My God!"s—such as one parent losing a job, leaving the state, or the death or prolonged illness of a family member.

**Separation Agreements–
By other names...**

"Separation agreement" is a generic term that refers to the writing that details your agreement about property and debt division, maintenance, child support, as well as parental decision-making and parenting time. In recent years some professionals put their agreement about parental responsibilities in a separate document called a "Parenting Plan," while others include the Parenting Plan as part of their Separation Agreement. Sample wording for writing your own Separation Agreement, including the Parenting Plan, is in Chapter 12. When you develop your agreement in mediation, the mediator prepares a "memorandum," usually called a "Memorandum of Understanding," or "Memorandum of Agreement", and that serves as your Separation Agreement. It may or may not include your parenting plan.

P PARTNERS There is no body of law for the dissolving of personal relationship partnerships, as there is the Dissolution of Marriage Act for divorce. When dissolving partners go to court, one or the other is usually suing on contract, written and signed, or verbal, or even implied, and a legal theory called unjust enrichment. There is no right to an equitable portion of what is acquired during the relationship, as there is in marriage and divorce, unless you have made a prior agreement that says so.

P PARTNERS To terminate a Designated Beneficiary Agreement (see pages 7–8), one (or both) of the beneficiaries simply signs the Revocation of Designated Beneficiary form in front of a notary, records it, and the Clerk mails a copy of it to the other beneficiary (if necessary). That's it! (See a sample form in Appendix E at the back of this book.)There is no court involvement, unless there is dispute about matters not covered in the Revocation.

Continuing jurisdiction: The ongoing power of the court where you obtained your divorce to hear requests to enforce or change its orders made at the time of the decree.

You can choose to file, or not file, your completed separation agreement with the court (see about privacy and enforcement), but you must at least show it to the court when you ask for your final decree. Some people prefer to get everything worked out, written up, and even signed before they file the petition. Others file the petition first and then use the waiting period to work things out. Use this time wisely. Provisions and agreements which are acceptable when you have just separated may not be workable months later. It is very hard, and not always possible, to change your agreement after it is approved by the court. You may therefore want to make tentative agreements before or at the time you file and then use the mandatory waiting time to try living with them—to "get the bugs out." Remember that the court will want to know your progress, or lack of progress, on resolving these issues at the initial status conference.

You must also show the court sworn financial statements detailing the financial circumstances of each of you before you ask for your final decree, usually at your first status conference. These affidavits provide the basis for the court to *find* your separation agreement to be *fair,* and to *enter* a decree of dissolution of marriage or legal separation after the 91 day period has run.

WHAT IF WE DON'T AGREE ON EVERYTHING?

If you are not in agreement with all issues before the initial status conference, the court facilitator will want to know when you will resolve those issues, and will set a date for another status conference or a hearing to resolve contested matters. This may be the time to consider mediation, something you may begin at any time—before or during this process—with or without lawyers.

OBTAINING YOUR FINAL DECREE

You may obtain your final decree in one of two ways:

1. If you **do not** have minor children, or if you do and you are both represented by an attorney, **AND** you agree on all aspects of your divorce or separation, you qualify for a Divorce or Legal Separation by Affidavit. You can mail or deliver all of your final papers, along with a signed *Affidavit for Decree Without Appearance of Parties,* to the court. The court will read your papers after your 91-day waiting period and, if they approve, will sign your Decree. If you file all your papers before your initial status conference, you will not have to attend. See Chapter 12 about how to do this.

2. If you do not qualify for a decree by affidavit, you have agreed to everything, and you have all your papers filed, you still must appear at a final non-contested hearing in court.

THE COURT'S CONTINUING JURISDICTION

After your divorce or legal separation has been granted, the court retains *continuing jurisdiction* over your children (parental responsibilities, parenting time, child support). If you have filed your separation agreement, the court also keeps jurisdiction over any future payments and promises which are contained in it, such as a payment due when the house is sold or open-ended maintenance (spousal support). If after your divorce you wish to change one of the provisions of your separation agreement, the court keeps jurisdiction over that too. Even if one or both of you moves out of the state, the original court keeps jurisdiction until another court formally takes over.

The court will not interfere in your personal family matters unless one of you asks it to. If you can cooperate with each other, and be reliable—keeping all your agreements, in spirit and letter—neither of you will have to ask the court to do anything but approve your agreement.

Chapters 5 through 12 of this Guidebook cover each step of the non-contested court process, from first papers through the final decree.

A Word About the Law

Many people, both laypersons and lawyers, assume that all parts of the law apply to everyone. In family matters this may not be true. The question of how much of the law of divorce applies to people doing their own divorce in a friendly way is unsettled.

Statutes—bills that are passed by the Legislature and signed by the Governor—apply differently to different people. According to the divorce statute (The Uniform Dissolution of Marriage Act, Colorado Revised Statutes 14-10-101, et seq.), if you want a divorce you must go through the court system. That applies to everyone. There is no other way to obtain a divorce. There is common law marriage, but there is no common law divorce.

"But to live outside the law you must be honest..." Bob Dylan, "Absolutely Sweet Marie".

The divorce statute lists the factors that the judge must consider when dividing property in a divorce. The statute does not say that you must consider those same factors when you divide your property yourselves. What the judge must consider is the law that applies if you and your spouse cannot agree. For example, the statute defines *marital* and *separate* property. You may agree to define these terms the way the statute does, but you are free to define them your own way. For another example, the Dissolution of Marriage Act tells the court the factors it must listen for in allocating parental responsibilities. You may consider these same factors, if you wish, or decide for yourselves what factors are important to you.

How to Win in Court – Not!

Since this Guidebook is about friendly and cooperative divorce, it offers no advice or tips about how to "win" in court.

The court system produces a second part of the law called case law or precedent. If, after a trial, one or both parties are unhappy with the judge's decision (juries are not used in family law matters in Colorado) they may appeal to the Colorado Court of Appeals. If they challenge the results from the Court of Appeals, they may further appeal to the Colorado Supreme Court. The appeal process reviews only the transcript of the trial, and hears arguments by the lawyers. The appellate court then decides whether the trial court made an error, or *abused its discretion,* meaning that the trial judge wandered too far beyond the boundaries of other similar cases. The appellate court either *affirms* the trial court's decision, *reverses* it, or sends it back *(remands)* to be tried again. The appellate courts publish their rulings in those cases they decide are significant. These published opinions are what lawyers call "precedent."

"The notion that most people want black-robed judges, well-dressed lawyers & fine-paneled courtrooms as the setting to resolve their disputes is not correct. People with problems, like people with pains, want relief, and they want it as quickly and inexpensively as possible." Warren E. Burger, Chief Justice, United States Supreme Court

In the area of divorce, these opinions are law in that they create legal *presumptions* for people in similar circumstances. Since most of these precedent cases arise from trials, and not from cases in which the parties reached agreement, there is a very real question whether such case law applies to people who do their own divorce.

Occasionally, however, cases settled by the spouses themselves are appealed. This usually occurs when the court does not approve the proposed separation agreement or when one of the spouses has a change of heart immediately after the agreement is approved. For example, there are a number of cases where the parents initially agreed to no child support, the trial court would not approve it, and the parties appealed. The Colorado Court of Appeals affirmed, refusing to permit the parties' agreement. The same thing has happened to agreements which do not provide for parenting time for both parents. Both trial and appellate courts agree that support from, and time with, parents are rights of the child—even the parents cannot take them away.

This Guidebook distinguishes between legal definitions and procedures which you, *if you do your divorce yourself,* must follow, and those areas in which you can make your own definitions and agreements.

Privacy

The United States conducts its legal business in public. All courts are open to the public, except juvenile court and certain specific cases that are closed due to especially sensitive testimony. Some trials are broadcast live on television. Many small towns in Colorado still publish a list of just-granted or just-filed divorces in the local newspaper.

A little-known result of this openness is that your divorce file may be asked for, read, and even copied by anyone—including the media, credit reporting agencies, real estate brokers, insurance salespersons, and your children, friends, and neighbors. Some courts are limiting what the public can look at in a court file, including the entire financial statement. The Court is prohibited by Federal law from revealing Social Security numbers.

"The human animal needs a freedom seldom mentioned, freedom from intrusion. He needs a little privacy quite as much as he wants understanding or vitamins or exercise or praise." Phyllis McGinley, "A Lost Privilege," *The Province of the Heart.*

Even in a non-contested, non-adversarial divorce the court must review the economic circumstances of the spouses in order to determine if their separation agreement should be approved. What do you do if you do not want your financial circumstances to become public knowledge? The way to keep your privacy and still be sufficient in your divorce papers is to provide the minimum amount of specific information for the court to understand your agreement and why you think it is a good one.

Following are some suggestions that may help you keep your private matters private while still providing necessary information to the court:

- Consider bringing necessary but sensitive documents with you to the final hearing for the court to review, but ask that they be returned at the end of the hearing, i.e., you do not file them. Psychological evaluations, profit and loss calculations for your business, trust account data, medical reports, criminal actions involving you, all are examples of things you may wish returned to you, and not left in a court file which is open to the public.

CAUTION

Whether or not you incorporate your agreement into the decree, a) the decree will indicate your parenting arrangements, and, b) the support order will recite the amount of child support being ordered. This is because the court keeps jurisdiction over minor children.

- Consider not incorporating into the decree all or part of your separation agreement. If you do not incorporate your agreement into the decree, you lose your right to enforce it through the court. You will have to decide how much your privacy is worth when measured against ease and sureness of enforcement. See Chapter 13 for more on enforcement.

- Consider asking the court to seal your file, or parts of it. To do this, you must satisfy the court that your, or your children's, need for privacy outweighs the public right to know. Such confidential sealing is routinely done with parenting evaluations filed with the court.

How Do You Want to Conduct Your Divorce?

Most people want to end their marriage as inexpensively as possible and not make difficult matters worse. At a time when there may not be enough money to support a family in two homes, no one wants to make unnecessary payments to parenting evaluators, lawyers, appraisers, tax accountants, career counselors, business consultants, mediators, arbitrators, or fact-finders.

Money isn't the only issue. How do you want to conduct your divorce? How do you want it to be conducted? Here are some examples of how a divorce can be done, from the simple to the complex, from the friendly to the more adversarial, as well as from the inexpensive to the costly.

DIVORCE PROCESS OPTIONS

DO IT YOURSELVES

There is a list of all the published forms you might need for non-adversarial divorce in Chapter 6 of this Guidebook. You must fill out the forms correctly, file them in the correct sequence and pay the correct filing fee.

CAUTION

"Should I use an Agreement Form?"

When we wrote the first edition of this book in 1990-1993, we decided not to include a sample separation agreement, and for good reason. On the one hand, forms are attractive because they make a difficult thing look relatively simple, and offer the opportunity to get a painful process over with quickly. On the other hand, any separation agreement form that just requires you to fill in the blanks has already made some decisions for you, either by what is implied in the words of the form and how it is set up, or by what is not said. In truth, you have much more latitude and many more choices than is implied in any separation agreement form.

Use any such form, including our sample wording at the end of Chapter 12, with caution. It's always wise to have a separation agreement read by an attorney—one for each spouse—before you sign it.

You must negotiate and prepare a separation agreement for the court to review at the time of your decree. You can negotiate your separation agreement at home.

- You will need to create you own agreement, perhaps using the sample language in Chapter 12.

If you have no children and little property or debts, you may have a separation agreement of only a few lines or paragraphs which you can create on a separate sheet of paper and attach to the decree, or you can use the form JDF 1215. Not many qualify for this simple method since most married couples have some joint obligations or separation-year tax filings that require a more detailed written understanding between them.

ASSISTANCE FOR DO-IT-YOURSELFERS

If you need some help in working out the separation agreement, there are some low-cost resources available to you.

There are a number of books and manuals which will help you complete the forms and the process. This Guidebook is one.

There are classes on do-it-yourself divorce in most counties, and at many of the community colleges and adult education centers.

There are legal centers and some private attorneys who will, for a flat fee or an hourly rate, fill out the forms and review your agreement to see that it is complete and in a form acceptable to the court. Generally these fees include consultation, and sometimes filing of the forms in court—but they do not include mediation or negotiating your agreement for you.

DO IT YOURSELVES WITH MEDIATION

In mediation the two of you negotiate with each other in the presence of the mediator—who is neutral. After you gather all the papers that show your incomes, assets and debts, you bring them to the mediation meeting, put all the cards on the table, so to speak, and then negotiate with each other to form your agreement, and your parenting plan if you have children. The mediator's function is to help focus the conversation, explain the process, show you different ways to do things so you can consider a variety of options, and help each of you hear what the other is saying. But YOU make the decisions. Mediation is a good way to stay in charge of making your own decisions, and at the same time to get help on how to put an agreement together.

As the two of you begin to come to agreement and the agreement begins to take shape, the mediator puts your agreement in written form, so you can see how it looks in writing, and to give you further opportunity to consider it. You can go through as many drafts as you need as you become progressively clearer about what you want to do, until it finally says exactly what you want. Usually only one or two drafts are needed, but some couples require several. The written agreement that emerges from mediation is usually called a *Memorandum of Understanding* and you can use it as your separation agreement in court.

It is always recommended that each of you have the agreement reviewed by your own attorney, before it is signed. Sometimes those reviews raise issues that need to be further discussed in mediation. If decisions are changed, then the *Memorandum* is revised.

Working together with a mediator allows you to be directly involved in the process of arriving at every decision. Sometimes if you are not in the thick of the decision-making process yourself, the results may not fit you. The agreement someone else may reach on your behalf may be the best they can envision – but they do not see with your eyes. If you want to have an agreement which is uniquely suited to you and to which you will commit with your

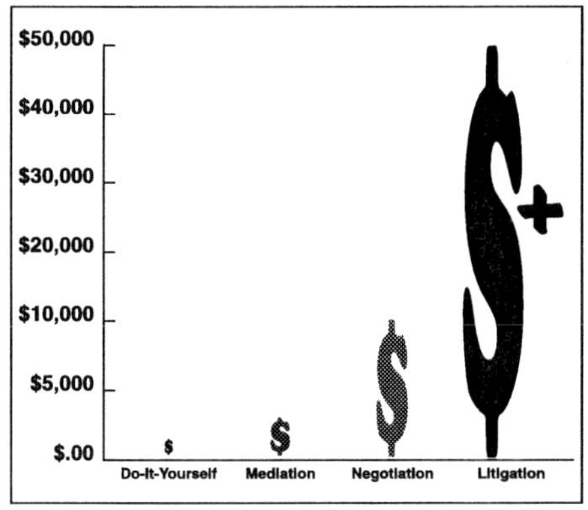

P PARTNERS A partnership can end far more quickly and abruptly than a marriage, and often does, leaving feelings wounded and often financial matters unresolved. Mediating the untangling of your blended personal and financial matters can help you to come apart without increasing the amount of emotional baggage you already have.

How do we know if we can mediate?

You may be good candidates for the mediation process if

- You can trust each other to be forthcoming about all your facts and circumstances, financial and otherwise, and not hide anything.
- You care about being fair to the other as well as yourself.
- You can communicate with each other reasonably well, with the assistance of a mediator.

whole heart, you will have to feel that YOU negotiated it. You are more likely to be satisfied with your agreement—and with yourself—and more likely to abide by the agreement if YOU BOTH walk through each step and negotiate each issue.

When to Use a Mediator

You can hire a divorce mediator to work with you both right from the beginning of your decision to separate to help you make your decision about who will move out and where, who will be responsible for what expenses and bills, and how you will manage the children from two locations, until you make some final decisions. Once temporary agreements are made—your agreed upon holding pattern, so to speak—you can move forward to working on long term solutions.

Do I have to mediate?

Many courts now order mediation in nearly every case where parenting or change of parenting is an issue, or for modification (change) of child support or maintenance. If you wish to be excused from a court ordered mediation due to recent domestic violence or fear of it, you must bring a motion to the court.

Some people come to mediation after they discover that the attorneys they have hired are more contentious than they are, and they decide to take back being in charge of their divorce. Still others, having begun a contentious divorce process, change their minds, and are able to instruct their lawyers to shift gears to assist them in the mediation process. Still others, doing their divorce themselves, discover that with only a few weeks to go they can't seem to manage it themselves, and so they go to mediation to get assistance in putting their final agreement together. Mediation can be an excellent choice in all these different situations.

In mediation, are we in one room or two?

Usually both spouses are in the same room, at the same table with the mediator. Occasionally the mediator may find it helpful to talk with you individually for a few minutes, to *caucus* with each of you separately, and then go back to all three of you together. Sometimes that's all it takes to get through a sticking point. In more hostile cases, and in most cases where clients bring their own attorneys, usually the husband and wife are in different rooms and the mediator goes back and forth. When one or both parties are at a distance, or do not want to see each other, mediation can be done by conference call.

Choosing a Divorce Mediator

There are many different kinds of divorce mediators with different kinds of backgrounds. While most are lawyers or mental health professionals, you will find a wide variety of other backgrounds as well.

A divorce mediator can help you decide how you are going to approach and do your separation and divorce. For example, whether to be petitioner and co-petitioner, or petitioner and respondent. A divorce mediator who is trained in law, can help you understand the forms and how they fit into the process you have selected. A divorce mediator can help you throughout to evolve a collaborative bargaining process which you can use well into the future.

The mediator is not an expert to tell you the "right things to do." There is no right or wrong answer in divorce. There are probably a number of possible solutions, many of which would work for both of you.

Consider the two basic styles of divorce mediation. One is based on problem solving, which is the style of mediation we have described here. The other is more structured, focusing more on reaching specific agreements around what they believe to be the likely outcome in court. This style is more narrow, the former more broad in focus.

Select a mediator who has experience in the areas that you are discussing, such as parenting plans and their relation to child development, divorce taxation, financial planning, business or pension valuation and division. The more expertise the mediator has in the areas you are negotiating—especially those areas where you are unsure—the more efficient and less expensive your mediation is likely to be.

Questions to Ask a Prospective Divorce Mediator

Ask the following questions of any mediator you are considering until you find one who answers them to your satisfaction.

- Are you a specialist in family matters? How many families have you assisted in the divorce process? How long have you been a mediator?
- How much do you charge? Do you charge per couple per hour, or per person per hour? Do you meet with the parties together or separately? How long does the average divorce mediation take in your practice?
- How available are you? How quickly do you return phone calls? How long does it take to schedule an appointment?
- Do you mediate within the legal context of the outcome in court? How important is it to you that the results in mediation be similar to the probable results in court?
- Do you have a problem-solving style, or it is more outcome oriented?

Med-Arb

Some mediators offer a hybrid process called *med/arb.* You initially work with the professional as a mediator, then, after a time, if you do not reach agreement on any given issue the mediator becomes an arbitrator and makes that decision for you. If you are interested in med/arb, be sure you make that clear to the mediator you hire.

How to Find a Divorce Mediator

- Ask friends or professionals whom you trust for a personal recommendation or referral.
- Google "divorce mediator" or "divorce mediation" plus your location, city or county.
- Look in the Yellow Pages under "Mediation Services."
- Ask at your local courthouse if they maintain a list of mediators available in your judicial district.

"If we don't work everything out in mediation, the mediator will decide for us."

A mediator does not make any decisions for you. Rather, he or she works with both of you to help you come to agreement. You keep your power to decide in mediation.

Arbitration is a very different process where you each present your "side," and the arbitrator decides.

Arbitrators

An arbitrator, like a judge, makes the decisions for you. You argue, the arbitrator decides. An arbitrator can decide your whole divorce for you, or any single issue on which you get stuck. You can make the decision binding, that is, it becomes a court order immediately as though you had gone to court on that issue. Or, you can make the decision of the arbitrator advisory, so that you are not bound by it, but you incorporate it into your thinking as you work on developing your final agreement. You must decide before the arbitration begins whether the decision is to be binding or advisory.

Fact-Finder, Special Master

You can ask the court to approve a person, often a lawyer with special expertise in the area in which you are stuck, to investigate and collect data and then recommend a decision to the judge or to you about these issues. Sometimes this will save you the cost of lengthy litigation, in part because you can ask for this service very early on and then use the recommendation as the starting point for building the rest of your settlement. Lawyers who specialize in family law are probably the best source for knowing who provides these services.

HIRE AN ATTORNEY

You can hire an attorney to conduct your divorce right from the beginning. You can learn the lawyer's view of the law as it applies to you and your situation. An attorney can relieve you of having to meet face to face with your soon-to-be-ex; protect you if you feel you need it; sue the blankety-blank for everything you can get, if that's what you want to do.

There are several ways to use a lawyer in divorce, but they can be classified into two fundamental categories: lawyer as *consultant*, and lawyer as *representative*. Within these two categories you have further options. Ask yourself, how much authority, responsibility, and control do I want my attorney to have? Here are some examples.

Lawyer As Consultant

- You can learn a lawyer's view of the law as it applies to you and your situation before you start the legal process, or during it, including the likely outcome in court should you ask the court to decide any issues for you.

Should I Hire an Attorney?

In Colorado, whether and how you use a lawyer in your divorce is up to you. The statutes allow you to conduct your divorce "pro se" – the Latin phrase for "for yourself."

The question of whether to hire an attorney is not, in and of itself, the same as whether you are going to be friendly or adversarial, or whether you are going to keep control through the divorce process. These are determined by which lawyer you hire, and what you ask, or allow your lawyer to do for you.

- You can do the paperwork yourselves, including your separation agreement and each run it all by a lawyer before you finalize and file your agreement.

- If you have reached agreement in mediation, you may want a lawyer to review your agreement before you sign it. The lawyer can tell you if he or she believes it to be sound and in your best interests, and make suggestions for additions and changes.

- In some instances an attorney can fill out the official court forms for you without becoming your representative. Many lawyers aren't willing to do this.

- You can work out an agreement yourselves, and one or both of you hire an attorney to do the paperwork. This may or may not include translating your agreement into legal language. Depending upon how much you ask the attorney to do for you, this could be consultant or representative. Most lawyers will not work for both of you, but only for one, which can lead to some unwanted one-sidedness in the writing. Many in this situation prefer to have a law-trained mediator, a neutral who works for both of you, prepare the written agreement.

Lawyer As Representative

- Having a lawyer as your representative means he or she is your official representative to the court. Anything you want to file with the court must be filed by your lawyer. Your representative must be present with you any time you appear in court.

- A lawyer as representative will speak to your spouse's attorney, or your spouse directly if he or she is not represented, and negotiate with them for you.

- Some lawyer representatives require you not to speak to your spouse to ensure that all communications are through lawyers. This may or may not be what you need or want, so make your wishes known before you hire someone.

- A lawyer as representative will require you to bring in all the papers from the checklist in Chapter 6, although in a more formal way, and require your spouse to produce them too. This can be helpful if you fear someone is hiding something.

BUNKY **"I'll wait until we have our agreement signed and sealed, and then show it to an attorney."**

Noooooo! It's best to do all your consulting and information gathering before you sign something. Find out about your mistakes before you make them.

P PARTNERS Partners can hire attorneys to handle their financial separation.

CAUTION **"That's just my lawyer talking."**

Don't kid yourself. If you hire an attorney, he or she becomes your representative. You are responsible for the way your divorce is conducted, including what your lawyer says, as well as how, when and where it is said. Your lawyer works for you.

How to Find a Lawyer for a Family Matter

- Ask everybody you know who has hired a family law lawyer recently if they recommend anyone. Word of mouth from a person you trust is still the best recommendation a family lawyer can have.
- Ask your marriage counselor, mediator, social worker, or pastor to make a recommendation.
- Look up "Lawyers" or "Attorneys" in the Yellow Pages, under the sub-heading "Divorce" or "Family Law".
- Call Metropolitan Lawyer Referral Service: (303) 831-8000.
- To check out the lawyers you are considering, call the Colorado Supreme Court, Attorney Registration Office. They will tell you if the lawyer is registered (which is mandatory for lawyers) and whether there is a public censure (discipline) on his/her record. This is the equivalent of a Better Business Bureau for lawyers.
- Look up the lawyer's name in the Martindale Hubbell lawyer directories available at your library. Lawyers and firms are rated by other lawyers for experience and expertise.

- Mediation is still available for those with lawyers representing them. You and your attorney can decide whether it's important for your attorney to attend mediation sessions with you.

- You can each hire a lawyer as a representative who is specially trained in Collaborative Law, a recent innovation in legal representation. Attorneys who practice collaborative law agree, in writing, at the time they accept the case that they will work together towards settlement, and they work together with you as a team. If there is a need for 3rd party opinions or experts, such as an appraiser, or parenting evaluator, they are retained by the team and not by one side. If later it becomes clear that the matter should go to court, the attorneys and the experts are disqualified from the case and must resign.

- As your representative, a lawyer can direct operations right from the start all the way through your Decree. A lawyer can argue in court as your advocate, for your rights and interests, to maximize your outcome.

Helping Your Lawyer Work For You

The information in this book about separation agreements and divorce will help you help your attorney work for you. Knowing about many of the details in advance will save your attorney time in explaining things to you. That will save money on hourly fees. Your knowledge of the tax rules and divorce procedure will also increase your attorney's bargaining power because more options will be understood by you. Thoroughly reviewing the chapters that deal with your most difficult points can put you in a position to understand and contribute to the negotiations.

Which functions do you want your lawyer to fill for you? How much control do you wish to have over your divorce and your role in it? Before you begin interviewing attorneys, clarify what you want and expect from a legal professional. Following are some suggestions about things to consider.

Questions to Ask Any Lawyer You Are Considering

Ask the following questions of any lawyer you are considering until you find one who answers them to your satisfaction.

- Are you a specialist in family law? How many family law cases have you handled? How long have you been a lawyer?

- How much do you charge? Hourly? Retainer? Additional rate for paralegal, associate or clerical staff?

- How available are you? How quickly do you return phone calls? How long does it take to schedule an appointment?

- How adversarial or non-adversarial are you?

- Are you supportive of the mediation process? How much experience do you have assisting clients in mediation?

- Are you willing to work with me as a consultant rather than a representative? Will you allow me to negotiate directly with my spouse?

- Do you practice Collaborative Law? See sidebar

D DEFINITION

Collaborative Law

Collaborative law is an attorney-based dispute resolution process where each spouse has his or her own specially trained collaborative law attorney. Each of the lawyers must commit to the non-adversarial resolution of all issues, meaning resolved out of court. Typically they then hire a collaborative law mediator. Any other experts needed are hired only as both sides agree. If the process fails to reach resolution and moves on to court, the collaborative law attorneys must resign, and clients must seek new counsel for court proceedings, or go forward unrepresented.

Divorce Services and Consultants

Whatever process you choose to achieve your divorce, there are a number of services you can hire to help make the final result more complete and workable. Some of these services may help you with the process of coming to an agreement. They range from those who work with you both to develop your own solutions, to those who decide some of the outcome for you. You may or may not need any of them, but read through the entire list to see if any of them might be helpful to you.

PARENTING EXPERTS AND RESOURCES

There are many resources and services available to help you with issues concerning your children. The following are some things you can do, as well as kinds of professionals and resources concerning children:

- Together, speak with a *parenting consultant* about how your children are doing and for assistance in working together as parents. This professional can help you understand your own needs and feelings, together and separately, and those of your children, and your legal needs. This person can assist you in planning what would be most helpful for you and your children during this confusing time.

- Hire a parenting consultant, an individual or a team, to advise you and your spouse about what kind of parenting plan is best for your family. You can do this informally where the consultant(s) reports directly to you, or to you in a mediation session. You can decide in advance how binding or not you want their recommendations to be.

P PARTNERS

All of these services and consultants are available to partners who need these kinds of professional input.

- Speak to the *school psychologist* about how your children are doing. Also ask about the kinds of difficulties which other children experience when their parents separate.

You can divorce a spouse but you cannot divorce a child.

- If your child or children are experiencing protracted difficulty adjusting to the divorce, you might hire a *therapist* for them.
- Ask the court to appoint a *Child and Family Investigator* (CFI) to investigate, report, and make recommendations to you and the court regarding such things as where the children should live, how much time they should spend with each parent, who should make decisions about them and how to address any special needs of the children. This may be an attorney, a mental health professional, or a layperson.

MANDATORY PARENTING CLASS

Nearly all jurisdictions in this state require divorcing parents to attend a three to four hour parenting-after-divorce class to learn the latest on the effects of divorce on children at different developmental levels. The cost varies, but is about $50-$60 for each parent.

- Ask the court to appoint an attorney to be a representative of your children to advise the court as to what he or she determines is in your children's best interest.
- Hire an attorney for the child. This is a legal representative for your child to advocate your child's wishes.
- Find a divorce recovery group for your children through your school, church, community center, local mental health center, or one of the many services—public or private—which specialize in assisting children when their parents divorce.

P PARTNERS Partners with children who file their parenting plan with the court may be ordered to take the mandatory parenting class, as above.

- There are a number of excellent books that may help both you and your children. See the bibliography at the end of this Guidebook for some suggestions.

Decide what you want from a professional. Do you want advice about your children to go directly to you? To the children? To your attorney? To the court? Do you want a professional to help you make your decision(s), or do you want someone to decide for you?

FINANCIAL CONSULTANTS

This category includes various experts who can help you unravel your money issues. You can find financial consultants by asking for recommendations from friends, lawyers, mediators or other financial consultants; through the yellow pages; or through the classified section of your local newspaper.

- Certified Public Accountant. A CPA experienced in divorce taxation issues can be a tremendous help in planning your settlement. Having an experienced CPA review several proposed settlements may save you money in the future by avoiding errors or inadequate tax planning.

- Certified Financial Planner. A CFP can project any settlement you are considering, to give you an idea of your earnings and net worth years from now. Some are certified divorce planners. This can be especially useful for those who have income-producing assets that one or the other plans to live on, or a long-term debt to pay after the divorce.

- Employment Counselor: If either or both of you are re-entering the job market after being away for some years, or are changing careers during the divorce process—whether or not by choice—some employment testing and counseling can be very useful. There are resource centers in a number of community colleges available to both men and women, which will assist you in aptitude testing, skills evaluation, resume writing, and other job-seeking skills. $5.00 of your divorce court filing fee funds these centers.

- Employment Evaluator. This service can evaluate your current skills and training and can estimate the cost of, and increased earnings from, additional training and education. Lawyers who do personal injury work are probably the best source for finding these services.

ASSET EVALUATORS

- Real Estate Appraisers. Real estate appraisers determine the value of your home, or other real estate, based on current construction costs as well as comparable properties which have sold recently. An appraiser adjusts the sold values of comparable properties by using certain industry standards, for example, a certain amount for a garage, so much for brick vs. wood, etc. Real estate appraisers are certified for certain specialties, such as residential, commercial, or agricultural. Ask their fee before they begin their work.

- Real Estate Market Analysts. A real estate salesperson or broker provides this service. He or she will review the properties sold recently in the same area and compare your property in a less formal and technical manner than the appraiser. The market analysis is usually much less expensive than an appraisal, and is often free.

- Personal Property Appraisers. These are specialists who will appraise anything from antiques to fine art, pin ball machines and beer can collections, juke boxes, pedigreed livestock, and beer steins. Sometimes it is useful to ask for the same three values suggested in the real estate market analysis.

If you request a real estate market analysis, consider asking for three values:

- High sales value (also often the recommended listing price) the most you can get if you are willing to wait for just the right buyer.
- Fair market value – the probable value of your property if you and a willing buyer are able to compromise.
- Fire sale value – the quick sale value.

- Business Appraisers: These are usually CPAs who specialize in valuing sole proprietor businesses or closely-held corporations. This is often the only way to obtain a value for the goodwill of a business—what it is worth above and beyond assets minus liabilities. See Chapter 7 for more on this.

- Pension Plan Evaluators. These services are necessary only if you need to know the present value of a future income stream. For example: what is the present value of a pension which will pay only when you retire or after you reach a certain age? What is the present value of the matching portions of a defined contribution plan? See Chapter 7 for a more complete discussion of the division of future assets such as retirements, pensions, and annuities and for more about property and valuations. There are computer programs available that can evaluate a future income stream. Many lawyers and mediators have these programs.

As you can see, there is a great range of choices in how you conduct your divorce and who you select to help. The choices you make now will determine cost, duration and the over-all tone of your transition to single lives. Keep all these options in mind as you work through your own situation.

CHAPTER 3

TAKING CARE OF YOURSELF

TAKING CARE OF YOURSELF

Keeping Yourself Together So You Can Work Together

"It is a common tendency for us to misinterpret spiritual or relationship hunger for physical hunger. When we are 'unconscious' of the distinction, we move like robots to the refrigerator every time we feel a lack of something." Thomas F. Crum, *The Magic of Conflict.*

Now that you have a better understanding of the legal system and your options for navigating through it, you will soon be taking some life-changing steps to plan for the future. As you go through this process, it is important to keep track of how you are doing.

PARTNERS: This chapter is just as relevant for partners as it is for married couples.

Disconnecting a marital relationship is not easy, whether you are the initiator of it, the receiver, or even when it is mutual and simultaneous. No matter which way you do it, feelings abound. Grief, hurt, fear, a sense of loss, a sense of failure, guilt, and of course anger. Many also feel relief, sometimes even joy that it's over, or that they have at last stopped denying that it's over. It's not unusual to feel grief and relief or joy at the same time.

CAUTION: People in divorce are much more accident prone, injury prone, and illness prone, than the general population. Be careful. Feeling edgy? Don't drive. You don't even have to be drinking for driving to be dangerous for you. Avoid other potentially dangerous activities, too, such as using knives and other sharp objects, heavy machinery, heavy anything, fast skiing or cycling. This is not the time to try bungee jumping or sky diving. Be careful around alcohol, medicine, and drugs. Even your ordinary day-to-day tasks that you take for granted can become challenging, if not dangerous, as you may find yourself forgetful, or easily distracted.

Take good care of yourself. Be patient with yourself. Try a relaxing warm bath, a cup of herb tea, soothing music, a massage. Don't be afraid to ask your friends to drive and for other help, until you calm down. Often, much of your physical and emotional energy can be so consumed by coping with the separation – actual or impending – that there is almost no energy left for taking care of yourself.

"When people fall in deep distress, their native sense departs." Sophocles.

Working out your own divorce plan with your spouse requires some important skills, such as the ability to focus and concentrate, to understand the issues – especially about money and property – and to learn more about them. You will also need the ability to communicate in ways that do not close off discussion, and the ability to take responsibility for your participation and whatever you agree to without creating the foundation for future anger and regret. These skills are all needed at a time when you feel ready to explode with some of the most difficult and intense feelings ever.

The information in this chapter about knowing yourself and understanding your feelings will help you to think clearly and participate effectively in your negotiations. Commit to yourself and to each other that you will negotiate and respond from a rational/logical place rather than an emotional one. If any position you take or compromise you make is based on anger, or hurt, or intimidation, or revenge, or guilt, or determination to be a victim, you are likely to conclude the divorce process with far more emotional baggage than you entered it with. It is better to do your divorce well now so that you don't remain stuck in it for years after it's over.

Just about everyone going through divorce could use psychotherapy at least part of the time. If you answer YES to any of the following questions, you might consider consulting a professional:

- Am I having trouble taking adequate care of myself (bathing, buying groceries and eating, putting gas in the car, and the like)?
- Am I having trouble meeting my obligations to my family?
- Am I having trouble carrying out my responsibilities at work?
- Am I having trouble sleeping?
- Am I having trouble starting and finishing my tasks each day?
- Do I experience anger or sadness that is out of proportion to the apparent cause?
- Do I hear myself saying things that I don't believe, or I know to be untrue, but I can't stop myself?
- Am I taking physical chances like driving too fast, not using potholders, not wearing warm enough clothing, and the like?
- Am I drinking more than usual, or does using drugs sound inviting?
- Am I stuck thinking thoughts of revenge or acting on such thoughts?
- Am I unable to separate from my emotions in order to discuss rationally with my spouse?

How to Find a Divorce Therapist

1. Get a referral from a friend you trust who can make a recommendation based on personal experience.
2. Ask your pastor, social worker, lawyer, or mediator to make a recommendation.
3. Search online or in the Yellow Pages under the following headings:

   Divorce Therapists

   Marriage and Family Counseling

   Psychotherapists

   Psychologists

   Divorce Mediation Services
4. Inquire at your neighborhood or county mental health center.
5. See pictures and information about therapists in your area by visiting http://therapists.psychology-today.com.

Whether or not you are seeing a professional therapist, consider finding someone to talk to during this time – a friend, neighbor, pastor, or find a divorce group to join for awhile. Remember, it is not okay to use your children as your emotional sounding board. Find a healthy adult or professional to provide you with this kind of support.

"If you do not go within, you go without." Neale Donald Walsch in *Conversations with God.*

The Emotional Divorce Sequence

For most people, the emotional divorce follows a fairly typical pattern. The timing of the phases may be very different for each spouse, but everyone goes through them all.

1. First is the crisis, the critical point in time when the relationship is coming apart – one of you leaves or announces that it's over, or you both decide that it's over. This recognition may be experienced by one spouse significantly before the other.

2. The second phase is the reaction to the initial crisis, which frequently just feels "crazy." This phase usually extends over several months, and has identifiable stages of its own. Knowing these stages and their sequence can help you through them. See below.

3. Then, at last, comes the recovery – the healing, the sense of peace. Now, you can get on with your life.

The middle reactionary phase has five recognized stages, which are actually the stages of grief. As you read them, see if any of them seems to be where you are. (This information is from *Rebuilding,* and *When Your Relationship Ends,* by Dr. Bruce Fisher. Dr. Fisher has found that the stages of the emotional divorce parallel the five stages of grief as outlined originally by Dr. Elizabeth Kubler-Ross. Used here by permission.)

"Give sorrow words; the grief that does not speak / Whispers the o'er-fraught heart and bids it break." Shakespeare, *Macbeth.*

Grief has many faces besides full blown sorrow. It frequently appears as a feeling of loneliness, difficulty in concentrating, and a sense of being weak and helpless. Sometimes it will bubble up as a kind of anger, not so much anger at the sorrow but at the inability to "be yourself" and get things done like you usually do. When you feel unable to control your mood swings or your ability to be responsible and productive, it can be frightening.

"We cannot direct the wind but we can adjust our sails." *City of Hope.*

Stage 1: The first stage of grief is emotional shock. "This isn't happening to me." "This isn't real." There is a numbness about it. We suppress the anger and hurt and act as though nothing has happened. We put on our best manners. We keep it all inside and don't tell anybody, and put up walls and protect ourselves.

The next four stages are each steps toward accepting the end and letting go.

Stage 2: Anger appears in the second stage – anger turned outward towards others. It's easy to lash out angrily and inappropriately in a variety of situations. Much of the anger, about "how terrible it was to be married to him/her," is expressed to friends and others and not to the spouse. The anger, however, is a "Catch 22" because of fear that if we are too angry at the departing spouse (or the one we are leaving or think we should leave) there will be no getting back together. The emotional door is usually still open at this stage – there is strong ambivalence about wanting the spouse back.

Look in The Mirror

If you feel tempted to blame your present misery on your spouse, look in the mirror and pretend you see your spouse there as your reflection. You might notice that when you think or say, "I hate it when you do that" is really code for "I hate it when I do that, and I keep doing it."

Stage 3: The third stage is yet another attempt to prolong the relationship. We repeatedly bargain and compromise – we try to make deals with our spouse, in thought if not in action. This can be a "teddy bear" stage (see chapter 3) where we are willing to accommodate almost anything in order to have the relationship continue. This can be a dangerous stage because many couples get back together at this point by agreeing to be teddy bears, yet most of us can't stay that way for very long before emerging angrier than before. Frequently people get back together at this point because they can't stand the loneliness and the unhappiness of ending the relationship – choosing the spouse again as the lesser of two evils.

Stage 4: The fourth stage is the "blahs," a kind of depression and internal questioning: "Is this all there is to life?" This is the darkness before the dawn. It's a stage of growth where we build a stronger identity, and find life more meaningful, more purposeful. However, some people in this stage become suicidal when they find themselves discouraged at having worked so hard on this relationship which they now must let go. This stage frequently comes a long time after the actual separation – we are often surprised to find ourselves depressed about it all over again. Research has found that people who are aware of this stage get through it more easily.

Peggy Lee sang: "Is that all there is? If that's all there is, then let's keep dancing."

Stage 5: The last stage brings acceptance of the loss of the love relationship. We are finally free of the pain of grief. The end of grief is the acceptance of the end of the relationship. We find internal peace, become centered, and once again move on in our lives.

Rate Your Fears

Directions: Each of you list the fears you have relative to your separation or divorce, and rate each on a scale of 1-10.

My worst fears are: Rating

My worst fears are: Rating

Distinguish between a good belly laugh and cynicism. Cynicism is not funny.

Paste your favorite family or divorce cartoon here:

It's wise to get through all five stages of grief before entering a new relationship. You may experience them in a different order, and they may overlap. Many who work professionally with people in the divorce process say the grief process takes eighteen months to two years for most people.

Staying Sane Under Insane Conditions

Passing through the five stages of grief is like navigating your ship through a storm in the Twilight Zone. Try to recognize where you are in relation to these stages. Pay close attention to yourself throughout, and expect to be surprised. Here are some tips to help you along the way.

- *Fear* is often the trigger for doing some of the craziest or most hurtful things. It can lure you away from your deepest sense of yourself. Tell your worst fears to someone, or write them for yourself. To ensure that the fears do not control your choices, examine each fear. Rate just how realistic or likely an eventuality it is, on a scale of one to ten (ten being the most likely). For those fears you've rated over 5, ask yourself what you can and should do to minimize the risk. For example, as a marriage ends we might harbor a deep fear of "being a bag lady/bum." To minimize this risk, be responsible for budgeting your post-divorce life style and realistically assessing how much of that you can earn.

- *Let them flow,* strange as it may seem, is the way to deal with grief and its component emotions. Cry, weep, wail, however it is you do it, in ways that don't hurt yourself, or anyone else. Avoiding these emotions takes all our available energy, like trying to hold the door shut in a tornado, leaving us exhausted and depressed. Acknowledging them is the only way to release them. You must let them pass through, like opening both the front door and a window so the breeze can flow through. You can maintain yourself in your job, and perform better at work, by actually allocating time before or after, for expressing strong emotions in a non-destructive manner, without making anyone wrong. You can do this in a number of ways. Play music that helps you weep. Write a letter expressing your anger, but do not send it. Write or call a close friend. Therapy can help too.

- *Find your sense of humor,* even if you think there isn't anything in your situation to laugh about. Think back to the last ridiculous thing you did. If you cannot find anything to laugh about in yourself, find something out there, somewhere, that will help you have at least one good belly laugh. Find something to laugh about at least once a day. Cartoons, comedy videos, animals, pets, children – all of these can be of help.

Whining doesn't solve anything.

- *Blame is a black hole.* Allow your feelings to flow without placing blame for them – especially on your spouse. Keep acknowledging your emotions (grief, anger, hurt, fear, etc.) within yourself, without focusing on your spouse, or anyone else.

Healing Has its Ups and Downs

Healing, or recovering, from the pain of separation and divorce would be so much easier if it were a steady and consistent improvement from miserable to "feel good". But it's not. You might have one really good day followed by three depressing and confusing downers. Sometimes when you're feeling buffeted about by emotions you don't understand, you think you're going nuts. Know that progress from misery to complete recovery is a zigzag, not a straight line. Whether you're feeling better or worse than yesterday, or a few minutes ago, know that even as you feel like you're bouncing around, your recovery is under way.

- *Guilt is the desire to blame yourself.* Take responsibility for whatever you did or didn't do in your relationship without judging any of it as wrong. Figure out what you need to learn from it. Try to see your own actions and omissions in terms of their results, both in your relationship and inside yourself. This step is vital to moving on to a new relationship, one that won't be a repeat of the one that's ending.

- *Be patient.* The phases of the emotional divorce, although easily described, take time to live through. To rush through them is to try to push the river or rush the harvest. Allow each stage the time it needs.

- *Celebrate when you can.* Give yourself exactly what you want for birthdays and Christmas, Hanukkah, or Kwanzaa. Recognize your wedding anniversary. Don't set yourself up to receive nothing on important occasions. Don't abandon yourself. Celebrate your successes, no matter how small.

- *Create your own support system.* Maintain connection with several people with whom you can discuss anything. Be sure you find people who are genuinely caring, compassionate, and not just blindly militant on your behalf.

Being a Good Parent is Part of Taking Care of Yourself

Part of taking care of yourself is to be sure that you do your very best as a parent at this difficult time. It goes without saying, children need and deserve good parenting. Your own sense of self-esteem will plummet if you feel in any way that you are neglecting or harming your children. See How to be a Good Parent Through the Divorce Process in Chapter 8.

You can divorce a parent, but you cannot divorce a child.

Automatic Injunction:
(From the Petition in Chapter 5)

Both of you are bound by the terms of the following injunction the moment your case is filed and served (see Chapter 5). If you are filing as co-petitioners, you are *presumed* to be bound by it as soon as you sign the Petition.

"AUTOMATIC TEMPORARY INJUNCTION

1. Both parties are restrained from transferring, encumbering, concealing, or in any way disposing of, without the consent of the other party, or an Order of the Court, any marital property, except in the usual course of business or for the necessities of life. Each party is required to notify the other party of any proposed extraordinary expenditures and to account for all extraordinary expenditures made after the injunction is in effect; and

2. Both parties are enjoined from molesting or disturbing the peace of the other party or the minor child(ren); and

3. Both parties are restrained from removing the minor child(ren) of the parties, if any, from the state without the consent of the other party or an Order of the Court; and

4. Both parties are restrained, without at least 14 days advance notification and the written consent of the other party or an Order of the Court, from canceling, modifying, terminating, or allowing to lapse for nonpayment of premiums, any policy of health insurance, homeowner's or renter's insurance, or automobile insurance that provides coverage to either of the parties or the minor child(ren) or any policy of life insurance that names either of the parties or the minor child(ren) as a beneficiary.

Nothing in this automatic injunction shall prohibit either party from applying to the Court for further orders, an expanded automatic temporary injunction, or orders modifying or revoking this injunction."

How to Handle Potential Violence and Other Stressful Encounters

Fear, panic, feeling frozen emotionally and intellectually, are all results of relationships which are on the edge of violence. Both spouses may feel these, and both or only one may react with violence. Such violence, the experts say, is very often a result of feeling out of control (not necessarily that someone else is controlling you, but that you aren't in control of you). Some people use violence to make their partner feel helpless, in order to feel powerful.

If you feel, at any time in the course of your separation, that you or your spouse are to the point of violence or abuse, whether physical or extreme verbal assault, then do the following:

- *Get physically separated.* Go to solid friends or family. Some may need to go to the nearest safehouse.

- *If there is a neutral place where your children can go,* take them there. Grandparents can be a Godsend or a real curse. If they will defend the children's peace against both of you, they are the ones to go to. Neutral, mutual friends with children your children's age are often best. Sometimes, if you leave and take the children with you – especially to a secret place – that, too, can feel violent to the person left behind.

- *Do not destroy, sell, give away, or hide any property* which the other party is likely to feel is marital. Such unilateral action often feels like violence at the receiving end and generally escalates hostility.

- *Do not try to move the divorce along too fast.* Jumping into the adversarial process or even forcing yourself into mediation or counseling when you are still hurt and fearful may only convert anger to rage and rage to more violence.

- *Establishing certain agreements will go a long way* toward helping you get back in control of your individual lives: mutual agreements to stay apart, pay certain debts, preserve certain property; agreements about seeing the children without seeing each other; mutual promises of no violence or derogatory comments about each other. Try writing down what you yourself are willing to do along these lines. Make no demands about what you expect your spouse to do. Then sign it and give it to a trusted friend to give to your spouse. Such a proposal may open a door to settlement.

If none of these suggestions works or is even possible, and you fear that violence is imminent or inevitable, then you may need to use the courts to protect you. You should know that, in practice, a court order is a piece of paper. Sometimes it can push someone over the edge, so they no longer can be controlled by law. Sometimes the order is ignored.

There is a county court procedure for dealing with domestic violence. Forms and instructions may be obtained through the county court or Bradford Publishing.

Protection order: Written action by a court which prohibits a person from doing certain acts, for example from entering a certain property. Doing the prohibited act is then punishable by the court.

Protection orders are also available through your divorce action in district court. If you need more information on this subject, take care of yourself by consulting with an attorney who has expertise in the area of domestic violence and abuse.

If violence happens, or is threatened, call the police to report it immediately, and be willing to follow through with your charges. When it gets to this point you must seek intervention.

Restraining or protection orders are available to partners through a county court procedure under the Domestic Abuse statute.

Spouses in marriages in which there has been actual violence may still be able to have a friendly divorce, usually with the assistance of a mediator with experience in this area. A great deal of self-knowledge and insight on the part of both spouses has to occur, however, before this is possible.

Beware the Eternal Return

Humans are creatures of habit, and beliefs are mostly unconscious. Statistics show that without some introspection, self-reflection, and change, most of us will form a new relationship with someone almost exactly like the person we just ended with, like the divorced couple who were matched with each other through a dating service.

With honest self-examination you can make conscious changes in yourself and your patterns that can lead to an entirely new experience in relationship. Or, unchanged, you may find yourself attracted to the same dynamic you thought you left behind.

Notes:

CHAPTER 4

MOVING FROM ONE HOUSEHOLD TO TWO

MOVING FROM ONE HOUSEHOLD TO TWO

If you have decided to move apart—whether you are doing a trial separation, a legal separation, or a dissolution of marriage—you will be faced with a number of immediate choices. There will be some choices which you will want to make, but shouldn't; there will be others which you will not want to face, but should. This chapter is designed to help you to choose wisely for the short term.

You must make sure that as you separate nothing falls through the cracks. The children must be cared for on a daily basis; your bills must get paid; your property must be maintained. It is vital that at this difficult time you keep your communications open so that you can make clear agreements about all of these matters.

A useful first step is to decide the time frame for each of your interim agreements. You may make an agreement about paying the bills, for example, for three or six months, and an agreement about managing the children day to day for only one month or six weeks until you see how it works for everyone. Now is a good time to try different schemes to discover what works and doesn't work for you.

If you are planning a legal separation or divorce, and will therefore be filing papers in court, the interim agreements you make in this chapter may be made into a temporary order of the court, as explained at the end of this chapter. Many couples do not need to write down their temporary arrangements because their communications are clear and there is complete trust and reliability. Others want something written, more formal or official.

Your financial separation should be carefully planned. A common problem results when, sensing an imminent separation, one spouse fears that the other will do something that will cost a lot of money. So, to "protect" the money, he or she closes the joint account and puts the money in a separate account. The other spouse then panics, matters get out of control, and the legal fees soar.

Sometimes instead of fear, anger takes over. The working spouse will disallow the non-working spouse from using credit cards or bank accounts. This will nearly always result in bad things happening to the targeted spouse's credit rating and ability to survive financially. Judges usually frown on that.

Temporary agreement: Formal accords, usually written, between spouses concerning use of property, payment of debts, children and their support, temporary maintenance and taxes, to govern or affect the time stated in the agreement, which is generally from the time of the agreement until the final decree.

Temporary orders: Court orders that affect divorcing or legally separating spouses from the date of the order until their final decree; may be the result of a status conference, court hearing, or trial, or an order approving the spouses' temporary agreement.

"Once you are physically separated you are legally separated."

This assumption is incorrect, and can be very costly. You are legally separated only if and when you receive a signed decree of legal separation from a court.

Temporary Responsibility and Use, Not Permanent Ownership

Your temporary agreement does not decide who ultimately gets what, only the use of property, responsibility for keeping it up, and who will make what payments. Even the court is cautioned by statute not to let temporary agreements dictate the way things should be permanently. Temporary agreements are opportunities for you to experiment and try out ideas.

Partners can avoid much difficulty, and save money too, by carefully planning your separation so that neither of you gets in over your head, and no one is out on the curb either. You can make temporary agreements between you, as suggested in this chapter, making clear to each other just how long you mean "temporary" to be.

Residence Checklist – Short Term

Fill in the property address, occupant and the amount of the payment in the appropriate column for which of you will be responsible for making the payment in the short term. At this point the person who occupies a residence does not necessarily have to be the one responsible for all its expenses. Make two copies so you can repeat for a 2nd home or for non-residence real estate, such as rentals, or a vacation condo.

Address: ______________________

Occupant: ______________________

	Husband	Wife
Mortgage/ Rent	________	________
Mortgage (2nd)	________	________
Property Tax (if not in mtg.)	________	________
Insurance (if not in mtg.)	________	________
Homeowners Dues	________	________
Repairs	________	________
Capital Improvements	________	________
Regular Upkeep and Maintenance	________	________
Utilities	________	________
Appliance & Utility Repair	________	________

If you feel the need to have a written agreement, transfer the agreements on this checklist, as you reach them, to your Temporary Agreement, using the Sample Wording for Temporary Agreements at the end of this chapter.

These and other kinds of unilateral actions, without discussion or notice—let alone agreement—usually escalate the situation from very warm, to a mild simmer, to a fast boil. Suddenly your separation is no longer a private change of life, but a very expensive and public war. The more your early actions are based on joint decisions, made ahead of time, the more chance you have of finishing your divorce in peace, if not in harmony.

Who Uses What and Who Pays for It

In order for a couple to begin to live apart as satisfactorily as possible, they need a clear understanding of who will get to use what property, who will live in the home, how the mortgage or rent will be paid, who will drive which car, and who will be responsible for the car and other expenses. There are usually several major items of personal property about which you need understandings. For example, the computer, the washer and dryer, the ski condo time-share, the camping gear. Even if you are separating within the same residence, you will need to face these same questions.

You are not deciding ownership at this point, only temporary use. Do not try to resolve the entire property picture right at the beginning. Just settle who uses what, and who makes what payments for now.

Be certain that you plan clearly how long your temporary agreement is to last. Having a definite cut-off point (3-6 months is a likely term) helps you stay focused on finishing the final agreement. Be certain to define what circumstances will send you back to the bargaining table (loss of job, for example).

HOMES

Who will stay in the family home and who will move out? The answer to this question has serious financial consequences, both short term and long term. This chapter is about the short term.

If one or both of you wants to keep the house in the long term, test this plan for at least a month or two before committing to it. Use your temporary period to experiment. This is especially important if you're not sure whether you want to do this "for the sake of the children," or because you love the house so much.

For example, the lower income spouse may want to stay on in the house since this spouse might have difficulty qualifying for a new home loan. If the house is very large, very expensive or difficult to keep up, the burden may not be worth it. If the spouse who wants to keep the home is not the one who usually did the repairs or tended the lawn, the amount of headache involved may be an unpleasant surprise.

How will you as a couple finance the additional expense of a new home or apartment along with the expenses of the family home? Some people find they have to spend savings, sell stock, or take out a loan. If so, begin thinking about who will repay the loan, or whose share of your property the repayment will come from.

Even for the short term, be sure you list all the expenses of a family home, plus those of a new second home for the spouse who is moving.

You may wish to consider whether either of you may have another adult living with you to help with the expenses. Are there any restrictions between you as to who this person may be? Do any of your children contribute anything toward the costs or the upkeep of either home in money or in labor?

CARS AND OTHER MOTOR VEHICLES

Make clear agreements with each other about who will drive which car for the time being. Nothing needs to be done at this point about changing the names on the title. Car loans and automobile insurance should be unchanged and payments must be kept current. You may need to talk about joint use of a single car. Think in terms of problem solving—what's going to work—and a reasonable sharing of comforts and conveniences along with burdens and inconveniences.

In the permanent property division, the spouse who gets the car ordinarily gets the loan on it too. But you do not have to do it that way in the short term. You can usually keep both cars on the same insurance policy until the date of the divorce or until the next time the premium comes due after the date of the divorce. Discuss who will be responsible for paying the premium, or whether and in what proportion it will be shared. Once your case is filed, the Temporary Injunction in the petition restricts you from canceling insurance without following a detailed procedure.

OTHER PROPERTY AND OTHER REGULAR EXPENSES

You may wish to clarify which of you gets to use other items during this period, such as the computer, sound system, TV or home theater, pets, RV, microwave, camping and other sports equipment. Make an agreement that whoever gets to use these items for now will maintain them until you reach a final decision. Remember, you are not deciding ownership, only use.

Motor Vehicle Checklist – Short Term

Directions: Fill in the vehicle year and make and the amount of each expense in the appropriate column for which of you will pay it in the short term. At this point the person who has the use of a vehicle does not necessarily have to be the one responsible for its expenses. Repeat for additional vehicles.

Year & make of vehicle ________________

	Husband	Wife
Loan/lease payment	________	________
Insurance	________	________
Gas & Oil	________	________
Maintenance	________	________
Other	________	________

Year & make of vehicle ________________

	Husband	Wife
Loan/lease payment	________	________
Insurance	________	________
Gas & Oil	________	________
Maintenance	________	________
Other	________	________

If you feel you need a written temporary agreement, transfer the agreements on this checklist, as you reach them, to your Temporary Agreement, using the Sample Wording for Temporary Agreements at the end of this chapter.

Other Property Checklist – Short Term

Directions: List in the left hand column those items of property which are important to both of you. Then put a check in the "Husband" or "Wife" column to indicate which of you will have the use of it for the time being, and be responsible for maintaining it.

Item	Husband	Wife
________	___	___
________	___	___
________	___	___
________	___	___
________	___	___
________	___	___
________	___	___
________	___	___
________	___	___
________	___	___
________	___	___
________	___	___
________	___	___
________	___	___
________	___	___

Similarly, you must decide who will make your fixed payments, such as life and medical insurance, installment loans and credit cards, and student loan payments. Once you file your case, you must follow the Temporary Injunction regarding cancellation of any insurance.

CAUTION: It is essential at this time that you either agree not to use any credit cards except together, or that you each choose one or more credit cards to use and be responsible for their payment. For example, you may wish to retain the use of an oil company credit card for your car expenses.

Whatever your agreement about use and payment of credit cards or payment of debts, creditors are not bound by your agreement. They will still have the right to "come after" both of you for any missed payments. See Temporary Teeth, page 63.

Fixed Payments Checklist

List your creditors in the left column. For each creditor, write the amount of the payment in the column of the spouse who will be responsible for making the payment. Be sure to indicate the time period for any payment that is not monthly.

Creditor	Husband	Wife
________	$ ______	$ ______
________	$ ______	$ ______
________	$ ______	$ ______
________	$ ______	$ ______
________	$ ______	$ ______
________	$ ______	$ ______
________	$ ______	$ ______
________	$ ______	$ ______
________	$ ______	$ ______
________	$ ______	$ ______
________	$ ______	$ ______

If you feel you need a written temporary agreement, transfer the agreements on these checklists, as you reach them, to your Temporary Agreement, using the Sample Wording for Temporary Agreements at the end of this chapter.

NECESSARY PURCHASES

Whenever a family expands from one household to two, some items will need to be duplicated. Such items might be: children's furniture, couch, bed, washer/dryer, towels, sheets, coffee pot, iron, tools, stereo, TV.

CAUTION Purchasing these items could easily swallow your budget. You may need to limit this list to essentials, with each household bearing some burden of doing without. You might color-code different items—red for essentials needed right away; green for things needed soon, etc.

Consider sharing instead of duplicating. Alternate times with the washer/dryer. Use the camper on alternate weekends. Mow your lawns on different days with the same mower.

Share the burden of being without or being inconvenienced. For example, if one of you has no washer/dryer and must use the laundromat, perhaps the other could do without the stereo. Some couples prefer to separate within the same residence in order to save on these items and not have to incur this expense right at the beginning.

Agree that neither of you will make major purchases other than those on the DIN List below. This will help you build trust in one another's sense of what is necessary. Agree that neither of you will borrow any money, or use any credit cards, without the consent of the other.

Duplicate Items Needed List ("DIN" List)

Directions: List in the "Item" column those things which you will want to acquire to make your two households complete. Work together on this. Under the heading "Husband" or "Wife," list the maximum cost for each item that you agree needs to be duplicated for that person's household.

Category	**Item**	**Husband**	**Wife**
Furniture			
Linens			

Category	Item	Husband	Wife
Appliances			
	______	______	______
	______	______	______
	______	______	______
	______	______	______
Kitchen items			
	______	______	______
	______	______	______
	______	______	______
	______	______	______
	______	______	______
	______	______	______
	______	______	______
	______	______	______
	______	______	______
Children's things			
	______	______	______
	______	______	______
	______	______	______
	______	______	______
Other			
	______	______	______
	______	______	______
	______	______	______
	______	______	______
	______	______	______
	______	______	______
Total Cost		______	______

This DIN list is an example of a private agreement between you and your spouse that will probably not find its way into a formal Temporary or Permanent Agreement or form, unless you feel the need to make lists and file them with the court.

YOUR CREDIT AND YOUR DIVORCE

Without credit, you can't get a credit card. Without a credit card, you cannot rent a car, make hotel or travel reservations, buy a truck or furniture on time, or have that margin of borrowing power for emergencies. In short, it is very important that you protect your credit in your divorce. This section is about how to emerge from a divorce with the highest possible credit ratings for each of you.

You should each immediately obtain your individual credit rating as soon as you decide to separate. This way you have ample time and the legal right to remedy any errors between you, and to add any missing accounts for either of you. Look under "Credit Reporting Agencies" in the Yellow Pages and call at least one. A recorded message will tell you how to obtain your credit report. Be sure that you request your individual reports, not your joint report, and that you each give any previous name(s).

Credit ratings are the history of the way you pay your bills. This history is kept by a number of credit reporting agencies to which the individual creditors (credit card companies, department stores, banks, credit unions) report the relative regularity and promptness of payments by those who owe them money. Marriage and divorce affect credit ratings indirectly, but profoundly.

If the debt or credit card was applied for by both of you and based on both your incomes, then it is a pretty good bet that it has been reporting in both your names and contributing to both your individual credit ratings. You will see the debt on both your credit reports.

If, however, one of you had the card or debt before the marriage, or it was applied for by one of you based on only that one income, then the credit may not be reporting in both names. This often happens when one spouse is the primary wage-earner. In such cases, the non-wage-earning spouse may well not have a credit rating at all or have an inadequate one because it does not contain some of the major credit accounts used during the marriage. You will know this is the situation if your credit report comes back blank, or does not contain any information about debts you know were paid on jointly.

The only way an account that is in one name only will report into both your credit ratings is if the person to whom that card was issued requests in writing, before the divorce is final, that their spouse receive credit on that account. The spouse who wants the credit cannot do this. So, if you are agreeing to finish paying off a debt or credit card as part of your settlement, be certain that

BUNKY **"I signed all the checks to pay the bills and they were all written on our joint account, so I know I have good credit."**

The correct information: Credit is reported automatically only in the name of the person who applied for the account or loan and on whose income it was based. If you did not sign the application, then this record of payments on your marital debt may not be reporting in your name at all.

Notes:

particular debt or credit card is reporting on your own credit rating. Otherwise, you may pay off a bill which will not establish or benefit your own credit.

You may build up a credit rating for a low- or non-income spouse by making certain all the high-rated credit cards are reporting in his or her name before the divorce. Then, pay off the balances on these cards at the time of the divorce. Have the low-income spouse keep at least one of the best-rated cards—with a provision that he or she will 1) use the card for small purchases that will be paid off quickly, 2) apply for a card in his or her own name within a certain number of months or years after the final decree, and then 3) close the old joint account.

If you close any high-rated credit card accounts before the divorce, or notify the issuing bank to "take my spouse off the card," you may have sabotaged your spouse's ability to build a satisfactory credit rating. A better arrangement is to put all the credit cards in a sealed envelope and leave it with a trusted friend or in a safe deposit box out of sight, and agree not to charge anything until you finish your agreement. Then make clear agreements about all the cards as part of your temporary agreement. See the bibliography to read more about credit.

Notes:

Children

The time when parents begin living apart is one of the most stressful for children. Their worst fear is of losing a parent. They need both parents to stay actively involved in their lives at this time. Children can readily adjust to the separations and transitions involved in two-household parenting. They adjust better when their parents work together to support each other's relationship with them. You might wish to read through the information about how children react to the divorce process in Chapter 8 of this book. It is full of useful tips about putting together a parenting plan that will work for your children.

HOW TO BE A GOOD PARENT THROUGH THE DIVORCE PROCESS

Children feel more secure when they are confident that their parents can take care of themselves. If they feel you are not doing that, they will try to take care of you, and the parent-child relationship becomes reversed. Therefore taking care of yourself at this difficult time is not only good for you, it is in the best interest of your children.

Critical to good parenting throughout the divorce process is insulating the children from any hostilities between the parents. This means managing your own conflict well. Work toward strengthening your children's sense of security while they navigate their own choppy waters as you separate and divorce. It's a time to be very careful what you say, and to whom you say it. Think your conduct through carefully.

WHO MAKES WHAT DECISIONS ABOUT THE CHILDREN

The two major kinds of decision-making about children are day-to-day decisions, and major decisions. Day-to-day decisions—menus, schedules, bed times, transportation—are made by the parent who has the children at the time.

The divorce statute suggests that the major decisions include "the health, education, and general welfare of the child." Most divorcing parents find this definition unworkably inclusive. It is important that the two of you evolve your own more specific list of decisions which you agree you must share during this interim period. Some examples are:

- activities of our children which will take place on both parents' time with them.
- major expenses for our children which we expect the other parent to share.

BUNKY

"Divorce always hurts children." "You just can't possibly be a responsible parent and get a divorce."

The truth, shown by extensive research, is that divorce does not necessarily hurt children. What does hurt them is ongoing hostilities between their parents, whether or not there is a divorce. Research shows that children of divorcing parents who stopped fighting were as well adjusted as those raised in successful marriages. The same research also shows that children of parents who stayed together, but who continued to fight, had as much trouble adjusting as children of the continually hostile divorce. So it's not the divorce that hurts the children, it's the ongoing anger and hostility that are harmful.

Parenting-After-Divorce Classes

Just about all Colorado courts now require divorcing parents to attend a one-time class about the effects of divorce on themselves and their children. These classes teach coparenting skills and strategies. The court will require a certificate of completion to be in your court file before it will determine parenting issues and before it will enter a final decree. Usually the parties are responsible for mailing or bringing the certificate to the court. In some jurisdictions, the instructor will take care of this. The cost of the class is usually $35 to $60 each, which can be waived by the instructor upon a showing of serious need.

P PARTNERS

Partners who are parents have all the same concerns and responsibilities as married parents when moving from one household to two. You may not be ordered to take a parenting-after-divorce class, but you aren't prohibited from taking one, and you might find it helpful.

D DEFINITION **Temporary Parenting Plan: Parental Responsibility.** Designates the way parents will make the major decisions about their children during the time between their separation and divorce.

They can agree that one parent will be responsible for making the decisions or that both parents will share all major decisions. Or, parents may select certain decisions to be made by one parent and certain other decisions to be made by the other parent—with or without negotiation beforehand. Other decisions may be made jointly.

"Children have never been very good at listening to their elders, but they have never failed to imitate them."
James Baldwin, "Fifth Avenue, Uptown."
Nobody Knows My Name.

- major planned elective medical or dental care, but not emergency medical care.
- how we will share or divide birthdays and holidays which occur during this interim period.

Shared or mutual decision-making means you keep talking until you reach agreement. You may agree that some or all of the major decisions, or categories of decisions, will be made by one or the other of you. Even if you are agreeing that one parent alone will make particular decisions, you may list matters about which the decision-maker must consult with the other parent. This means you must discuss it beforehand, even though the decision-maker still makes the final decision. For example, one parent might make all the clothing purchases, but discuss ahead of time the limit on spending and how to pay for it.

Naming one parent to make certain decisions and the other parent to make others allows some parents to share this important aspect of parenting without creating endless confrontations. If one of you has historically made the decisions about medical care, and the other has always had the last word about education issues, you can continue this way of doing things in your temporary agreement.

Whatever your choices, being clear about who makes what decisions about your children helps them feel secure, and to know that you are in control.

Notes:

Temporary Parenting Decisions List

Directions: List in one of the categories below, the decisions concerning your children which you anticipate must be made during this interim period.

We will make the following decisions together, jointly:

1.

2.

3.

Mother will make the following decisions:

1.

2.

3.

Mother must consult Father on (all) (#).

Father will make the following decisions:

1.

2.

3.

Father must consult Mother on (all) (#).

If you feel you need a written temporary agreement, transfer the agreements on this list, when completed, to the Sample Temporary Agreement at the end of this chapter.

Temporary Parenting Plan: Physical Residential care. Where the children of separated parents live between the time of separation and final decree.

"Children should have only one home."

Research shows that children adjust better to divorce when they continue to have stable and loving relationships with both parents. This can be accomplished in two homes.

"Children get confused when their parents' lifestyles are too different."

Not necessarily. Some experts do say that for two households to work well together, they shouldn't be too terribly far apart in value systems. For example, if one parent lives a "laid-back" lifestyle and the other household uses linen napkins, the child may begin to wonder whether to be like Mom and her household, or Dad and his. Studies show that children can make these kinds of transitions – but not frequently and with support and preparation from their parents in every transition.

WHERE WILL THE CHILDREN STAY

The temporary period is an excellent time to try out various parenting plans. Put together a consistent schedule for six weeks or so, try it out, and then assess it. You may discover that some aspects of your plan do not work well for your family. Talk about it with each other; then listen to the children's input; reach agreement and make the needed changes and adjustments. Don't expect to know right away what arrangements are going to be best for your children in the long term. Your first plan may well not be your final agreement. You will need flexibility.

Some parents want equal time sharing when it may not be in the children's best interest at this time. For example, infants and very young children may not be developmentally ready for two homes on a 50-50 basis. Small children may be better served by gradually expanding the overnights with the other parent, with a goal of reaching 50-50, or roughly equal time sharing by a certain age, such as 5, or 6, or 7. However, a younger child may do quite well in equal time sharing if his or her connections have been strong with both parents, and/or if there is an older sibling making the same transitions on the same schedule. Teenagers, who can do well with equal time sharing, need to have a great deal to say about where and how they spend their time.

Children who are more mellow, even young ones, can be transferred back and forth a lot. The younger the child, the more frequently visits are needed with each parent. A week seems like a year to them. Frequency of contact is more important to them than duration. Children who are more hyper may need more structure and consistency, meaning they need to be more anchored in one place.

Another factor to consider is "work time" and "play time" which, for most, is the work week and the weekend. It's best for children if each parent has both work time and play time with them. Having one parent do all the work and the other all the play gives children a skewed idea of roles to identify with.

Recent research shows that children can handle up to three living environments, such as Mom's house, Dad's house, and daycare. More than three is challenging for children and they become confused and disorganized. Stay aware of your children's needs during this time, and keep evaluating how your current plan is working for them.

For more on the significance of your child's developmental age for your parenting plans, see Chapter 8. This would be an excellent time to read *Children of Divorce,* by Baris and Garrity, or any other books listed in the bibliography at the end of this Guidebook which relate to your circumstances.

P PARTNERS All the information here about temporary decision making and temporary parenting time is relevant for partners.

HOW TO TELL THE CHILDREN

How do you tell your children about your separation? Have both parents there, if possible, and tell the children not only your decision to separate, but also your plan. Help them understand that you are not separating from or "divorcing" them. Tell them that you will always take care of them, no matter what. Parents might stop loving each other, but they never stop loving their children. Tell them how important it is to both of you that they continue to have both of you. Be concrete with them about your plans. Children function better if they know the physical plan, such as where their room will be and who keeps the dog.

"The ones that matter most are the children. They are the true human beings." Lakota proverb

When appropriate, share your six-week calendar with your children and ask for their input. Listen to their concerns about the mechanics: "Where will my bicycle live?" "How will my ice skates get from one house to the other?" "I only have one computer, how will I do my homework?"

If you can, discuss in advance the physical plans for your separation with the children. Involve them in the doing—take them with you to see possible new apartments or homes so they can participate in the creation of their second home. They will have their own ideas about which toys and books should be at which place and how they want their spaces to look. You may have to override some of their choices, but they should be allowed to participate and to express themselves, and even to carry out some of their wishes in their own way.

Notes:

Six Week Parenting Plan and Calendar

Directions: Using the material from the following page, fill in your parenting time for the next six weeks. This calendar ends the week with Saturday and Sunday together. Most published calendars divide the weekend by placing Sunday as the first day of the week, and Saturday the last—a picture which is generally confusing when working out parenting times.

Mon.	Tues.	Wed.	Thurs.	Fri.	Sat.	Sun.

USING YOUR SIX-WEEK CALENDAR

Fill in the following information on the calendar on the previous page. Make several photocopies first for your rough draft(s). (Sometimes it is useful to use different colored pens for each parent, or each member of the family.)

1. The dates for the six-week period you are planning, and any holidays or other special days, such as a child's birthday.

2. Parents' fixed schedules. For example: work hours, fixed meetings and appointments.

3. Children's fixed schedules, such as school hours, and planned regular activities such as soccer practice, piano lesson, Cub Scouts. Discuss whether a change in the children's day care schedule is desirable. On the one hand it may be just the time to make a needed change; on the other hand, if both of you are moving, keeping the day-care schedule the same may help a young child feel more secure at this difficult time.

4. Appointments (doctor, dentist) and special events already committed to (recital, track meet, reunion).

5. Looking at the six-weeks as a whole, begin to discuss and even pencil in some possible parenting times. For example, school nights with one parent, weekend or vacation nights with the other; alternating weeks with each parent; dividing each week 4-3, 5-2, or 6-1; dividing each two week period in half with a 4-3-3-4 schedule; dove-tailing with one or both parents' variable work schedule. A 2-2-3 schedule can work well for small children: Monday and Tuesday with mother; Wednesday and Thursday with father; Friday-Sunday with mother; then reverse this for the following week. Some children struggle with a 14-day plan, however, needing instead to be with the same parent on the same day of each week ("I'm with Mommy/Daddy on Monday"). So observe your children's needs carefully.

6. Be sure you take into account your children's ages and stage of development. Your time plan for an infant will be very different from the plan you would make for a teenager.

7. Indicate on the calendar who will provide the transportation each time, who will pick-up or drop-off. The further apart you live, the more important the transportation issue will become. Whenever you bring your children to their other parent, you demonstrate your support and willingness for your children to leave you and to relate to their other parent.

8. Write or at least discuss any items which must move back and forth with the children, such as clothing, boots, homework, and musical instruments.

If you feel the need to have a written temporary agreement, transfer the agreements you make about the residential physical care of your children into to your Temporary Agreement using the Sample Wording for Temporary Agreements at the end of this chapter.

The Budget Crunch

Two together still live more cheaply than one. Two apart are more expensive than one. Negotiating early through the stark reality of the high cost of two households is a major key to keeping peace throughout the separation and divorce process. As you separate, it is important that you and your spouse have a complete understanding of which income will pay for which expenses.

The purpose of this section is to help you keep track of your incomes and budget your expenses as your family moves from one household into two.

TRACKING YOUR INCOMES

The word "income" can mean very different things to different people. To the worker it probably means spendable earnings. To the IRS it means what is taxed. In the Colorado Child Support Guideline, it can mean potential earnings that are not actually coming in, and even imputed income nobody actually receives.

Using the "Income Tracker," write down the income each of you expects to receive during the interim period you are planning for. List both incomes you are certain of receiving, and that which you might receive. Definite income includes your base pay before commission, salary, draw, guaranteed hours, required overtime, regular bonuses. Possible income may include commissions, bonuses, one-time sales or liquidation, irregular overtime, irregular bonuses.

Write down both your gross and net incomes. The gross is the larger number, before anything is withheld. The net number is the amount you bring home, after all the withholding and deductions from your paycheck. This number may change as you make agreements about tax planning and saving for your futures, but use the present actual numbers for now.

If you are self-employed, your gross income is your business net, i.e., your total business receipts less your total necessary business expenses. The information on your Schedule C from your last several income tax returns is an excellent place to start. In most instances, the bottom line on that form, your business income, will be your own personal gross income—the number to use for figuring family support during this period.

Income Tracker

Husband *expects* to receive the following regular income (averaged per month) for the next __________ months:

$_________ gross; $_________net.

Husband *may* receive the following additional income (averaged per month) over the next _________ months:

$_________ gross, $__________net.

Wife *expects* to receive the following regular income (averaged per month) for the next __________ months:

$_________ gross; $_________net.

Wife *may* receive the following additional income (averaged per month over the next _________ months:

$_________ gross, $__________net.

Look at a Week Instead of a Month?

Cheryl had managed the household, but had never been responsible for paying the bills. When she and Mike separated, she was starting at the beginning when it came to thinking about a monthly budget. In fact a month was too large for her to start with. So they began with a weekly budget. After a few weeks of experience, Cheryl, was ready to begin looking at the monthly picture.

EXPENSES

The purpose of this section is to budget your expenses as your family changes from one household to two. You will have the on-going expenses of both households, plus any debt payments you may have.

The ongoing expenses for two households can be divided into two categories:

1. bare bones: necessary expenses during this period of time ("survival");
2. discretionary: expenses which either of you could live without, albeit with difficulty ("lifestyle"); and

Your Monthly Budget is the chart that begins on page 121 in Chapter 6. It lists your expenses in the categories described above. Make several photocopies of the budget and complete one for each household. You may need some now for your rough drafts, and to prepare again toward the end of your interim or temporary period (and at the time of your decree), as your circumstances change.

Be sure that between your two spouse's budgets, you include all your expenses and debts for both households, and that you do not duplicate any of them. Do these budgets separately even if you are physically separating within the same residence. You will still have to decide how to share the expenses of the home.

Notes:

Notes:

P PARTNERS The Budget Crunch and the following Budget Analysis can be just as relevant for parent-partners as they are for married parents.

BUDGETING YOUR SEPARATION

Now you are ready to compare your expected incomes with your expected expenses for this interim period.

Directions: Have in front of you the following:

1. Your DIN (Duplicate Items Needed) List, pages 43-44.
2. Your Income Tracker, page 54.
3. Both of Your Monthly Budgets (from Chapter 6). Use them to complete the following chart. You may want to make several photocopies of this for rough drafts.

Budget Analysis Chart

HUSBAND:

Basic Income (Inc. Tracker)	$ ____________	Extra Income (Inc. Tracker)	$ ____________	Total Income	$ ____________
Bare Bones Expenses (Monthly Budget)	$ ____________	Discretionary Expenses (Monthly Budget)	$ ____________		
DIN List Expenses (Monthly Budget)	$ ____________			Total Expenses	$ __________

WIFE:

Basic Income (Inc. Tracker)	$ ____________	Extra Income (Inc. Tracker)	$ ____________	Total Income	$ ____________
Bare Bones Expenses (Monthly Budget)	$ ____________	Discretionary Expenses (Monthly Budget)	$ ____________		
DIN List Expenses (Monthly Budget)	$ ____________			Total Expenses	$ __________

BUDGET ANALYSIS

Step 1. A Look at your Combined Picture.

Add your combined total incomes: $ ____________________

Add your combined total expenses: $ ____________________

Subtract expenses from incomes: +/–$ ____________________

If your result is a positive number, this means that you have enough take-home money at the present time to meet the total short term expenses for both households. Make a clear agreement about what you will do with the surplus, so that the whole family can benefit from it during this time. You are not unusual if you have a negative number here. Most people do not have enough income to meet the total "wish lists" of two households.

Step 2. One Household Shortfall.

If you have a combined negative number, go to Step 3. If you have a combined positive number, you must now check if you individually have a positive number. Subtract your individual total expenses from your individual total income as follows:

Husband's Total Income	$ ________________	Wife's Total Income	$ ________________
Husband's Total Expenses	$________________	Wife's Total Expenses	$ ________________
Difference:	+/–$ ________________	Difference:	+/–$________________

If one of you has a positive difference, and the other a negative, some money must change hands between you to enable both households to meet all expenses. It is possible to increase the net income to your whole family by decreasing income taxes in this situation. In principle, this type of planning lowers the tax burden of the higher income spouse by allocating some of his or her income to the lower income spouse who is in a lower tax bracket. This can generate significant savings from which you can both benefit. See the next section of this chapter and Chapter 10 (Maintenance) and Chapter 11 (Taxes) for more about this.

Step 3. Mutual Belt-Tightening.

If the result in your Budget Analysis is a negative number, there is not enough combined income to meet your total combined expenses. Look at both of Your Monthly Budgets and your DIN List. What can you agree together to cut back on? The discretionary column on Your Monthly Budget is the most likely place where you can cut. If by doing this you can break even in your combined numbers, then go back to Step 2.

Step 4. Rethinking Your Budgets.

If Step 3 does not bring you back to break-even or a positive number, then you will probably need to take a hard look at the assumptions underlying your two-household monthly budgets:

- Can either of you increase your income by decreasing your withholding, working additional hours, or taking interest or dividend incomes which you would normally not do?
- Is this the time for either of you to go from part time to full time employment, or to find employment?
- Is this the time to sell the house?
- Is this really the time to buy the second home? Can one or both of you rent or lease-with-option-to-buy for a time?
- Is this the time to sell an asset, or use a savings account?
- Is this the time to borrow against an asset: take a second mortgage on the house, borrow against your life insurance, or your car?
- Are there friends or relatives who will help you through this interim period?
- If your short-fall is primarily due to large debts or bill payments, is this the time to call Consumer Credit Counseling, or to consider a Chapter 13 Bankruptcy?

This is a difficult time for everyone who faces these circumstances. This may be the time when you are most tempted to give up working together and let someone else take over. Don't panic. Be careful not to lose yourself in fear about money. Keep focused on the good that will come to your family by separating cooperatively.

If you can agree on a solution like the suggestions above, thereby bringing your combined totals to break-even, then go back to Step 2.

Step 5. "Oh My God!"

If there is nothing you yourselves can do to make your two-household budgets happen, then ask:

- Must you separate at this time? Can you put off the separation until one of you finishes school, or is no longer laid off? Is this the time to reconsider sharing the house "upstairs/downstairs?"
- Can you resolve the situation itself: place the disabled child or elderly family member in a care facility, or delay your separation until the difficulty is resolved?
- Is this the time for a Chapter 7 Bankruptcy?
- Is there a source of community, church, or family assistance? (Food Stamps, Unemployment Compensation, Social Security, Supplemental Security Income?)

Temporary Support Between Spouses

TEMPORARY MAINTENANCE

If your budget analysis on the previous page shows that some money needs to change hands between you in order that you may both meet your on-going living expenses, you may need to agree on temporary support. Here are two basic ways.

1. *Higher income spouse pays some or all of lower income spouse's expenses directly.* One expense may be the mortgage. If the mortgage is still in the paying spouse's name and he or she doesn't have another primary residence, and you file separate returns (including married filing separately), this spouse can take the tax deduction for the home mortgage interest. Other expenses might be insurance, credit card bills and utilities.

   The paying spouse can also pay directly some of the children's expenses, such as day care, babysitting, medical and dental bills. The child care credit, available to single working parents, may then be taken by the paying spouse IF AND ONLY IF you file separately (including married filing separately), the paying spouse has been separated for more than 6 months before the end of the year, and has sufficient parenting time to qualify as head of household. This is an easy rule to miss and a costly one.

2. *Higher income spouse pays temporary maintenance, each party pays their own bills.* If you structure your agreement so that the bills the lower income spouse is paying are tax deductions (like the mortgage interest and property tax) or lead to a credit (like work-related child care), then the receiving spouse off-sets these against the taxable payments from the paying spouse. And everyone saves money. If the lower income spouse is the primary residential care parent, remaining in the family home, this way of doing things may be tailor-made for you.

As you move towards a decision on the amount of your temporary maintenance, if any, and your combined annual gross income is less than $75,000, there is a statutory formula which the court must follow if you asked the court to decide it for you (see sidebar). You may wish to include this as part of your thinking.

Once you have decided on the amount of your temporary maintenance, whether it's a fixed amount throughout or one amount for certain months and another amount for other months, or

D DEFINITION

Alimony

Same as maintenance. Also called Section 71 payments, referring to the section in the Internal Revenue Code.

IR$

Temporary Maintenance

Payments made by one spouse to the other, prior to the final decree, are deductible from the income of the paying spouse, included in the income of the receiving spouse, and are subject to federal and state income tax, but not Social Security taxes.

Temporary Maintenance Formula

Higher monthly gross income
x 40% __________

minus lower monthly gross income
x 50% - __________

Result is Temporary Maintenance
= __________

If 0 or minus number, no presumed payment

Tax filing status during separation.
If there are no children, you must file married (jointly or separately). If you are still married but have been living separately for more than six months, and if you have a child in your household to whom you are entitled a dependency exemption (even if you have waived your right to it), you may file as head of household. If so, the other spouse must file married filing separately unless he or she also qualifies for head of household. Or, instead of this arrangement, you may still file married filing jointly no matter how long you have been separated. See Chapter 11 Taxes.

If partners choose to pay some short term support, there is no tax effect. The paying partner pays in after tax dollars, and the receiving partner may owe income tax on it. Nevertheless this is a solution for some, often until the receiving partner obtains employment. The word "temporary" meaning "before the Decree" in the divorce process, has no parallel meaning for partners.

When partners separate, their tax filing status does not change unless a dependent for head of household filing status is no longer in their household.

simply one lump sum, you must decide whether you want it to be a private agreement between the two of you, or a court order.

1. Temporary maintenance by private agreement. Write an agreement that states your names, that you are husband and wife, the date of your marriage, and the date of your separation—you must be living apart in order to have a temporary maintenance agreement. Then write the amount of the maintenance, whether it's per month, per quarter, one lump sum, and when it is due to the receiving spouse (for example "on or before the 4th day of each month starting in July 2007"). Write how long you want it to go—often "until entry of our Decree," or "until we agree otherwise in writing and signed by both of us." Then each of you sign it in front of a notary, and each keep a copy or the original in your tax file. Such an agreement must be signed and dated before you make any of the maintenance payments in order to shift the taxes. Temporary maintenance paid according to a private agreement IS NOT an exception to the steep stair-step recapture rule test calculations (see Chapter 11). Read the rule and decide whether it makes any difference in your situation.

2. Temporary maintenance by Temporary Order of the Court. Temporary maintenance paid according to a court order IS an exception to the steep stair-step recapture rule test calculations (see Chapter 11). Check the rule to see if you need to go this route. If so, see the end of this chapter for how to make your Temporary Agreement into a Temporary Order of the Court. If your combined annual gross income is less than $75,000, you will have to show the calculation of maintenance according to the statutory formula and either use that number, or explain why a deviation from the formula is fair in your particular circumstances. If you have children, you will also need a child support worksheet and an agreement about temporary child support. Calculate maintenance first, then child support.

IR$ TAX CONSIDERATIONS

The date of your physical separation affects the options you have about your filing status, as does the date of your final decree.

If it is less than 91 days between your time of filing for dissolution or legal separation and the end of the calendar year, you must file married filing jointly or married filing separately. (You cannot file as Single.) If you wish to have temporary maintenance that is taxable, you must file married filing separately. If your temporary maintenance is non-taxable, you can file married filing jointly.

If you have been separated for more than six months before the end of the year (i.e., you physically separated before July 1 of this year) you have another option. Any separated person who has provided a home for his or her dependent child for more that six months of the year, may file as head of household. If you have more than one child and are sharing residential care parenting time, you might each have this option and each get the child care credit for that child. This may save money over filing jointly. If only one parent can qualify as head of household, the other must file married filing separately while you are still married.

If your 91 day waiting period will finish before the end of the year, then you have the option of completing your final decree in this tax year, and will be able to file as single or head of household for the tax year.

Agreeing to temporary maintenance can help you avoid the "recapture problem" if you have one (see Chapter 11). If you can reach agreement quickly about high-end temporary maintenance—even large lump-sum maintenance—ask the court to approve your written agreement as an order of court, then any amounts will not count in the steep stair-step recapture rules.

Temporary Child Support

If you wish to have the court approve your temporary agreements you must use the Colorado Child Support Guideline to calculate child support and include a child support worksheet and financial affidavits. See chapters 6 and 9 for instructions on these forms. This means that some of the money changing hands will probably have to be labeled child support, thus losing some of the tax planning opportunity of calling it maintenance. You can still do some tax planning by subtracting the amount of temporary maintenance from the income of the paying spouse and adding it

Checklist of Temporary Maintenance and First Year Filing Status.

☐ **We plan to obtain our final decree of dissolution of marriage (legal separation) this calendar year.**

We will file our taxes this year as:

Wife: ☐ Single ☐ Head of Household

Husband: ☐ Single ☐ Head of Household

________________ (paying spouse) will pay $ ____________ per month as temporary maintenance to ________________ (receiving spouse) starting __________ (date), until the decree. ________________ (paying spouse) will pay $ __________ per month as maintenance between the final decree and the end of the calendar year, for a total of $ __________.

We ☐ will ☐ will not make our temporary maintenance agreement into a court order, so that the total paid before the decree ☐ will ☐ will not be counted in the first separation year maintenance total for testing under the recapture rule (see Chapter 11).

☐ **We don't plan to obtain our final decree this calendar year.**

We will file our taxes this year as follows:

☐ Married filing jointly.

☐ Married filing separately.
☐ Wife ☐ Husband

☐ Head of Household.
☐ Wife ☐ Husband

________________ (paying spouse) will pay to ________________ (receiving spouse) $ __________ per month for temporary maintenance ☐ by ☐ not by court order for a total of $ __________ which ☐ will ☐ will not be our first separation year for maintenance recapture test calculations (see Chapter 11).

If you feel you need a written temporary agreement, transfer the agreements on this checklist, when completed, to the Sample Temporary Agreement at the end of this chapter.

to the income of the receiving spouse on the child support worksheet. This will alter the ratio of your incomes, thereby reducing the child support of the paying spouse—often significantly.

If you are bargaining between yourselves about how to get the bills paid, and you feel no need to have your temporary agreement made into a court order, you do not have to follow the Colorado Child Support Guideline in calculating support.

Once you have agreed to an amount for temporary support and other temporary arrangements and if you prefer a written agreement, you may transfer the information to the sample Temporary Agreement at the end of this chapter.

The Temporary Agreement

HOW FORMAL DOES OUR TEMPORARY AGREEMENT NEED TO BE?

Many couples do not need to write down their temporary arrangements. Others want something more formal, or official. This is your call. If you want to make your agreements firm, write them down and have your signatures notarized to show the strength of your intent. You are bound by this agreement just as you would be by any contract, such as a contract for purchase of real estate, a car or a sofa.

IR$ If you make your temporary maintenance agreement into a court order, any maintenance payments that are made DO NOT count in the maintenance considered in the steep stair-step rule (See Chapter 11). Therefore you can transfer large lump sums as temporary maintenance without recapture (pulled back into the payor's income for taxation).

If you DO NOT make your temporary maintenance agreement into a court order, these payments DO count in the maintenance considered in the steep stair-step rule, and it may be recaptured. Be sure to do the calculation before you decide.

If your temporary agreement includes maintenance to shift income tax, your agreement must be in writing and signed by both of you. The IRS must honor a designation of payments as temporary maintenance (even if you don't file your Petition), so long as you have separate addresses and file separate tax returns within certain limits that are discussed in Chapter 11, the section about Maintenance Recapture. See also the sidebar on this page.

Not everyone needs temporary orders. Many couples work together through the temporary period (the time between filing your petition and the entry of your Decree) in a cooperative way, and do not have a need for a formal written agreement, let alone a court order.

WHAT IF YOU NEED AN AGREEMENT ABOUT TEMPORARY ORDERS AND CAN'T GET ONE?

If your spouse will not agree to work out a temporary plan with you, or has chosen not to be involved in the divorce negotiations at this stage, you can still obtain some temporary orders. When you file your petition, ask the clerk if you can motion the court for temporary orders at the initial status conference.

Fill out form JDF 1109, *Information for the Court,* to detail what temporary orders you would like the court to order. The court may require that you send your spouse formal notice of a status conference or contested hearing to obtain temporary orders, and will tell you which forms to use. This information may be detailed in your Case Management Order.

File the Petition First

In order to make your Temporary Agreement a Temporary Order of the Court, you *must* file your Petition so that you have a case number and an action in court. See Chapter 5. You may file your Petition and your Temporary Agreement at the same time if you wish.

TEMPORARY TEETH

If you are worried that the agreement might not be kept by either or both of you, consider writing in some "teeth". In a maintenance agreement, for example, some teeth to help the paying spouse keep his or her promises would be to agree that if a payment is missed, that money, when paid, is not counted as maintenance. The paying spouse loses the tax deduction, and the receiving spouse does not pay tax on it. (The IRS permits you to say whether or not something that looks like maintenance to the IRS will receive the deductible/taxable treatment.) In this case, make the tax consequences strictly contingent on prompt payments.

"My object all sublime I shall achieve in time – To make the punishment fit the crime." Sir William Schwenk Gilbert, *The Mikado.*

Teeth to help the receiving spouse keep his or her promises would be to agree that if the money he or she receives from the paying spouse is not used to pay for the home or car, as agreed, that asset will be immediately placed on the market. It may or may not be appropriate for you to put such strict punishments in your own agreement. That's your decision. But, if you begin right away treating your agreement as a very serious bargain between you, there will be less chance that you will be tempted to take it lightly later on.

You may also give your temporary agreement legal teeth by making it an order of the court. If you do this, your agreement is then enforceable directly by the court. When you make your agreement an order of the court, the obligations in the contract become court orders, and therefore enforceable through judgments and contempt. See Chapter 13.

MAKING YOUR AGREEMENT INTO A COURT ORDER

Before you can ask the court to approve your temporary agreement, you must have already filed your petition. See Chapter 5 for how to do this. Be sure you put your case number on everything you file with the court, and each keep a copy for yourselves.

If you want to ask the court to approve your temporary agreement and make it into a court order, the steps are:

A. If you have not filed your petition:

1. File your petition and temporary agreement at the same time, along with both of your completed, signed and notarized Sworn Financial Statements (see Chapter 6), and a completed Child Support Worksheet, if any (see Chapter 9).

2. Follow your court's procedure for setting your status conference as soon as possible.

3. At the status conference, request that your Temporary Agreement be made an order of the court, if that has not already been done.

B. If you have already filed your petition:

1. Take your Temporary Agreement, both of your completed Sworn Financial Statements (see Chapter 6), and a completed Child Support Worksheet, if any (see Chapter 9) to the status conference with you.

2. At the status conference, request that your Temporary Agreement be made an order of the court.

Sample Wording for Temporary Agreements

Directions: to write your own temporary agreement, use your notes and agreements from this chapter while making appropriate use of the samples below that apply to you.

If you use any of these samples, be sure to change them to express your own agreements precisely.

To make your agreement into a court form, you will need to add a caption to the top of the sheet. If you are using your computer, copy the caption from your petition into a new document and type your agreement below it. If you are hand writing your agreement, copy the caption on page 317 onto a blank sheet of paper and then insert your agreement. Add signature lines at the end and sign it in front of a notary.

General Statements and Agreements

1. We, ____________________ *(full name, how you will be referred to in this agreement),* and ____________________ *(full name, how you will be referred to in this agreement),* agree to the following:

2. We were married on ____________ *(date)* and separated on ____________ *(date).* Our current addresses are *(as stated in the petition)* ____________________ , and ____________________ , respectively.

3. Our children are: ____________________ *(name),* ______ *(age),* ____________________ , ______ , and ____________________ , ______ .

4. We intend this agreement to stay in effect from the date we sign it until our final decree of ____________ or (for   months/days) or (until ____________ *[date]*). We will agree to any changes in writing, signed and dated.

5. We agree to the following ground rules for conduct between us during this interim period:

6. We agree that the terms of this temporary agreement are fair to both of us and in the best interests of our children.

Who Uses What and Who Pays for It

7. ____________________ will remain in the family home at ____________________ *(address),* and will be responsible for paying the following expenses at that address *(list the expenses that you agreed to in the Residence Checklist – Short Term):*

_______________ *(other spouse)* will be responsible for the following expenses at the family home _______________ and/or will be solely responsible for all living expenses at _______________ *(address) (Repeat here information from your Residence Checklist – Short Term):*

8. We will separate within our residence as follows: _______________ will occupy the _______________ bedroom and _______________ bath / the finished basement / the _______________ floor and _______________ *(Repeat for other spouse).*

9. We will share the common areas of the house as follows:

10. _______________ will drive the _______________ automobile(s) and will be solely responsible for paying the following expenses for it (them) *(list from Car Checklist – Short Term): (Repeat for other spouse.)*

11. The next premium for car insurance is due _______________ *(date)* and _______________ will be responsible for paying it.

12. We agree to be responsible for our bills and other expenses during this period as follows:

13. _______________ will be responsible for paying the following during the period covered by this agreement *(list credit card and loan payments not listed above; children's expenses such as school, day care, medical and dental; family expenses such as health and life insurance, and any other expenses either of you is paying from Your Monthly Budgets): (Repeat for other spouse.)*

14. _______________ will have the exclusive use of the following credit cards and may use them only for the following purposes: *(Repeat for other spouse.)*

15. ______________________ agrees to contact the following creditors and ask to have __________________ *(other spouse)* designated as a person to receive credit on this account: *(Repeat for other spouse.)*

16. Neither of us will sell or mortgage any of our assets except as we specifically agree in writing.

17. We specifically agree to sell or mortgage the following for the following purpose:

    Item:

    Anticipated Sales/Mortgage Proceeds:

    Money to be Used for:

18. Neither of us will incur any debt, including charging anything else on our credit cards, except as we specifically agree in writing.

19. We specifically agree to borrow $______________ from ___________________________ , for the purpose of _____________________________ on the following re-payment terms: ___________________________ .

Children: Parental Responsibilities, Decision Making
Transfer here your parental decision making agreements

20. We will share the following decisions about our children:

21. ________________________ , mother, will make the following decisions about our children: Mother will consult with father on (all) (#   ).

22. ______________________________, father, will make the following decisions about our children: Father will consult with mother on (all) (#   ).

23. For the purposes of the IRS, school registration and interstate custody laws, we designate _______________ _________________________________ (*parent*) as the residential home of___________________________

(child) and____ *(parent)* home as the residential home of ______________________________*(child)*

24. We will use the following process if we can't reach agreement:

Residential Care, Parenting Time
Transfer your parenting time decisions here

25. We agree to the following schedule of time with our children during the period covered by this temporary agreement *(copy or re-write the schedules, including holidays, which you agreed to in your Six-Week Calendar extending it, if necessary, to cover the whole period of your temporary agreement):*

26. We agree to the following about transporting the children between us, changing the schedule, notifying of significant events, etc. *(copy or re-write here any other agreements you have reached about your children):*

Budgeting Your Separation
Transfer your budgeting agreements here

27. ______________________________ expects to receive regular income of $_______________ per month from __________________________ *(source).* ___________________________ *(same spouse)* may also receive occasional income of $_________________________ per month from __________________________ *(copy or re-write here your information from the Income Tracker). (Repeat for other spouse.)*

28. We agree that ___________________________ need not seek employment outside the home at this time (in order to be at home with our children) (in order to complete school or training at _______________________) (due to ____________________ [illness] or __________________________________)

29. __________________________ will pay as Temporary Maintenance *(spousal support, Section 71 payments)* to _________________________ *(other spouse)* $______________ per (month)(quarter)(lump sum). This is to be paid on ___________________________________ *(dates),* by ___________________________________ *(check) (direct deposit) (money order) (voluntary income assignment)(other).* (*If applicable)* Our motion for Temporary Maintenance is attached. We agree that this maintenance will be deductible from income by _______________________ and taxable as income to ____________________ for income tax purposes.

30. _______________________________ will pay to _______________________________ $ ___________ per (month) (week) (twice monthly) (every other week) as temporary child support. This amount will be paid on

_______________ *(dates)* and/or by (check) (money order) (direct deposit) (voluntary income assignment) (other).

31. _______________ will pay $_______________ per _______________ to (child) (other parent) (institution) as post-secondary education costs for our child _______________.

32. _______________ *(other parent)* will pay $_______________ per _______________ to (child) (other parent) (institution) as post-secondary education costs for our child _______________.

33. In addition to the above child support, we agree that we will share the following extraordinary expenses for our children which are not included in the calculations for child support *(indicate each category of expense and who will pay it, or in what proportion you will each pay it.*

34. We anticipate that we will file as separate taxpayers beginning with the year_______________. We anticipate that _______________ will file as Head of Household for _______________ *(child),* and may claim the Child Care Credit for this child. *(Repeat for other spouse if applicable.)*

35. _______________ may claim _______________ *(child)* as tax exemption and receive the child care credit for the____ tax year. *(Repeat for other spouse as agreed.)*

36. _______________ may have as a deduction _______________% of the mortgage interest and property taxes on the family home for the year_______________.

37. We ☐ agree ☐ do not agree to ask that this Temporary Agreement be made an order of the court.

38. *(Add any additional agreements you have made at this time.)*

Add your signatures, the date you sign, and a notarization.

Notes:

CHAPTER **5**

THE FIRST COURT PAPERS

THE FIRST COURT PAPERS

Who May File in Colorado

In order for you to obtain a Colorado divorce or legal separation, one of you must have been domiciled in Colorado for at least 91 days before filing your first papers with the court. "Domicile" is "residence" (you live here), plus the intent to make it your primary residence. If you are new in Colorado, you may file your divorce on day 92 after your arrival in the state. Voter registration or transferring your driver's license to Colorado indicates your intention to make Colorado your home. If you are leaving Colorado and you want to keep jurisdiction in this state, file your divorce before you go.

Divorce and legal separation are not available in Colorado for same-sex couples.

When to File

There are many factors to keep in mind when deciding *when* to file your petition. The timing of your grief processes may be different. In this case frequently one spouse will wait until the other is "ready". Parents sometimes wait until the end of the school year, or other time they feel is better for the children. If you're concerned about either of you running up debt or spending assets, sooner can be better. Your tax status changes (from married to single or head of household) in the year of your decree (not the filing of the petition). So you may want to file sooner (in order to become separate taxpayers for this year), or later (in order to file one more time as joint taxpayers), if it will save significant money. All of this is personal choice.

Keep in mind that once you file your petition, you will have no more than 42 days to gather and exchange all the information described in Chapter 6. You now have work to do, deadlines to meet, and meetings to attend. (See next section for details.) Some work well with deadlines, others do not. So be prepared. You can get most or all of this done before you file your petition, if you wish.

What's the best order for doing things in a friendly divorce?

First is always to gather and exchange your information, as explained in Chapter 6. After that, many negotiate their agreement, and then prepare their court forms, including the petition and sworn financial statements. Others prefer to finish their sworn financial statements first, and then negotiate. This is your personal choice. The latter option may lead to having to update your sworn financial statements. But remember, once you have filed your petition, your sworn financial statements are due within 42 days, whether or not you have begun your negotiations.

What Happens When You File Your Petition?

When you file your Petition, the court will issue a *Case Management Order* to you both. The court will assign your case to a Magistrate or Judge, and to a Family Court Facilitator or other person in the court who will manage and facilitate your case through the court process. The Order will tell you how to

D DEFINITION **Venue:** The location where a case will be heard; often refers to a choice of several available courts, those with ties to this family.

To Locate Your Court

To locate your court, see the "District Courts" list in Appendix B in the back of this book, or look in the blue pages of the phone book for the county where you want to file. Then find the sub-heading "District Court – Civil Division." Larger judicial districts may have a special Domestic Relations Division or Clerk. Asking for the Domestic Relations Clerk when you call, or addressing your correspondence to the Domestic Relations Clerk is likely to be helpful, even if there is not a specific clerk or court for divorces in your particular district.

Application for Waiver of Court Costs

If your financial situation is such that the filing fee is too much for you to pay, then you may apply to the court to waive (not pay) the filing fee (currently $195 for divorce or legal separation). When you go to file your case, ask the clerk of the court for a form for you to fill out called Motion to File Without Payment of Filing Fee and Supporting Financial Affidavit. The judge will review your application and decide if you should be relieved of paying.

reach the facilitator, what that person's role will be, and that they cannot give you legal advice.

Case Management Orders vary from court to court, but all detail many things that you must do and deadlines by which they must be done. The Order requires that you exchange certain documents and papers, called Mandatory Disclosures (discussed in Chapter 6), and that you attend an initial status conference, **both within 42 days of filing the Petition**. The Order may include any requirements for parenting classes, mediation if you can't resolve issues, experts you may use, and motions you may file. It will tell you when you must file your completed sworn financial statements with the court, usually before the initial status conference. If you haven't begun your negotiations, it's certainly time now to talk with each other toward reaching agreement, or to step up your mediation process. You now have deadlines.

Where to File

Where do we file? The legal term for this is *venue*. Divorces take place in the state court, as distinguished from federal or municipal court. The state court in Colorado is divided into 22 judicial districts. Each judicial district contains at least one county, and maintains both district and county courts. Divorce cases are filed and heard in the district court.

Which district should you file in? In legal terms, this is also a *venue* question. As a practical matter, you may file your case in any district court in Colorado. Your case will stay where you file it unless your spouse or the court disagrees. Civil cases (divorce is a civil rather than a criminal matter) are supposed to be heard in the judicial district where you both live, where the respondent lives, or where the marital home was, or is. Sometimes, court administrators "clean house" and try to move all "alien" filings. It's best if the two of you agree on which district you will use before you file. You may pick the court that is most convenient for both of you. If your divorce remains friendly and cooperative, you won't have to spend much time in court anyway.

What Forms Do We Need?

You will need some, but not all of these forms, depending on your circumstances. Read the entire list and the corresponding chapters that detail how they are used, and check off the ones you will need.

Practice copies of most forms are printed in the indicated chapters, along with line-by-line instructions for completing them. The forms marked with an asterisk (*) in the list below are included with your purchase of this book. Instructions to access these fillable Word template and PDF documents can be found on the sticker on the inside back cover. Complete sets of divorce and legal separation forms with and without children are available at www.bradfordpublishing.com.

Use the boxes below to check the forms you need, and again later when completed and filed.

STEP 1 THE INITIAL PAPERS—This Chapter

* ☐ **Petition:** Every action for divorce or legal separation needs this. Bradford form No. 248A if you have children of this marriage, and 248B, if you don't.
* ☐ **Case Information Sheet:** Many courts require this form be filed with the Petition to summarize the information about the parties. Social Security Numbers are gathered here, rather than on the Petition, to protect them from public view.
* ☐ **Summons:** You will need this if you are not filing as co-petitioners, i.e. if you are not both signing the Petition. Bradford form No. 254.
* ☐ **Waiver and Acceptance of Service/Return of Service:** If one spouse signs the Petition, the other spouse can sign the Waiver and Acceptance of Service, and not have to be personally served with a Summons. Use the Return of Service – to be filled out by the person who serves the papers – if the spouse will not sign the Waiver and Acceptance of Service. Bradford form 254, page 3.
  ☐ **Petitioner's Verified Motion and Order For Publication:** You will need these two forms if only one spouse is filing the Petition and you do NOT know the street address or whereabouts of your spouse. Bradford form Nos. 250 and 250A.
* ☐ **Response:** If both of you signed the Petition, you don't need this form. If only one spouse signed and filed the Petition, the spouse who did not sign may use this. Bradford form No. 249.
* ☐ **Notice to Set:** The court may require that this form be used to notify the other spouse of a time that both can contact the court to set a status conference or hearing date. The Case Management Order will give this information. Bradford form 1195, shown in Chapter 12.
* ☐ **Notice of Domestic Relations Initial Status Conference:** Most courts will require that you give formal written notice of this conference. JDF 1120.
  ☐ **Temporary Orders Agreement and Temporary Orders forms:** If you want to formalize your Interim Agreement, you may use the Temporary Agreement you wrote in Chapter 4, or use the following forms: JDF 1115, JDF 1109, and JDF 1110. See Chapter 4.

STEP 2 MANDATORY DISCLOSURE FORMS—Chapter 6

* ☐ **Sworn Financial Statement and Supporting Schedules for Sections F, G, H, and I (if applicable):** Each party is required to prepare, sign, and file this form with the court, and to provide a copy of the completed form to the other spouse. Bradford form Nos. 253 and 253-SS.
* ☐ **Certificate of Compliance with Mandatory Financial Disclosures:** Each party is required to prepare, sign and file this form with the court certifying that he/she has exchanged the information required in the list of mandatory disclosures in Chapter 6, and provide a copy of this completed form to the other spouse. Form JDF 1104.

STEP 3 THE FINAL COURT PAPERS—Chapter 12

* ☐ **Decree:** Everyone needs this. Bradford form No. 251.
* ☐ **Affidavit for Decree Without Appearance of Parties:** You must use this form if you are obtaining your divorce or legal separation decree "by Affidavit" rather than by a court hearing. You qualify to avoid a hearing if:
  a. there are no minor (under 21) children of this marriage; or
  b. you have minor children and each of you is represented by your own attorney.
  c. you agree on all matters related to your legal divorce.
  Bradford form No. 252.
- ☐ **Separation Agreement:** Everyone needs this in non-contested cases. You may write your own agreement using the sample wording at the end of Chapter 12, elements of which can be found in Chapters 7 through 11, or use JDF 1115, or have a mediator or attorney write it for you.
- ☐ **Qualified Domestic Relations Order:** There is no pre-printed form for this. You'll find a sample in Chapter 7. You may use this to transfer an interest in certain retirement plans from one spouse to the other when agreed to in your final separation agreement.
* ☐ **Notice to Set Hearing** (form 1195) and **Notice of Hearing** (form 1196): The court may require these forms to notify your spouse about your final hearing.

If you have children or you will pay maintenance—Chapters 8, 9 and 12

* ☐ **Worksheet A – Child Support Obligation: Sole Physical Care:** You will need this if your children spend less than 25% of the overnights (92 or less) per year with one of the parents. Bradford form No. 1170. See Chapter 9.
* ☐ **Worksheet B – Child Support Obligation: Shared Physical Care:** You will need this if you have a shared physical care arrangement—93 or more overnights per year with each parent. Bradford form No. 1171. See Chapter 9.
* ☐ **Support Order:** Use this form if payment of child support and/or maintenance is part of your agreement. Bradford form No. 251A.
- ☐ **Parenting Plan:** You will need a parenting plan if you have children, or you may include this information in your separation agreement.
- ☐ **Notice to Withhold Income for Support:** You will need this if you want payment of child support and/or maintenance to be made by means of an income assignment. Bradford form No. 1155.
- ☐ **Notice to Employer to Deduct for Health Insurance:** You will need this if your agreement requires a working parent to provide health insurance for the children as a deduction from pay. Bradford form No. 1162.
- ☐ **Notice to Insurance Provider of Court-ordered Health Insurance Coverage:** You will need this if your agreement requires that a parent provide insurance for children when he or she is not currently covered. Bradford form No. 1164. See Chapter 12.

Preparing Your Papers for the Court

You must file original forms with the court, keeping photocopies for your records. Most of the forms shown in this Guidebook are downloadable free as shown inside the back cover. Other forms are available at www.bradfordpublishing.com.

There are some procedures that vary with each district court. The best way to be certain you are doing things correctly for your particular court is to find out what information they provide and if they require any specific forms or instructions.

TYPING/PRINTING

All courts prefer typed or computer-generated papers. If you do not have your own computer, you might see if your local library or "quick" print store has public computers that you can use. Most courts will accept forms that are neatly hand printed in black ink.

TRUTH

On any paper you file with the court, write only what you know or believe to be true. If the form asks for something not part of your case, write "no" or "none", as appropriate. Deliberately not telling the truth to a court, especially if signed under oath, is a crime.

Filing Your Petition

Give the clerk of the district court where you have chosen to file your case:

- Your completed Petition, signed by you and notarized, or signed by both of you and notarized if you are co petitioners. If you are signing at different times, there can be two notarizations. If you submit two copies of the Petition and stamped envelopes, the clerk will sign, date, and return the copies for your records.
- The filing fee (as of the publication of the 8th edition of Guidebook) is $195 for dissolution of marriage and for legal separation. This fee is subject to change. Most courts prefer cash, money orders, or certified funds, but many will accept your personal check. Call ahead to be safe.

When you file your petition, the clerk will give or mail you a Case Management Order detailing the next steps you must take and your deadlines. *Be sure to read it carefully.*

Case Number

When you file your petition with the court there will be a case number, or "docket" number on your receipt. Example: 11 – DR – ______ , followed by division or courtroom number, or the judge's initials. The first two digits represent the year you filed your petition, and "DR" means Domestic Relations. *Be sure to make note of your case number because you must write it at the top of any correspondence and all forms and papers you file with the court about your case.* This is the only way to be sure that your document will find its way into your file, and not get lost.

District Court, ______ ❶ ______ County, Colorado Court Address: ❷	❺ ▲ COURT USE ONLY ▲
❸ **In re the Marriage of:** Ⓐ **Petitioner:** and Ⓑ **Co-Petitioner/Respondent:**	
Attorney or Party Without Attorney (Name and Address): ❹ Phone Number: E-mail: FAX Number: Atty. Reg. #:	Case Number: ❻ Division: Courtroom:
❼ **PETITION FOR:** ☐ **DISSOLUTION OF MARRIAGE** ☐ **LEGAL SEPARATION (WITH CHILDREN)**	

❼ 1. This Petition is for ☐ Dissolution of Marriage or ☐ Legal Separation.

2. The Marriage is irretrievably broken.

❽ 3. **Information about the Wife:** ☐ Petitioner ☐ Co-Petitioner/Respondent ☐ Check if in Military

Full Legal Name: ______ Date of Birth: ______

Length of **Current Residency in Colorado:** ______ (Years/Months) Dates: ______

Current Mailing Address: ______

City, State & Zip Code: ______

E-mail Address: ______

Home Phone #: ______ Work Phone #: ______ Cell #: ______

4. **Information about the Husband:** ☐ Petitioner ☐ Co-Petitioner/Respondent ☐ Check if in Military

Full Legal Name: ______ Date of Birth: ______

Length of **Current Residency in Colorado:** ______ (Years/Months) Dates: ______

Current Mailing Address: ______

City, State & Zip Code: ______

E-mail Address: ______

Home Phone #: ______ Work Phone #: ______ Cell #: ______

❾ 5. Date of the Marriage: ______ Place of Marriage: ______ (City/State)

❿ 6. Date the parties separated: ______

⓫ 7. The Wife is ☐ pregnant ☐ not pregnant.

Bradford Publishing, 1743 Wazee St., Denver, CO 80202 — 303-292-2590 — www.bradfordpublishing.com

8. The following child(ren) was/were born or adopted of this marriage (attach a second sheet, if necessary):

12

Full Name of Child	Present Address	Sex	Date of Birth

13 9. The child(ren) listed above have lived in Colorado for a minimum of 182 days prior to the filing of this Petition or since birth if under six months of age. ☐ **Yes** ☐ **No** If **No**, please state the name of child, name of person child lived with and the month, date and year when each child most recently moved to Colorado.

Full Name of Child	Name of Person Child Lived with	State Moved From	Month	Day	Year

14 10. I/We understand that a request for genetic tests shall not prejudice the requesting party in matters concerning allocation of parental responsibilities pursuant to §14-10-124(1.5), C.R.S. If genetic tests are not obtained prior to a legal establishment of paternity and submitted into evidence prior to the entry of the final decree of dissolution or legal separation, the genetic tests may not be allowed into evidence at a later date.

11. **Each party has a continuing duty to inform the Court of any proceeding in this or any other state that could affect the current proceeding.**

12. **I/We understand that the Court may review any case involving the children, Petitioner, Co-Petitioner/ Respondent and other parties named in this Petition that have been filed in any Court.**

13. I/We have participated in the following proceeding(s) regarding the child(ren) as a party or a witness, or in any other capacity concerning the allocation of parental responsibilities including decision-making, child support and parenting time with the child(ren). Identify name of court, case number, state, date, and type of proceeding if any.

15

Name of Court	Case Number	State	Date of Proceeding	Type of Proceeding

14. I/We know of the following proceeding(s) that could affect the current proceeding including, but not limited to proceedings relating to domestic violence or domestic abuse, enforcement of Court orders, protection/restraining orders, termination of parental rights, and adoptions. Identify name of court, case number, state, date, and type of proceeding if any.

16

Name of Court	Case Number	State	Date of Proceeding	Type of Proceeding

15. The following people are not parties in this matter, but have physical custody of the child(ren) or claim rights of parental responsibilities, legal custody or physical custody, or visitation/parenting time with the child(ren). Identify name and address of those persons, if any.

17

Full Name of Person	Address (City/State/Zip Code)

16. **Required Notice of Human Services Involvement.**

18 The parents or dependent child(ren) listed on this Petition has/have received within the last five years, or is/are currently receiving benefits or public assistance from the state Department of Human Services or the County Department of Social Services. ☐ **No** ☐ **Yes** If your answer was **Yes**, complete the following:

Name of Person Receiving Benefit	Name of County and State	Case Number	Month/Year

17. **Required Notice of Prior Protection/Restraining Orders.**

Have any Temporary or Permanent Protection/Restraining Orders to prevent domestic abuse or any Criminal Mandatory Protection/Restraining Orders (MRO) or Emergency Protection Orders been issued against either party within two years prior to the filing of this Petition?

19 ☐ **No** ☐ **Yes** If your answer was **Yes**, complete the following:

20 The Protection/Restraining Order was ☐ Temporary ☐ Permanent ☐ MRO and issued against ______________ ______________________________ in a ☐ Municipal Court ☐ County Court ☐ District Court in the County of ______________, State of ______________, in case number __________ on ______________ (date).

21 What was the subject matter of the Protection/Restraining Order or Emergency Protection Order?

____

____

____

____

____

____

22 18. **Notice of Existing Case with Child Support Enforcement (CSE)**
The parents have filed a case with CSE? ☐ **No** ☐ **Yes** If **Yes**, identify the case number: ______________

23 19. I/We ask that the Court enter orders regarding the ☐ status of the marriage, ☐ best interests of the child(ren), ☐ maintenance (spousal support), ☐ child support, ☐ division of property and debts, ☐ attorney fees and costs, if appropriate, ☐ restoration of the previous name of a party, ☐ and any other necessary orders.

24 20. The ☐ Petitioner ☐ Co-Petitioner requests that the Court restore his/her **prior full name** to
____

25 ***Notice:*** Colorado Revised Statutes §14-10-107, provides that upon the filing of a Petition for Dissolution of Marriage or Legal Separation by the Petitioner or Co-Petitioner, or upon personal service of the Petition and Summons on the Respondent, or upon waiver and acceptance of service by the Respondent, an automatic temporary injunction shall be in effect against **both parties** until the Final Decree is entered, the Petition is dismissed, or until further Order of the Court. Either party may apply to the Court for further temporary orders, an expanded automatic temporary injunction, or modification or revocation under §14-10-108, C.R.S. or any other appropriate statute.

1. **Both parties are restrained from transferring, encumbering, concealing, or in any way disposing of, without the consent of the other party, or an Order of the Court, any marital property, except in the usual course of business or for the necessities of life. Each party is required to notify the other party of any proposed extraordinary expenditures and to account for all extraordinary expenditures made after the injunction is in effect; and**

2. **Both parties are enjoined from molesting or disturbing the peace of the other party or the minor child(ren); and**

3. **Both parties are restrained from removing the minor child(ren) of the parties, if any, from the state without the consent of the other party or an Order of the Court; and**

4. **Both parties are restrained, without at least 14 days advance notification and the written consent of the other party or an Order of the Court, from canceling, modifying, terminating, or allowing to lapse for nonpayment of premiums, any policy of health insurance, homeowner's or renter's insurance, or automobile insurance that provides coverage to either of the parties or the minor child(ren) or any policy of life insurance that names either of the parties or the minor child(ren) as a beneficiary.**

Nothing in this automatic injunction shall prohibit either party from applying to the Court for further orders, an expanded automatic temporary injunction, or orders modifying or revoking this injunction.

Petitioner and Co-Petitioner, if any, acknowledge that he or she has received a copy of, has read, and understands the terms of the automatic temporary injunction set forth in this Petition and the Summons.

VERIFICATION AND ACKNOWLEDGMENT

I swear/affirm under oath that I have read the foregoing Petition and that the statements set forth therein are true and correct to the best of my knowledge.

26 ______________________________
Petitioner Signature Date

27 ______________________________
Co-Petitioner Signature Date

28 ______________________________
Petitioner's Attorney Signature, if any

28 ______________________________
Co-Petitioner's Attorney Signature, if any

29 Subscribed and affirmed, or sworn to before me by ______________________________ in the County of ____________________, State of ____________________, this ________ day of ____________________, 20______.

____
Notary Public/Clerk

My commission expires: ____________________

Subscribed and affirmed, or sworn to before me by ______________________________ in the County of ____________________, State of ____________________, this ________ day of ____________________, 20______. 29

____
Notary Public/Clerk

My commission expires: ____________________

The Petition

The Petition for Dissolution of Marriage or Legal Separation is the first document that you must submit to the court. It is your official request for dissolution of marriage or legal separation.

INSTRUCTIONS TO FILL OUT THE PETITION (form 248A, with children). If you do not have children, use form 248B, and skip instructions 12–17, and 22.

1–6 of the instructions contains the information the court requires to keep track of your case. It goes in the top portion of the form known as the "Caption." You will fill out the caption on every form the same way.

1. Fill in the county in which you will file.
2. Insert the mailing address for the court where you are filing. To find this, see Appendix D in the back of this book.
3. A. Type the full name of one of you. This person is now the "petitioner" (the person petitioning for a dissolution or separation).

   B. Type the full name of the other spouse. A spouse joining in the initial petition for dissolution or legal separation is the Co-Petitioner. A spouse not joining in the initial petition is the Respondent.
4. Type the name, address and phone number, including area code, of the petitioner or co-petitioner. Include your fax number if you have one at home. Fill in your e-mail address if you have one, and leave Att. Reg.# blank or put N/A.
5. Leave this space blank for the court stamp.
6. The case number and the division, courtroom, or judge, will be assigned to you when you give the petition to the clerk of the district court and pay your filing fee. Put this information on all subsequent forms.
7. Check the appropriate box, depending on whether you are seeking a dissolution of marriage (divorce) or legal separation. If there are no children, use the form Petition for Dissolution of Marriage or Legal Separation (Without Children).

   Be sure you understand the difference between a Dissolution of Marriage and a Legal Separation (see Chapter 1).

   If you are asking for a legal separation, and your reason is that you are not convinced the marriage is irretrievably broken, you may draw a line through line #2 on the petition.
8. Fill out this information for each of you. Check the applicable box for each of you for Petitioner or Co-Petitioner/Respondent and if you are in the military. Fill in your full legal name, spelling out each name and insert your dates of birth. In most cases, the current length of residence in Colorado is simply how long (in months or years) you have lived here this time only. If you have lived in Colorado more than once, in the second blank insert the range of dates such as 1996-1998 and April 2006 to present. Fill in your current mailing addresses. Write in your email address if you have one, or write "None". If you do not know your spouse's email address, write "Unknown". If you both still have the same address, type it in both places. If you do not know your spouse's current address type "unknown" in the lines for address and city. Insert home, work, and cell phone numbers for each of you. If you do not have one of them, write "None". Write "unknown" if you don't know your spouse's phone numbers.
9. For "Date" and "Place of Marriage" indicate the date of the ceremony, and the city, county and state (or country, if you were married outside the U.S.A.) where your marriage ceremony was performed. If you are common law married, write the date you became married and add "by common law."

10. "Date the parties separated" is the date you stopped living with your spouse. If you are still living at the same address, type "We are not yet separated" or just leave blank.
11. Check the appropriate box stating whether or not the wife is pregnant.

If the Wife is Pregnant

A child conceived by the wife during the marriage is presumed, by law, to be the child of that marriage. If the child the wife is expecting is not the husband's child, you must tell the court. Be certain your final agreement and decree say that this child is not from this marriage. Some people also make a notation to this effect right on the petition, next to the box which tells the court that the wife is pregnant, to say "but expected child will not be child of this marriage." A child of the husband with a woman who is not the wife, is not a child of the marriage.

---

12. List all children of the marriage, natural and adopted, even if they are now adults, and provide all the information requested. If they are married, put their married name too. If there are no living children of this marriage, write "None" or use the form Petition for Dissolution of Marriage or Legal Separation (Without Children).
13. Check whether all your minor children have lived in Colorado for at least six months or since birth if under six months of age. If no, list only the names of minor children who have not lived in Colorado, the person the child lived with, and the date the child moved to Colorado.
14. This paragraph, added in 2006, gives notice to all alleged or presumed fathers of their right to dispute their paternity and request genetic testing, that doing so will not prejudice their parental rights, and that they may not raise the question of their paternity later after a decree of divorce or legal separation is signed. Thus it requires that the paternity questions be settled before the Decree.
15. Fill in information about any legal action in which you participated concerning any of the minor children of this marriage. This could include a custody or visitation case, allocation of parental responsibilities, parental decision-making, child support, parenting time, an adoption, or a non-support, delinquency, or dependency and neglect action. If the case was closed or dismissed, be certain to include this information. If there has been no such legal action, type "None".
16. Fill in the requested information about any case anywhere in the world that could affect this court case. If there is no such case, write "None."
17. If someone other than you (the parents) has cared for your minor children for any significant length of time (such as a grandparent who has always kept the children for the summer), you should list them here. In Colorado, grandparents have a right to see their grandchildren. They are sometimes given consideration in determining parenting time. If you are fairly certain there is a relative or former caretaker who will wish to be considered for parenting time or physical care of your children it is probably wise to anticipate it here. If no one fits this category, write "None."

    CAUTION: This information is required by both state and federal law. You will be signing this petition under oath and therefore swearing to the truth of this information. Be sure that it is accurate and complete to the best of your knowledge and belief.

18. Check the appropriate box to indicate whether you or any of your dependent children have received any benefits or public assistance from either the state Department of Human Services or any county Department of Social Services. If you checked "yes", list the name of the person receiving that benefit, his or her relationship to you, the location (county and state) of the agency that paid it, the case number, and the month and year.
19. Check the appropriate box to indicate whether either of you has had any protection or restraining orders issued against you in the last 2 years.

20. If you answered "yes" to number 19, you must check whether the protection/restraining order is temporary or permanent.
    A. Check whether it was temporary, permanent or MRO.
    B. Write the name of the person the order was against.
    C. Check whether it was issued in Municipal, County, or District Court.
    D. Put here the name of the county it was issued in.
    E. Write the state in which it was issued.
    F. Write the case number in which the order was issued.
    G. Write the date the order was issued.
21. Write here what actions or behaviors are restrained or prohibited in the order. Attach a separate piece of paper if there is more than one restraining order, providing the same information about each of them.
22. Indicate whether either of you has a case with Child Support Enforcement (which need not be about any of the children of this marriage, if any). If so, write the case number.
23. This is where you tell the court the general areas that your divorce is about, whether you reach agreement about them or ask the court to decide for you. Check only the boxes that apply to you.
    A. Check this box to show whether you are seeking a divorce or a legal separation.
    B. If you have minor children, check this box.
    C. If you are co-petitioners and you have agreed that one of you will pay maintenance to the other, check this box. If you are the sole petitioner and are requesting maintenance, check this box.
    D. If you have minor children, check this box.
    E. Check this box if there are any assets or debts of your marriage.
    F. You will probably not check this box if you are doing your divorce together. If you are the sole petitioner and you want your spouse to pay your lawyer or the costs of the case (like the court filing fee, appraisals, counseling professionals, financial advisors, mediators), then check this box.
    G. Check this box if one or both of you wants to return to your name before the marriage.
    H. Check this box if you want the court to have the power to enter other orders about things you may have omitted, or which you learn about later. If you are doing your divorce together you will probably not check this box.
24. Check which of you, if any, wants to return to your name before the marriage. Then type the complete restored name(s) in the space. The final Decree will reflect the restored name(s) and, when signed by the judge, becomes the official document which you may use to change your Social Security card, your driver's license, bank accounts, etc. You may use the divorce proceeding to restore your name before the marriage, but not to change to an entirely new name. To do that you must file an action for change of name in the county court where you live.
25. Read the Temporary Injunction carefully. It applies to both of you the instant the court has jurisdiction in the case.

26\. and 27. You must sign in the presence of a notary. Be sure to include the date. If you are co-petitioners, you both sign in front of a notary or notaries, and fill in the date.

28. If either or both of you is represented by an attorney who wants to sign the petition, they may sign here.
29. Leave blank. This is for the notary to fill in and sign.

☐ District Court ☐ Denver Juvenile Court ______________ County, Colorado Court Address:	
❶ ☐ **In re the Marriage of:** ☐ **In the Interest of:** ☐ **In re the Parental Responsibilities concerning:** ______________, **Petitioner:** and **Co-Petitioner/Respondent:**	▲ COURT USE ONLY ▲
Attorney or Party Without Attorney (Name and Address): Phone Number: E-mail: FAX Number: Atty. Reg. #:	Case Number: Division: Courtroom:

CASE INFORMATION SHEET

❷ **Full name of Petitioner**: ______________
Date of birth: ______________ Social Security Number: ______________
Residential address: ______________ Apt. # ______
City: ______________ State: ______ Zip Code: ______
Mailing address (if different from residential address): ______________ Apt. # ______
City: ______________ State: ______ Zip Code: ______
Telephone Numbers: Home ______________ Work ______________ Cell ______________

❸ **Full name of Co-Petitioner/Respondent**: ______________
Date of birth: ______________ Social Security Number: ______________
Residential address: ______________ Apt. # ______
City: ______________ State: ______ Zip Code: ______
Mailing address (if different from residential address): ______________ Apt. # ______
City: ______________ State: ______ Zip Code: ______
Telephone Numbers: Home ______________ Work ______________ Cell ______________

Names of children (attach a second sheet, if necessary):

❹

Full Name of Child	Present Address	Sex	Date of Birth	Soc. Sec. No.

❺ ☐ The Petitioner is planning to be self-represented.
❻ ☐ The Co-Petitioner/Respondent is planning to be self-represented.
❼ ☐ Both you and the other party have retained an attorney.

❽ Date: ______________ ______________
☐ Petitioner ☐ Co-Petitioner/Respondent

Bradford Publishing, 1743 Wazee St., Denver, CO 80202 — 303-292-2590 — www.bradfordpublishing.com

The Case Information Sheet

Most courts require the Case Information Sheet, shown on the following page, not only to have certain information up front, but also because of their obligation to redact (hide or remove) a Social Security Number before allowing the public to have access to a file. Having the Social Security Number only on this Sheet makes it easier for them to find and redact. The Petitioner should complete and sign this form. If you are co-petitioning then prepare this form together and both sign it on the signature line 2. Most of the information needed for this form can be copied from the Petition.

INSTRUCTIONS FOR FILLING OUT THE CASE INFORMATION SHEET

1. Fill out these lines the same as you did on the Petition. Check "In re the Marriage of:"
2. Fill out your personal information the same as on the Petition, but this time include your Social Security Number.
3. Fill out your spouse's personal information the same as on the Petition, but this time including the Social Security Number.
4. List here all the information required for any children of this marriage the same as on the Petition, but this time include their Social Security Numbers. If you have no children of this marriage write "None".
5. Check this box if you (the Petitioner) do NOT plan to hire an attorney to represent you. (You may change your mind later.)
6. Check this box if the Co-Petitioner or Respondent, your spouse, does NOT plan to hire an attorney to represent him/her. If you don't know, do not check the box, but write "unknown" at the end of the sentence.
7. Check this box if both of you have hired attorneys for representing you in this case.
8. Sign and date the form. Both, or either of you, may sign.

Jurisdiction

If you and your spouse are filing as *petitioner and respondent*, the information in this section applies to you. If you are both signing the Petition, you may skip ahead to page 109.

Jurisdiction is the legal word for the power of the court to take action about something. The court's jurisdiction in a divorce or legal separation case usually begins when both spouses file jointly as co-petitioners, OR when one spouse (petitioner) files with the court and completes service on the other spouse (respondent).

How you serve your spouse determines the type of jurisdiction (power) the court gets over your divorce case. Most cases result in either, ***in personam*** (personal jurisdiction), or ***in rem*** (jurisdiction over the matter, in this case over the legal marital status). The court has personal jurisdiction when the spouse has been served personally. The court has ***in rem*** jurisdiction when the whereabouts of the spouse is unknown and he or she cannot be served personally.

If the court has personal jurisdiction it can order either of you to transfer property, make payments on debts, or pay maintenance or child support. If the court has only ***in rem*** jurisdiction it cannot order these things. Whether Colorado courts, without personal jurisdiction over both parents, can enter orders granting custody of children located in Colorado is an unsettled legal question. Courts generally enter custody orders anyway and sometimes order support or transfer of property with the reminder that the absent spouse could come in later and re-open the matters that require personal jurisdiction.

If the court has entered such an order in your case and your spouse reappears, immediately serve him or her with all the court papers that have been filed, or ask him or her to sign the waiver of service and then ask the court to deal with the personal jurisdiction matters it could not determine earlier.

If the court has only *in rem* jurisdiction, and you must have clear title to rcal or other property, you must get ***quasi-in-rem*** jurisdiction. This procedure has specific requirements explained briefly in this chapter, and in Chapter 12.

D DEFINITION **Jurisdiction:** Power of the court to enter orders; can also refer to which court is the proper place for this kind of case (i.e., juvenile court has jurisdiction over persons under 18 years); can also refer to the parties having been properly notified of the court action (see "Service of Process," this chapter).

D DEFINITION **Personal jurisdiction:** Power of the court to enter orders which must be personally carried out; derives from the person(s) affected having received personal notification of the case.

D DEFINITION **In rem jurisdiction:** Power of the court to enter orders only concerning a legal status; derives from those affected having received no personal notice of the case.

D DEFINITION **Quasi-in-rem jurisdiction:** Power of the court to enter orders affecting some limited in-state property; derives from the request for title to that property having been specifically described in the initial papers and then published.

P PARTNERS Since Colorado does not recognize same-sex marriages, Colorado courts do not have jurisdiction to dissolve them.

Notifying Your Spouse/Service of Process

In the American civil legal system, the court cannot enter an order against anyone unless the court is certain that the person had notice of what was going on. If you decide to file for a divorce and your spouse does not go along with it, then you are responsible for proving to the court that your spouse was properly notified about what you filed and what you are asking for. The paper which notifies your spouse of what you have filed is the summons. Proving to the court that your spouse got a copy of the summons and petition is called service of process.

There are several ways to notify your spouse of what you have filed. To determine which procedure you should follow, complete the following checklist.

JURISDICTION AND SERVICE OF PROCESS CHECKLIST

Directions: Check the statement which fits your situation. Then, see the instructions in this chapter for that procedure.

☐ **Co-petitioner filing:**
You and your spouse are co-petitioners and each signed the petition in front of a notary. You do not need to "serve" a summons. The court has personal jurisdiction over both spouses, the children and all your property and can enter any order. You may go to Chapter 7.

☐ **Only one spouse is filing the petition and you know the whereabouts of your spouse:**
You will need to fill out the summons and then choose one of the two following methods of service:

☐ **Waiver and Acceptance of Service:**
You may ask your spouse to "sign" for the papers. This means that your spouse waives his or her right to be handed the papers by a third party and acknowledges receipt of a copy of both the petition and the summons. The court has jurisdiction over both parties, the children and all your property even if the respondent is out of state or in the military. If you use this procedure, your spouse must complete and sign the waiver on the back of the summons. You may then skip the section on personal service and go to Chapter 7.

☐ **Personal Service:**
You may have your spouse personally served with the papers and then prove to the court how service was completed. See "Personal Service" (page 94) and complete the return of service (page 97) on the back of the summons. The court has jurisdiction over both parties, any children and all property unless you served out of state on a non-resident, in which case the jurisdiction may be limited to *quasi-in-rem* (previous page). You may then go to Chapter 7.

☐ **Only one spouse is filing the petition, and you do NOT know the whereabouts of your spouse:**
If you have only a post office box or general delivery address for your spouse, or you absolutely do not know the whereabouts of your spouse, you must fill out the summons and serve your spouse by constructive service (see page 98). You must obtain permission from the court to serve in this manner by filing a Verified Motion and Order (see pages 101 and 103).

☐ **Response filing:**
If your spouse filed the petition, but you do not agree, see page 105 for issues that you may respond to. Filing of a response gives the court personal jurisdiction even if the manner of service of process did not, unless the response is specifically limited to the jurisdictional issue.

District Court, ______________ County, Colorado Court Address: ❶	
In re the Marriage of: **Petitioner:** ❷ and **Co-Petitioner/Respondent:**	
Attorney or Party Without Attorney (Name and Address): ❶ Phone Number: E-mail: FAX Number: Atty. Reg. #:	▲ COURT USE ONLY ▲
	Case Number: ❸ Division: Courtroom:

❹ **SUMMONS FOR ☐ DISSOLUTION OF MARRIAGE ☐ LEGAL SEPARATION AND TEMPORARY INJUNCTION**

TO THE RESPONDENT NAMED ABOVE – This Summons serves as a notice to appear in this case.

If you were served in the State of Colorado and if you wish to respond to the Petition, you must file your Response with the clerk of this Court within 21 days after this Summons is served on you. If you were served outside of the State of Colorado or you were served by publication, and you wish to respond to the Petition, you must file your Response with the clerk of this Court within 35 days after this Summons is served on you.

Your response must be accompanied with the applicable filing fee.

After 91 days from the date of service or publication, the Court may enter a decree affecting your marital status, dividing marital property, and addressing parental responsibilities, child support, maintenance, and attorney fees and costs, to the extent the Court has jurisdiction.

If you fail to file a Response or enter your appearance in this case, any or all of the matters above, or any related matters which come before this Court, may be decided by default without further notice to you.

This is an action to obtain a Decree of: Dissolution of Marriage or Legal Separation as more fully described in the attached Petition, and if you have children, for orders regarding the children of the marriage.

NOTICE: Section 14-10-107, Colorado Revised Statutes, provides that upon the filing of a Petition for Dissolution of Marriage or Legal Separation by the Petitioner or Co-Petitioner, or by a legal guardian or conservator on behalf of one of the parties, or upon personal service of the Petition and Summons on the Respondent, or upon waiver and acceptance of service by the Respondent, an automatic temporary injunction shall be in effect against **both parties** until the final Decree is entered or the Petition is dismissed, or until further Order of the Court. Either party may apply to the Court for further temporary orders, an expanded temporary injunction, or modification or revocation under §14-10-108, C.R.S., or any other appropriate statute.

No. 254. Rev. 7-12. SUMMONS FOR DISSOLUTION OF MARRIAGE/LEGAL SEPARATION (Page 1 of 4)

Bradford Publishing, 1743 Wazee St., Denver, CO 80202 — 303-292-2590 — www.bradfordpublishing.com

❺ **Automatic Temporary Injunction – By Order of Colorado Law, You and Your Spouse are:**

1. Restrained from transferring, encumbering, concealing or in any way disposing of, without the consent of the other party or an Order of the Court, any marital property, except in the usual course of business or for the necessities of life, and requiring each party to notify the other party of any proposed extraordinary expenditures and to account to the Court for all extraordinary expenditures made after the injunction is in effect;
2. Enjoined from molesting or disturbing the peace of the other party;
3. Restrained from removing the minor child or children of the parties, if any, from the State without the consent of the other party or an Order of the Court; and
4. Restrained, without at least 14 days' advance notification and the written consent of the other party or an order of the Court, from canceling, modifying, terminating, or allowing to lapse for nonpayment of premiums, any policy of health insurance, homeowner's or renter's insurance, or automobile insurance that provides coverage to either of the parties or the minor children or any policy of life insurance that names either of the parties or the minor children as a beneficiary.

❻ **ADVISEMENT:** A request for genetic tests shall not prejudice the requesting party in matters concerning allocation of parental responsibilities pursuant to §14-10-124(1.5), C.R.S. If genetic tests are not obtained prior to a legal establishment of paternity and submitted into evidence prior to the entry of the final decree of dissolution or legal separation, the genetic tests may not be allowed into evidence at a later date.

❼ Date: ____________________

____
☐ Signature of the Clerk of Court/Deputy

____
☐ Signature of Attorney for Petitioner, if any

This Summons is issued pursuant to C.R.C.P. 4 and Article 14, of Title 10, C.R.S. A copy of the Petition must be served with this Summons. This Summons should not be used where publication is desired.

The Summons

If you and your spouse are co-petitioners you do not need this form or service of process. Go to Chapter 7.

The summons for dissolution of marriage or legal separation and temporary injunction is the official document used to notify your spouse of your request (petition) for a divorce or legal separation. In legal terms you are the "petitioner" and your spouse is the "respondent." This means that you are the one who is initiating the request to dissolve the marriage and that your spouse chooses not to join in the request from the beginning. This does not necessarily imply that your spouse is contesting or disagreeing with your request. For more information on responding, see the end of this chapter.

INSTRUCTIONS FOR FILLING OUT THE SUMMONS

1. Fill out these lines the same as you did on the Petition.

2. Type your name in the space for petitioner and your spouse's name in the space for respondent, just as you did on the Petition.

3. Leave these spaces blank until you take your petition to the clerk of the district court. Once the clerk has assigned you a case number, it is a good idea (although not technically required) to include the case number on the summons before it is served.

4. Check the appropriate box, depending on whether you are asking for a dissolution of marriage (divorce) or a legal separation.

5. Read the Temporary Injunction carefully (also on the petition). It applies to both of you the instant the court has jurisdiction in the case.

6. This paragraph gives notice to all alleged or presumed fathers of their right to dispute their paternity and request genetic testing, that doing so will not prejudice their parental rights, and that they may not raise the question later after a decree of divorce or legal separation is signed. Thus is requires that any paternity issues be settled before the decree.

7. Do not date or sign the Summons. These spaces are for the signature of the clerk of the court or your attorney, if any. Obtain the signature of one or the other.

WAIVER AND ACCEPTANCE OF SERVICE

Waiver: The giving up of a legal right. In waiver and acceptance of service, the respondent is giving up the right to require the petitioner to have the papers personally delivered by a third party to him or her.

If your spouse does not want to be a co-petitioner, but is willing to accept service by "signing" for the papers, then your spouse is said to be "waiving" (giving up) the legal right to be "served" (handed the papers by the sheriff or a neutral third person). In signing the waiver, your spouse is not agreeing to the truth of anything you wrote in the petition—including arrangements you say have been already made and the "relief" you requested. By signing the waiver, your spouse only acknowledges receipt of a copy of both the petition and summons and acknowledges and accepts the court's power (jurisdiction) to issue a decree that will be binding on both of you. If your spouse is not living in Colorado, using the waiver can substantially decrease the time involved to obtain a divorce or separation because you can avoid time-consuming out-of-state service. A signed waiver may also give the court personal jurisdiction over the Respondent, where even personal out-of-state service might not.

If Your Spouse Is In the Military Service

A spouse on active duty in the military, starting on the date active duty orders are received, has some protections under the federal Servicemembers (formerly Soldiers and Sailors) Civil Relief Act. He or she may request to postpone court proceedings for a mandatory minimum of 91 days, and even request further postponements as long as that duty prevents attendance or participation in those proceedings. If you are on active duty, consult with your legal assistance office about the jurisdictional meaning of signing the waiver and acceptance of service, about the paperwork you will need to file with the court, and your deadline for doing so, if you want to request such a postponement — it is not automatic. If your spouse is on active duty, away from home, and will not sign the waiver, your divorce case may be very difficult to accomplish at the present time. You may wish to consult an attorney if this happens. In practice, most military persons sign and return the waiver promptly.

"If I sign the Waiver, I am signing away all my rights."

Not so. What you give away in signing the Waiver, is your right to make your spouse hire the sheriff or process server to give you the papers. You still have the right to participate in every phase of the negotiations.

"My 91-days started when I filed the Petition."

Not necessarily. The 91-days begins only when both filing and service of process are complete. Both are completed at the same time when you file as co-petitioners, but at different times in all other circumstances.

91 Days Begins

If your spouse signs the Waiver, the 91-day waiting period begins the date the Waiver is signed in front of a notary, provided that you have already filed the Petition with the court or do so within 14 days of the signing of the Waiver. In practice, the signed Waiver may become void if your Petition has not been filed within 14 days of the signing of the Waiver.

District Court, ______________________ County, Colorado Court Address:	
In re the Marriage of: **Petitioner:** 1 and **Co-Petitioner/Respondent:**	▲ COURT USE ONLY ▲
	Case Number: Division: Courtroom:
2 **WAIVER AND ACCEPTANCE OF SERVICE**	

I declare under oath that I am the Respondent in this case, that I have received and accept service of the Summons, a copy of the Petition, and if applicable the ☐ Case Management Order, ☐ Notice of Initial Status Conference, and ☐ Other (Please identify): ______________________________ in this case, and consent to the jurisdiction of this Court to determine all issues raised in the pleadings as if I were served by personal service within the State of Colorado.

Check one:

☐ I am not in the military service. This waiver of service shall not be construed as an admission by me of the truth of the allegations in the Petition and I reserve the right to receive notices of settings and the right to respond and appear in person.

or

☐ I am in the active military service of the United States of America. After consultation with the base legal officer or other counsel of my choice, I have decided to waive the stay (or postponement) provisions of the Soldiers' and Sailor's Civil Relief Act, 50 U.S.C. § 520 et seq., as well as my right to court-appointed counsel under the Act and permit the action to proceed. This waiver of service shall not be construed as an admission by me of the truth of the allegations in the Petition.
☐ I reserve the right to receive notices of settings and the right to respond and appear in person.
☐ I waive my right to receive any further notice of the proceedings.

3 Dated: ____________________________

____
Signature of Respondent

Subscribed and affirmed or sworn to before me in the County of ______________, State of ______________, this ______ day of ______________, 20____.

____
Notary Public/Clerk
My commission expires: ______________

I received and accepted service of the Summons, Petition, and all other documents checked above on behalf of the Respondent.

____
Attorney for Respondent

INSTRUCTIONS TO FILL OUT THE WAIVER AND ACCEPTANCE OF SERVICE

1. Fill in the names of the Petitioner and Respondent and the Case Number the same as on the Petition and Summons.
2. The rest of this form is to be completed by your spouse, NOT BY YOU. Have your spouse check the boxes for any forms or other papers that are included with the Summons and Petition, and also check the boxes that indicate his/her military status.
3. Your spouse must sign in the presence of a notary. Once your spouse signs and returns the waiver, you may go to page 109.

Personal service: Having legal papers handed to and left with a party or witness. Must be served by a *disinterested* (not connected to the case) person over 18.

Not So Friendly

It is not a good idea to have your new "significant other" or a close personal friend serve the papers on your spouse. It may create hard feelings which could add to an already difficult time and make a friendly settlement less likely.

PERSONAL SERVICE

If you know where your spouse is and he or she did not sign as co-petitioner, and did not or will not sign the waiver and acceptance of service, you must have your spouse served with the summons and petition. If your spouse is in Colorado, you may use a friend to serve, or use a private process server in the same locale. Whether your spouse is in Colorado or some other state, you may use the sheriff in the county where your spouse lives.

Using a Friend to Serve Your Spouse

You may ask an acquaintance to give your divorce papers to your spouse. This is a lot to ask of a friend. To serve this way, give your friend a **COPY** of the Petition, and a **COPY** of the Summons, marked (with pencil, or with a sticky note) "to be served." Also give the friend the **ORIGINAL** Summons, showing on the back where the friend will fill out the Return of Service.

Using the Local Sheriff or Private Process Server to Serve Your Spouse

If you are having your spouse served locally, check the government section of the phone book for the sheriff's number or the yellow pages for a "process server." If you are having your spouse served out of town or out of state, call directory assistance in that area code and ask for the sheriff's office for that county. Call and obtain their rates for Civil Service of Process. Then send a **COPY** of the petition, and a **COPY** of the summons, marked (with pencil, or with a sticky note) "to be served." Also send the **ORIGINAL** summons, indicating on the back where the process server is to fill out the return of service. Enclose a stamped envelope, addressed to you, and a check for the amount they charge for service. You may write a cover letter to the process server like the following sample. Including the Spouse's Whereabouts Information Sheet, which follows, will give the server valuable information.

91 Days Begins

If you serve your spouse by personal service, the 91-day waiting period begins on the date personal service is completed as written on the Return of Service by the process server, provided that the Petition has already been filed with the court or is filed within 14 days of the personal service. If you have not previously filed your Petition with the court, you must do so within 14 days of personal service, or the service becomes void.

Sample Cover Letter to Process Server

Your name
Your address
Date of your letter:

Dear Sheriff/Process Server,

Please serve the enclosed copies of a Petition for Dissolution of Marriage or Legal Separation, and the Summons on ______________________________ (name of your spouse).

Information for locating ______________________________ (name of your spouse) is on the attached Spouse's Whereabouts Information Sheet.

I have enclosed a photograph to help you identify him/her.

After you have completed the Return of Service on the back, please return the original Summons to me in the enclosed stamped legal size envelope.

My check to you for $_________ is enclosed.

Sincerely,

Enclosures:

Original Summons
Photocopy of Summons
Photocopy of Petition
Spouse's Whereabouts Information Sheet
Your check to the Process Server
Stamped legal size envelope addressed to you

SPOUSE'S WHEREABOUTS INFORMATION SHEET

If you are using personal or constructive service, you will find it useful to complete this form. It will help you to gather and clarify the information needed for personal or constructive service. Copy this form, complete the information, copy the information onto the Motion if doing constructive service, or give it to the server if doing personal service. It is helpful to include a recent photograph of your spouse for the server. Any sheriff will charge by the number of attempts to serve and mileage so efficient service is much less costly.

Spouse's full name: ____________________

Other names used by spouse: ____________________

Last known address: ____________________
Street, Apt. #

____
P.O. Box

____
City, State, Zip

When there: ____________________

Work information:

Company name: ____________________

Company office address: ____________________

____

Position/title ____________________

Hours: ____________________

Supervisor: ____________________

Physical Description: ____________________

____

Family members who might know where spouse is:

Name ____________________ Relationship ____________________

Address ____________________

Phone: Home ____________ Work ____________ Cell ____________

Name ____________________ Relationship ____________________

Address ____________________

Phone: Home ____________ Work ____________ Cell ____________

<table>
<tr><td>District Court, ____________________ County, Colorado
Court Address:</td><td rowspan="2">

▲ COURT USE ONLY ▲</td></tr>
<tr><td>In re the Marriage of:
Petitioner:

and
Co-Petitioner/Respondent:</td></tr>
<tr><td></td><td>Case Number:

Division: Courtroom:</td></tr>
<tr><td colspan="2">RETURN OF SERVICE</td></tr>
</table>

❶

❷ I declare under oath that I am 18 years or older and not a party to the action and that I served this Summons, a copy of the Petition, and if applicable the ☐ Case Management Order, ☐ Notice of Initial Status Conference, and ☐ Other (Please identify): ______________________ in this case on the
❸ Respondent in ____________ (County) ____________ (State) on __________ (date) ______ (time) at the following location: ______________________________

❹ **By (Check one):**

☐ by handing it to a person identified to me as the Respondent.

☐ By leaving it with ______________________ (Type or write name legibly), who is designated to receive service for the Respondent because of the following relationship with the Respondent: ______________________ as provided for in C.R.C.P. 4(e).

☐ I attempted to serve the Respondent on _____ occasions but have not been able to locate the Respondent. Return to the Petitioner is made on ______________ (date).

☐ I attempted to leave it with Respondent who refused service.

____
Signature of Process Server

❺ ☐ Private Process Server
☐ Sheriff, ______________ County
Fee $________ Mileage $________

____
Name (Print or type)

Subscribed and affirmed or sworn to before me in the County of ______________, State of ______________, this ______ day of ______________, 20____.

____
Notary Public/Clerk
My commission expires: ______________

INSTRUCTIONS TO FILL OUT THE RETURN OF SERVICE

Instructions 1 and 2 are for you to do. 3–5 are to be done by the person who serves the documents on your spouse, NOT BY YOU, to detail how he/she served, or attempted to serve the papers on your spouse.

1. Fill in the names of the Petitioner and Respondent and the Case Number at the top of the page the same as on the Petition and Summons.
2. Check the boxes for any forms or other papers that are included with the Summons and Petition and write in the title of any other documents that are included.
3. Indicate the date and time (including a.m. or p.m.) and the location where the documents were served by you (the process server) on the Respondent.
4. Check the Appropriate box. Check the third box and fill in this section only if you (the process server) were not able to locate the Respondent.
5. The person who served your spouse, or attempted service, signs in this space and dates his/her signature, in the presence of a notary, and checks the correct box.

Constructive service: Serving papers when papers can't be served, a "legal fiction," refers to publishing notice of the case in a newspaper and/or sending the papers to a post office box or other non-specific address.

CONSTRUCTIVE SERVICE – DIVORCING THE ABSENT SPOUSE

There are three ways to get jurisdiction for the court so your divorce can proceed even if you cannot actually serve your spouse personally.

Certified Mail allows you to send the petition and summons to your spouse's last known address.

Publication by Consolidated Notice permits the court to include your names and docket number in a group publication in a local paper so you can obtain a decree of dissolution.

If you can only do published or mailed service, the court only gets jurisdiction over the marital status and sometimes over in-state property. The same is true for out of state service on a spouse with "no contacts" with the state of Colorado.

Publication of Summons (Individual) enables you to publish your whole summons in a local paper so that the court can give you not only the final decree but also title to in-state real estate, cars, and other titled assets. Some of the larger courts have their own instructions about how they want this done. Ask about this when you file your petition.

Why Should I Bother With Constructive Service?

If you can serve your spouse only by constructive service, the court only gets jurisdiction over the legal marital status and if you follow some additional procedures, over certain in-state titled property. So, why bother? Why not stay married?

Marital Obligations Continue After Separation

So long as you are legally married, you are potentially obligating each other on every debt you make and arguably sharing all property you acquire, regardless of the names on either. Any children born or conceived by the wife are presumed to be fathered by the husband, even if the real father is present at the delivery and wants the child to carry his name.

"It's okay to tell the court that you don't know where your spouse is, even when you actually do know or could easily find out."

This is not only a bad idea, it's also a crime, which is why it requires a Verified (sworn) Motion to get permission to serve your case by constructive service. Lying about this might get you a divorce without initial hassle, but your divorce is null and void (can be wiped out) if your spouse finds out about it and can prove to the court that you knew his or her whereabouts all along, or could have discovered it.

Certified Mail

If you have only a post office or general delivery address for your spouse, you will need to get permission from the court to serve by certified mail. To do this, prepare the Verified Motion shown below. Take or mail the original and a photocopy of your verified motion along with a stamped envelope addressed to you, to the clerk of the district court where you filed your case.

Different courts handle service by certified mail in different ways. Some courts do the certified mailing for you, and some ask you to do it yourself. You must ask which procedure your court uses.

1. *If your court does the mailing,* then you must pay the court a small fee to do this for you. The court will then mail back to you, in the envelope you provide, a receipt showing the dates the petition and summons were mailed to your former spouse. Sometimes the court will post notice of your divorce on a bulletin board or other public place at the courthouse, so do not be startled if you see it there.

2. *If your court does not do the mailing for you,* then you should expect to receive, from the clerk, the copy of the verified motion and order showing the date the judge signed the order. You then send your spouse, by certified mail, RETURN RECEIPT REQUESTED (forms available at the post office), one copy each of the petition, the summons, and the verified motion and order as signed by the judge. You will eventually receive in the mail either the green receipt card signed by your spouse, or the original envelope you mailed showing that it was never picked up. Be sure you put your case number on everything, including both post office forms.

D DEFINITION **Service by Certified Mail:** The Clerk of the Court mails a copy of the summons and petition to the respondent's last known address, or to an address such as a post office box or general delivery, when no address for service of the respondent is known. Requires court permission.

If you get back the signed green card, file it with your case in the court file, and you have completed service sufficiently to obtain a final decree of dissolution of marriage. **For service by certified mail, the 91-day waiting period begins the date your spouse signed the certified envelope.**

If the entire envelope is returned to you, this indicates that certified mail was not accomplished, and that you did not get service on your spouse. You must file another verified motion and order asking this time for permission to publish, which is covered in the next section.

Publication by Consolidated Notice

For publication by consolidated notice, the clerk groups together all the cases for divorce filed that week or month which request service by publication, and runs them in a "consolidated notice" in the newspaper. To participate in this, give the clerk the original and a copy of the verified motion and order, the original summons, a stamped envelope addressed to you, and the amount of money the clerk requests. The clerk will publish the consolidated notice, sign a certificate of publication, put the original of this in your file, and send you a copy. **In consolidated notice publication, the 91 day waiting period starts on the last date of publication.**

D DEFINITION **Service by Publication (Consolidated Notice):** clerk of the court supplies a general notice to newspapers listing all similar actions filed in that court on or by a certain date. Lists only names of parties and case numbers of all actions for dissolution of marriage, etc. Requires court permission.

Service by Publication (Individual)

DEFINITION

Publishing your entire Summons in a newspaper, usually in the county where the case is filed, once a week for four weeks. Necessary to obtain *quasi-in-rem* jurisdiction.

Publication of Summons (Individual)

There are several reasons why you might want to serve your spouse by publication of summons (individual).

a) If you want the court to have jurisdiction over title to in-state property (see Jurisdiction, this chapter), then you must publish your whole Summons, individually, not a consolidated notice with other cases.

b) If you are reasonably certain of your spouse's whereabouts, but do not have an exact address, then you may want to publish the summons in a newspaper in that locale. The consolidated notice is published only in the county where the case is filed.

c) The jurisdiction where your case is filed may not have a consolidated notice option.

This process is rarely used and may be best handled by an attorney. However, to do service by individual publication yourself, complete the verified motion and order for publication and give the original and a copy and a stamped envelope addressed to you, to the clerk of the district court. Ask the clerk to send the copy back to you indicating when the judge signed the order which gives you permission to publish.

You must publish your entire summons in a newspaper of general circulation five times, one week apart. The newspaper may be located either where the respondent is located or in the county where your case is filed. As a general rule, local papers are much less expensive than the big dailies. Call and find out what they charge. You may choose the least expensive if you wish. Send the newspaper a copy of the summons and petition and a copy of the signed order for publication, along with their fee, and a stamped envelope addressed to you. After the publication is completed, the newspaper will send you "proof of publication" in the envelope you provided. Send the proof of publication and the original Summons to the court for filing in your case. (You have already filed the Petition.) **In individual publication, the 91-day waiting period begins on the last day of publication.**

☐ District Court ☐ Denver Juvenile Court ____________________ County, Colorado Court Address: **In re:** ❶ ☐ **The Marriage of:** ☐ **The Parental Responsibilities concerning:** ____________________ **Petitioner:** and **Co-Petitioner/Respondent:**	▲ COURT USE ONLY ▲
Attorney or Party Without Attorney (Name and Address): Phone Number: E-mail: FAX Number: Atty. Reg. #:	Case Number: Division: Courtroom:

❷ **PETITIONER'S VERIFIED MOTION:** ☐ **PUBLICATION OF SUMMONS**
☐ **SERVICE BY CERTIFIED MAIL**
☐ **PUBLICATION BY CONSOLIDATED NOTICE**

The Petitioner moves for an Order to serve the Respondent by the method checked above for the following reasons:

❸ **1.** Petitioner has filed: ________________________________ (identify type of case or action)

❹ **2.** Petitioner has been unable to locate an address for service and/or complete personal service of the Respondent despite diligent efforts, as follows:

☐ Personal Service unsuccessful – documentation attached.

☐ Internet search (Provide site names, dates of search, and briefly describe findings):

____

____

____

____

☐ Contacted family, friends, and employer. (Provide names, dates of contact and briefly describe findings):

____

____

____

____

☐ Other: ____________________________________

____

☐ Respondent's known address is a post office box.

Bradford Publishing, 1743 Wazee St., Denver, CO 80202 — 303-292-2590 — www.bradfordpublishing.com

❺ **3.** ☐ Respondent's last known mailing address is as follows:

____

❻ **4.** Petitioner last saw Respondent on ____________________ (date) at ________________

____ (location/place).

❼ **5.** ☐ This action involves property located in the State of Colorado in which the Respondent has an interest.

6. ☐ This involves issues relating to allocation of parental responsibilities (decision-making and parenting time) of minor children, in which the Respondent has an interest.

VERIFICATION AND ACKNOWLEDGMENT

I swear/affirm under oath that I have read the foregoing Motion and that the statements set forth therein are true and correct to the best of my knowledge.

❽ Date: ______________________ ______________________

Petitioner's Signature

____

Signature of Petitioner's Attorney

❾ Subscribed and affirmed, or sworn to before me by ______________________ in the County of ______________, State of ______________, this ____ day of __________, 20___.

____

Notary Public/Clerk

My Commission Expires: ______________

☐ District Court ☐ Denver Juvenile Court __________________ County, Colorado Court Address:	
10 **In re the Marriage of:** **In re Parental Responsibilities concerning:** ______________________________ **Petitioner:** and **Respondent:**	▲ COURT USE ONLY ▲
	Case Number: Division: Courtroom:

ORDER FOR: ☐ **PUBLICATION OF SUMMONS**
☐ **SERVICE BY CERTIFIED MAIL**
☐ **PUBLICATION BY CONSOLIDATED NOTICE**

11 **This Matter comes before this Court on Petitioner's:**

- ☐ Verified Motion for Publication of Summons
- ☐ Verified Motion for Service by Certified Mail
- ☐ Verified Motion for Publication by Consolidated Notice

The Court, having reviewed the Motion finds the following:

- ☐ That the Petitioner has used due diligence to obtain personal service upon the Respondent and that all such efforts have failed.
- ☐ That the Petitioner has not used due diligence to obtain personal service upon the Respondent.

Therefore, the Court Orders:

- ☐ The Motion is denied.
- ☐ The party shall complete service by publication in a newspaper published in this county or as otherwise specified by the Court. Such publication shall be made once weekly for five successive weeks from the date of the Order.
- ☐ The Clerk shall send by certified mail a copy of the process to each person whose address or last known address has been stated in the motion in accordance with §14-10-107(4), C.R.S.
- ☐ The Clerk shall send the information to his or her local paper to be published by consolidated notice in accordance with §14-10-107(4), C.R.S. and shall post a copy of the process on his or her local bulletin for 35 consecutive days.

Date: ________________________ ____________________________________

☐ Judge ☐ Magistrate

CERTIFICATE OF MAILING AND POSTING

I certify that I posted a copy of the process on the court bulletin board from _________________ (date) to ____________________ (date) and I certify that on _____________________ (date), I mailed, faxed, e-filed, or hand-delivered a copy of this Order to the Petitioner or Petitioner's Attorney and I mailed a copy of the Petition and Summons to the Respondent's last known address as follows:

____
____
___________________________________ ____________________________________

Clerk

No. 250A. Rev. 7-12. ORDER FOR PUBLICATION

Bradford Publishing, 1743 Wazee St., Denver, CO 80202 — 303-292-2590 — www.bradfordpublishing.com

The *Petitioner's Verified Motion and Order for Publication* are to be used to meet the service requirement only if, with due diligence, you have been unable to locate your spouse after a good faith effort to find him or her. You will have summarized this information if you filled out the Spouse's Whereabouts Information Sheet.

INSTRUCTIONS TO FILL OUT THE PETITIONER'S VERIFIED MOTION AND THE ORDER FOR PUBLICATION

1. Fill out these lines the same as on the Petition. Be sure to include the case number and the division or courtroom number. Fill in your name for petitioner and your spouse's name for respondent as they appear on the Petition.

2. Check the correct box: "Publication by Consolidated Notice" or "Publication of Summons," depending whether you need the court to have the power to give you title to property; "Service by Certified Mail" if you know your spouse's mailing address or post office box but can't get a street address.

3. Fill in whether you are asking for a dissolution of marriage or a legal separation.

4. Check the appropriate boxes. If you have not been able to locate your spouse's address, describe in detail all efforts you made to determine his or her whereabouts. IF YOU KNOW YOUR SPOUSE'S OUT OF STATE ADDRESS, YOU MUST PERSONALLY SERVE HIM OR HER IF POSSIBLE.

5. Type your spouse's last known address.

6. Fill in the date, city, state, and address, if possible, of the place where you last saw your spouse.

7. Check the first box if you have property in Colorado. Check the second box if you listed children in the Petition.

8. Sign and date in the presence of a notary.

9. Leave blank. This is for the notary to fill in and sign.

10. Fill out the caption the same as on the Motion, except that the information for attorney or *pro se* party is not needed.

11. Leave blank. The order will be completed by court personnel.

The Response

This form is for the spouse who did not sign the petition.

When the petitioner asks the court for a dissolution of marriage, he or she says to the court that the marriage is "irretrievably broken." But, what if you really do not want the divorce, and instead believe the relationship can be reconciled? In that case, you may wish instead to be a respondent (responding to the Petition).

You may use the Response to say any of the following:

- That you disagree that the marriage is irretrievably broken. If you are using the Response to urge the court to find that the marriage is not broken, and that there is a chance for reconciliation, then you MUST sign the Response in front of a notary.
- That you think any of the factual data on the Petition is incorrect.
- That you disagree with what the petition said were temporary arrangements.
- That you want results different from those requested in the final paragraph of the Petition.

If you are using the Response for any purpose except to urge that the marriage is not irretrievably broken, your signature does not have to be notarized. But, you may wish to do so anyway, to show the seriousness of your intent.

If the Response asks for a reconciliation, the court may postpone signing the decree for up to an additional 63 days and order the spouses to try marriage counseling. If the court does so and the petitioner still wants the divorce at the end of 63 days, the divorce will go through.

To file the Response, send or give the original Response to the clerk of the district court along with the current filing fee ($116) in cash, certified or cashier's check, or money order. Give or send a copy to the petitioner. To prove to the court that you have given or mailed a copy of the Response to the petitioner, fill out the Certificate of Service/Mailing on the original Response form to show when you gave your spouse a copy or mailed one to him or her or the petitioner's lawyer. Use certified mail, return receipt requested, to prove to the court that you did this. File the green card, which the post office returns to you, or take it personally to your final hearing. Be sure to write your case number on it.

Contradiction?

Is it contradictory to file a Response asking for a reconciliation of your marriage while at the same time using this guidebook to reach a settlement? Not necessarily. You may feel strongly against the divorce, but still be sufficiently realistic to know it will happen, and sensible enough to want to keep control over how it happens. The initial papers to the court, the Petition and Response, tell the court and anyone who reads your file, how you each felt at the time the Petition was filed.

Filing the Response

Ordinarily you must file your Response within 21 days of service (or publication) if this occurred within the State of Colorado, and within 35 days if outside the state. If your relationship is amicable and you both want to work on your divorce agreement together, whether or not in mediation, then obtain the petitioner's signed agreement to waive your deadline for filing a response until he/she revokes it in writing, to give you time to work on your agreement. If you come to complete agreement and file all of your final papers (see Chapter 12) you won't need to file a response and can save the fee.

District Court, ____________________ County, Colorado Court address:	
❶ **In re the Marriage of:** **Petitioner:** v. **Respondent:**	▲ COURT USE ONLY ▲
Attorney or Party Without Attorney (Name and Address): Phone Number: E-mail: FAX Number: Atty. Reg. #:	Case Number: Division: Courtroom:

RESPONSE TO THE PETITION FOR
☐ DISSOLUTION OF MARRIAGE OR ☐ LEGAL SEPARATION

❷ The Respondent states that:

☐ The marriage is irretrievably broken.

OR ☐ The marriage is not irretrievably broken.*

☐ There is a possibility of reconciliation.

☐ The parties should seek counseling.

The information in number(s) ____❸________ of the Petition is incorrect. The following information is correct:

❹ The Relief Requested is that the Court enter orders regarding the following:

Ⓐ ☐ A finding that the marriage is not irretrievably broken

Ⓑ ☐ That the Court suggest to the parties that they seek counseling

Ⓒ ☐ A Decree of ☐ Dissolution of Marriage ☐ Legal Separation

Ⓓ ☐ Allocation of parental responsibilities: ______________________________

Ⓔ ☐ Child Support: ______________________________

Ⓕ ☐ Maintenance: ______________________________

Ⓖ ☐ Property and/or debts: ______________________________

*Sign before a notary if you deny that the marriage is irretrievably broken.

H ☐ Attorney fees and costs: ____

I ☐ The Respondent requests that the Court restore his/her **prior full name** to:

____

J ☐ Other orders the Court finds appropriate:

5 ___________________________________
Attorney Signature, if any

6 ___________________________________
Signature of Respondent Date

____
Address

____
City, State, Zip Code

____
(Area Code) Home Telephone Number

____
(Area Code) Work Telephone Number

7 STATE OF COLORADO
_____________ County of _______________ } ss.
Signed under oath before me on ________________________.

____
Notary Public
My commission expires: _______________

8

CERTIFICATE OF SERVICE

I certify that on ________________________ (date) a true and accurate copy of this Response was served on the other party by:

☐ Hand Delivery OR

☐ Faxed to this number _____________________________ OR

☐ placing it in the United States mail, postage pre-paid, and addressed to the following:

TO: __________________________________

____

____

____
Your Signature

No. 249. Rev. 7-09. RESPONSE TO PETITION FOR DISSOLUTION OF MARRIAGE OR LEGAL SEPARATION (Page 2 of 2)

INSTRUCTIONS TO FILL OUT THE RESPONSE

1. Fill out this entire top section of the form the same as the top of the Petition. If there are misspellings or other errors in this material, include your corrections under number 4 below.
2. If you agree that your marriage is irretrievably broken, check the first box. If you do not agree, check the second box, then check the third box if you think there is a possibility of reconciliation, and the fourth box if you think you and your spouse should seek counseling.
3. If the petitioner has made any factual errors in paragraphs 3 through 11 of the Petition, write the number of the paragraph you are correcting in the space indicated and any corrections or missing information you want the court to know in the space below. Repeat as needed for every paragraph for which there is a correction.
4. This is where you tell the court what you want the court to order. If you and your spouse are in agreement, check only those boxes that are consistent with those that your spouse checked on the Petition.
    - A. If you believe your marriage is not irretrievably broken and you want the court to agree, check this box. This will probably not apply if you are doing your divorce together.
    - B. If you want the court to suggest that you and your spouse seek counseling, check this box.
    - C. If you want the court to enter a Decree of Dissolution of Marriage at your final hearing, check the first box. If you want the court to enter a Decree of Legal Separation at your final hearing, check the first and third boxes.
    - D. If you have minor children, check this box. If you and your spouse have agreed to your parenting arrangements, type that information in the space provided, which should agree with the parenting arrangement requested in the petition. If you do not agree with what is stated in the petition, write either "to be determined," or the parenting arrangements you wish to have, such as "the respondent," "the petitioner," or "the parties mutually.
    - E. If you have minor children check this box and fill in the amount you have agreed to and who will pay it, or write "to be determined", or the amount you wish.
    - F. If you want to either receive maintenance from or expect to pay maintenance to your spouse, check this box and fill in the amount you have agreed to and who will pay it, or write "to be determined", or the amount you wish and who will pay it.
    - G. Check this box if there are any assets or debts of your marriage. Fill in the blank with what is on the petition if you agree with it.
    - H. You will probably not check this box if you are doing your divorce together. If you want your spouse, the petitioner, to pay your lawyer or the costs of the case (like filing fee, appraisals, counseling professionals, financial advisors, mediators), then check this box and complete it.
    - I. Write your former name if you want it back.
    - J. Check this box if you want the court to have the power to enter other orders about things you may have omitted, or which you learned about later. If you are doing your divorce together you will probably not check this box.
5. If you have a attorney representing you, he or she signs here.
6. Put your signature here and write the date in the space provided. If you have written in step 4 that you do not agree that your marriage is irretrievably broken, you must sign this line in front of a notary. Otherwise you do not need a notary.
7. The notary will fill out this part, if necessary.
8. Complete the Certificate of Service on the back of the Response to prove to the court that you have given or mailed a copy of the Response to your spouse.

Setting the Initial Status Conference

The court will require both of you to attend an initial status conference within 42 days of filing the Petition. They may give you a date and time for it when you file your petition, or give you a phone number to call to set it, or some other procedure. How the conference gets scheduled differs from one court to another, but will likely be spelled out in your Case Management Order. If one of you will be out of town, you may request to attend your status conference by telephone.

If you did *not* file as co-petitioners, it may be your (the Petitioner's) responsibility to notify your spouse (the Respondent) about how this conference will be set (Notice to Set) or when it will happen (Notice of Domestic Relations Initial Status Conference). You may provide the notice of the initial status conference by sending it with the Petition and Summons when they are served. Both of these forms are in Chapter 12.

Those who have no minor children, are in complete agreement about everything, and file all their final papers (including the Affidavit for Non-Appearance of the Parties – see Chapter 12) with their petition, soon after, or before any status conference, are exempt from all status conferences.

What If You and/or Your Spouse Have a Change of Heart?

What if you wake up the morning after filing your case with a heart full of regrets? What if you feel you might not need a legal separation or a divorce after all?

If your case has not been served yet, you can call the sheriff and tell him to hold off while you re-think. He will send you back your papers and your down payment—with a bill for his time.

If you, the Petitioner, want to drop the divorce before the other side has filed a response, double check yourself to be sure that this is what you truly want. In many families, especially those experiencing domestic violence or abuse, the morning after remorse and guilt may be very powerful. If you are the victim, you may be under tremendous pressure from your spouse, friends and family to drop the divorce, forgive, and give the abuser another chance. Only you have the right to determine how many chances are enough. Statistically, sadly, the odds are not with reformation.

If you and your spouse both agree that the divorce is a bad idea at this time and want to have it dismissed—knowing you will have to start all over if the reconciliation does not work out—you may ask the court for the forms you need to accomplish this.

The case management procedure requires you to move your divorce or legal separation along and complete it in a timely fashion. The days when you could file your case and then let it sit there for weeks, months, even years, while you think about it, are gone. If the court finds that you are not taking action in a timely manner or using "due diligence," such as failure to appear for a hearing or status conference, late cancellation, or missed deadline, it can dismiss your case and you will not be divorced. The Court may dismiss your case outright, or give you a Notice of Dismissal for Failure to Prosecute, or an Order to Show Cause why your case should not be dismissed, which may give you up to 35 days to correct the problem and if not done, then dismiss it. If your case is dismissed and you still want to be divorced, you will have to file a new Petition and pay a new court filing fee.

CHAPTER **6**

GATHERING INFORMATION, PREPARING SWORN FINANCIAL STATEMENTS, AND MANDATORY DISCLOSURES

Page

GATHERING INFORMATION, PREPARING SWORN FINANCIAL STATEMENTS, AND MANDATORY DISCLOSURES

If you want to negotiate and resolve all or part of your separation agreement before you file your petition in court, this is the place to start. In order to negotiate with each other, you both must know exactly what is and isn't in your financial picture.

If you have already begun the court process and established the court's jurisdiction over both of you, your marriage, and any children, it's time to pull together, and make available to each other, all the information about your financial circumstances, even those matters you are certain both of you already know.

Working through this chapter will help you gather the information you need. You can make your own checklist of all the documents for your situation or just use the checklists in this chapter. You will both need all this information before beginning to negotiate your agreement about division of debts and assets, how to raise and support your children, or to help each other out financially. You will also need it to complete the court's disclosure requirements, prepare a budget, and fill out your sworn financial statements.

Your agreement should not be based on guesswork. For instance, knowing that the balance in your spouse's IRA is $13,857.95 as of September 30, 2012 gives you much more confidence in your discussions than estimating it's somewhere around $10,000 or $15,000. Your current statement will have the most accurate numbers. You should have clear and accurate paperwork to back up every number you use in your final settlement.

Your check register and credit card statements are good sources of information about your monthly expenses and spending habits. Some people keep track of their household expenses using software like Quicken, and portfolio software to keep track of their investments. Many people keep records by throwing receipts, canceled checks, and statements of all kinds into a shoe box or file folder, sometimes marked "House", "Car", "Bills", "Taxes", or "Kids". Important papers like Deeds and Wills, and insurance policies are often kept in a fireproof box or a safety deposit box at the bank.

Assemble all of these things ready to take to wherever you are going to begin talking—around the kitchen table, mediator's office, or lawyer's office. Gather as much of this information as possible before you begin any discussions. You might find it helpful to make two photocopies of everything, one for each of you (and a third for any mediator you may use). This will give you something to make notes on as you continue working through this book and as you begin your negotiations.

This chapter lists the information you will need to gather in order to negotiate your divorce agreement. It begins with information about income, then your budget of monthly expenses, and then unsecured debts. This is followed by a checklist of your assets—anything of value—whether it's yours personally, your spouse's, or joint. Use this checklist to remind yourself of everything you need to pull together to make a complete picture of all your financial facts and circumstances.

CAUTION

You may have to prepare your financial statement more than once.

How can that be? Some couples have finished with their agreement, or nearly so, in the 42 days after filing the petition, while others are still at the beginning and haven't even moved apart yet. So the financial picture you present at 42 days may be very different from the one that exists by the time you are ready to finalize. You have the duty to update your financial information when it changes significantly.

The Sworn Financial Statement and instructions for filling it out follow the checklist. It is arranged, for the most part, in the same order as the Income Chart, Budget and Checklist. Each spouse must prepare a sworn financial statement. It is your personal choice whether you fill it out before, during, or after your negotiations. Regardless, it is due in the court at or before your initial status conference, and no later than 42 days after you file your petition.

Next in this chapter are the Mandatory Disclosures, those items the law requires you to gather and present to each other, including your completed sworn financial statement. The Certificate of Compliance follows. Each of you must complete and sign a Certificate of Compliance, and swear that you have presented certain information to each other. Out of all of this documentation, only the Certificates of Compliance and your Sworn Financial Statements get filed with the court.

Lastly in this chapter is more information about your status conference, and direction as to what to do after you have gathered all your information.

Information About Income

The word "income" can mean different things to different people. To the worker it probably means spendable earnings. To the IRS it means what is taxed. For calculating child support (see Chapter 9), income may include earnings based on earning capacity rather than actual current earnings. The list of items below and the Income Chart that follows are designed to help you assemble and organize your various kinds of income.

Directions: Initial each item that applies to you. This means that you are responsible for obtaining this information, statement, data, or item. Write the date you receive the information and put it in your joint file or the date you put it in your own file and make a photocopy for your spouse.

Initials/Date	Initials/Date	
		1. If you have a salary or regular pay (whether or not you receive additional income from commissions, tips, or performance-bonus), provide:
________	________	a. Paycheck stubs for the last 3-6 months.
________	________	b. Any employment contract or letter that states your salary or hourly pay and what you must do to earn it.
		2. If you are self-employed, put together, summarize, and average monthly:
________	________	a. Gross business receipts.
________	________	b. Necessary expenses to earn this income. (For ideas about categories see IRS Schedule C. Do not factor in depreciation on business assets, but consider allocating something for replacing equipment and/or repairs.)
________	________	c. Estimated tax payment and tax rate you are using.
________	________	d. Average take-home pay.
________	________	3. If your business is a corporation or limited liability company, provide the last year's corporate or company tax return. Your gross (before tax) income should appear under officer's pay, while your benefits (insurance, retirement, etc.,) will appear as corporate expenses. The corporate tax return will also show any income you received from the profits as an owner.
________	________	4. If your business is a partnership, provide the IRS Schedule K-1 form, Partner's Share of Income, Credits, Deductions, etc., to show your actual income received, if any.
________	________	5. List any monthly reimbursed expenses and in-kind payments to the extent that they reduce your personal living expenses.
________	________	6. If you have income from investments, including dividends, interest, and capital gains, assemble at least a year of monthly or quarterly reports. Summarize the earnings, even if you left them in the account, and any expenses, and average them monthly. Do the same for any interest on bank accounts.

Initials/Date Initials/Date

_____________ _____________ 7. If your income for this last year included a one-time windfall such as profits from the sale of a home or stock, lotto winnings or an inheritance, assemble all the information about this income, including any taxes paid at the time or which you expect to pay.

_____________ _____________ 8. Put together documentation of any additional income, other than that listed above, that you received during the last year. See the Income Chart for a list of other income sources you may have.

_____________ _____________ 9. Provide the last three year's income tax returns, including all attached schedules, W-2, 1099, and K-1 forms.

Notes:

DIRECTIONS TO COMPLETE THE INCOME CHART

Make two copies of the Income Chart—one for each of you. Use this chart to show your respective incomes from all sources. When completed, the information in this chart can be transferred to your Sworn Financial Statement, later on in this chapter where several of the categories will be combined.

1. This section asks you to detail all your sources of income on a *monthly* basis. If you receive a payment twice a month, then the amount is the sum of those two. If you receive several payments each year in a particular category, then add them up and divide by 12. Write "0" if you have none. If you are self-employed, enter your net income *after* necessary business income and *before* you take out for taxes.

    a. Write the total of any child support and/or maintenance you receive from another relationship or marriage. If you have no such income from others, but you have already agreed to your child support and/or maintenance from this marriage, write that total. Check the box that applies to your situation. If you have both sources, write the grand total, and check the box for "both".

    b. Add up your total monthly income from both columns and write that number here.

2. This section is where you record all the deductions from the income you declared in Section 1. These are actual deductions from your paycheck, and not an estimate of what the future tax will be. Be sure to adjust them to *monthly* amounts or averages. If you are self-employed, write the monthly average of your estimated taxes.

    a. Add up your total monthly deductions in these two columns and write that number here.

    b. Subtract your total monthly deductions (step 2a) from your total monthly income (step 1b) and write that number here. This is the total amount of money (net) that you bring home each month, on average.

Income Chart

❶ **1. MONTHLY Income Chart:** (Convert annual, bi-monthly, and weekly amounts to monthly amounts.)

Gross Monthly Income (before taxes and deductions) from principal employment	$	Royalties	$	
Second job		Trust Income		
Self employment income (after necessary business expenses, before taxes)		Investment Income		
Unemployment		Dependent Children's Income		
Veterans' Benefits		Rental Net Income		
Pension & Retirement Benefits (including Social Security retirement)		Child Support ☐ this marriage ☐ other marriage ☐ both		a
Public Assistance (TANF)		Maintenance ☐ this marriage ☐ other marriage ☐ both		a
Social Security Benefits (SSA) ☐ SSDI (Disability insurance entitlement program) ☐ SSI (supplemental income – need based)		Contributions from Others		
Disability Income		Expense Accounts or Reimbursed Expenses		
Workers' Compensation		Other: ____________		
Interest & Dividends		Other: ____________		
		Total Monthly Income	$	b

❷ **2. MONTHLY Deductions:**

Federal Income Tax	$	Life Insurance	$	
State Income Tax		Disability Insurance		
Social Security Tax (FICA)		Health Insurance		
Medicare Tax		Dental Insurance		
PERA/Civil Service		Vision Insurance		
Local Tax		Child Care		
Flex Benefit Cafeteria Plan		Stocks/Bonds		
Retirement & Deferred Compensation		Credit Union (savings)		
		Credit Union (loan)		
Other: ____________		Other: ____________		
		Total Monthly Deductions	$	a
		TOTAL MONTHLY NET INCOME	$	b

Your Monthly Budget

The purpose of this section is to budget your expenses as your family changes from one household to two. Each spouse needs to do one of these. You will have the on-going expenses of two households, plus any debt payments you may have (see the Debts Chart following the Budget).

The ongoing expenses for two households can be divided into two categories:

a. bare bones: necessary expenses during this period of time ("survival"); and

b. discretionary: expenses that are in addition to bare bones items that either of you could live without, albeit with some difficulty ("lifestyle").

Use this distinction to sort out what you absolutely need, plus what you would like to have, or are used to having in your lifestyle. If you find you need to cut back, look to the discretionary column.

DIRECTIONS TO COMPLETE YOUR MONTHLY BUDGET

The Monthly Budget is designed to help you organize information for your planning, your negotiations, and your Sworn Financial Statements. It lists the categories noted above and a total column. Work with these until you are satisfied that you have a budget that you can truly live with.

You should each do one of these to represent your own separate household. Make a photocopy of the Monthly Budget for each of you. You may want to make several additional copies for rough drafts in order to look at different possibilities (such as renting an apartment versus buying a condo) and to update them as your circumstances change.

You may prepare these separately and then share them with each other, or you may prepare them together. As you do so, try not to let this process become an opportunity to tell each other how to spend. Write down the information that is true for you, or as best you can project for the expenses in your future households. Be sure that between your two budgets, you include all your expenses for both households, but that you do not duplicate any of them.

If you have not yet separated or have recently separated, much of the information you have will be based on your expenses when you were together. If you have been separated for some time, the information you have will be based on some individual experience.

If you are physically separating, but will share the same residence long-term, do separate budgets. You must decide how you will share the expenses of the home.

THINGS TO GATHER FOR YOUR MONTHLY BUDGET ARE AS FOLLOWS:

1. Using your check register(s), list all the expenses you have had in each of the categories on the Monthly Budget over a period of time (6 months to 2 years), then divide the total by the number of months. Write the number in the appropriate place on the Budget, allocating it, if necessary, among bare bones and discretionary. For example, the base rate for your telephone is bare bones; long distance and other services may be discretionary, in whole or in part.

2. If you have no experience with an expense on this Budget, do some investigation:

   a. To determine rent or a mortgage, drive around the area you want to live in, and call about homes for rent or sale. Be sure you ask about the average monthly cost of utilities and the cost between number of bedrooms

   b. Buy a simple budget book at your local office supply or discount store. Each day, write down every penny you spend.

   c. Super market spending is rarely limited to groceries and often includes cleaning supplies, sox, toiletries, and batteries. These are real expenses and can be grouped in the groceries/supplies category on your budget.

   d. Obtain information regarding the balance you can expect to pay for any ongoing treatment for any members of your family, such as dental care, mental health, physical therapy, and the like.

   e. Find out about one-time children's expenses such as prom, yearbook, school pictures, school trips, summer camp.

3. Don't forget to include expenses that might not be paid monthly or weekly, such as car insurance, life insurance, or property taxes if they are not included in the mortgage payment.

4. Be sure you average expenses that vary with the time of year: heat, water, birthday expenses, Christmas gifts, summer activities, school clothes in the fall.

5. If you included your entire expense allowance you receive from your employer in your Income Chart, then be sure to include those expenses on this Budget.

6. If you participate in a "cafeteria plan" pre-tax medical or day care expense program, show your contribution to the cafeteria plan as a deduction from your income, then when you show the expenses it pays for in your budget, mark them "pre-paid" and do not add them into the total expenses (this would be deducting them twice).

Your Monthly Budget

Expenses	Bare Bones	Discretionary	Total
A. Housing			
1st Mortgage	$	$	$
2nd Mortgage			
Rent			
Property Taxes (not included in mortgage payment)			
Insurance (not included in mortgage payment)			
Condo/Homeowners' Fees			
Other:			
B. Utilities and Miscellaneous Housing Services			
Gas & Electricity	$	$	$
Water/Sewer			
Trash Removal			
Home telephone, local and long distance			
Cell phone, pager			
Internet, Cable & Satellite TV			
Lawn Care, Snow Removal			
Cleaning Services			
Security System			
Household Maintenance			
Other:			
C. Food & Supplies			
Groceries/Supplies	$	$	$
Dining Out			
D. Health Care Costs (Co-pays, out of pocket costs, insurance premiums)			
Doctor	$	$	$
Vision Care			
Dentist			
Orthodontist			
Medicine/RX Drugs			
Therapist			
Premiums (if not paid by deduction from paycheck)			
Other:			
Subtotal	**$**	**$**	**$**

Expenses	Bare Bones	Discretionary	Total
E. Transportation and Recreation Vehicles (Motorcycles, Motor Homes, Boats, ATV, Snowmobiles, etc.)			
Primary Vehicle Payment	$	$	$
Other Vehicle Payment(s)			
Fuel			
Parking			
Maintenance			
Insurance			
Registration/Tax			
Bus & Commuter Fees			
Other:			
F. Children's Expenses and Activities			
Clothing and Shoes	$	$	$
Child Care (work related)			
Child Care (education related)			
Child Care (for other reasons)			
Special Needs			
Tuition			
Lessons			
Tutor			
Books/Supplies			
Activities			
Uniforms & Equipment			
School Lunches			
Car Insurance			
Allowance			
Other:			
Other:			
G. Education for You			
Tuition	$	$	$
Books & Supplies			
Other:			
Other:			
Subtotal	**$**	**$**	**$**

Expenses	Bare Bones	Discretionary	Total
H. Maintenance & Child Support (that you pay)			
Spousal Maintenance (This family)	$	$	$
Spousal Maintenance (Other family)			
Child Support (This family)			
Child Support (Other family)			
I. Miscellaneous (List here on-going expenses not covered above.)			
Clothing and Shoes (for you)	$	$	$
Hair & Nail Care			
Recreation/Entertainment			
Legal/Accounting Fees			
Subscriptions			
Charity/Worship			
Movie & Video/DVD Rentals			
Vacation/Travel			
Hobbies			
Investments (not part of payroll deductions)			
Memberships/Clubs			
Home Furnishings			
Pets/Pet Care			
Sports Events/Participation			
Other:			
Other:			
Other:			
Other:			
Other:			
Other:			
Subtotal	**$**	**$**	**$**
Subtotal (Page 123)			
Subtotal (Page 124)			
Total Monthly Expenses	**$**	**$**	**$**

Unsecured Debt

The purpose of this section is to gather information about your unsecured debts. Now that you know about your income and expenses, this step will help you complete your financial picture to see if you will have enough funds to provide for the future as budgeted or if a shortfall will occur.

Assemble all the current debt, credit card, and loan statements you have, including those since your separation. This section does NOT include your mortgage(s), or car payment(s), or any other secured debt (meaning tied to an asset) that already appears in your budget.

Include all debts, whether joint or in separate names. The goal is to list all debts, not just the ones you are paying or willing to pay.

You will need to know the balance of any debts incurred during the marriage and their monthly payments to complete that section of the Sworn Financial Statement. Deciding how you will divide these debts can be an important part of your negations and your separation agreement.

Using the information you have gathered, complete the Debts Chart. You can both use a single chart to list all of your debt. If you have already agreed on who is responsible to pay which debt, you can each make your own chart—just be sure your two charts together include all your debt.

To complete the summary at the bottom of the Debts Chart, pull your Net Monthly Income from the Income Chart, your Total Monthly Expenses from your Budgets. Subtract the Minimum Monthly Payments you have calculated on the Debts Chart to arrive at your shortfall or excess.

On a separate piece of paper, make a list of all the payments and charges you have made since your separation. Include any debt you incurred to acquire items identified on your DIN (Duplicate Items Needed) List in Chapter 4. This may be important in your negotiations.

Debts Chart

Debts (unsecured)

(List **unsecured** debts such as credit cards, store charge accounts, loans from family members, etc. Do **not** list debts that are liens against your property, such as mortgages and car loans, because their payment is already listed as an expense above, and the total of the debt is shown elsewhere as a deduction from value where that asset is listed, such as under Real Estate or Motor Vehicles.)

Creditor	Account Number (last 4 digits only)	Name on Account	Date of Balance	Balance	Minimum Monthly Payment Required	Principal Purchase(s) for Which Debt Was Incurred
				$	$	
			Unsecured Debt Balance	$	$	Total Min. Mo. Pmt.

Summary of Total Net Income, Expenses, and Monthly Debt:

Total Monthly Net Income	$
Less Total Monthly Expenses	$
Less Min. Mo. Debt Payment (from above)	$
Shortfall or Excess	$

Assets

Assemble all the documents you have showing the current fair market value or balance of your major assets. This includes items titled in either of your separate names, titled in your joint names, or titled to either or both of you jointly with others. If you still own assets you entered the marriage with, you may want to document their value at the time of your marriage. As you will see in Chapter 7, you are free to make your own distinctions between marital and separate property. Gathering this data, *if you have it*, will help you focus on your specific situation. Each of the types of asset below is discussed in detail in Chapter 7. If you need to know more about that asset as you gather these items, turn to the page number listed below each of these headings.

Directions: Initial each item that applies to you. This means that you are responsible for obtaining this information, statement, data, or item. Write the date you receive the information and put it in your joint file or the date you put it in your own file and make a photocopy for your spouse.

A. REAL ESTATE
(Also see page 162)

Initials/Date	Initials/Date	
		1. Family Residence.
____________	____________	a. Your Warranty Deed.
____________	____________	b. Purchaser's closing statement, or cost of construction.
____________	____________	c. Documentation of your cost of any capital improvements.
____________	____________	d. Current balance, interest rate, and number of payments remaining for each mortgage or equity line of credit of all mortgages.
____________	____________	e. Market analysis or bank appraisal showing current market value.
____________	____________	f. County tax assessment valuation.
____________	____________	g. IRS form 2119 for all previous primary homes sold by either of you showing any capital gain rolled over into this home. If you don't find any 2119s, gather your purchaser's closing statements and your seller's closing statements, records of any capital improvements, and costs of sale on those homes. ***There is no need to do this if your primary residence (home) has increased less than $250,000 in value (including any amount rolled into it).***
		2. Other real estate.
____________	____________	a. Warranty deed or other deed to you.
____________	____________	b. Purchaser's closing statement or 1031 documents to ascertain purchase or "start-up" value.
____________	____________	c. Any depreciation taken by you if you have been renting the property or using it for business.
____________	____________	d. The cost of any capital improvements, or cost of construction if you built it.
____________	____________	e. Current balance, interest rate, and number of payments remaining for each mortgage or equity line of credit of all mortgages.
____________	____________	f. Market analysis or bank appraisal showing current market value.
____________	____________	g. County tax assessment valuation.

B. MOTOR VEHICLES

(Also see page 168)

Initials/Date Initials/Date

__________ __________ Look at the NADA Blue Book at your local library or online at (nada.com) or Kelley Blue Book online (kelleybluebook.com) for retail and wholesale values, and/or ads for similar cars from the newspaper classifieds. Find out loan balance owed, the date of the balance, and the names on the loan. Unless your lender is holding it, provide the title.

C. CASH ON HAND, BANK, CHECKING, OR SAVINGS ACCOUNTS, CDS

(Also see page 169)

__________ __________ If you keep on hand more than small amounts of pocket money, make a list, whether it's in a safe, mattress, or buried in the backyard. Gather current statements for each of your bank accounts and certificates of deposit.

D. LIFE AND HEALTH INSURANCE

(Also see page 169)

Most of the information you need to answer the questions in this section may be in a benefits booklet from your employer. If you do not have a benefits booklet, ask your employer to provide the information to you in writing. If you have private insurance, provide the policies.

1. For each life insurance policy you have, gather this information:
   - __________ __________ a. The company name and policy number
   - __________ __________ b. Whose life does the policy cover?
   - __________ __________ c. Is it whole life, term, hybrid (mixture of several kinds), or universal life?
   - __________ __________ d. Who is the owner of the policy?
   - __________ __________ e. Who are the beneficiaries of the policy? (Get a copy of the actual beneficiary designation.)
   - __________ __________ f. What is the cash value, if any?
   - __________ __________ g. What is the cash surrender value, if any?
   - __________ __________ h. What is the loan balance, if any?
   - __________ __________ i. What are the current and future premium payments?
   - __________ __________ j. What is the death benefit?
2. __________ __________ For each health or medical insurance policy you have (medical, dental, vision, etc.), gather this information:
   - __________ __________ a. Who is covered?
   - __________ __________ b. What is the premium for each person or category of person?
   - __________ __________ c. What is the coverage for each kind of medical expense? Dental? Eyeglasses? Preventive care? Office visits? Prescriptions? Chiropractic? How much is the deductible, or the co-pay?
   - __________ __________ d. When does the spousal coverage end as a result of the divorce? The date of the Decree? The end of that month? The end of the following month? This information will tell that spouse when to start the new coverage.
   - __________ __________ e. Obtain the details on the COBRA option that permits a former spouse to purchase separate coverage of the same insurance, for up to three years after the divorce. (See Chapters 10 and 12 for more on this.)

E. FURNITURE AND HOUSEHOLD GOODS

(Also see page 170)

Initials/Date Initials/Date

________ ________ 1. Furniture, appliances and household goods. List every item of significant value—you decide what significant value means to you. Remember, value may not be monetary. Something may be valuable to you because of its utility or that it reminds you of a person, or the place where you acquired it. It is often useful to make your list with columns: "I want," "You want," "Both want," "Nobody wants." You can make a fifth column for value or comments if you wish. You can make columns for whether something was yours before the marriage or was a gift or inheritance or for some other reason feels more like "mine" than "ours." An interesting way to gather this information is to each do a list and compare them. Be sure you allow time to walk through the house individually (or together if you wish) to prepare the list. If you are separated, walk through each other's homes, listing the items you acquired together.

Many people do not detail their division of these assets in their settlement. It is possible to keep this as a private agreement after you physically divide the items between you. Therefore, this is an early agreement you can be working on while you gather data necessary to complete your larger settlement.

If you use a monetary value for these items in your settlement, use street value—what you would get for an item if you sold it yourself.

________ ________ 2. Art, antiques, collectibles. Start making a detailed list of these items with a description and value for each.

________ ________ 3. Necessary purchases of duplicate items needed for two households. As the two of you move from one household to two, inevitably you will need to acquire some new furniture and household goods. If you envision some necessary purchases in this vein, complete the Duplicate Items Needed ("DIN") List in Chapter 4.

F. SECURITIES AND/OR INVESTMENT ACCOUNTS (NON-RETIREMENT)

(Also see page 172)

If all of your securities are in a brokerage account or mutual fund, or an employee stock purchase plan, provide a current statement. For each security that you own, whether in a brokerage account or as a separate certificate, including restricted stock, stock options, and similar interests, provide the following:

________ ________ a. Name of company, and number and type of shares or bonds.

________ ________ b. How titled.

________ ________ c. Value/cost at acquisition and value now.

G. PENSION, PROFIT SHARING, OR RETIREMENT FUNDS — DEFINED CONTRIBUTION PLANS — INCLUDING SEPS, IRAS, KEOGHS, 401(k)s, 403(b)s, AND OTHER ACCOUNTS THAT HAVE AN ACTUAL BALANCE TODAY

(Also see page 173)

1. Your current and previous employers, plan administrators, or trustees have been giving you, or should have been giving you, the following documents regarding your, profit sharing, retirement, 401k, thrift savings, and IRAs. Provide the most current:

________ ________ a. A benefit statement telling what kind of retirement or tax-deferred benefit you have.

Initials/Date	Initials/Date	
________	________	b. A current statement of the amount that is vested for you or in your name.
________	________	c. Is your plan subject to a Qualified Domestic Relations Order ("QDRO")? If so, are there written information and "in house" forms available from your employer or plan administrator? If so, provide them.
		2. Check the accuracy of the factual data in the plan (since small discrepancies can create huge problems, including with the Social Security Administration). Not all this data will appear in every plan, but check your plan for the accuracy of the following data:
________	________	a. Participant's name, address, Social Security number, birth date, and the exact date you began participating in the plan.
________	________	b. The exact name of the surviving spouse, alternate payee, or beneficiary, and his or her address.
________	________	c. The date of your marriage.
		3. Make a photocopy of this question for each retirement, tax deferred savings plan, IRA, 401(k), thrift savings or other defined contribution plan, either of you has. Then, for each plan, answer the following questions. If you don't know the answers to these questions, you can get help from the benefits office at work, or your account executive.
________	________	a. Who is the named beneficiary upon death of the participant?
________	________	b. What portion of the funds held in this plan are tax-deferred?
________	________	c. What portion of the funds held in this plan have already been taxed?
________	________	d. Can the participant receive a lump sum payout? If so, when, and under what circumstances?
________	________	e. Is any benefit or amount available to the participant now? Is there a "hardship" clause which permits a partial payout for
________	________	1) purchase of a primary residence
________	________	2) college or higher education (self, spouse, or children)
________	________	3) medical emergency
________	________	4) divorce
________	________	5) other ____
		____
________	________	f. May the participant borrow from the plan? If so, under what circumstances?
________	________	1) purchase of a primary residence
________	________	2) college or higher education expenses (self, spouse, or children?)
________	________	3) medical emergency
________	________	4) divorce
________	________	5) other ____
		____
________	________	g. What is the participant's expected date of retirement?
________	________	h. What is the participant's earliest possible date of retirement?

H. OTHER PENSION OR RETIREMENT FUNDS — DEFINED BENEFIT PLANS — INCLUDING PERA, CIVIL SERVICE, FFPA, UNION OR MILITARY RETIREMENT, ETC.)

(Also see page 173)

Initials/Date Initials/Date

1. Your current and previous employers, plan administrators, or trustees have been giving you, or should have been giving you, the following information about your pension or other defined benefit plan. Provide the most current:

______ ______ a. Name of your employer and division or department, or military service.

______ ______ b. Name of the retirement plan.

______ ______ c. Address and telephone number for the plan or retirement authority.

______ ______ d. Your date of birth

______ ______ e. Your spouse's date of birth

______ ______ f. Date of hire or enlistment

______ ______ g. Your plan entry date (if not date of hire)

______ ______ h. Date of marriage

______ ______ I. Your rank (if military), or your job description

______ ______ j. Date first eligible to receive retirement

______ ______ k. Expected amount of lump sum or monthly payments.

______ ______ l. The exact name of the surviving spouse, alternate payee, or beneficiary, and his or her address.

______ ______ 2. Is your plan subject to a Qualified Domestic Relations Order ("QDRO")? If so, are there written information and "in house" forms available from your employer or plan administrator? If so, provide them.

3. Make a photocopy of this question for each pension or defined benefit plan either of you has. Then, for each plan, answer the following questions. If you don't know the answers to these questions, you can get help from the benefits office at work.

______ ______ a. How is the plan funded? Does participant contribute? Does the employer contribute? If so, how much, and when?

______ ______ b. How and when does the employer's contribution vest?

______ ______ c. When and under what circumstances does the plan pay out?

______ ______ d. Is the plan subject to divestment? Total? Partial? If so, when and how?

______ ______ e. Does the plan have a pre-retirement death benefit? If so,

______ ______ 1) What is the benefit?

______ ______ 2) Who is the named beneficiary of this benefit?

______ ______ f. Does the plan have a death benefit after the monthly payments begin? If so,

______ ______ 1) What is the benefit?

______ ______ 2) Who is the named beneficiary of this benefit?

______ ______ g. What is the participant's expected date of retirement?

______ ______ h. What is the participant's earliest possible date of retirement?

Initials/Date	Initials/Date

i. What change in benefits, if any, results from early retirement?

j. Is any portion of this plan in lieu of Social Security (i.e., participant does not pay F.I.C.A. and does not have F.I.C.A. paid on his/her behalf)?

k. If the answer to the previous question is yes, what is the value of the portion of the plan that is in lieu of Social Security?

l. Are any of the benefits described above affected by participant's Social Security benefits, estimated or received? If so how? In what amount?

m. Is the participant presently eligible for Social Security benefits? If so, what is the present anticipated monthly benefit? If not, how many more quarters are needed.

4. If you have worked for 40 full-time quarters (10 years), you will probably be eligible to receive Social Security—unless you work for a public entity which has a plan in lieu of Social Security, such as P.E.R.A. Call the local Social Security office and ask them to send you a statement of your present earned credits and probable benefit.

I. BUSINESS INTERESTS

(Also see page 185)

If either spouse owns a business, or part of a business, gather any documents that you have that give some indication of the value of the business. Consult with a lawyer, CPA, and/or business appraiser regarding the value of these assets. See Chapter 7.

J. MISCELLANEOUS AND OTHER ASSETS OR INTERESTS

(Also see page 190)

The rest of your assets may include a variety of things like tools, sports equipment, livestock, crops or frequent flyer miles. Start gathering titles, descriptions, and costs to acquire or maintain these items. The paper work should be ready to give to whoever will keep that asset after the divorce. Now is the time to start assembling everything so you avoid lost documents and nerve-wrenching last minute scrambles.

K. RECENT TRANSACTIONS

The period of the break-up of a marriage, and especially the physical separation, are times of high stress when people are likely to be less careful than usual—including about finances. Keep track of all your recent transactions.

Provide documentation of any large withdrawal from, or sale of, an account or asset you made during this last year, especially since or around the time of your separation. If you can show the money you received went into a current asset (for example: home, car, furniture) then also provide that documentation (for example: bank statement, sales receipt, closing statement). If the money went into your own account, try to show what you used it for through your check register or other written records.

L. LOANS, GIFTS AND INHERITANCES

______ ______ If anyone gave you a gift or loan of money during the last year, or especially since or around the time of your separation, then obtain a written statement from the person who gave you the money showing their understanding of the amount and whether they expect it to be paid back, and the interest rate if any.

If anyone gave you a gift of an item of significant value since or at about the time of your separation (car, jewelry, antiques, pedigreed animal), then obtain written proof of the gift and the value.

If you inherited or received by gift any money or property during the marriage, provide written documentation of the date you received it, the value when received, and the value now.

M. PROPERTY OWNED BEFORE THE MARRIAGE

______ ______ If you owned property of substantial value before the marriage that you still own, or can trace, provide documentation of the property, the value at the time of the marriage, and the value now.

N. CREDIT REPORT

______ ______ If you have any concerns about your credit, or if you are not sure that credit has been established in your name, Look under "Credit Reporting Agencies" in the yellow pages or Google and call at least one. Obtain your individual (not joint) credit reports. See "Credit and your Divorce" in Chapter 4 for why this can be important.

The Sworn Financial Statement

INSTRUCTIONS TO FILL OUT THE SWORN FINANCIAL STATEMENT—INCOME AND DEDUCTIONS

Now that you have gathered all the information about your income and deductions, you are ready to complete that portion of the sworn financial statement. Use the numbers from your Income Chart. Follow the directions on the form carefully, as well as the instructions below. Note that different categories on the Income Chart are combined on the Financial Statement.

1. Check the first box, District Court, and enter the county where you filed your petition. Enter the street address of your court, and all the other information the same as on your petition.
2. Check the first box "The Marriage of". Fill out these lines the same as you did on your petition and all previous forms.
3. Insert the full name of the person filing this Statement. Check the appropriate boxes about your employment, hours, and pay. Insert the number of hours you actually work each week. If it varies, calculate the average.
4. Insert the date your employment began, your job title or a description of your employment, and the name and address of your employer.
5. If you are unemployed, insert the date of your last employment, and state the reason why you are now unemployed.
6. Insert the number of adults and children in your household. Include any children who are with you part time.
7. Insert what you believe your spouse's monthly gross income is (before taking out for taxes and other deductions). Insert the annual gross income for each of you for last year (again before taking out for taxes and other deductions).
8. This section, in two parts (Monthly Income and Miscellaneous Income), asks you to detail all your sources of income on a monthly basis. Insert the total of your before-tax monthly income from all your employments. If you receive a payment twice a month, then the amount is the sum of those two. Be careful here. Twice monthly is not the same as every other week. For the latter, take each paycheck amount times 26, then divide by 12. If you are paid weekly, multiply the amount by 52, and then divide by 12. Include self-employment income here after deducting for necessary business expenses, but not for taxes. If you receive several payments each year in a particular category, then add them up and divide by 12.

Be sure to insert any income you have in each of the other categories listed in two parts (Monthly Income and Miscellaneous Income), averaged monthly. Write "0" if you have none.

9. Add up your total monthly income from both columns and write that number here.
10. Add up your total monthly miscellaneous income and write that number here.
11. Add the Total Monthly Income (step 9) and the Total Monthly Miscellaneous Income (step 10) together and write the sum here.
12. This section 2 is where you record all the mandatory and voluntary deductions from the income you declared above. These are actual deductions from your paycheck, and not an estimate of what the future tax will be. Be sure to adjust them to monthly amounts or averages, as in step 8 above. If you are self-employed, insert the monthly average of your estimated tax payments.
13. Add up your Total Mandatory Deductions from both columns and write the sum here.

14. Add up your Total Voluntary Deductions from both columns and write the sum here.
15. Add the Total Mandatory Deductions (step 13) and the Total Voluntary Deductions (step 14) together, and write the sum here.

INSTRUCTIONS TO FILL OUT THE SWORN FINANCIAL STATEMENT—EXPENSES AND DEBTS

Use your Monthly Budget and Debts Chart to complete this part of the Sworn Financial Statement. Some separate categories on the Budget are combined on the Financial Statement. Then do the calculations for the Summary.

16. In Section 3, list your regular monthly expenses in subsections A through I. If an expense does not occur every month, use an average. You can take the total for a quarter and divide it by 3, or for the year and divide it by 12.
17. Write the total from both columns for each subsection A through I and put them in the Total column for the subsection.
18. Add up all the subsection totals in subsections A through I, and insert that total here.
19. Be sure to list complete information here about all your debts, making sure you don't repeat mortgages and car loans, and check the appropriate box to show the name(s) on the account.
20. Add up all the balances in this column and insert the total here.
21. Add up all the minimum monthly payments in this column and insert the total here.
22. Insert the number from Total Income (step 11).
23. Insert the number from Total Monthly Deductions (step 15).
24. Subtract the deductions (step 23) from your income (step 22) and insert that number here.
25. Insert the number from Total Monthly Expenses (step 18).
26. Insert the number of your Total Minimum Monthly Payments (step 21).

    If you have an explicit agreement with your spouse about who is responsible for which debts, insert the total of only the ones you are responsible for. If you do not have an explicit agreement, insert the total number.
27. Add together steps 25 and 26, and insert that total here.
28. Subtract the amount in step 27 from step 24. If the number is negative, you have a shortfall, so put it in parentheses like this: ($1,032). If it is positive, you have an excess or surplus, and you do not use parentheses.

INSTRUCTIONS TO FILL OUT THE SWORN FINANCIAL STATEMENT—ASSETS

29. In Section 5 you list all assets - anything of value - of yours and of your spouse, whether marital (joint) or separate, regardless of how titled and regardless of when or how you acquired it. Then check "J" if you acquired it during the marriage but not by gift or inheritance; check "P" or "C/R", as appropriate, if it was acquired by one of you before your marriage, or during the marriage by gift or bequest. If an asset is part marital and part separate, check each box that applies. If an asset was acquired during the marriage from proceeds from other separate assets, check "P" or "C/R" for whose separate property it is.

    See pages 157–161 for more information about marital and separate property.

    If you have no assets in any subsection, check "None".
30. List the address or property description and the lender for any mortgages and/or lines of credit for each piece of real estate. Keep each parcel of real estate on one line.

31. Write the amount owed on each property. If there is more than one mortgage, or a mortgage and a line of credit, add them together and insert the total.
32. Write what you believe to be the fair market value for each property.
33. Subtract the Amount Owed (step 31) from the Estimated Value as of Today, and write the result here. If it is a negative number, put it in parentheses like this ($3,500).
34. Write the totals for subsection A in each of the three columns.

    Note: If one or both of you owns 25% interest in a rental condo, put 25% of the amount owed, 25% of the estimated value, then subtract to determine the net value/equity of the 25%.
35. Provide all the information requested for each vehicle that either, or both of you, own, and enter the "Amount Owed" and the "Estimated Value as of Today". Subtract the amount owed from the estimated value to obtain the "Net Value/Equity."
36. Write the totals for subsection B in each of the three columns.
37. Provide all the information requested for your cash on hand, bank, checking, savings, certificates of deposit, or health accounts, including medical savings accounts and flex plan balances.
38. Write the totals for subsection C in each of the three columns.
39. List each life insurance policy owned by either of you, and the type of each (whole life, term, universal life, etc. The "Face Amount of Policy" is the death benefit. A term policy has no cash value, so put zero in the last column. For a policy with a cash value, list the cash value in the last column less any outstanding loan balance.
40. Write the totals for subsection D in each of the three columns.
41. List by groups all the items you have in this category, such as "dining room furniture", "electronics", or "tools." Remember in the first set of columns headed P, C/R and J you are telling the court whether it is your joint property or separate because it was previously owned by one of you before the marriage, or gifted to, or inherited by, one of you during the marriage. The second three columns are for telling the court which of you currently has physical possession of these items. This is about current physical possession only, and does not reflect a final settlement. Be sure to estimate the value.
42. Write the total for subsection E.
43. If you have none of the items listed here check "None". If you do, check the second box and complete Schedule F on the last page of the Financial Statement (called Supporting Schedules for Assets in Sections F, G, H, and I). For an investment account with several holdings, don't list the number of shares. This section is only about non-retirement non-tax-deferred assets.
44. Insert the total for subsection F from the Supporting Schedule F.
45. If you have none of these items check "None". If you do, check the second box and complete Schedule G on the Supporting Schedule. See Chapter 7, pages 171-184 about valuing retirement assets.
46. Insert the total for subsection G from the Supporting Schedule G.
47. Check the appropriate box for any asset you have not listed on any previous schedule, and provide the detail on the Supporting Schedule H, or on a separate piece of paper. If you have none of these, check "None".
48. Insert the total for subsection H from the Supporting Schedule H.

49. If you claim no separate property, check the first box. If you claim any separate property (that is not marital), check the second box, and then list what portion of the property listed in Section 5 Schedules A through H you assert or believe to be your separate property. Detail these in the Supporting Schedule for Assets under Subsection I. To help you determine which assets are separate property, see pages 157–161.

    Note: There is a potential ambiguity in the Sworn Financial Statement form. First you list all your assets, marital and separate, in sections 5.A–H. Then you list all separate property in 5.I, thus potentially counting separate property twice. Therefore, any separate property you list in 5.I, write the value again, but do not add it into your total a second time. You may write a note: "value included above at 5.___", the section where you previously listed it.

50. Insert the total for subsection I from the Supporting Schedule I.
51. Add the totals of all the subsections A through I and insert the total of all assets here.
52. Read the oath and, when you are ready, sign in front of a Notary or a Court Clerk.

1 ☐ District Court ☐ Denver Juvenile Court
______________________ County, Colorado
Court Address:

2 ☐ **In re the Marriage of:**
☐ **In re the Parental Responsibilities concerning:**
____

Petitioner:

and
Co-Petitioner/Respondent:

Attorney or Party Without Attorney (Name and Address):

1

Phone Number: E-mail:
FAX Number: Atty. Reg. #:

▲ COURT USE ONLY ▲

Case Number:

1

Division: Courtroom:

SWORN FINANCIAL STATEMENT

3 I, ______________________________ (full name), ☐ am ☐ am not currently employed.
I am employed ______ hours per week. I am paid ☐ weekly ☐ bi-weekly ☐ twice a month ☐ monthly.
My pay is based on a ☐ Monthly Salary ☐ Hourly rate of $_________ ☐ Other: ______________
4 Date employment began: ______________________
My occupation is: ____________________ Name of employer: ____________________
Address of employer: ____
5 If unemployed, what date did you last work? ______________________
I am unemployed due to ☐ disability ☐ involuntary layoff at work ☐ other: ______________
6 This household consists of _____ adult(s), and ______ minor child(ren).
7 I believe the monthly gross income of the other party is $___________.
Annual gross income (last tax year 20____) for Petitioner $___________, ☐ Co-Petitioner/Respondent $___________.

8 **1. Monthly Income (Convert annual, bi-monthly, and weekly amounts to monthly amounts.)**

Gross Monthly Income (before taxes and deductions) from salary and wages, including commissions, bonuses, overtime, self-employment, business income, other jobs, and monthly reimbursed expenses.	$	Social Security Benefits (SSA) ☐ SSDI (Disability insurance – entitlement program) ☐ SSI (supplemental income – need based)	$
Unemployment & Veterans' Benefits		Disability, Workers' Compensation	
Pension & Retirement Benefits		Interest & Dividends	
Public Assistance (TANF)		Other:	
		Total Monthly Income	$ 9

Bradford Publishing, 1743 Wazee St., Denver, CO 80202 — 303-292-2590 — www.bradfordpublishing.com

8

Miscellaneous Income				
Royalties, Trusts, and Other Investments	$	Contributions from Others	$	
Dependent Children's monthly gross income. Source of Income: ______		All other sources, i.e. personal injury settlement, non-reported income, etc.		
Rental Net Income		Expense Accounts		
Child Support from Others		Other:		
Spousal Support from Others		Other:		
		Total Monthly Miscellaneous Income	$	10
		Total Income	$	11

12 **2. Monthly Deductions (Mandatory and Voluntary)**

Mandatory Deductions	Cost Per Month		Cost Per Month	
Federal Income Tax	$	State/Local Income Tax	$	
PERA/Civil Service		Social Security Tax		
Medicare Tax		Other:		
		Total Mandatory Deductions	$	13
Voluntary Deductions	**Cost Per Month**		**Cost Per Month**	
Life and Disability Insurance	$	Stocks/Bonds	$	
Health, Dental, Vision Insurance Premium		Retirement & Deferred Compensation		
Total number of people covered on Plan		Other:		
Child Care		Other:		
Flex Benefit Cafeteria Plan		Other:		
		Total Voluntary Deductions	$	14
		Total Monthly Deductions	$	15

16 **3. Monthly Expenses**

Note: List regular monthly expenses below that you pay on an on-going basis and that are not identified in the deductions above.

A. Housing

	Cost Per Month		Cost Per Month	
1st Mortgage	$	2nd Mortgage	$	
Insurance (Home/Rental) & Property Taxes (not included in mortgage payment)		Condo/Homeowner's/ Maintenance Fees		
Rent		Other:		
		Total Housing	$	17

B. Utilities and Miscellaneous Housing Services

	Cost Per Month		Cost Per Month	
Gas & Electricity	$	Water, Sewer, Trash Removal	$	
Telephone (local, long distance, cellular & pager)		Property Care (Lawn, snow removal, cleaning, security system, etc.)		
Internet Provider, Cable & Satellite TV		Other:		
		Total Utilities and Miscellaneous Housing Services	$	17

No. 253. Rev. 4-10. SWORN FINANCIAL STATEMENT (Form C.R.C.P. 35.2) (Page 2 of 8)

C. Food & Supplies

	Cost Per Month		Cost Per Month
Groceries & Supplies	$	Dining Out	$
		Total Food & Supplies	$

17

D. Health Care Costs (Co-pays, Premiums, etc.)

	Cost Per Month		Cost Per Month
Doctor & Vision Care	$	Dentist and Orthodontist	$
Medicine & RX Drugs		Therapist	
Premiums (if not paid by employer)		Other:	
		Total Health Care	$

17

E. Transportation & Recreation Vehicles (Motorcycles, Motor Homes, Boats, ATV, Snowmobiles, etc.)

	Cost Per Month		Cost Per Month
Primary Vehicle Payment	$	Other Vehicle Payments	$
Fuel, Parking, and Maintenance		Insurance & Registration/Tax Payments (yearly amount(s)÷12)	
Bus & Commuter Fees		Other:	
		Total Transportation	$

17

F. Children's Expenses and Activities

	Cost Per Month		Cost Per Month
Clothing & Shoes	$	Child Care	$
Extraordinary Expenses, i.e. Special Needs, etc.		Misc. Expenses, i.e. Tutor, Books, Activities, Fees, Lunch, etc.	
Tuition		Other:	
		Total Children's Expenses and Activities	$

17

G. Education for you - Please identify status: ☐ Full-time student ☐ Part-time student

	Cost Per Month		Cost Per Month
Tuition, Books, Supplies, Fees, etc.	$	Other:	$
		Total Education	$

17

H. Maintenance & Child Support (that you pay)

	Cost Per Month		Cost Per Month
Spousal Maintenance	$	Child Support	$
☐ This family		☐ This family	
☐ Other family		☐ Other family	
		Total Maintenance and Child Support	$

17

I. Miscellaneous (Please list on-going expenses not covered in the sections above.)

	Cost Per Month		Cost Per Month
Recreation/Entertainment	$	Personal Care (Hair, Nail, Clothing, etc.)	$
Legal/Accounting Fees		Subscriptions (Newspapers, Magazines, etc.)	
Charity/Worship		Movie & Video Rentals	

No. 253. Rev. 4-10. SWORN FINANCIAL STATEMENT (Form C.R.C.P. 35.2) (Page 3 of 8)

I. Miscellaneous (Cont'd)

	Cost Per Month		Cost Per Month
Vacation/Travel/Hobbies	$	Investments (Not part of payroll deductions)	$
Membership/Clubs		Home Furnishings	
Pets/Pet Care		Sports Events/Participation	
Other:		Other:	
Other:		Other:	
Other:		Other:	
Other:		Other:	
		Total Miscellaneous	$ 17
		Total Monthly Expenses (Totals from A – I)	$ 18

19 **4. Debts (unsecured)**

List unsecured debts such as credit cards, store charge accounts, loans from family members, back taxes owed to the I.R.S., etc. **Do not** list debts that are liens against your property, such as mortgages and car loans, because that payment is already listed as an expense above, and the total of the debt is shown elsewhere as a deduction from value where that asset is listed, such as under Real Estate or Motor Vehicles.

For name on account, "P" = Petitioner, "C/R" = Co-Petitioner or Respondent, "J" = Joint.

Name of Creditor	Account Number (last 4 digits only)	P	C/R	J	Date of Balance	Balance	Minimum Monthly Payment Required	Reason for Which Debt Was Incurred
		☐	☐	☐		$	$	
		☐	☐	☐				
		☐	☐	☐				
		☐	☐	☐				
		☐	☐	☐				
		☐	☐	☐				
		☐	☐	☐				
		☐	☐	☐				
		☐	☐	☐				
		☐	☐	☐				
		☐	☐	☐				
		☐	☐	☐				
					Unsecured Debt Balance	$ 20	$ 21	→ **Total Minimum Monthly Payment**

SWORN FINANCIAL STATEMENT SUMMARY (INCOME/EXPENSES)

Total Income (from page 2)	22	$ ____________	A		
Total Monthly Deductions (from page 2)	23	$ ____________	B		
Total Monthly Net Income (A minus B)				$ ____________	24
Total Monthly Expenses (from page 4)	25	$ ____________	C		
Total Minimum Monthly Payments Required – Debts Unsecured (from page 4)	26	$ ____________	D		
Total Monthly Expenses and Payments (C plus D)				$ ____________	27
Net Excess or Shortfall (Monthly Net Income less Monthly Expenses and Payments)		(+/-)		$ ____________	28

29 **5. Assets**

You MUST disclose all assets correctly. By indicating "None," you are stating affirmatively that you or the other party do not have assets in that category. Please attach additional copies of pages 5 & 6 to identify your assets, if necessary.

If the parties are married, check under the heading Joint (J) all assets acquired during the marriage but not by gift or inheritance. Under the headings of Petitioner (P) or Co-Petitioner/Respondent (C/R), check assets owned before this marriage and assets acquired by gift or inheritance.

If the parties were NEVER married to each other or are using this form to modify child support, list all of each party's assets under the headings of Petitioner (P) or Co-Petitioner/Respondent (C/R).

("P" = Petitioner, "C/R" = Co-Petitioner or Respondent, "J" = Joint.)

	A. Real Estate (Address or Property Description and Name of Creditor/Lender) ☐ None	**P**	**C/R**	**J**	**Estimated Value as of Today** Value = what you could sell it for in its current condition.	**Amount Owed**	**Net Value/ Equity** (Value minus amount owed)
30		☐	☐	☐	31 $	32 $	33 $
		☐	☐	☐			
	34 **Total**				$	$	$

	B. Motor Vehicles & Recreation Vehicles, including Motorcycles, ATV's, Boats, etc.) (Year, Make, Model) (Name of Creditor/Lender) ☐ None	**P**	**C/R**	**J**	**Estimated Value as of Today** Value = what you could sell it for in its current condition.	**Amount Owed**	**Net Value/ Equity** (Value minus amount owed)
35		☐	☐	☐	$	$	$
		☐	☐	☐			
		☐	☐	☐			
		☐	☐	☐			
	36 **Total**				$	$	$

C. **Cash on Hand, Bank, Checking, Saving, or Health Accounts** (Name of Bank or Financial Institution) ☐ **None**	**P**	**C/R**	**J**	**Type of Account**	**Account #** (last 4 digits only)	**Balance as of Today**
37	☐	☐	☐	$	$	$
	☐	☐	☐			
	☐	☐	☐			
	☐	☐	☐			
	☐	☐	☐			
					38 **Total**	$

D. **Life Insurance** (Name of Company/Beneficiary) ☐ **None**	**P**	**C/R**	**J**	**Type of Policy**	**Face Amount of Policy**	**Cash Value Today**
39	☐	☐	☐	$	$	$
	☐	☐	☐			
	☐	☐	☐			
					40 **Total**	$

E. **Furniture, Household Goods, and Other Personal Property, i.e. Jewelry, Antiques, Collectibles, Artwork, Power Tools, etc.** (Identify Items and report in total.) ☐ **None**	**P**	**C/R**	**J**	**Current Possession Held By**			**Estimated Value as of Today** Value = what you could sell it for in its current condition.
				P	**C/R**	**J**	
41	☐	☐	☐	☐	☐	☐	$
	☐	☐	☐	☐	☐	☐	
	☐	☐	☐	☐	☐	☐	
	☐	☐	☐	☐	☐	☐	
	☐	☐	☐	☐	☐	☐	
	☐	☐	☐	☐	☐	☐	
	☐	☐	☐	☐	☐	☐	
						42 **Total**	$

43 F. **Stocks, Bonds, Mutual Funds, Securities & Investment Accounts** ☐ **None** ☐ **If owned please attach the Supporting Schedule.**	44 **Total**	$
45 G. **Pension, Profit Sharing, or Retirement Funds** ☐ **None** ☐ **If owned please attach the Supporting Schedule.**	46 **Total**	$

No. 253. Rev. 4-10. SWORN FINANCIAL STATEMENT (Form C.R.C.P. 35.2) (Page 6 of 8)

47 **H. Miscellaneous Assets**
☐ **None If you own any of the assets identified below, please check the appropriate box and attach the Supporting Schedule to report the value.**

☐ Business Interest	☐ Stock Options	☐ Money/Loans owed to you	☐ IRS Refunds due to you
☐ Country Club & Other Memberships	☐ Livestock, Crops, Farm Equipment	☐ Pending lawsuit or claim by you	☐ Accrued Paid Leave (sick, vacation, personal)
☐ Oil and Gas Rights	☐ Vacation Club Points	☐ Safety Deposit Box/Vault	☐ Trust Beneficiary
☐ Frequent Flyer Miles	☐ Education Accounts	☐ Health Savings Accounts	☐ Mineral and Water Rights
☐ Other:	☐ Other:	☐ Other:	☐ Other:
		48 **Total**	$

49 **I. Separate Property**
☐ **None** ☐ **If owned please attach the Supporting Schedule to identify the property and to report the value.** 50 **Total** $

Total Value/Balance of All Assets (A–I) $ 51

I swear or affirm under oath that this Sworn Financial Statement, attached schedules, and mandatory disclosures contain a complete disclosure of my income, expenses, assets, and debt as of the date of my signature.

I understand that if the information I have provided changes or needs to be updated before a final decree or order is issued by the Court, that I have a duty to provide the correct or updated information.

I understand that this oath is made under penalty of perjury. I understand that if I have omitted or misstated any material information, intentionally or not, the Court will have the power to enter orders to address those matters, including the power to punish me for any statements made with the intent to defraud or mislead the Court or the other party.

52 Date: ______________________________

____
Signature of ☐ Petitioner or ☐ Co-Petitioner/Respondent

Subscribed and affirmed, or sworn to before me in the County of ______________, State of ______________, this _______ day of ____________________, 20____.

My Commission Expires: ______________________

____
Notary Public/Deputy Clerk

CERTIFICATE OF SERVICE

To be completed if the Sworn Financial Statement is not being filed with JDF 1104 – Certificate of Compliance with Mandatory Financial Disclosures

I certify that on _________________________ (date), a true and accurate copy of the ***SWORN FINANCIAL STATEMENT*** was served on the other party by:

☐ Hand Delivery, ☐ E-filed, ☐ Faxed to this number: ___________________, **or**

☐ By placing it in the United States mail, postage pre-paid, and addressed to the following:

To: ______________________________________

____

______________________________________ ______________________________________

Your signature

_______________ and _______________ Case Number: _______________
Petitioner Co-Petitioner/Respondent

Supporting Schedules for Assets in Sections F, G, H, and I.

Attach this supporting schedule to the Financial Statement ONLY if you have assets in sections F & G, any additional assets to report in section H, and/or separate property to report in section I. In addition, report totals from this document to the appropriate sections on the Financial Statement.

43

F. **Stocks, Bonds, Mutual Funds, Securities & Investment Accounts** (Name of Item or Fund)	**P**	**C/R**	**J**	**Number of Shares**	**Account Number** (last 4 digits only, if applicable)	**Current Values as of Today**
	☐	☐	☐			$
	☐	☐	☐			
	☐	☐	☐			
	☐	☐	☐			
	☐	☐	☐			
	☐	☐	☐			
	☐	☐	☐			
	☐	☐	☐			
					Total	**$**

45

G. **Pension, Profit Sharing, or Retirement Funds** (Defined Contribution and/or Defined Benefit Plans)	**P**	**C/R**	**J**	**Type of Plan** (401K, IRA, 457, PERA, Military, etc.)	**Account Number** (last 4 digits only, if applicable)	**Current Values as of Today**
	☐	☐	☐			$
	☐	☐	☐			
	☐	☐	☐			
	☐	☐	☐			
					Total	**$**

47

H. **Miscellaneous Assets** (Identify Type of Asset)	**P**	**C/R**	**J**		**Estimated Value as of Today**
	☐	☐	☐		$
	☐	☐	☐		
	☐	☐	☐		
	☐	☐	☐		

Bradford Publishing, 1743 Wazee St., Denver, CO 80202 — 303-292-2590 — www.bradfordpublishing.com

H. Miscellaneous Assets (Cont'd) (Identify Type of Asset)	**P**	**C/R**	**J**		**Estimated Value as of Today**
	☐	☐	☐		$
	☐	☐	☐		
	☐	☐	☐		
	☐	☐	☐		
	☐	☐	☐		
	☐	☐	☐		
	☐	☐	☐		
	☐	☐	☐		
	☐	☐	☐		
				Total	**$**

49 **I. Separate Property** (Identify Type)	**P**	**C/R**	**J**		**Estimated Value as of Today**
	☐	☐	☐		$
	☐	☐	☐		
	☐	☐	☐		
	☐	☐	☐		
	☐	☐	☐		
	☐	☐	☐		
	☐	☐	☐		
	☐	☐	☐		
	☐	☐	☐		
				Total	**$**

No. 253-SS. 3-06. SUPPORTING SCHEDULES FOR ASSETS (Form C.R.C.P. 35.3) (Page 2 of 2)

Mandatory Disclosures

Parties to a divorce or legal separation in Colorado must provide certain information to each other—whether or not they have lawyers, and whether or not the other spouse asks you for it. You have an affirmative duty of full and honest disclosure of all the facts that materially affect each other's rights and your children's interests. You must give each other all of the items that are listed in the following Mandatory Disclosures form that apply to you, usually within 42 days of filing the petition, and at any rate, before the first status conference.

Once you have exchanged this information, you should each have a complete set of all the papers. You each must then prepare, sign and file with the court the Certificate of Compliance that follows the Mandatory Disclosures in this chapter, and give a copy of the completed/signed form to your spouse.

YOUR CHECKLIST FOR MANDATORY DISCLOSURE

(Complete and accurate copies may replace originals. Children refers to minor children of both parties.)

☐ (a) Sworn Financial Statement. Each party shall provide a complete and signed Sworn Financial Statement in the Supreme Court approved form. See Appendix to Chapters 1 to 17A, Form 35.2, C.R.C.P. [Bradford form no. 253 in this book]

☐ (b) Income Tax Returns (Most Recent 3 Years). Provide the personal and business federal income tax returns for the three years before filing of the petition or post decree motion. The business returns shall be for any business for which a party has an interest entitling the party to a copy of such returns. Provide all schedules and attachments including W-2s, 1099s and K-1. If a return is not completed at the time of disclosure, provide the documents necessary to prepare the return including W-2s, 1099s and K-1s, copies of extension requests and estimated tax payments.

☐ (c) Personal Financial Statements (Last 3 Years). Provide all personal financial statements, statements of assets or liabilities, and credit and loan applications prepared during the last three years.

☐ (d) Business Financial Statements (Last 3 Years). For every business for which a party has access to financial statements, provide the last three fiscal years' financial statements, all year-to-date financial statements, and the same periodic financial statements for the prior year.

☐ (e) Real Estate Documents. Provide the title documents and all documents stating value of all real property in which a party has a personal or business interest. This section shall not apply to post decree motions unless so ordered by the court.

☐ (f) Personal Debt. Provide all documents creating debt, and the most recent debt statements showing the balance and payment terms.

☐ (g) Investments. Provide most recent documents identifying each investment, and stating the current value.

☐ (h) Employment Benefits. Provide most recent documents identifying each employment benefit, and stating the current value.

☐ (i) Retirement Plans. Provide most recent documents identifying each retirement plan, and stating the current value, and all Plan Summary Descriptions.

☐ (j) Bank/Financial Institution Accounts. Provide most recent documents identifying each account at banks and other financial institutions, and stating the current value.

☐ (k) Income Documentation. For each income source in the current and prior calendar year, including income from employment, investment, government programs, gifts, trust distributions, prizes, and income from every other source, provide pay stubs, a current income statement and the final income statement for the prior year. Each self-employed party shall provide a sworn statement of gross income, business expenses necessary to produce income and net income for the three months before filing of the petition or post decree motion.

☐ (l) Employment and Education-Related Child Care Documentation. Provide documents that show average monthly employment-related child care expense including child care expense related to parents' education and job search.

☐ (m) Insurance Documentation. Provide life, health and property insurance policies and current documents that show beneficiaries, coverage, cost including the portion payable to provide health insurance for children, and payment schedule.

☐ (n) Extraordinary Children's Expense Documentation. Provide documents that show average monthly expense for all recurring extraordinary children's expenses.

INSTRUCTIONS TO FILL OUT THE CERTIFICATE OF COMPLIANCE

1. Complete the box at the top the same as on your petition.
2. Check whether you are the petitioner, co-petitioner, or respondent.
3. Check each box in the list to indicate DOCUMENTS THAT YOU HAVE PROVIDED to your spouse. You can asterisk the ones that your spouse provided to you, and explain that in the space provided. You can double asterisk the ones that don't even apply to you, and explain that as well.
4. Sign on the appropriate signature line and date your signature.
5. Fill out the Certificate of Service to explain how you gave a copy to your spouse, and the date you filed the original with the court.

☐ District Court ☐ Denver Juvenile Court ____________________ County, Colorado Court Address:	
1 ☐ **In Re the Marriage of:** ☐ **In Re the Parental Responsibilities concerning:** ____________________, **Petitioner:** and **Co-Petitioner/Respondent:**	▲ COURT USE ONLY ▲
Attorney or Party Without Attorney (Name and Address): Phone Number: E-mail: FAX Number: Atty. Reg. #:	Case Number: Division: Courtroom:

CERTIFICATE OF COMPLIANCE WITH MANDATORY FINANCIAL DISCLOSURES
*******EACH PARTY MUST COMPLETE AND FILE THIS FORM WITH THE COURT*******

2 I, the ☐ Petitioner ☐ Co-Petitioner/Respondent (check one) hereby certify that I have sent the other party the following Mandatory Disclosures as required by Rule 16.2(e)(7) of the Colorado Rules of Civil Procedure.

See JDF 1125: Mandatory Disclosure – Form 35.1 for explanation on what is required by the disclosures being listed. Check those that you have furnished to the other party. (***Note: Only the Sworn Financial Statement and Child Support Worksheet should be filed with the Court.***)

3 ☐ Sworn Financial Statement
☐ Income Tax Returns (most recent 3 years)
☐ Personal Financial Statements (last 3 years)
☐ Business Financial Statements (last 3 years)
☐ Real Estate Documents (Appraisal, Title, etc.)
☐ Personal Debt (Loans, Title, Credit Card Statements, etc.)
☐ Investments
☐ Employment Benefits
☐ Retirement Plans
☐ Bank/Financial Institution Accounts
☐ Income Documentation (Pay Stubs, etc.)
☐ Employment and Education – Related Child Care Documentation
☐ Insurance Documentation
☐ Extraordinary Children's Expense Documentation

If I have not provided information, it is because: ____________________
____

I hereby certify that, to the best of my knowledge, information and belief, the disclosures I have made are complete and correct as of this date.

4
____
Petitioner/Co-Petitioner/Respondent Signature Date

____
Attorney Signature, if any Date

You must complete the Certificate of Service below:

5 **CERTIFICATE OF SERVICE**

I certify that on ____________________ (date) a true and accurate copy of the ***CERTIFICATE OF COMPLIANCE WITH MANDATORY FINANCIAL DISCLOSURES*** was served on the other party by:
☐ Hand Delivery, ☐ E-filed, or ☐ Faxed to this number ____________________, **or**
☐ by placing it in the United States mail, postage pre-paid, and addressed to the following:
To: ____________________
____
____

____
(Your signature)

About Status Conferences

If you have filed your petition and received your Case Management Order, you will know when to expect your Initial Status Conference. Status conferences will be conducted by a judge, magistrate, or family court facilitator. Things that you may do or that may occur at a status conference are:

- You will hand in your original, signed and notarized Sworn Financial Statements and Certificates of Compliance, if you haven't already done so.
- You may ask to make your temporary agreements into a court order, if you wish (see Chapter 4).
- You will tell the facilitator what agreements have reached and what still needs to be decided, what needs to be done in order for you to reach agreement, and your timeline for completion.
- You will tell the facilitator if you are in mediation, or if you would like to be. Some courts will order mediation to help you resolve issues. (See Chapter 2 about how to select a mediator who specializes in divorce and legal separation.)
- You may be given deadlines for things to do before your next status conference.
- You may be given a date for your next status conference or court hearing.
- You may want to ask that your file be sealed (made unavailable to the public), or for your financial statements to be sealed.

Once all your papers are finalized and filed with the court, and the 91-day waiting period has run, the court *may* sign your decree at a later status conference. Check with the court to see if this is possible. If not, a Permanent Orders hearing will be set as described in Chapter 12.

Where Do We Go From Here

With all this information gathered and shared, you are now ready to begin your negotiations. You need to reach agreement about the division of your assets and debts (Chapter 7), a parenting plan for your children (Chapter 8), and whether you will have maintenance, also called alimony (Chapter 10). Begin thinking about the financial consequences of becoming separate taxpayers (Chapter 11). With your parenting plan in place, along with the financial information you have pulled together, you will be ready to negotiate your child support (Chapter 9).

One More Thing

"Force, no matter how concealed, begets resistance." Lakota proverb

Sorting out the details of your financial past and future can take its toll on your emotions. This might be a good time to go back and reread Chapter 3 and do something nice for yourself.

"The great strength is gentleness." Iroquois proverb

Notes:

CHAPTER 7

ASSETS AND DEBTS SEPARATION AGREEMENT – PART I

Separation Agreement: The written (typed) document, filed with the court that sets out how the parties are dividing assets and debts, planning to parent their children, paying support and maintenance, and any other agreement between them which they want the court to approve.

Separation Agreements–By other names...

"Separation agreement" is a generic term that refers to the writing that details your agreement about property and debt division, maintenance, child support, as well as parental decision-making and parenting time. In recent years some professionals put their agreement about parental responsibilities in a separate document called a "Parenting Plan," while others include the Parenting Plan as part of their Separation Agreement. When you develop your agreement in mediation, the mediator prepares a "memorandum," usually called a "Memorandum of Understanding," or "Memorandum of Agreement". This book assumes that your parenting plan is part of, or included in, your separation agreement.

ASSETS AND DEBTS SEPARATION AGREEMENT: PART I

Introduction to the Separation Agreement

Before the court can give you a final decree of dissolution of marriage or legal separation, you must resolve and put in writing all the financial and parental issues remaining from your marriage. This written summary is called the separation agreement whether you are obtaining a divorce or a legal separation. It must be read and approved by the court.

Your separation agreement must include the following:

1. Assets you have accumulated must be accounted for and divided (this chapter).
2. All debts, including taxes, must be acknowledged and paid or the responsibility for paying them allocated between you (this chapter, and Chapter 11, Taxes).
3. You must establish a parenting plan for your children—decision-making and parenting time—and make commitments about their support (Chapter 8, Children, Chapter 9, Child Support, and Chapter 11, Taxes).
4. If either spouse is to assist in supporting the other—spousal support, maintenance—the amounts and duration must be set (Chapter 10, Maintenance, and Chapter 11, Taxes).
5. You must arrange to pay for any costs of the divorce itself: the court filing fee, mediators, lawyers, accountants, recording fees, and the like, if any (this chapter).
6. You must agree when and under what circumstances any of your agreements change or terminate (Chapters 7-10 and Chapter 13).

The five separation agreement chapters (7-11), plus Chapter 13, designed to help you write your separation agreement, are full of technical terms and legal requirements. The information you will need for your separation agreement is listed in Chapter 6. Gathering this information now will make all your bargaining more effective and more complete. Using this checklist will ensure that you don't omit anything vital to a comprehensive agreement. Much of the information you gathered in Chapter 6 will be especially helpful for this chapter.

Chapter 12 contains sample wording for a wide variety of options in writing a separation agreement, drawn from the topics discussed throughout this Guidebook. As you complete your agreement about each topic, you might wish to read the relevant sample wording in Chapter 12 for ideas about writing your own agreement.

Assets—Marital and Separate

Nearly anything of value is considered an asset. Assets may include: real estate, furniture, household goods, art, musical and sporting equipment, any personal items, cars, trucks and other motor vehicles, cash, bank accounts, stocks and bonds, investments, retirement and pension plans, profit sharing, business interests including accounts receivable, furniture and fixtures, and good will. You must divide all your marital assets in your separation agreement. Similarly, you must divide all your marital debt.

Your first task is to distinguish separate from marital assets. By definition, separate assets belong to one of you only. Marital assets belong to both of you together. The only assets that must be allocated or divided between you in your divorce are what you determine to be marital. You may define separate and marital assets any way you wish. If you do write your own definitions, they must be included in your separation agreement. If you choose **not** to distinguish between separate and marital assets, you must say so in your separation agreement.

Similarly, you must distinguish between marital and separate debts. For example, you might agree that any debts incurred by either of you after your physical separation are the separate debt of that person; or, agree that these are still marital. Most couples agree that a debt related to a separate asset is a separate debt.

Bear in mind, an asset or debt may be part marital and part separate. For example, a spouse may have a retirement plan, part of which was accumulated before the marriage. A credit card may have been used for both marital and separate purposes.

If you do not use your own definitions of marital and separate assets and debt, or state that you do not want to distinguish between them, the court will presume you used the following definitions:

Marital Assets Division is Not a Taxable Event

Division of assets in a divorce does not result in taxable income for anybody, even if one spouse pays off the other in cash, as long as the transfers are directly between the two spouses, either before the divorce is final, or after, according to the terms of a written separation agreement. The transaction is seen by the IRS as the division of something you already own, not as a taxable "sale."

"We have to divide our assets equally. That's the law."

Nowhere is it written in Colorado that your marital assets must be divided equally. The word used in the statute is "equitable" which means fair.

Pre- and Post-Marital Agreements

If you and your spouse have a signed agreement written before or after your marriage which defines "marital" and "separate" assets and/or debts, it will control your definitions of these terms, unless you agree otherwise now. This is especially true if you were both represented by counsel.

Gifts to Each Other

While a gift to one of you from a third party is treated as separate property, recent legislation now makes gifts to each other marital property. This ticklish area may well be one in which you would rather make your own definitions.

Separate Assets:

Anything brought into the marriage.

Anything acquired during the marriage by gift or inheritance, except gifts to each other.

Anything purchased with the sale or trade of separate assets.

Marital assets:

Anything acquired during the marriage, regardless of whose name is on it or who paid for it.

Increase in the value of separate assets during the period of the marriage.

Gifts to each other

Marital debt:

Any debt incurred during the marriage, regardless of whose name is on it (remember your marriage continues until the court approves your separation agreement and signs your Decree).

Notes:

BRAIN TEASER
MARITAL OR SEPARATE? YOU BE THE JUDGE

How would you define the following assets (remember, there is no right or wrong answer here).

A. Wife's aunt brings over a rocking chair with a card that says: "Dear kids, this is wife's grandmother's chair. Thought you should have it." Is the chair

_____ Separate _____ Marital _____ Other ______________________________

B. A 5-year marriage. Husband quits job he had for ten years, and therefore keeps only his contribution to his retirement. He takes it out in cash. Is it

_____ Separate _____ Marital _____ Other ______________________________

C. Wife's previous divorce "awarded" her the house in which she and present husband have been living. Three years ago they re-financed, putting the home in both names. Is the home

_____ Separate _____ Marital _____ Other ______________________________

D. Husband uses a credit card in his name to pay for furnishings for his new home on the day of physical separation. Is the debt

_____ Separate _____ Marital _____ Other ______________________________

A strict reading of current statutes and case law would probably suggest the following answers:

A. Marital gift to both husband and wife. Not an inheritance, unless you agree otherwise.

B. Part marital, part separate. The portion earned during the marriage is marital, the rest is separate. An accurate way to determine the portions would be to find out the amount (value) of husband's contribution as of the date of the marriage. That much is his, the rest is marital.

C. Marital? A strong, much-quoted case Moncrief, Colorado Court of Appeals, May 1975, says putting assets into joint tenancy makes it a "gift to the marriage." But the Rhoades case, Colorado Supreme Court (the higher of the two courts), same month and year, says that separate money put into the home at the time of marriage is separate and comes back to the spouse who contributed it.

D. Marital, unless you agree otherwise.

OUR AGREED-UPON DEFINITIONS OF MARITAL AND SEPARATE

Directions: Write your own agreed-upon definitions of marital and separate assets and debts:

Marital assets are:

Separate assets are:

Marital debts are:

Separate debts are:

MARITAL OR SEPARATE ASSETS AND DEBTS ORGANIZER

Directions: You may photocopy the chart below, or copy it onto a larger piece of paper if you need more room. List each of your assets and debts, by **name** (not value), in one or more of the columns below. For example, the Marital column may include "Husband's retirement during marriage," and the Husband's separate column may include "Husband's retirement before marriage." The Marital column may include "Wife's student loan during marriage," while Wife's Separate column may include "Wife's student loan before marriage."

ASSETS and any SECURED DEBT	WIFE'S SEPARATE	HUSBAND'S SEPARATE	MARITAL
Real Estate			
Motor Vehicles			
Cash, Bank Accounts, CDs			
Life Insurance			
Furniture and Household Goods			
Stocks, Bonds, and Other Securities			
Pensions, Profit Sharing, or Retirement Funds – Defined Contribution Plans			
Other Pension or Retirement Funds – Defined Benefit Plans			
Business Interests			
Other Assets			
UNSECURED DEBTS			
Loans			
Credit cards			
Tax Debt			
Divorce Expenses			

Valuing Your Assets

You may list your division of assets and debts on the 2-page Division of Marital Assets and Debts Chart near the end of this chapter. The value of an asset, or the amount of a debt, will probably be an important part of this division. The next section of this chapter describes each kind of asset that may be part of your marital estate. Each discussion contains suggestions about how to find values for that particular kind of asset. Following are some thoughts about value to keep in mind as you read this chapter.

"If we can't agree on values, we can't agree on anything. We'll never be able to settle."

This is not true. You may elect to divide anything and everything without regard to monetary value. There are many kinds of value; dollars is only one of them. You are only required to divide your assets "equitably" – in a fair manner.

What if the two of you are unable to agree on a value? This is not a reason to give up, or to stop negotiating. Put down both values and agree that the value of that asset falls somewhere in between. It is possible to put together an asset settlement in which several assets are assigned range-values only. Some assets are extremely difficult to value, such as a small business. Bringing in a professional to tell you a value could cost hundreds, if not thousands of dollars. You may list the value of such an asset for now as simply "unknown," and decide later, if your negotiations necessitate, to hone in on a precise number or range.

You have the right to decide to allocate any or all of your assets between you without regard to monetary value at all. Value is not always monetary. The value an item has for you may be the memories it contains, its usefulness, or its beauty. Value to you may mean your need for an asset. For example, you might decide that certain items of furniture, such as the washer and dryer, may need to remain in the home with the children. You do not have to inventory and place values on such items.

Kinds of Assets

REAL ESTATE

Real estate includes your family home, condo, vacation home, time-share, commercial real estate, raw land, and real estate partnerships, as well as a contract for the purchase of real estate. Most people value real estate at current fair market value (the amount a willing buyer would pay a willing seller). There are three resources which may help you in determining fair market value: real estate appraisal, market analysis, and county tax assessment value. To help you decide whether you need either of the first two of these, see Asset Evaluators in Chapter 2. The tax assessment value, which is an appraisal done by the county for determining the property tax, may be a reasonable approximation

Real Estate Gross Equity Calculation

(Complete for each asset)

Fair Market Value (FMV)	______________
Less: 1st Mortgage Balance	______________
Less: 2nd (& 3rd) Mortgage(s)	______________
Gross Equity	______________

of fair market value if it is not more than a year old. You can obtain it at no cost.

Getting the fair market value of your real estate is only the beginning. This is not the value to you in the divorce. You must take into account what is owed against the property: mortgages, liens, etc. The fair market value minus the amount owing is the gross equity. This is the most this asset could be worth to the two of you.

You may wish to adjust the gross equity value of your real estate for selling costs and capital gains taxes.

Selling Costs

Selling costs typically include real estate sales commission, title insurance, and fix-up and repairs to make the property saleable. If the property is to be sold immediately, or in the near future (especially if the selling costs would wipe out the equity and the person keeping the property is not certain whether he or she can hold on to it for very long), it makes sense to take out the costs of sale in arriving at what the value really is for you. Some selling costs to consider are:

- *Real Estate Sales Commission.* To estimate this, multiply the probable sales price times 7%—or other rate (the commission on farm, ranch, mountain, or commercial properties may be as high as 10%). There are services which will assist you in selling your home yourself so that the real estate commission may be as little as 2-3%.
- *Points, if any, when the seller pays them.* These represent seller's agreement to discount the sales price by a percentage —one point is one percent. Points are likely in some markets, especially if you need a quick sale.
- *Title insurance and deed recording fees.* $1000–$1500 is a good ball-park for these last two items, but you should check with professionals in your area.
- *Cost of fix-up for sale.*

If the spouse receiving the property is likely to keep it for a number of years, for example until the children are grown, then you may not wish to subtract future selling costs now.

Whether or not you subtract the costs of sale to determine the equity is up to you. Making a clear agreement about selling costs is one of the ways in which you can fine tune your settlement.

"I don't have to worry about capital gain because I'm not going to make any money on the sale."

This belief could be fatal to your financial health, particularly with regard to investment real estate. The warning signs of this disease are: equity loan, rolled over capital gain from previous exchange, second mortgage, depreciation over many years. Your capital gain may be many times larger than your "profits."

The tax on capital gains is a "hidden" cost of real estate sales.

Capital Gains Taxes on Real Estate

The capital gains tax is a real cost that stays with a piece of real estate and that will have to be paid when the property is sold, unless you fit into one of the exclusions. Whoever keeps the property will ultimately be responsible for this tax. If you sell the property now, the persons whose names are on the deed are responsible for this tax.

Capital gain is the difference between the adjusted selling price and your investment in the property. You will pay income tax on the gain as though it were additional income earned by you in the year of sale. The amount of your investment for tax purposes is called the *basis.*

If you bought your property, your original basis is the purchase price. If you acquired the property by means other than a purchase (built it yourself, hired someone to build it for you, or received it as a gift or inheritance), see IRS Publications 523 and 551 for how to determine your original basis. The bibliography at the end of this Guidebook will tell you how to obtain these publications.

While you owned the property you may have increased or decreased your basis. You may have *increased* the basis by additions or capital improvements; you may have *decreased* the basis by rolling over a prior capital gain, or depreciation. The lower your basis, the greater your gain, and the greater your tax on the gain. See IRS Publication 551 for a detailed discussion of these, and other adjustments to basis.

To determine your likely capital gain, subtract your adjusted basis from the fair market value. Then you may adjust for probable selling costs. Next step, figure your tax on it.

1) If the real estate is your personal residence:

Married homeowners who own their home jointly may exclude up to $500,000 of gain from the sale of a principal residence; $250,000 for single taxpayers. This effectively eliminates capital gains tax on the sale of a personal residence for most individuals. There is no age requirement and the exclusion is reusable every two years. You can claim the exclusion if, during the five year period ending on the date of the sale, you have: 1) owned the home for at least two years (the ownership test), and 2) lived in the home as your main residence for at least two years (the use test). This tax break allows most homeowners to sell a more expensive home and purchase a less expensive one, or even to sell and not repurchase, without incurring a capital gains tax, and relieves most homeowners of the burden of keeping paperwork on capital improvements.

If there is any question in your mind that this new rule might not apply to you; your gain might exceed these limits (including any rolled over gain); you are concerned about property other than your personal residence; or you don't know enough about capital gains to know whether you qualify or not, then read the rest of this section. Making a mistake about capital gains tax can be very costly. Consult your tax lawyer or accountant for clarification about your situation.

2) If the real estate is not your personal residence, or if you have gain on your residence beyond what can be excluded:

A good rule of thumb is that your tax is approximately 1/5 (19.63%) of your capital gain (15% for federal tax, plus 4.63% for the State of Colorado). If your total taxable income for the year of sale has not filled the 10% and 15% tax brackets, the tax on your capital gain will be less. See Chapter 11 Taxes.

It is crucial that you take into account the tax consequences of the eventual sale of real estate before you make decisions about it in your property settlement.

The following worksheet is for investment or rental property. Do one worksheet for each piece of real estate you own that is not your personal residence—whether or not you plan to sell. Take the worksheet line by line, reading the instructions as you go. If you get frustrated, stop and come back later, or consult an accountant.

Even if you're not selling the property right now, you can use these forms to estimate how much you would clear after a sale, taking into account capital gains tax. Naturally, you'll be estimating certain items and some items may not apply if you're not going to actually sell the property now.

NOTE: Use only the total column now and fill in the Husband's and Wife's shares after you determine how you will divide your assets and debts using the chart at the end of this chapter.

To Estimate the Capital Gain on Your Personal Residence

Selling price	________
Less:	
Brokerage fees	(________)
Closing costs	(________)
Original purchase price	(________)
Original closing costs	(________)
Cost of improvements	(________)
Depreciation deducted on previous returns	(________)
Capital Gain	________

A zero or negative number means no capital gain. If you have a positive number, determine whether you qualify for the exclusion ($250,000 or $500,000), and if so, reduce your gain accordingly. If you do not qualify for the exclusion, or still have a positive number then calculate your tax, if any, at 15% if you are in the 25% tax bracket or above, and 0% if you are in the 10% and 15% tax brackets until those brackets are filled, and the rest at 15%. Absent further legislation, the 15% tax rate will rise to 20% in 2013, and the 0% rate to 10%.

Capital Gains Tax Worksheet for Rental or Other Investment Real Estate

The Property	Total	Wife's Share	Husband's Share
1. Selling Price of this Property			
2. Brokerage commission (usually 6%):			
3. Closing Costs on sale (usually ±1%):			
4. Amount Realized for Capital Gains Tax purposes (Line 1 minus Lines 2 and 3):			
5. Mortgage Balance and any other liens: *(Not part of capital gain calculation)*			
6. Net cash before taxes (Line 4 minus Line 5):			
CAPITAL GAINS TAX			
7. Original Price of this Property:			
8. Improvements and Original Closing Costs on purchase or refinance:			
9. Depreciation deducted on previous returns:			
10. Adjusted Basis of Property Sold (Line 7 plus Line 8 minus Line 9):			
11. Capital Gain (Line 4 minus Line 10):			
12. Capital Gains Tax (multiply Line 11 by your est. tax rate):			
13. Net cash after taxes (Line 6 minus Line 12):			

Instructions for Equity and Capital Gains Tax Worksheet for Rental or Other Real Estate

Line 1: Estimate a realistic sales price, or use the actual price if you have already sold this property.

Line 2: This item is optional if there's no actual sale contemplated. But some people still include it if they think a later sale is inevitable.

Line 3: Closing costs for a sale usually include title insurance and recording fees. They may include advertising, a survey, and mortgage points paid by you. This item is also optional if there's no actual sale contemplated. But some people still include it if they think a later sale is inevitable.

Line 5: Mortgage amounts are not included in capital gains tax calculations.

Line 7: Put in the total price you paid for this property.

Line 8: Improvements are things that add to the permanent value of the property, such as additions, paving a driveway, a new roof, or an intercom system. Usually, maintenance and repairs of existing features do not count as improvements. Also include here the closing costs you paid when you bought this property.

Line 9: If you took any depreciation on this property, put it back here.

Line 11: If this is zero, or a negative number, there's no capital gain and no tax, and no problem. Line 6 is your actual net.

Line 12: If you are in the 25% marginal tax bracket or above, use 19.63% (15% for federal, 4.63% Colorado). If your income is a lower tax bracket, only that portion of your capital gains that reaches into the 25% tax bracket and above is taxed at that rate.

After you have calculated your costs and any capital gains tax, decide for each piece of real estate the value which you will use in negotiating your total marital assets division. This information will be helpful in deciding how to divide your real estate using the chart at the end of this chapter.

WHAT TO DO?

If one of you retains real property in your divorce settlement, consider decreasing your equity—the value you are working with in your settlement—by the estimated tax on the capital gain to date, or some portion of it, for the person who takes this property.

Different Ways to "Divide" Real Estate

Before you take out the chain saw or sign the listing agreement, think about all the possible ways you might "divide" real estate. There are many workable options:

1. Sell it together now, and determine how you will handle the capital gain (see previous section).

   Divide the proceeds. Dividing responsibility for the capital gain does not mean you have to divide the proceeds in the same proportion. Responsibility for tax on your share of any gain is an IRS requirement. This has nothing to do with how you choose to divide the proceeds between you. You may:

   - Give more than half to the spouse who needs more down payment in order to qualify for a mortgage; and/or
   - Off-set some or all of the proceeds with some other kind of asset to the other spouse, business interests for example, or savings, stocks, or present value of retirement; and/or
   - Use the proceeds to pay off marital debts.

2. One of you keeps the home or other real estate.

   - The other gets some other asset of like value; or
   - The other gets cash or other liquid assets; or
   - The other gets a promissory note (with or without interest) promising to pay at some later date (a balloon payment), due on sale, or even amortized over a period of time (months or years). This promise to pay may be secured by a deed of trust (to the public trustee) which would be recorded with the clerk and recorder in the county in which the assets is located, and then become a mortgage or lien against the home. Although the principal

The IRS Never Gives Anything Away
If you have maintained a rental home or business property during your marriage, you have probably been depreciating it. (Even if you haven't, the IRS may.) The total amount of the depreciation for all the years you have rented the property becomes a capital gain which is taxable at the time of sale.

Difference Between Joint Tenancy and Tenancy In Common
Joint tenancy means that you each own an undivided 50% interest in the property, and the whole property comes to the survivor upon the death of the other joint tenant. Tenancy in common is a divisible interest, presumed to be 50-50, unless otherwise specified (60-40, 72-38) and each owner's share passes at death with his or her estate (does not go automatically to the other owner). Most couples own their family home in joint tenancy.

CAUTION If you have already done your sworn financial statements (Chapter 6), you may use them instead of the various assets checklists we have provided in this chapter. If you have not done your sworn financial statements yet, using these checklists can be a handy way to begin your negotiations as well as preparation for your sworn financial statements.

Motor Vehicle Checklist

Provide the following information for each of your motor vehicles:

Make and Model:

Blue Book Value:

Trade-in:

Retail:

Private party:

Loan balance:

How titled:

Make and Model:

Blue Book Value:

Trade-in:

Retail:

Private party:

Loan balance:

How titled:

amount of these payments is not taxable, the interest on them is taxable to the recipient in the year it is received.

3. You can retain the home or other real estate together.

- If the property is your personal residence, one of you can live in the home, and you can agree to keep it for a time, even for many years, and then sell it and share the profits at a later time.

- You can rent it to a third party and wait for a better market, both can depreciate your share of the home, and pay tax on the capital gain when the property is sold. If the property is not your personal residence, you have the option of continuing joint ownership of it after your divorce is final.

In either case, be sure you make clear agreements about who will pay the following: the mortgage, property taxes, insurance, homeowners association dues, day-to-day upkeep and repairs, major repairs, capital improvements, selling costs. Be sure you agree about how to share the profits when you sell, taking into account who has been paying what.

If you have now decided how you want to divide all or some of your real estate, write the appropriate information on the Division of Marital Assets and Debts Chart at the end of this chapter. You may do this even if you are not certain this is your final agreement. Noting your interim thinking in pencil is a good idea. You will probably look at several different assets divisions before you reach final agreement.

CARS AND OTHER MOTOR VEHICLES

Motor vehicles include: car, pick-up, RV, boat, cycle, trailer, and aircraft. You may divide these by value, need, or any other measure you agree to.

If your vehicle is leased, you do not own it, and therefore you cannot divide it. You should state in your agreement who will be responsible for the remainder of the lease payments and who owns the buy-out option.

To divide by economic value, you may start with the automobile values obtained from the NADA (National Automobile Dealers Association) *Blue Book* (www.nada,com), available at any Public Library, car dealer, bank, or lending institution or from the Kelley Blue Book (www.kelleybluebook.com). This will give you three different values that parallel the retail, trade-in, and private party sales values. "Retail" is the price a dealer would get. Likewise, "trade-in" is probably too low, as it is the price a dealer would pay. Private party is usually the highest of the three values. The value of your automobile is probably somewhere in the ballpark of these three numbers. You can further refine these values by looking for used cars like yours in the weekend classified ads of your local newspapers or on www.craigslist.com.

For other motor vehicles, you can call and survey dealers and brokers, especially of used items like yours, and find out what they are asking. You can find these dealers and brokers through Google, other search engines, or the yellow pages, under the type of item you are valuing, such as "Aircraft," or "Boats." You may also compare your vehicle with those offered for sale in www.craigslist.com or classified ads in local newspapers. To get a professional appraisal, you can start your search by Googling or looking in the yellow pages under "Appraisers." See also Asset Evaluators in Chapter 2.

If you have now agreed on how you are going to divide your motor vehicles, you may enter the appropriate information on the Division of Marital Assets and Debts Chart at the end of this chapter. If you have agreed not to value your motor vehicles monetarily, there is no need to enter the information. If you have not yet reached agreement, just read on.

LIQUID ASSETS: CASH, BANK ACCOUNTS, AND CDS

Cash, the most liquid of assets, is easiest to value. Bank accounts and certificates of deposit, are also "liquid" assets. You may include money market accounts here too. Savings accounts, certificates of deposit, and some checking accounts earn interest, and money market accounts increase in value. See your most recent statements for their current values. Remember to take into account amounts that are in a form which has not yet matured, bonds and certificates of deposit for example. You may want to adjust your valuation of these assets in your settlement if the person keeping them will have to cash them out soon—therefore realizing less than face or full value.

If you have now agreed on how you are going to divide your liquid assets, you may enter the appropriate information on the Division of Marital Assets and Debts Chart at the end of this chapter. If you have not yet reached agreement, just read on.

LIFE INSURANCE

There are two basic kinds of life insurance policies, "whole life," and "term", and there are many hybrids. Whole life policies have

Liquid Assets Checklist

Bank name:
Type of account:
Name(s) on the account:
Balance:
Date of balance:

Bank name:
Type of account:
Name(s) on the account:
Balance:
Date of balance:

Bank name:
Type of account:
Name(s) on the account:
Balance:
Date of balance:

Bank name:
Type of account:
Name(s) on the account:
Balance:
Date of balance:

Life Insurance Checklist

Complete the following for each life insurance policy on either of your lives, or owned by either of you on anybody's life.

Company:

Person insured:

Death benefit:

Accidental death benefit?

Beneficiary(ies):

Type of policy:

Cash value:

Surrender value:

Personal Assets Checklist

Directions: Check or complete those statements below which are true. Use a separate piece of paper for any itemized lists.

- ☐ We will divide our personal assets by value.
- ☐ We will divide our personal assets by need.
- ☐ We have set aside the separate personal assets for each of us.
- ☐ We have agreed to walk through the house together on ______________ (date).
- ☐ We will create THE LIST of items we both want by ______________(date).
- ☐ We will divide the items on THE LIST by means of ____________________ ____________________________, on ____________________________(date).

These personal assets have debts against them:

Item	Amount of Debt

cash value, which is an asset. The value is often stated in the policy, or can be learned by asking your insurance agent. Usually two values will be given: the cash value which is the actual value of the policy in place, and the lesser surrender value, which is the amount of money you would receive if you cashed in the policy.

Term policies, including most group policies offered by employers, have no cash value and are not valued in the division of assets. These policies are useful to "secure" or "underwrite" your agreements about child support, and/or maintenance (see Chapters 9 and 10).

Many so-called insurance policies are really annuities, similar to a retirement plan. You may want to include these policies, or portions of these policies, in your discussion of retirement.

If you have now agreed on how you are going to divide your insurance policies, you may enter the appropriate information on the Division of Marital Assets and Debts Chart at the end of this chapter. If you have decided to divide some or all of your insurance policies according to some value other than monetary, you do not need to make an entry on the chart. If you have not yet reached agreement, just read on.

PERSONAL ASSETS (Furniture and Household Goods)

Your personal assets include furniture, appliances, computers, stereo system and TV, linens, all your kitchen items, musical instruments, art, collectibles, sporting equipment, pets and animals, and all the stuff in the basement and the garage. This section is about how to allocate these things.

Personal assets usually do not include your personal clothing and jewelry. Yours is yours, and your spouse's is your spouse's. An exception might be if you choose to treat certain gifts to each other as marital property. Another exception might be if you have treated gems, jewelry, or furs as an investment or as a collection, and therefore as marital assets. Personal assets do not include business personal assets, such as the computer or the copier or the desk that is part of one's business. Business personal assets are included as part of Business Interests below.

The division of personal assets is often a discussion one spouse wants to avoid completely. "He/she can have it all! I just want out!" This is usually a great mistake. Both of you probably need some continuity with your things, even though the thought of having any of them may be painful at first.

Sometimes things become "larger than life." An item can become a metaphor for your time together, or for your marriage or divorce. If you feel yourselves stuck on items of personal assets, it is probably because this has happened. Take a little time to figure out what this hard fought-for item really represents for one or both of you.

Some people list all their personal assets, place values on them, and then divide the value in some agreed upon proportion. Most people who do this use fair market value, which for most of us is the likely price at a garage sale. For more expensive items, such as musical instruments, art, antiques, collections of any kind, you may want to pay for an appraisal. The importance you put on the value of items is up to you.

Another approach is to divide things by need. Walk through the house together and see if you can agree on who gets what with a view to setting up two households that are as complete as possible. Inevitably some new purchases will be necessary. See the "DIN" list in Chapter 4. Many people try to find an equitable way to bear that burden/benefit too. It's a burden because you have to spend money, and can be a benefit or a burden because one of you gets the "new" item while the other gets the used one with all the memories. Remember, the replacement cost of an item is probably much higher than the fair market value of the existing one.

There may be items you don't agree on. You can always sell what neither of you wants, but what to do about items you both want? First of all, just list them—don't argue about them. When you have allocated everything else to your satisfaction, you can begin to deal with "The List." See if you can strike a bargain about any of those items. "You can have #4 if I can have #3." "I'll give you $40.00 if I can have #6." Agreements like these can shorten The List. Finally, you can flip a coin to decide who goes first to pick one item off The List. The other then takes the next two items from The List (in exchange for not being first). You then take turns until nothing remains on The List.

If you have now agreed to your division of personal assets, you may enter the appropriate information on the Division of Marital Assets and Debts Chart at the end of this chapter. If you have agreed not to value your personal assets monetarily, there is no need to enter the information. If you have not yet reached agreement, just read on.

We need to research the values for the following items of personal assets:

Who will do it? When will it be done?

☐ We have completed our DIN List (see Chapter 4), or will complete it by ____________________(date).

George's Tools

Mary thinks George spends all his time in the garage tinkering with small motors which appear to propagate overnight. She proves, through a review of the check register, that they have spent over $5,000 on his tools and equipment. She wants to value his things in the garage at the original cost. He says they "might be worth $500 on a good day," if he could find someone who wanted them.

Louise's Dining Room

Louise and Charles bought a Chinese Chippendale dining room set for $8,000, fifteen years ago, because it was "just like" the one Louise grew up with—and her parents gave to her sister when they retired. Charles has no objection to Louise keeping it, but wants to be allocated $8,000 to buy his dining room set. Louise says that it might bring $800 at a garage sale.

Stocks Checklist

Repeat as necessary, for each stock held.

Company:
# of shares:
Value per share:
Date of value:
How titled:
Who holds certificate:

Bonds Checklist

Repeat as necessary, for each bond held.

Name on bond:
Face value:
Date of maturity:
Estimated current value:
How titled:
Who holds the bond:

Options Checklist

Repeat as necessary for each grant.

1. Company:
2. Person granted to:
3. Date of grant:
4. Number of shares/options:
5. Exercise price:
6. Vesting schedule:
7. Expiration date:
8. Number vested during marriage:
9. Number that will not vest during marriage:
10. Are they qualified or non-qualified?
11. Will the company permit you to transfer them at divorce?

MUTUAL FUNDS, OPTIONS, AND OTHER SECURITIES

If your holdings are in an investment account at a brokerage, then the current fair market value will be given in your most recent statement. For individual stocks, bonds, and some limited partnerships, look up their values in the *Wall Street Journal.*

If stocks (or bonds) have increased in value during the time you have held them, then the spouse who keeps them will face a capital gains tax when they are sold. The top capital gains rate for most assets is 15% for those in the 25% tax bracket or higher, and 0% for those in the 10% and 15% tax brackets. The regular holding period for long-term capital gains is now more than 12 months. You must decide whether to factor this tax burden in your bargaining. If you have been carrying a loss on investment assets from year to year, you now must stop doing so at the time of divorce and factor the loss into the value of the asset. This may increase your capital gain considerably. Consult your tax lawyer or accountant for how this affects you.

Bonds carry a similar built-in capital gains tax burden. The face value of a bond is the amount it will pay on its maturity date. Before that date, bonds are usually worth less than the face amount; after that date, more.

Limited partnerships may be especially tricky to value. Some enable the owner to take depreciation year after year. This lowers the basis. The more the basis is lowered, the greater the gain when sold—and the higher the tax on the sale. Some call this "phantom income." You must investigate each limited partnership interest you own to discover its fair market value (what a willing buyer would pay for it currently), plus whatever the tax burden will be upon sale.

An option is a right to purchase a stock at a stated price, called the exercise price. The majority of these are typically granted by a company to an employee as an incentive, vest over a period of time, and are given an expiration date after which they may no longer be exercised. Usually options that vest before the end of the marriage are marital, and those, which vest later, are not. Vesting means you own it, but it will expire on the expiration date, or if the employee leaves the company. There is a method for determining the present marital value of unvested options, and if this is of concern to you, you need to consult counsel. There are qualifying and non-qualifying options, the former receiving more favorable tax treatment than the latter. Options may be transferable to your spouse, if the company that granted the options agrees—be sure to get any such agreement in writing. If you want to divide non-transferable options between you, the spouse they are granted to must hold the other spouse's options for him/her, and pay that spouse any net profit, or transfer the actual shares when the options are exercised. You will need to agree on who will decide when they will be exercised and who will pay the exercise price.

If you have now agreed on how you are going to divide your stocks, bonds, and other securities, you may enter the appropriate information on the Division of Marital Assets and Debts Chart at the end of this chapter. Your stocks and bonds information goes in Schedule F of your financial affidavit, while options information goes in Schedule I. If you have decided to divide some or all of your stocks, bonds, and options according to some value other than monetary, you do not need to make an entry on the chart. If you have not yet reached agreement, just read on.

RETIREMENT, PENSIONS, AND PROFIT SHARING

If you have completed the Checklist of things to gather, Chapter 6, you will have gathered all the information you will need to allocate or divide your retirements. If you have not done this, you may wish to refer to the "Pension, Profit Sharing, and Retirement" section of Chapter 6 to gather the information regarding your specific plans.

Retirement plans are of two general types: those **defined by the benefit paid** at retirement, and those **defined by the contributions made.** Many plans combine both these elements.

A plan defined in terms of its benefits is usually called a **pension.** It tells you what it will pay you at retirement, usually based on a percentage of your highest earnings at the time of retirement. Typically the employer contributes directly to this benefit, and nothing, as a rule, is withheld from your paycheck for this purpose. Sometimes these benefits are lost completely if you leave the employment before retirement age. Others vest over a period of years. Vesting means you own that portion and it cannot be taken away. If a plan vests gradually, you might own 20% of your plan after one year of employment, 40% after two years, etc.

Examples of this kind of retirement are: pensions, PERA, Civil Service Retirement System, Federal Employee Retirement System, Military Retirement, most Railroad Retirements, and many municipal and state employee group plans such as firemen, policemen.

A plan defined in terms of its contribution means there is a set amount which you contribute from your gross pay—often a combination of a required percentage of your pay plus an optional amount. Then your employer may "match" the amount you put in. The employer's contribution frequently does not occur until you retire, however, or may vest over time.

Retirements Checklist

Complete the following information for each retirement or pension plan either one of you has.

Name of Plan:

Kind of plan, if known:

Name of participant:

Vested?

Current vested value:

Date of vested value:

Future benefit?

At what age?

Monthly amount, lump sum or formula?

Reductions for early retirement?

Subject to divestment?

Divisible by QDRO?

Loans available?

Early payout option?

Preretirement survivor benefit?

Survivor benefit?

Name of Plan:

Kind of plan, if known:

Name of participant:

Vested?

Current vested value:

Date of vested value:

Future benefit?

At what age?

Monthly amount, lump sum or formula?

Reductions for early retirement?

Subject to divestment?

Divisible by QDRO?

Loans available?

Early payout option?

Preretirement survivor benefit?

Survivor benefit?

For additional retirements, repeat on a separate sheet of paper.

Sometimes there is a vesting schedule, similar to that in the defined benefit plan. The employer can provide a schedule or formula of their matching as well as of the vesting. If you leave employment before retirement, sometimes you lose a portion or all of the employer's contribution, but you do not lose your own.

The amount of your total contribution, plus accumulated interest, is yours when you leave the company, even if you do so before retirement. The amount in your account is shown at least once a year in a statement from your employer or the trustee or institution which manages your account or plan.

Examples of this kind of plan are: IRA, SEP, 401(k), Profit Sharing, ESOP, Tax Sheltered Annuities, Money Purchase Plans, Keogh, 403(b), TIAA-CREF, some profit sharing plans, (and TRASOP and PAYSOP which are no longer available).

The first step in negotiating about retirement plans is to find out exactly what you have. Most of us don't really know. Today's plans are often complex hybrids of the simple plans that existed only a few years ago. There are tax pitfalls to be wary of, some of very recent origin.

How Do We Value Our Retirements?

A defined contribution plan is easy to value. Just take the actual amount of your contributions, plus those of the employer which are vested to you (if any), plus accrued interest to date. This is the most readily obtainable value because it is on the periodic statement from the plan administrator, trustee, or agency holding your account.

A defined benefit plan—a pension—is valued by calculating the present value of a future flow of payments. For example, you will receive $680 per month starting at age 65. This amount can be translated into a current cash value: the amount of money you would need now, invested at 6% (or other interest rate), which would pay you your monthly pension amount starting at age 65 for 17.8 years. This is the life expectancy of men and women at age 65, according to the Colorado Mortality Table (C.R.S. 13-25-103). (Other mortality tables differ, showing longer life expectancies and are different for men and women.) Some of these plans include other valuable rights, such as cost of living increases, or the right to purchase certain health insurance. Most also have the opportunity for a joint and survivor annuity at retirement, so that payments to the survivor will continue after the death of the retiree, as well as a right to a preretirement survivor annuity in the event of the death of the employee prior to retirement. WARNING: These benefits are widely misunderstood by both professionals and lay people in dividing retirement bene-

Death Benefit

There are two kinds of death benefits often attached to retirement or pension plans. The first is the remainder of the retirement (if any) after the death of the participant, usually payable to the surviving spouse. The second is a separate amount, often about $10,000, which, like a life insurance policy, is payable in a lump-sum upon the participant's death to the designated beneficiary. Be certain your agreement is clear about what happens to any death benefit. Does it stay with the current spouse, or will it be available to a future spouse, if any?

Tax Status of the Money in the Plan

For the most part, contributions—whether yours or your employer's—will be carried in your account in tax-deferred status. This means that you did not pay income tax on this money, but that you will pay tax on it when you receive it—typically at retirement. Since you will usually be in a lower tax bracket at retirement than you are in now, you save money by deferring or putting off tax on this money until later. By contrast, some of your or your employer's contributions may have already been taxed, or be tax-free, and they should not be taxed again when those dollars are paid out to you. If you are considering an early payout, when you examine the present value of the plan be sure you understand which dollars are in which tax status because it will substantially change the value to you of each dollar.

fits between spouses. If either of you has a defined contribution plan, be sure to discuss it with an attorney or CPA who specializes in retirements before making your decision about it.

The plan administrator may or may not tell you the present value of your account. If it is provided to you, be sure you know what interest rate was used to determine it. (A low interest rate means a higher present value, and vice versa.) If your plan administrator does not provide the present value, you may need to hire a CPA, an actuary or an attorney who specializes in this kind of valuation, or there are computer programs which do this (see the bibliography at the end of this Guidebook). The values determined by any of these professionals may vary considerably since they are based on the evaluator's choice of what interest and discount rates to apply. (The discount rate is a number representing the probability that you will not exceed the life expectancy from the table, or that you will not continue in your job until retirement. Figuring this for a 35 year old is different from figuring it for a 55 year old.) Large amounts of time and money are being spent in divorce cases figuring out the present value of these assets which may or may not ever get paid. Sometimes it seems like so much smoke and mirrors.

There are other ways to factor your retirement into your negotiations than dividing it by present value. See the "How to Divide" section below for ways to divide such plans without spending money on present-day valuations.

EARLY PAYOUT OPTIONS

There are three typical early payout options: lump sum, hardship, and loans.

1. *Lump-sum.* Some plans offer a lump-sum payout at retirement, or on the occurrence of certain events, such as leaving the job. The lump-sum options on defined contribution plans are usually available at either retirement, leaving the employment, or at death. It is important in your bargaining and in your planning to know the options in your plan. Even if your periodic statement about your account gives your balance in projected monthly payout, or account balance, don't assume that this is the only option for you.

2. *Hardship.* Some plans offer a lump-sum payout of all or a portion of the balance on the occurrence of certain events. Most common are purchase of a primary residence, college or higher education expenses, medical emergency, and sometimes divorce. The payouts, if available, are taxable as additional income in the year you receive them. Some hardship option clauses allow you to get money out, but you have to

IR$ In some defined contribution plans, it is possible for an employee spouse to distribute retirement assets to a non-employee spouse as current taxable income at the time of the divorce or legal separation, but without a 10% penalty. The penalty on early withdrawal of funds does not apply to certain "qualified" plans when the distribution is made to the non-participant spouse under a divorce court order. If this would fit your situation, be sure to consult with your plan administrator to see if your plan qualifies for this exemption.

pay a penalty. Be sure you know which kind of hardship clause you have, if any.

3. *Loans from the Plan.* Some plans, especially those with actual present value, permit you to borrow against the balance, similar to borrowing against a whole life insurance policy. Often you must prove need. The terms are strict—usually repayment within five years but the interest rate is usually low. This can be a valuable planning tool for you to meet short-term emergency needs at the time of your separation or divorce.

Divestment

Whatever the nature of your retirement (defined contribution, defined benefit, or a hybrid) all or some of it may be subject to divestment (you may lose it) under certain circumstances. The most likely of these is if you leave the employment before your retirement date—by quitting, being fired, or death. If your retirement is subject to divestment, you may want to consider dividing it with an agreement that goes into effect only if it pays.

SOCIAL SECURITY

To be eligible for Social Security benefits, a worker must accumulate 40 full-time working quarters (3-month periods, 40 of them equals 10 years) in which the worker paid F.I.C.A. or Self-employment taxes. Until you have 40 quarters, you are not eligible for Social Security retirement in any amount. Once you become eligible, the amount of your benefit payable at retirement depends on your earnings during your working lifetime.

These payments represent a future income stream which may not be the same for each spouse. Most people use their estimated Social Security incomes when discussing whether maintenance or child support payments should survive or be payable after retirement of either the recipient or the payor. Some people, however, do ask for a present value of their future Social Security benefits, and treat it like an asset.

IRS regulations withhold 20% if YOU take money from an IRA, or other tax-deferred plan even for the purpose of transferring it into another IRA for yourself or your spouse. The trustee must take out the 20% and send it to IRS. You must then replace the 20% out of your own pocket to transfer to the new IRA, or pay tax on that 20% as though you had received it as income that year. You therefore not only lose this money from the IRA, but you also pay tax on it. If you do replace the 20% out of pocket, the IRS will then return the 20%, without interest, if you request it as a tax refund on your next income tax return. If you put it back into the IRA, you won't pay tax on it. The only way to avoid this 20% is to never let YOUR HANDS touch it. Have it transferred by the trustee, DIRECTLY to the trustee of another IRA for yourself or your spouse as part of your divorce agreement.

PLANS IN LIEU OF SOCIAL SECURITY

Some retirement plans take the place of Social Security. Common examples are PERA, Civil Service, Military Retirement, and some specific plans for groups of public employees, like firemen and police. The difficulty in valuation of these plans is that there is usually no way to accurately determine the equivalent Social Security portion. If, in your bargaining you choose to treat pension and other retirement benefits as assets but not Social Security, then set aside some part of any plan in lieu of Social Security as though it were Social Security. A ballpark way to do this is to take 7% of your salary over the time of your contribution to the plan, plus interest. (The present Social Security rate is 7.65%, 15.3% if you are self-employed.)

How May We Divide Our Retirements?

This section shows you the mechanics of how to divide your retirements if you choose to do so in your final separation agreement. You may choose, alternatively, not to "divide" them at all, but simply to allocate them—"You keep yours, and I'll keep mine." Some plans are divisible directly, some require a Qualified

Domestic Relations Order (QDRO), some are divisible by written agreement, and some are really not divisible at all.

PLANS WHICH ARE DIVISIBLE DIRECTLY

The most immediately divisible plans are those which are really tax-deferred savings plans, such as IRA's and SEP's. These may be divided by directly transferring all or some of the balance to a similar account in the name of the other spouse. Show your separation agreement to the plan administrator or account executive and ask them to carry out the transfer.

If you withdraw money from an IRA account to help finance your separation or divorce, you will pay a 10% penalty plus federal and state income tax on the amount withdrawn. You will pay this penalty unless you are at least 59½. There are no general "hardship" exceptions from the penalty for IRA withdrawals, but you can withdraw for deductible medical expenses, health insurance premiums if you are unemployed, higher education expenses for yourself or your dependent, or a first home purchase, all without the 10% penalty. Each of these is still subject to income taxes.

The IRS requires the IRA administrator to withhold 20% of the withdrawal (i.e. $2,000 withheld on a $10,000 withdrawal) to cover any taxes and penalty. You must report this on your income tax return, but you may be entitled to a refund of all or part when you file, depending on your incomes, withholdings, and tax brackets.

Not all plans are required by law to permit division on divorce. However, the number of plans allowing division is increasing. Nevertheless, an increasing number which are not required to do so are now permitting such division. The largest of these are the various military and civil service retirements. Some private plans offer their own process for dividing retirements at divorce, whether or not they are required to do so by federal law.

TIAA-CREF has permitted division for 40 years. CSRS (Civil Service Retirement System and FERS (Federal Employee Retirement System) are divisible under the Civil Service Retirement Spouse Equity Act of 1984.

For all of these, contact the accounting office for the military service in question, the plan administrator for TIAA-CREF, FERS, and CSRS, or your employer. Request information about the procedure and forms, if any, for division of your retirement at divorce, and talk to an attorney or CPA who specializes in this area to prepare the documents for you, including the appropriate language about this in your separation agreement.

Defined Contribution Plan QDRO Decisions Checklist

1. Amount in the plan:

2. Amount to be transferred to the non-participating spouse:

OR

3. Percentage of balance on date of Decree to be transferred to the non-participating spouse:

Defined Benefit (Pensions) Plan QDRO Decisions Checklist

1. Fraction to be used to calculate receiving spouses share at time of participant's retirement.

2. Preretirement survival benefit for receiving spouse?

3. Retirement survival benefit for receiving spouse?

4. Other benefits extended to receiving spouse?

PLANS DIVISIBLE BY QDRO

A 1986 amendment to the Retirement Equity Act, a federal statute, gives domestic relations courts the power to order the division of certain "qualified" pension and retirement plans. The divorce court signs a Qualified Domestic Relations Order (QDRO, pronounced "Q-dro" or "Quadro") that requires the plan administrator to divide the retirement account according to the to the terms stated in the order.

If your plan administrator provides a QDRO form for you, be sure to read it carefully. You must check that it does what you want it to do (transfers exactly what you want transferred to the person you want it transferred to), and that it does not add something that you do not want to do (pays out the money thus incurring 20% withholding, along with possible penalty).

The plans which are covered under this federal law are large public employers who are covered by Employee Retirement Income Security Act of 1974 (ERISA), and include both defined benefit and defined contribution plans.

Plans divisible by QDRO include defined benefit plan pensions (IBM, Lockheed Martin, Qwest, and many others); 401(k)s (thrift savings plans); some profit sharing and money purchase plans; Keogh plans; tax-sheltered annuities; ESOP's (Employee Stock Ownership Plans), and the old PAYSOP's and TRASOP's.

A QDRO for a defined contribution plan instructs the plan administrator to transfer a dollar amount or a percentage to the non-participating spouse. This can be done in several ways:

When you have completed your QDRO, be sure to send it to the plan administrator before you ask the court to sign it. Ask the plan administrator if he or she will carry it out as written. He or she must, by law, tell you specifically if there are any problems with it. You must be sure that you have time to correct any problems before giving it to the court for signature.

- pay out in cash, in which case the plan will withhold 20% of the amount in the QDRO and the receiving spouse will pay income tax on it.
- roll over into an IRA in the receiving spouse's name. No income tax is incurred when the transfer is directly from one account to the other, and doesn't go through your hands.
- open an account in the same plan (i.e., a separate 401(k), or other qualified plan) for the receiving spouse. This option is not always provided, so ask your plan administrator is this is available.
- a combination of the above.

"We have plenty of time to do our QDRO after our divorce."

This is incorrect. Each plan has its own deadline for when the QDRO needs to be signed by the judge and sent to the plan administrator. If you miss the deadline the order is void and the money cannot be transferred. It is best, therefore, to present your QDRO to the court for signature at the time of your final hearing, and then give a copy of the signed QDRO to your plan administrator immediately. Your plan administrator should have previously approved the form before signature, as above.

If your goal is to keep this money handy for emergency purposes, consider transferring it into an IRA, which usually has more flexibility for withdrawals than a 401(k) or other qualified plan. If your goal is to keep this money locked up so you can't touch it until retirement, then a 401(k) or other qualified plan may be best. Either way, be sure you read both plans so you are clear on your options. Sometimes couples take enough out of their 401(k) (or other qualified plan) for both spouses to have IRAs, rolling over the full amount first to the alternate payee's IRA, and then transferring half of that back into an IRA for the participant, without incurring any taxes. You can similarly take out cash for one or both of you, but remember the taxes will be incurred by the alternate payee.

A QDRO for a defined benefit plan is more complex than one for a defined contribution plan, and refers to future dollars and future payments. For many of these plans, you may create a formula that divides only the marital portion of the plan, and reserves any future contributions after the marriage for the participant spouse. The formula looks like this:

$$\frac{\text{\# years of marriage}}{\text{total \# years employed at retirement}} \times \text{50\%, (or other percentage you think is fair)}$$

You may give the plan administrator this formula as part of your QDRO, after filling in all the numbers (except the number of years employed if the employee-spouse is still working there). But you may determine whatever portion you think is fair for the non-employee spouse to receive. Some plans (military and civil service) may require exact numbers instead of formulas.

The receiving spouse has no more rights to the retirement benefit than the participating spouse has. The QDRO for a defined benefit plan, a pension, usually divides the retirement payments at the source, so that the receiving spouse will receive her/his own check from the retirement plan, but not until the participating spouse retires and starts receiving his/her payments. Both payments will end when the participant spouse dies, unless you also provide for a survivor benefit. Thus your defined benefit plan QDRO may also need to address

- Survival benefits
- Preretirement survival benefits
- Other benefits available through the plan.

CAUTION: Since is it possible that the spouse who participates in the defined contribution plan could die before the QDRO benefits are paid out, many couples agree to keep the receiving spouse as beneficiary of the plan until the QDRO transfer is complete (usually about 6 weeks).

If you are dividing more than one plan, you will need a QDRO for each plan. If you want a retirement plan to remain entirely the asset of the participant spouse, you need to say that in your separation agreement, and you will not need a QDRO.

If you are dividing a defined contribution plan, ask your plan administrator if they provide a QDRO form, and use that. If not, you can draft your own QDRO using the sample that follows.

If you are dividing a defined benefit plan, you are in a more complex and specialized area of both law and accounting, and your QDRO needs to be coordinated with the wording in your separation agreement. Be sure to have your defined benefit plan QDRO drafted or reviewed by one of these specialists to be sure you obtain the outcome you both intend.

Sample Language for a Qualified Domestic Relations Order for Defined Contribution Plan Only

Directions: This sample order is provided for you to prepare well in advance of your final decree, so that you may submit it to the plan administrator for review before you send it to the court for signature, at the time of your final decree.

<table>
<tr><td>☐ District Court
______________________________ County, Colorado
1 Court Address:</td><td rowspan="2">

▲ COURT USE ONLY ▲</td></tr>
<tr><td>☐ In re the Marriage of:

Petitioner:

3

v.
Respondent/Co-Petitioner:</td></tr>
<tr><td></td><td>Case Number:
2
Division: Courtroom:</td></tr>
<tr><td colspan="2">QUALIFIED DOMESTIC RELATIONS ORDER</td></tr>
</table>

This matter comes before this Court, pursuant to Paragraph 4 ___ of the parties' Separation Agreement, and pursuant to Section 206(d)(3) of the Employee Retirement Income Security Act of 1974, as amended (ERISA), and Section 414(p) of the Internal Revenue Code of 1986, as amended, for entry of a Qualified Domestic Relations Order ("QDRO"), the parties being in agreement and the Court being fully advised in the premises.

A. On ______5______________(date), this Court entered a Decree of Dissolution of Marriage 6 (Legal Separation) which incorporates the parties' Separation Agreement (the "Agreement dated ___7___________________, resolving between them the matters of assets division and maintenance pursuant to The Colorado Dissolution of Marriage Act. The Agreement further allocates to ______________________8______________, the Alternate Payee, benefits of his/her former spouse, which are carried out in this QDRO.

B. The name of the Plan to which this QDRO relates is ____

____,

9 which is referred to herein as "The Plan." The address of the Plan (and of the Plan Administrator) is

____

____.

C. The party entitled to benefits as a participant under the Plan, which benefits are subject to this QDRO, is referred to as the "Participant." The name, address, and Social Security number of the Participant is:

Name: ____

10 Address: ____

____

Social Security No.: ____

D. The party who will receive a right, as a result of this QDRO, to receive all or a portion of the benefits under the Plan, is referred to as the "Alternate Payee." The name, address, Social Security number, and date of birth of the Alternate Payee is:

11 Name: ______________________________

Address: ______________________________

____

Social Security No.: ______________________________

Date of birth: ______________________________

E. No portion of any benefit of the Participant under the Plan is presently required to be paid to any other Alternate Payee under a QDRO, and no such order has ever been entered with respect to any benefits of the Participant under the Plan.

F. This QDRO is intended by the parties to constitute a Qualified Domestic Relations Order under Section 206(d)(3) of the Employee Retirement Income Security Act of 1974, as amended (ERISA), and Section 414(p) of the internal Revenue Code of 1986, as amended.

THIS COURT THEREFORE ORDERS AS FOLLOWS:

1. The Alternate Payee, as the former spouse of the Participant, is hereby assigned the right to receive from the accounts of the Participant under the Plan:

12 a. _____% of the Participant's accounts, valued as of ____________________ (date), (Option 1). OR

$ ___________ to be charged against the Participant's accounts under the Plan (Option 2).

13 b. Alternate Payee shall (shall not) be entitled to Alternate Payee's pro rata share of earnings or losses on the amount determined under paragraph (a) from the valuation date specified above to the date of distribution.

2. Distribution shall be made to the Alternate Payee according to Alternate Payee's election.

3. Benefits paid to the Alternate Payee from the Plan shall not exceed the benefits to which the Participant is entitled under the Plan.

4. In the event of the Alternate Payee's death prior to receipt of all of the benefits hereunder, any remaining payments shall be distributed to the beneficiary of the Alternate Payee designated in writing to the Administrator of the Plan. If no such designation has been filed, or the designated beneficiary has predeceased the Alternate Payee, such payments shall be distributed to the Alternate Payee's estate.

5. The Alternate Payee shall not be entitled to Plan benefits that are already required to be paid to another Alternate Payee under another order previously determined to be a Qualified Domestic Relations Order (QDRO).

6. This QDRO shall remain qualified with respect to any successor plans to the Plans identified in this QDRO.

7. In case of conflict between the terms of the QDRO and the terms of a Plan, the terms of the Plan shall prevail. For example, if a Plan is terminated and all benefits are distributed, amounts due under this QDRO from that Plan shall be immediately distributable.

8. The court retains jurisdiction to amend this QDRO for the purpose of establishing or maintaining this Order as a Qualified Domestic Relations Order and/or to effectuate the parties' intention.

9. The Alternate Payee shall keep the Plan Administrator informed of his/her current address and telephone number until all transfers under this QDRO are complete. Notice of change of address or telephone number shall be made in writing to the Plan Administrator at the address given above in Paragraph B.

10. The Alternate Payee shall promptly serve a copy of this QDRO upon the Plan Administrator of the Plan.

SO STIPULATED:

14

______________________	____________	______________________	____________
Alternate Payee	Date	Participant	Date

15

Approved_________________________ (date) By ____
Plan Administrator

SO ORDERED this _______ day of ____________________ , ____ .

BY THE COURT:

16 ______________________________
District Court Judge/Magistrate

INSTRUCTIONS TO FILL OUT THE QDRO

1, 2, and 3. Fill out the same as on the Petition.

4. Type the number or letter of the paragraph in your separation agreement which states your agreement regarding the QDRO.

5. Type the date of the decree, or the date of your final hearing, or leave blank if you are obtaining your decree by affidavit and you intend for the QDRO to be signed at the same time as the decree.

6. Delete "Dissolution of Marriage" or "Legal Separation" as appropriate.

7. Type the date you signed your separation agreement.

8. Type the name of the spouse who is to receive a benefit from this QDRO.

9. Type the full name and address of the plan.

10. Type the name, address, and Social Security number of the spouse whose name is on the plan.

11. Type the name, address, Social Security number, and date of birth of the spouse who is receiving a portion of the plan.

12. If you have agreed on a percentage of the current balance to be transferred to the receiving spouse, write that percentage in Option 1 and delete Option 2. Enter the date of the decree or date you sign this or any date you choose for your final valuation. If you have agreed on a dollar amount to be transferred to the receiving spouse, write that amount in Option 2 and delete Option 1.

13. The receiving spouse's share may grow or shrink with the market it is in between the time of the valuation date or the date of your Decree and the time it is paid out. If you want that amount to adjust up or down accordingly, delete "shall not". If you don't want it to adjust, delete "shall".

14. Each of you must sign and date your signature.

15. Leave blank – this is for the Plan Administrator to date and sign.

16. Leave blank – this is for the court to sign.

PLANS DIVISIBLE BY WRITTEN AGREEMENT

The retirement plans of certain Colorado public employees can be divided in a divorce action. These plans include PERA and group funds such as police, fire, city and state employees who are not presently subject to ERISA (i.e., can not do a QDRO). BOTH spouses MUST agree to the division of the plan, in writing. The courts have no jurisdiction to order the division or modify the terms of the agreement if the couple does not agree.

If you are dividing a retirement plan by written agreement, you must give the plan administrator plenty of time to review and approve the plan before your court date. Without this approval, you would not be able to divide the this asset.

If you are considering dividing one of these plans, obtain any relevant forms and instructions from your plan administrator and then consult an attorney who specializes in retirement plans at divorce. (If you are not dividing your benefits under the plan, you may still need your spouse's signature on some official form.) Usually you will need a written agreement to submit to the plan administrator for approval, include language in your separation agreement, and then have a separate document, like a QDRO, for the court to sign. Be sure to allow enough time for all of these steps. Then take the agreement, signed by both of you, to the final hearing. Once it is approved by the court—which makes it an order—you usually have 90 days to submit the certified order to the retirement plan administrator.

PLANS NOT DIVISIBLE AT ALL

These include some plans of small employers not covered by ERISA or the "Colorado QDRO" above. For these plans, the best you can do in your negotiations is to balance them with other assets or income. If you can find a current value for the plan or a portion of it (for example, employee contribution to date), then you can set this aside for that spouse and offset it with other assets for the other spouse (after discounting it for a Social Security equivalent if you decide that is fair).

Future Income Stream as an Asset

If you treat a future income stream as an asset, the employee pays the tax on it when he/she gets it at retirement, and the payment from the retiring spouse to the former spouse is tax-free (in after tax dollars). These payments would not necessarily cease at either remarriage or death of the recipient.

You can set up a future payment in a lump sum, or as periodic payments, such as monthly or quarterly, by the retiring spouse to the non-employee spouse and call it a division of assets. You can set up a future payment in a lump sum, or as periodic payments, such as monthly or quarterly, and call it maintenance.

Future Income Stream as Maintenance

On the other hand, if you treat a future income stream as income, rather than an asset, the employee spouse may be able to deduct the payments to the ex-spouse. They then become maintenance payments, deductible by the employee spouse and taxable to the former spouse. Such maintenance payments are presumed to terminate on the former spouse's remarriage unless you state specifically that they are to continue beyond that event. In any event, such payments terminate at the receiving spouse's death.

If the plan is a pension, or contains the employer's promise to match it at a future date, then you may wish to treat that future portion as income rather than an asset, as you may do with Social Security. This means that when the benefit starts to pay, you can include in your separation agreement a promise that the retiree will pay to the former spouse a percentage of the amount received. You might consider using the formula shown earlier to determine what this percentage should be. Most people define such payments as maintenance, and therefore not payable if the recipient spouse remarries or dies.

If you are treating the payout of retirement as maintenance and this is the first time since your divorce that maintenance is being paid, then you MUST say in your separation agreement that this maintenance arises from the marriage and is part of the divorce agreement **and** the recipient must not waive his/her right to maintenance altogether in the separation agreement. If you are trying a late payout, you will do well to have your agreements double-checked by an accountant or attorney who specializes in this kind of long term financial planning.

If you have now agreed on how you are going to divide your retirements, you may enter the appropriate information on the Division of Marital Assets and Debts Chart at the end of this chapter. If you have decided to divide some or all of your retirements according to some value other than monetary, you do not need to make an entry on the chart. If you have not yet reached agreement, just read on.

BUSINESS INTERESTS

This section is about interests in business in which you play an active role. It could be a professional practice like dentistry, psychotherapy, massage, medicine, law, or accounting; the majority shares in a closely held corporation or family business; an active partnership or joint venture. For example, you might be an independent contractor or sole proprietor in a real estate business who pays rent and other fees to a broker with the franchise name. You might be a cosmetologist or stylist in a beauty salon. You and your brother might be running an old and very successful clothing store that has been in your family for three generations, owned by the two of you and your mother. One of you might sell Amway or Mary Kay products, either as supplemental or primary income. You might have a cottage industry, a small manufacturing or repair business in your home, or in a workshop, or be an artist, writer, or desk-top publisher.

Active businesses come in many forms:

- If your business is a *corporation,* your interest is a percentage of stock. In this case your actual assets is stock, and not the assets owned by the corporation itself—although the value of those assets is part of the value of the stock. If your shares constitute a *majority or controlling interest,* then your actions directly affect the conduct of business, and therefore the business is an asset to be considered in your settlement.

Business Interests Checklist

Directions: Complete the following information for each business interest either one of you has.

☐ Corporation (majority or controlling interest): _______________ (spouse) owns ________ shares of common/preferred/ other stock in ______________________ corporation, at _____________________ ______________________________ (address) constituting ____% majority or controlling interest. Shares are held by ______________________________ (broker or agent).

☐ Corporation (minority interest): We have listed these shares in our Stocks and Bonds Checklist.

☐ Limited Liability Company (LLC): ___________________________ (spouse) is a member with ____% ownership interest in_____________ LLC at__________ (address),with the right to________% of the profits.

☐ Partnership: ____________________ (spouse) is a ____% partner in _________ ______________________________ business, at ______________________ ___________________________ (address). Managing partner is ________________ ______________________________ at ______________________________ (address).

☐ Limited Partnership. ___________________________ (spouse) is a ____% limited partner in __________ ______________________________ (business) which we have listed in our Stocks and Bonds Checklist.

☐ Joint Venture. ___________________________ (spouse) is in a joint venture: ________________ __________________ (name of business) at ______________________________ ____________ (address) with ______ (other persons), whose names are:

☐ Sole Proprietorship: _____________ (spouse) is the sole proprietor of ________ ______________________ business at ______________________________ ___________________________ (address)

If you are a *minority shareholder,* the business is not directly affected by your actions. In this case, value your shares as stock—see "Stocks, Bonds, and other Securities."

- If your business is a *subchapter S corporation* it is a special kind of corporation in which the profits and losses of the corporation are attributed directly to the shareholder(s) as income.
- If your business is a *limited liability company,* you are a member with a certain percentage ownership interest in the business and entitled to a certain percentage (usually the same) of the profits.
- If your business is a *partnership,* your interest is your agreed percentage of that business. For example, if there are two of you, you may have agreed to be 50%-50% partners, 60%-40% partners, or some other proportion. You then own that agreed percentage of each of the assets of the business, and are responsible for that same agreed percentage of each of the partnership debts and obligations.
- If you are a *limited partner,* by definition you do not have any control over the operation of the business. In this case, value your limited partnership interest as stock—see "Stocks and Bonds."
- If your business is a *joint venture,* then each of those in the venture is a sole proprietor.
- If your business is a *sole proprietorship,* you personally own all the assets and are personally responsible for all the debts of the business.

Valuing a Business

There are appraisers who value businesses as a specialty. (See "Divorce Services and Consultants" in Chapter 2.) However, agree on a single appraiser who will be working for both of you, and be sure you tell him/her that this is a friendly divorce and you will not be asking for legal testimony as an expert witness. You should be prepared to put that in writing. You may be surprised how much it will reduce the price of the appraisal or valuation. If you wish to try to find a value acceptable to both of you on your own, begin by gathering all the fiscal year-end accounting and balance sheets, as well as tax reports, such as the corporate tax return, partnership K-1 tax forms, or Schedule C's.

There are some simple concepts which may make it possible for you to come to agreement about the value of your business. All businesses can be valued, at least in part, by adding up the business assets and subtracting the business debts. Business assets include: commercial real estate, unsold inventory, accounts receivable (money others owe the business for services rendered or goods purchased) which you may want to discount if they are old or you know the person or company that owes the money is having financial troubles; business equipment (copier, fax, car), furniture (desks, chairs), and supplies (paper, stamps, etc.). It is customary to use the fair market value of assets such as furniture, equipment and car—rather than what you paid for them, or what it would cost to replace them.

Business debts (liabilities) include: loan balances, the balance on leases (building, car), and bills not yet paid this month or quarter. The result, when you subtract the liabilities from the assets, will give you the minimal value of the business.

The difficult part of valuing a business is that the more established it is, the more likely that someone will buy it for more than the minimal value. The buyer is then paying for something called good will or blue sky. Good will is what makes the business desirable because it already has loyal customers, a good reputation, a known name, or those other qualities which make the consumer come to this business rather than any other offering the same service or selling the same goods. If your business is very new or very small or very shaky, you may agree that it has no, or very little good will, and therefore you will value it at assets minus liabilities.

If you think your business has good will, see some of the excellent books on the subject of valuing (usually for purposes of sale) a small or family business. These books are available both at local bookstores and at libraries. Several are listed in the bibliography. These books describe a variety of formulas for valuing businesses based on: personal income of the owner, how much more than the average business of this kind the particular enterprise earns, or the gross income stream of the business. There are many other formulas, and each industry lends itself to different ones. Trade magazines and journals will contain articles about buying and selling business in that particular field. This can be a good place to look for valuation formulas and how to use them for your particular business.

Business Valuation Checklist

Directions: Complete the following information for each business interest either one of you has.

☐ We will hire ____________________ (name of appraiser) to value our business ________________________ (name of business).

☐ We will try to value our business ________________________ (name of business) and will therefore need to gather the following:

Who will gather	Date Done	
_____	_____	P & L statement for ______________ (date/period of time) prepared by ______________ (accountant, if any)
_____	_____	Balance sheets for ______________ (dates) prepared by ______________ (accountant)
_____	_____	K-1 tax return for __________ years.
_____	_____	Income tax Schedule C for ____ years.

As a result of the above information gathered, we believe the following is true about ____________________ (business):

Assets are worth $ _________

Liabilities are worth $ _________

Value of business $ _________ (assets minus liabilities)

In addition, we agree this business has (does not have) a good will value of $_______________, figured using the following formula:

Don't kill the goose that lays the golden eggs.

Dividing a Business

If you are dealing with a very small family business, or a business which has been in one of your families for some time, you may feel like you are getting two divorces at once. If the business in question is also the primary support for the two of you, then it can be deeply threatening both emotionally and financially. A helpful technique might be to think of the business as a child of your marriage who must be shielded from your hostilities. Your business, like your child, must survive the divorce of its parents and must be given the opportunity to grow and flourish. Here are some suggestions for how to do this:

- Evaluate each possible way of allocating or dividing the business between you in light of which is most likely to enhance the business itself.
- Avoid any way of allocating or dividing the business which will or is likely to destroy it.
- Remember that you each have much more than money invested in this business.

Some Possible Ways to Divide Your Business

Following are some options for you to consider for dividing your business:

Your Business Is Your Baby

If your business was created by both of you, it may feel as though it were your child. If you cut it in half, as Solomon threatened, it won't survive. Better to work out for one or the other of you to have it, and then compensate the other in some way, or apply some of the ideas about joint custody, so that you both continue to own it.

1. *Don't divide it.* Plan to both be active in the business in either the short or long run. If you choose this, here are some things to remember:
   - *Protect the baby.* Don't allow your personal animosities or antipathy to overflow into your conduct of the business. If that keeps happening, despite your best efforts, then this is probably not a viable option for you in the long run.
   - *Try a plan* which allows you to re-evaluate at the end of 6 months or a year. This may be enough time for you both to go through the changes in yourselves which happen at the time of separation. You can then look at your changed relationship with each other and evaluate whether it will support your being business partners for the long term.
   - *Separate your roles* within the business as much as possible. Have separate offices or different hours. Share the necessary business travel, so one of you is always there,

but there are times when each of you is alone with the business. Be responsible for different departments or different functions. Try to be independent in your authority and responsibility within the business.

- *One of you takes an active role* (managing partner, runs the store) and the other keeps only a passive role (limited partner). The difficulty with this model is the possibility that the passive partner feels frustrated or is tempted to be critical of the active partner. Another consideration in this mode is whether the active partner should be paid the same in profits, and/or should be paid a salary or profit-based incentive or bonus if in fact he or she is doing all the work.

2. *Sell the business.*

   - If you have a *friendly buyer,* you can often keep control or feel as though you have. This is a viable option for some people, but it is very important to be clear about your on-going role in the business so that you do not "stick your nose in where it is not wanted." The friendly buyer, however, can enhance the likelihood of your being paid, since the buyer cares about you. The friendly buyer may also ease the transition for the clients and customers of the business, so that there is less danger of loss of business in the transfer.

   - If the *buyer is a stranger,* the transaction and the transition may feel like a terrible loss to you. However, this is often the surest way to solve the issue of valuation. If you cannot agree on a value between yourselves, despite your best efforts, you may need to sell in order to get on with your separate lives.

3. *One of you keeps the business.*

   - *Buy the other out* with cash or off-set with other assets, or a mix of cash and assets.

   - *Trade stock* in the business for other stock or assets.

   - *Do a long term buy-out.* You may do a long term buy-out as a straight assets settlement, or structure it like maintenance to provide some real tax advantages (see Chapter 11).

"Divorced people can't possibly go on sharing a business."

This is not necessarily true. It can be done successfully. The key is to differentiate between your relationship as spouses and your relationship as business partners.

"But screw your courage to the sticking place, and we'll not fail." Macbeth I, vii, 59

Don't Pay More Tax Than You Need To

Ted and Betty, husband and wife, and their friend Arthur founded Friendly Corporation, Inc., "FCI." After a few years Arthur wanted out, so their corporate attorney arranged for the corporation to redeem (purchase) Arthur's stock, resulting in Ted and Betty each owning 50% of the outstanding stock. This corporate redemption is taxed as a capital gain to Arthur.

When Ted and Betty divorced, they agreed that Betty would keep the corporation and Ted would start up his own company with the funds he would receive for his half of FCI. To save attorney fees, they followed the same paperwork their attorney had prepared when Arthur left. Ted paid capital gains tax on the increase in value of the shares he sold back.

If they had, instead, arranged for Betty to purchase Ted's shares directly from Ted, it would have been a transaction between husband and wife, "incident to divorce," and not taxable at all. Betty would keep all the shares at their original basis.

Other Assets Checklist

Directions: Complete the following information for each additional asset either one of you has.

We have the following additional assets to be divided in our agreement:

- ☐ Intellectual assets:
  - ☐ Patent #_______________ for _______________ in the name of _______________ (spouse).
  - ☐ Copyrighted (book, song, poem, art work, name, software, other) _______________ _________ (describe) in the name of _______________ (spouse).
- ☐ Priority rights:
  - ☐ Season tickets: _______________ _______________ (describe).
  - ☐ Fishing/hunting rights: _________ _______________ (describe).
  - ☐ Frequent flyer miles: _________ (# of miles) in name of _______________ _________ (# of miles) in name of _______________
- ☐ Membership in _______________ _______________ (club, organization).
- ☐ Accounts receivable $________ owed to _______________ (spouse) by _______________ (name of debtor) under the following terms:
- ☐ Other: Describe:

OTHER ASSETS

Other assets include intellectual property such as a patent or a copyright; Broncos, Rockies, and symphony tickets and ticket priorities; frequent flyer miles; hunting rights; club memberships; debts which people owe you; expected IRS refunds and estimated taxes paid ahead, security deposits, accrued paid sick leave, health savings accounts, and much more. These may all be mentioned in your separation agreement, even if you choose not to place a monetary value on them. Whether or not you mention them in your agreement, you must be clear about these items between the two of you.

If one of you has composed a song, authored a book or screenplay, written a software program, or painted a picture, then the rights to that creation have value. How can these rights be divided in a divorce? You can transfer ownership of patents and copyrights, and you can assign a certain portion of income from them, even a certain percentage of future income.

If you have rights to season tickets to the Broncos, the symphony, or hunting areas, you can alternate the use of these ("I'll take them this year, you take them next year,") or, divide the season or time they cover or trade them between you (I'll take the Bronco tickets, you take the rights to the duck blind.

If you belong to a private membership club, such as a country club, you may find these permit only one member of a divorced couple to continue the membership. You will have to reach agreement on this one. Trade for some other right or assets, or flip a coin if you have to.

Frequent flyer miles have value, but often cannot be transferred. A clever way to divide them is to use them for the benefit of both of you. Use them for your children's travel, for instance, or limit their use to the family business.

Suppose you loaned your best friend $1,000 when his car broke down. This is an informal but real loan, and his obligation to pay it back to you is an asset, as is a more formal loan with a signed promise to pay. Your friend's obligation to pay can be allocated to either one of you, or the payments may be divided between you when they are received, or used to pay one of your marital bills.

Kinds of Debts

Debts can be organized into four major categories:

1. debts which go with the assets—"secured" debts which are tied to an asset, like your mortgage to your house, or your car loan to the car;
2. freestanding or "unsecured" debts—not tied to any asset, like most credit cards;
3. tax debt;
4. divorce expenses.

SECURED DEBTS

The best examples of secured debts are the mortgage(s) on your home or other real estate, and loans on cars and trucks. For a loan to be secured, one of you must have signed a document that says that if you default on your loan payments the lender can take the asset. It's called foreclosure of a house, and repossession of a car.

Usually in divorce the person who gets the asset also gets the responsibility for the loan. Be sure in your negotiations you bear in mind that the value you place on any asset should take into account any outstanding loan balance on it. Keep in mind also any negative cash flow that goes with these assets. One way of managing both debt re-payment and negative cash flow is through maintenance (see Chapter 11).

In practice, only secured debt must be included in the division of assets. You may choose to deal with the following three types of debt as assets, or as a budgeting issue. If you chose to consider this a budgeting question, then hold your discussion of these debts until your discussion of support, maintenance and taxes, Chapters 9, 10, and 11.

UNSECURED DEBTS

Unsecured debts are those obligations which are not tied to an asset. They are "freestanding." Examples are most credit cards, personal bank loans, some lines of credit, and most loans from parents and friends.

TAX DEBT

Taxes rate their own category because Uncle Sam and the Colorado Department of Revenue are the most difficult creditors of all. One of your largest joint obligations may be your joint tax

Debts Checklist

Directions: Provide the following information for each secured or unsecured or tax debt either or both of you owes.

Creditor	Amount	Payment Terms

CAUTION

Uneasiness About Tax Returns

You are both legally responsible for any tax return you sign. Physical separation, when emotions are running high and expenses running even higher, is a time when people are tempted to be unwise on their tax returns (by exaggerating deductible expenses, claiming doubtful deductions, or "forgetting" to list income). If either of you is likely to be less forthcoming than the other, consider filing married/separately, so you are not legally bound by a tax return you are uncomfortable with. You may pay more tax this way, but the peace of mind may be worth it.

Divorce Expenses Checklist

Directions: Provide the following information for each divorce expense owed by either or both of you, or expected to be incurred by either or both of you.

Divorce Expense	Amount	Payment Terms

returns. The IRS can do random audits for 3 years after the filing, can question your return for good cause for 7 years, and forever for fraud. Therefore, your agreement should have some provision for what you will do about any additional taxes, penalties or interest, as well as the cost of a possible audit.

Your separation agreement should state clearly your plan for filing your taxes for the last full year of your marriage or before being legally separated. Your separation agreement should also state how you will deal with any audits or questions raised about tax returns which you filed together. See Chapter 11 Taxes. Sample clauses about taxes are included in Chapter 12.

DIVORCE EXPENSES

When you're focused on the marital debts, it's easy to forget that the expenses of the divorce must be negotiated as well. Be certain that your separation agreement contains your promises about which of you will be responsible for paying the direct and indirect costs of becoming separate. The most obvious ones are usually the court filing fee, appraisals, mediation, and attorneys. Some not so obvious divorce expenses are joint or individual accounting, financial planning, and counseling. To avoid having this become "the straw that broke the camel's back," try to treat these like any unsecured marital debt, regardless of whose lawyer's bill it is, or who ordered the appraisal.

Some of the divorce expenses may have been paid by one or both of you before you began bargaining together. You may want to remember these in your agreement by giving credit to the person who paid them (setting aside assets in that amount to the payor).

Some of the divorce expenses may take place after the decree. Examples of these are attorney fees for doing QDRO's and title transfers, tax preparation for the final joint return, mediation fees, and long-term divorce counseling for you or your children. You will need to be clear about these in your budgets and in your bargaining. You may wish to write these arrangements into your separation agreement.

Dealing with Debt

Talk about debts early on, since most must be paid regularly, or you risk a credit problem. It's very easy in a separation to have your debts fall through the cracks by assuming that your spouse is paying them all.

GATHER THE DATA

To avoid lots of heartbreak, expense, and recriminations later, begin by gathering all the information either of you has about your current and recently-paid debts, as delineated in Chapter 6. You must know whether bills such as the car insurance have been paid. If you are having any trouble agreeing about whether a certain purchase or expense was for the family, gather all the statements and/or charge slips which relate to that expense. Collect all this data before you begin talking about that debt.

Once you have collected all the data about the debts, agree which part of each debt is marital. For example, you may want to say that the expenses or charges incurred since your separation, or your charges for your own business, are your own and not marital. Remember, the presumption is that all charges during your marriage are marital. If you are agreeing to anything else, be very clear.

DEBT STRATEGIES

Try to pay off as many debts as possible before or at the time of the final decree. Consider using liquid assets (bank accounts, stocks, bonds) or other saleable assets (the extra car, the time-share condo, non-essential furniture) in order to do this.

If it is not possible to pay off your debts right away, then you must be clear about who will pay which debt and within what period of time. Debts are a good place to consider putting "teeth" in your agreement. If you fail to make a payment on a debt that is secured by an asset, you lose that asset to the other spouse. For example, if one of you fails to pay the loan on the washer and dryer, then the other spouse may have the washer and dryer and pay off the remaining debt.

To back-up your agreement about who will pay your unsecured debts, include a hold harmless clause in your agreement. This will *indemnify* the non-paying spouse. This means that the paying spouse gives the non-paying spouse the right to collect not only all missed payments, but also damages, interest and attorneys fees resulting from the failure to make the payment. Without a hold harmless clause, the non-paying spouse has only the right to collect the missed payments. With a hold harmless clause, the non-paying spouse has the additional rights.

Once you have divided the responsibility for paying the debts, examine the effect on your respective budgets. Some tax planning

"I'm not responsible for paying that VISA bill, my ex-husband/wife promised to pay it in our divorce agreement, and the judge approved it."

Any agreement you two make about who is going to pay this debt does not affect the creditor, because the person or company you owe a debt to is not a "party" to your divorce negotiation or agreement. If one of you defaults, the lender will attempt to collect from the other, and the default will be reported (to credit reporting agencies) in both your names.

through maintenance may be very helpful here to generate some cash with which to pay bills (see Chapters 9 and 10).

Failure to allocate all your debts between you and to give teeth to this part of your agreement may come back to haunt you years later.

BANKRUPTCY AT THE TIME OF YOUR DIVORCE

Hold Each Other Harmless

Here is a typical hold harmless clause: Wife will be solely and separately responsible for paying the loan at ABC Credit Union in our joint names, holding Husband harmless therefrom.

In the frustration over money issues, the threat of one or both spouses declaring bankruptcy may come up. Try approaching the discussion of possible bankruptcy as an "Oh my god!"—the kind of thing which might happen in spite of both of your best efforts—like being laid off at work, or becoming seriously ill.

There are four kinds of bankruptcy for individuals, called chapter 7, chapter 11 (a business reorganization bankruptcy that is also available to individuals), and chapters 12 (for family farmers and fishermen) and 13. Chapters 7 and 13 are by far the most common.

Chapter 7 provides a complete discharge of all dischargeable unsecured debts and the forfeiture of all assets over certain minimum protected amounts. Typical non-dischargeable debts are unpaid taxes and student loans, as well as unpaid child support and alimony/maintenance. To file for chapter 7 bankruptcy your income must be below the Colorado median income for individuals to file individually, and the Colorado median income for married couples to file jointly as married. For some it is beneficial to wait until their divorce is completed and two separate households are established because the threshold for two separate individuals is higher than the threshold for a joint filing.

Chapter 13 bankruptcy, often called the "Wage Earner Plan," and which establishes a payment plan over three to five years, requires that all priority non-dischargeable debt be paid in full, such as non-dischargeable taxes, child support and alimony/maintenance. It may, however, preserve the assets and allow the debtor to pay on mortgages and car loans, and discharge (erase) a portion of the unsecured debt.

Several things about bankruptcy should be taken into account in any settlement in divorce:

- If either spouse files for bankruptcy before, during, or after the divorce, the creditors will absolutely look to the other spouse to pay any of the originally joint debts, regardless of what you decided about them in your separation agreement.

- Once a bankruptcy petition is filed, all other legal actions are automatically *stayed* (halted). First, this means creditors can't sue the person who filed for bankruptcy (remember, they can still sue the other spouse). Second, it means that if you have filed for divorce but the final decree has not been entered, the divorce court must obtain written permission from the bankruptcy judge to rule or act on any matters which are also in the bankruptcy. Clearly, this will create chaos in your divorce negotiations if you don't know it is coming and haven't planned for it.

- When you file a petition in bankruptcy, the law imposes an *automatic stay* on all the creditors listed in the bankruptcy petition, as discussed above. This means that they are prohibited from attempting in any way to collect the debt from the bankruptcy petitioner as long as the stay is in effect, usually around three months. The automatic stay in bankruptcy can be a good planning tool. By filing a joint bankruptcy, you could use it to stop aggressive creditors and give yourselves time to reach agreement.

CAUTION If you think both or either of you might consider bankruptcy now, or could file for bankruptcy in the future, consult with a bankruptcy attorney and get some good advice BEFORE you file for divorce or legal separation.

Filing the bankruptcy and the divorce at the same time can be very beneficial, especially if there is a possibility of using a Chapter 13 plan to pay off your marital debts. It may take three lawyers to make this plan work smoothly – one for each of you in the divorce and one for you both in the joint bankruptcy filing. Don't discard this option just because it is initially expensive or distasteful.

Bankruptcy declared after your divorce does discharge (erase) unsecured debts and property settlement payments, but does not discharge maintenance or child support payments, either current or arrearages. You can anticipate a possible bankruptcy by saying in your separation agreement that if either declares bankruptcy within a certain period of time, you will agree to re-negotiate part or all of the separation agreement. See sample wording in Chapter 12.

Dividing Marital Assets and Debts

Many people try to divide each asset as they discuss it ("Your half the house is $4,000, my half of the house is $4,000"). Since you will rarely divide the house like this, this may not be the most useful way to go about it. It may be more practical, to begin with, to list each asset as a whole under the name of the person who will keep it. For example, in wife's column list the marital equity in the house if she is thinking of continuing to live there. List the entire value of the husband's retirement in his column, if that is

Defining Our Sense of Fairness

A. We agree our marital assets should be divided 50/50% because:

or

B. We agree that the first $__________ in value of assets should go to _______________ because:

or

C. We agree ____________ should get all the _____________ because:

and _____________ should get all the _______________ because:

or

D.

your initial inclination. An advantage to this method is that it allows you to see the balance, or lack of it, of your initial plan as you develop it.

If you want to know dollar values, you may need a third party, such as an appraiser, to help you determine them. In order to avoid expensive competing professional opinions, as discussed earlier, agree on who you will hire as your appraiser and how you will pay for it. Agree further how conclusive the appraised value will be for you.

As you divide the marital assets between you, remember that the value may be a range, or other than monetary. It is okay to bargain without fixed numbers for value.

This is the time for a real heart to heart about the range of your sense of fairness. Is the only possibility for you 50-50 division of things by value? By number? Are you more interested in cash than in things? Will you take less than 50% if your share is all cash? Are you more interested in future security than in present assets? If you are willing to wait for a buy-out of your share, such as house or retirement, are you looking for more than 50% to compensate you for waiting? Are you interested in a "lopsided" agreement (more to one than the other) to compensate for the larger earnings of one of you now? Do you want to be "made whole"—end up where you were at the beginning of the relationship? Do you need to be compensated "off the top" for some contribution you made to the acquisition of assets? If you can agree on a generic plan which meets each of your ideas of fairness, you will find you have an agreement which practically writes itself.

As you divide marital assets, write down on the Division of Marital Assets and Debts Chart which follows, the costs involved in maintaining each asset, the debt which comes with it, and the potential for growth or income. This will help you make a more balanced settlement.

As you allocate your other debts, decide first whether they are marital, separate, or a mix. Then agree who will pay off the balance of each. Remember that the problem of unsecured debts may be more easily handled as budget than division of assets. If you find yourselves getting stuck on the division of unsecured debts, including tax debt and divorce expenses, consider setting aside this issue for now. Look at these debts again in the context of maintenance and tax planning after reading Chapters 10 and 11.

Think beyond the short term to the long term effect of the division of assets and debts you are considering. For example, suppose one spouse gets all assets which appreciate slowly or depreciate, and which take money to maintain (home, car, furniture). Then suppose the other spouse takes all assets which increase in value or produce income (stock, retirement, rental home). In such a case, even a few years after the divorce, what in the short term appeared to be a "fair" or "equal" division will look quite different. The net worth of the second spouse will far exceed the net worth of the first – and the gap will just continue to widen. Be sure to consider this information before you decide what is really "fair" or "equal" in your situation.

DIRECTIONS FOR COMPLETING THE DIVISION OF MARITAL ASSETS AND DEBT CHARTS

Make several photocopies of each chart. Do your first drafts, preliminary bargaining, in pencil as you may want to try different possibilities.

Use the Marital Assets and Debts Chart to remind you of which assets and debts you have already agreed are separate, and list them in the appropriate column.

Now begin dividing the items you have agreed are marital. Use the checklists from throughout this chapter (a complete list of checklists and page numbers may be found at the end of the book) for the values and balances, to help you decide who gets the asset and the value of it, or the debt and its balance. Those checklists are:

Calculation of Your Value of Real Estate
Motor Vehicle Checklist
Liquid Assets Checklist
Life Insurance Checklist
Personal Assets Checklist
Stocks Checklist
Bonds Checklist
Options Checklist
Retirements Checklist
Business Interests Checklist
Business Valuation Checklist
Other Assets Checklist
Debts Checklist
Divorce Expenses Checklist

List under husband or wife, each marital asset and marital debt which that spouse will keep. Put debt balances in parentheses ( ).

For each asset or debt, whether marital or separate, anticipate and calculate the expected earnings or cost and increase or decrease in value in the cash flow/growth columns. Put decreases in brackets.

For example, if wife will be retaining the family home, all the costs of maintaining the home should be written in the cash flow column of the chart, along with the probable rate of increase in value (est. x % per year). You may wish to include the increase in equity as the mortgage is paid as part of the growth of that asset. If husband will retain his automobile, then the car payment, insurance, and costs of operating the car go in his cash flow column, as may also the rate of decrease in value of a depreciating asset, if you wish to include it. List debt balances in either the husband or wife column, as appropriate, and the monthly payment in the cash flow column. Remember to list any debts secured by an asset along with the asset.

When you have entered all your marital assets and debts, total the husband's marital assets minus husband's marital debts, and do the same for the wife. Then, for each spouse, total the cash flow column. These four totals will summarize your preliminary division of assets. Refer now to your answers to Defining Our Sense of Fairness. Review your division with this in mind, and make changes as you need to.

DIVISION OF MARITAL ASSETS AND DEBTS CHART

HUSBAND

ASSETS/DEBT	SEPARATE	MARITAL SHARE	CASH FLOW/GROWTH

DIVISION OF MARITAL ASSETS AND DEBTS CHART

WIFE

ASSETS/DEBT	SEPARATE	MARITAL SHARE	CASH FLOW/GROWTH

Finalizing Your Division

Use the Final Division Calculation to test whether the division of marital assets and debts which you have indicated on the Division of Marital Assets and Debts Chart is what you want to do.

Suppose your definition of a fair division of marital assets is 50-50. Add up the proposed assets and debts for each of you, in your separate columns, and compare these totals. If one of these totals is larger than the other, you will need to transfer one-half the difference to the spouse with the lower total. This can be done in a variety of ways. You can transfer an asset to effect this balancing, or actually pay it. This equalizing amount does not have to be cash. It could be a promissory note, amortized over time, or with a balloon payment when the home sells.

Whether you decide that your fair division is 60-40 or 70-30, the method is the same, only the arithmetic changes. For example, if you have agreed to a 60%-40% division, multiply the Net Marital Estate from the Marital and Separate Assets and Debts Chart times .6 to determine how many assets equals 60%. Then adjust the total for the spouse who is to receive 60% until you reach that number. This adjustment may be made by transferring assets, cash, or future payments, as discussed above.

Final Division Calculation

Directions: Enter the appropriate numbers from the Marital Assets and Debts Chart

	Wife	Husband
Total Marital Assets	______	______
Less Total Marital Debt	______	______
Total Net Marital:	______	______
Difference (Subtract the lower from the higher)	______	______
1/2 the Difference (to effect a 50/50 division)	______	

Making Things Happen: Enforcement

There are two ways to enforce your agreements about assets and debt division—voluntary and involuntary. The first we call teeth, which is voluntary but effective. The second is enforcement by the court.

VOLUNTARY ENFORCEMENT

Some people worry, from time to time, that they might not completely fulfill their end of the bargain they are negotiating. If your ex gets a new lover, will you be less likely to pay the old marital debts? If you lose your job or the bonus does not come through, will you look for a way out of your agreement? Most people would have to answer yes to at least one of these—or, at least admit that the possibility exists they could be tempted.

If you have any doubts about yourself, or some secret doubts about your soon-to-be-ex, then try putting in some creative incentives to do what you say you're going to do. These incentives to right behavior are called teeth and are limited only by your imagination. Try having the person against whom the penalty would act set the penalty. You may be surprised to learn what motivates each of you.

For example, pay the spouse-moving-out's equity in the home as described in a promissory note only if that person has paid all the marital obligations he or she agreed to pay. You can design baby teeth for minor misses. For example, the person who does not make a required mortgage payment on time owes the other spouse double the late fee if the other spouse "fronts" the payment. There are sample clauses about internal or voluntary enforcement included in Chapter 12. You may wish to review them after reading this chapter.

INVOLUNTARY ENFORCEMENT

The second kind of enforcement is the power of the court, or some other agency, to take remedial action if the promises you make are not kept. These are summarized in Chapter 13.

Conclusion

You have now finished your first rough look at your division of marital assets and debts. It will probably not be your final version. Go on to the next four chapters about the other essential components of your separation agreement. The agreements you reach as a result of each of those chapters may necessitate changes in the assets division you have worked out so far.

Take heart. Doing your own separation agreement is hard work. Don't expect to get it all done in one sitting. Don't even expect to complete the work of one of the separation agreement chapters in one sitting. Give yourself and each other the time you deserve to make the best decisions for both of you.

CHAPTER 8

CHILDREN
SEPARATION AGREEMENT – PART II

Page

CHILDREN
SEPARATION AGREEMENT - PART II

Before the court can give you a final decree of dissolution of marriage or legal separation, you must resolve and write out all the financial and parental issues remaining from your marriage. This written summary is called the separation agreement whether you are obtaining a divorce or a legal separation. It must be read and approved by the court.

Your separation agreement must do the following:

1. All property you have accumulated must be accounted for and divided (Chapter 7, Assets and Debts).

2. All debts must be acknowledged and paid or the responsibility for paying them allocated between you (Chapter 7, Assets and Debts, and Chapter 11, Taxes).

3. You must establish a parenting plan for your children—decision-making and parenting time—and make commitments about their support (this chapter, Chapter 9, Child Support, and Chapter 11, Taxes).

4. If either spouse is to assist in supporting the other—spousal support or maintenance—the amounts and duration must be set (Chapter 10, Maintenance, and 11, Taxes).

5. You must arrange to pay any costs of the divorce itself: the court filing fee, mediators, lawyers, accountants, recording fees, and the like, if any (Chapter 7, Assets and Debts).

6. You must agree when and under what circumstances any of your agreements change or terminate (Chapters 7-10 and 13).

The five separation agreement chapters (7-10 and 13), designed to help you write your separation agreement, are full of technical terms and legal requirements. The information you will need for your separation agreement is listed in Chapter 5.

Chapter 12 contains sample wording for a wide variety of options in a separation agreement, drawn from the topics discussed throughout this Guidebook. As you complete your agreement about each topic, you might wish to read the relevant sample wording in Chapter 12 for ideas about writing your own agreement.

BUNKY **"Divorce always hurts children." "You just can't possibly be a responsible parent and get a divorce."**

The truth, shown by extensive research, is that divorce does not necessarily hurt children. What does hurt them is on-going hostilities between their parents and loss of contact with one of the parents, whether or not there is a divorce. Research shows that children of divorcing parents who stopped fighting, and who maintained continuing contact with both parents, were as well adjusted as those raised in successful marriages. The same research shows that children of parents who stayed together, but who continued to fight, had as much trouble adjusting as children of the continually hostile divorce. So it's not the divorce that hurts the children, it's the ongoing anger and hostility, and the loss of contact with one of the parents, that are harmful.

Who Is a Child?

For purposes of your divorce petition, a child is any person born to, conceived by, or adopted by both of you during your marriage, which is why you list all your children, whether or not emancipated.

Emancipation: When your child is no longer your legal or financial responsibility.

The word *child* in Colorado law means anyone under the age of 21, with some exceptions. This is different from most other states, where the age of emancipation for all purposes is 18. Until your child reaches 19 in Colorado, you, the parents, may be liable for the child's financial needs, emotional welfare and perhaps for his or her actions. There are some circumstances in which a child never emancipates, such as severe disability.

"The age of emancipation in Colorado is 18."

Not exactly, Colorado law is confusing here. A person is no longer a juvenile for Juvenile Court when he or she reaches the age 18. A person is deemed old enough to make contracts and be held liable, to manage his or her estate, and vote, at age 18. The age of 18 is often referred to as the age of majority in Colorado. But, then again so is 19, when parents are no longer required to provide child support. 19 is often referred to as the age of emancipation.

At age 18 children can do many things without their parents' consent, some of which emancipate them. For example, they can go into the military or marry, either of which emancipates them. If the marriage is annulled, or if they leave the service before age 21, they may become unemancipated again. At age 18 anyone can sign a contract—to buy a car, for example—and be bound by their signature (they can be sued on the debt). They can make a will and inherit. The jurisdiction of the juvenile court ends at age 18, so anyone over 18 is treated like an adult in court. The terms *delinquency and dependency and neglect* do not apply to anyone over age 18.

Dates We Expect Our Children to Emancipate

We expect each of our children to emancipate on approximately the following dates, for the following reasons:

Name	Date of Birth	Expected Date and Circumstance of Emancipation

At age 19 the duty of child support as calculated by the Colorado Child Support Guideline ends. Divorcing people cannot be made to pay each other money to support a child over the age of 19, unless the child is mentally or physically disabled or still enrolled in high school or an equivalent program. The duty to pay child support may end before age 19 if the child emancipates.

People sometimes use the terms *"emancipated minor,"* and *"emancipated in fact."* An emancipated minor is someone whom an institution (usually a school) has decided to treat as an adult, so they can live independently of their parents and/or sign their own permissions for absences and trips, etc. Usually, this is an arrangement between the institution and the child, and does not emancipate the child for any other purpose. Emancipation in fact is a determination by a court for a specific case or set of circumstances. For example, if a person under 21 causes an automobile accident and is uninsured, the injured party is likely to seek damages from both the child and his or her parents—on the so-called deep pocket theory that the parents are more likely to have money. The judge in this case might determine that the child was "emancipated in fact," if he or she lived away from home, was totally self-supporting and had no ties of any kind to the parents, and that therefore the parents are not liable. This emancipates that child for that case only.

As you can see, the age of emancipation in Colorado is far from a fixed point in time. Watch for this to change (probably to 19 or even 18 for all purposes) in the near future.

P PARTNERS This entire chapter is relevant for separating parents who are partners.

How to Be a Good Parent Through the Divorce Process

The time when parents begin living apart is one of the most stressful for children. Their worst fear is of losing a parent. They need both of you at this time. Each of you has a clear and distinct role to play. Children really can adjust to the separations and transitions involved in two-household parenting. They adjust best when you work together to support each other's relationship with them.

D DEFINITION **Emancipated minor:** Special status of a child with an institution, such as a school, which allows that child to be responsible for him or herself in matters of permission to attend certain events, participate in sports, absences. Juvenile court can also recognize this status.

Children feel more secure when they are confident that their parents can take care of themselves. If they feel you are not doing that, they will try to take care of you, and the parent-child relationship becomes reversed. Therefore taking care of yourself at this difficult time is not only good for you, it is in the best interests of your children.

Critical to good parenting throughout the divorce process is insulating the children from any hostilities between the parents. This means managing your own conflict well. Work toward strengthening your children's sense of security while they navigate their own choppy waters as you separate and divorce. It's a time to be very careful what you say, and to whom you say it. Think your conduct through carefully. It's definitely not a time to introduce a new significant other.

Parenting-After-Divorce Classes

Most Colorado courts now require divorcing parents to attend a class about the impact of divorce. The class is a one-evening or Saturday meeting usually lasting three hours, which costs $35-60 in most jurisdictions. You may apply to have the fee waived if you cannot afford it. You will receive a written order from the court when you file your case, or shortly thereafter, if the class is mandatory, and, if so, how to apply to attend without cost, and who is in charge of filing the certificate of attendance—you or the instructor. If the class is required, the certificate must be in your file before the court will issue a final decree. Some judicial districts require minor children to attend a divorce class for children while their parents are attending their parenting after divorce class.

Parental Responsibility Law

Colorado has a better way of talking about what used to be called "custody" of minor children. It was clear to a great many people for a long time that using the word custody to refer to children implied what lawyers call "possession and control" (as in, "You take custody of the airplane tickets, Dear, I'm afraid I might lose them"). For a long time in this country and in Colorado the legal system did, indeed, use very odd words about where children would live and how they would be cared for after their parents' divorce. The court was said to "award" the children to one or the other parent. One parent would have "legal custody" or the power to make all the major decisions. Or, the parents could elect to share legal custody which meant they were yoked in a double harness on all major decisions: pull together, or pull against each other until everything was at a dead stop and no decisions got made until a mediator, arbitrator or court stepped in. There were no other choices about the power to make decisions.

D DEFINITION **Allocation of Parental Responsibilities:** This term means the manner in which parents agree or courts order that children shall be cared for following a divorce. Correlates to the former term custody.

The law now uses the phrase "allocation of parental responsibilities" to mean the manner in which the court or the parents determine how the children should be raised. Strongly implied in this choice of wording is the idea that the worthy upbringing of children is a responsibility of the parents to the children—a responsibility that the state, in the person of the court, has the mandate to enforce. This is a far cry from the idea that children are a prize to be won by the parents. Most people welcome this change.

P PARTNERS Partners who are parents may go through the court for orders regarding parental responsibilities if you wish. Many partners want to have the formality and official nature of court orders regarding their parenting plan, as well as the opportunity for enforcement if needed. But you may also create your parenting plan and child support arrangements by private agreement. If you go through the court, the Colorado Parental Responsibility law and the Colorado Child Support Guideline will apply. You can go through the court and still do it all by agreement.

"Allocation of decision-making responsibilities" refers to your agreement or the court's order about who decides such things as education, health and religion for minor children. "Determination of parenting time" refers to where minor children will live. When the statute refers to child support, the phrase becomes "residential care." You will need to cover both decision-making and residence of your children in your agreements. The next section concerns decision-making, the following section covers the topic of where the children will live. You will present these agreements to the court at the final decree hearing in the form of a Parenting Plan or Separation Agreement or both. The appropriate forms are referred to in this chapter as each topic is discussed.

Who Will Make the Decisions Regarding Issues that Affect the Children?

This section of this chapter concerns the "allocation of decision-making responsibilities."

It is a generally accepted rule that when the child is with one parent, that parent will make any day to day decisions about the child. Some examples of this would be bedtimes, school vs. sack lunch, dress, hygiene, manners and discipline. Activities which take place only during one parent's time with the child would also be assumed to be the decision of that parent.

What the court concerns itself with are the so-called major decisions affecting the children. The previous law defined these as "major decisions affecting the health, education and general welfare." The new law simply refers to "each issue affecting the child."

D DEFINITION **Allocation of decision-making responsibilities:** This term refers to how parents will make the major decisions about their children. Correlates to the former term Legal Custody. Choices include: one parent makes all these decisions, the parents make them all together, or each major decision-making area or category may be decided differently.

You or the court may list the important decisions you anticipate making about your children and then decide if you will make these decisions together (the law uses the term "mutual"), or if one or the other of you will make them (the law uses the term "individual"). You can mix and match. You may agree to make some decisions together, and turn some decisions over to one or the other of you. An example would be that you decide you will be mutual decision-makers regarding discipline and after-school sports, but that the mother will be the individual decision-maker about health matters and the father about education matters.

The law says that the court should take into account, when considering mutual decision-making, the present ability of the parties to share decision-making about their children and the history of same, and whether such sharing might enhance the contact between the child and both parents. If there is proven child abuse or neglect or spousal abuse then the court is not encouraged to order mutual decision-making unless both parties want to try it.

P PARTNERS If both partners are already on the child's birth certificate, and you want to put your parenting plan and child support arrangement through the court, you would file a Petition for Allocation of Parental Responsibilities. You can do this in full agreement, or have the court decide things for you. To do it yourselves, you will need a parenting plan, as explained in this chapter, as well as child support worksheets as explained in Chapter 9. If one of the partners is the natural father but is not listed on the child's birth certificate, you will need to file a Petition in Paternity along with a Petition for Allocation of Parental Responsibilities. All of these forms are available at Bradford Publishing (www.bradfordpublishing.com).

A provision in the law states that conduct by a parent that does not relate to a child is not germane to a determination of decision-making ability. As with much of family law in Colorado, you are not bound by the considerations the court must take into account, but knowing what might be in the judge's mind is useful as you try to put together a parenting plan that will be approved.

You are not limited strictly to the exact terms used by the statute. If you have an agreement that says you will share certain decisions, or that the wife will make all the major decisions, the court will get the idea.

HOW DO WE DECIDE?

The following questionnaire may help you decide whether you are good candidates to make mutual decisions about your children. Select the six (or more, if you wish to expand the graph) important decisions you believe will have to be made regarding your children—for example, which schools to attend, which doctors to see, which activities and lessons, drivers license, car insurance, birth control.

a.
b.
c.
d.
e.
f.

In the table below, each of you, using different colored pens, answer "Yes" or "No" for each question in the left column regarding each anticipated decision you have listed above.

Parental Decision-Making Questionnaire

Decisions:	a	b	c	d	e	f
1. Can I bear to be left out of this decision?						
2. Must I have veto power over this decision (if I don't agree, it does not happen)?						
3. Is it sufficient that I am consulted about my opinion?						
4. Is it sufficient that I be informed of the decision before the fact?						
5. Do I have to be part of the fact-gathering (interviewing day care providers, pediatricians, checking out ballet school or karate class, visiting colleges, etc.)?						
6. If I'm not part of the decision, am I willing to pay my fair share of the cost?						

Interpreting the Parental Decision-Making Questionnaire

- For any decision about which you both answered "no" to 1 and "yes" to 5, you are probably good candidates to make that decision mutually.
- For any decision about which either of you answered "yes" to 3, 4, and 5, this probably indicates it is acceptable to that parent that the other parent may make that decision individually.
- For any decision about which either of you answered "no" to 1 and "yes" to 2, this probably indicates that the parent will wish to be in charge of that decision individually.

CAN WE DO MUTUAL DECISION-MAKING?

Can parents who could not get along during their marriage really make mutual decisions? The answer to this question depends on whether the mutual decision-making becomes a vehicle for continuing the marital hostilities. In fact, making mutual decisions does not require that you get along, or even that you like each other. It requires respect for each other and maturity—the ability to trust and to cooperate. Ask yourselves whether you can discuss and negotiate fairly with each other, keeping your children's interest utmost.

Research has shown there are some qualities which enable parents to overcome their hostilities and to work together as mutual decision-makers.

Should We – Can We?

For most parents, the issue is not whether you should make mutual decisions about your children after your divorce, the issue is whether you can.

Notes:

CAUTION

Who Is Not (Quite) Ready for Mutual decision-Making?

Parents who have great difficulty making decisions together have many of these characteristics:

- They maintain intense, continuing conflict and hostility which they are unable to divert from the children.
- They exhibit overwhelming anger and the continuing need to punish the former spouse.
- There is a history of physical abuse.
- There is a history of substance abuse.
- One or both maintain a fixed belief that the other is a bad parent.
- One or both is unable to separate his or her own feelings and needs from those of the children.

If any of these apply to you or your spouse, doing mutual decision-making may still be a possibility for you if your determination is great enough, but you will probably require some professional help. There are therapists who specialize in teaching parenting skills. See "Divorce Services and Consultants" in Chapter 2.

Parenting Qualities Chart

Directions: Rate yourselves, and each other, individually and as a team, on a scale of one to ten, ten being excellent, on the following chart using different colored pens.

Mom	Dad	Team	Qualities of Parents who can make mutual decisions
			1. Makes clear to our children that he/she values their relationship and time with self and with other parent, despite all his/her anger and disappointment from the ending of our marriage.
			2. Maintains some objectivity throughout our divorce process, and insulates our children from our conflicts.
			3. Empathizes with our children's point of view, and with that of other parent.
			4. Successfully shifts his/her emotional expectations of the other from the role of mate to that of co-parent, and recognizes the boundaries of the new roles.
			5. Maintains high self-esteem, shows flexibility, and is open to both giving and receiving help from outside sources and especially from the other parent.

Interpreting the Parenting Qualities Chart

- If your evaluations of yourselves and each other coincide, and the estimate of your mutual functioning is 5 or better you are probably candidates for successful mutual decision-making.
- If your evaluation of yourselves and each other directly contradicts, and the estimate of your mutual functioning is 4 or less, then mutual decision-making might be difficult for you.
- If your answers are not consistent, and you still want to try major decisions together, then you've got your work cut out for you. The aspect of the new law that permits you to allocate certain decisions to one of you and other decisions to the other might be just right for you. You would then both stay involved in making decisions about your children, but you would not have to make any decisions together.

HOW TO MAKE MUTUAL DECISION-MAKING WORK

If you have agreed to be mutual decision-makers, it is crucial that you define the decisions which you will make together, and decide the process you will use if you do not initially agree.

Use the following shopping list together to write your Must-Share Decisions List.

Shopping List of Mutual Decisions

1. Any major expense (whether one-time or on-going) which you expect the other parent to share in. "We define a major expense as anything over $__________." For example: your child's teacher says you should enroll him or her in piano lessons and buy or rent a piano in each home.

2. Any activity which will or may take place on the other parent's time. For example: soccer league where the games are every Saturday and you plan on alternate weekends with each parent.

3. Any major change in your basic plan for time you each spend with the children and/or the basic support plan.

4. Choice of private or public schools, or which school.

5. Orthodontia.

6. Mental health counseling.

7. When do your children drive, whose car, and who pays for the extra insurance.

8. The birth control teaching and decisions of your children.

9. In-school electives and activities, whether or not they cost more money.

10. Parent-teacher conferences.

11. Results of medical/dental exams and recommended treatment.

12. **Elective** medical or dental treatment. Be sure you say that either parent is able to sign for **emergency** medical care when the other parent cannot be reached immediately. State that any follow-up care is a joint decision.

Mutual Decisions List

Our list of decisions which we both agree are to be made together.

1.

2.

3.

4.

5.

6.

7.

8.

Any decisions not on this list will be made by the parent who has the children at the time.

You may transfer this list to your Separation Agreement using the sample separation agreement provisions in Chapter 12.

AVOIDING DEADLOCK THROUGH GOOD COMMUNICATION

One key to making your mutual decision-making agreement work is to write out in detail your communication process.

This may sound too silly to work, but it usually does. Some couples find this very helpful at the beginning of their separation. It is up to you. It is also up to you whether you wish to include any of your agreements about process in your final separation agreement.

Communications Process Checklist

Initial

Directions: Discuss each of the following carefully, and decide which, if any, will work for you. Alter them as needed. Initial those statements below which you both agree will work for you.

______ ______ 1. We agree to meet at the same time, same place, for at least 15 minutes a week (every other week, month), whether we have anything earthshaking to report or not. (This will get you in the habit of talking face to face and listening carefully, before you have to do it "for real" when a problem comes up.)

______ ______ 2. We agree that our communication about the children will be only by email or texting until we both agree that we are ready for direct contact. (Note: this method, handy for some, also creates a "paper trail" to minimize who said what and when.)

   ______ ______ We will email acknowledgement of receipt immediately upon receiving an email from the other.

   ______ ______ We agree to respond to the matter raised in the email within ____ hours.

______ ______ 3. We agree to share (or exchange) a written agenda in advance of our meetings. (Big surprises are nearly always unpleasant and difficult.)

______ ______ 4. Each of us agrees to present the issue without our own "pet" solution already in place. Instead, each of us will keep an open mind and suggest a number of options.

______ ______ 5. If we really get stuck on something, we will each produce two alternate plans, solutions, or suggestions which each of us can live with, in the event one's favorite solution does not meet with the other's favor.

______ ______ 6. We agree to rank the three best solutions, any one of which is do-able by both of us, and let the children select.

______ ______ 7. If we agree, we may invite the child in question to the discussion.

______ ______ 8. We agree that unless there is real time urgency, we won't shake hands on the deal on the spot. We will write it up and exchange drafts the next day, then meet again.

______ ______ 9. We agree to suspend discussions until both of us have had time to cool off, if necessary, to gather more data, to get other input, to ask the children. We agree to look past our initial reaction and develop still more alternatives.

______ ______ 10. We agree to together seek the opinion of someone with special knowledge about the problem, such as a teacher, counselor, pediatrician, pastor.

______ ______ 11. We agree to initiate a short-term trial to gain more information and to check out our assumptions. For example: we agree to re-evaluate the school at the end of the semester, or re-evaluate after three sessions with the counselor.

LONG DISTANCE JOINT OR MUTUAL DECISION-MAKING

Can "long distance parents," parents too far apart geographically to meet face to face on a regular basis, be effective mutual decision-making parents? Yes, with great commitment by both parents. In fact, just as time heals much, so also may some significant mileage between the two of you greatly benefit your communication process. Distance may lend clarity and lessen pressure.

Following is some suggested language which you may wish to include in your agreement if you are considering becoming long distance mutual decision-makers. It's up to you whether to include any provisions about long distance communication in your agreement.

1. We will work together to make our list of must-share decisions as clear and well-defined as possible.
2. We agree to develop, at the outset, a communication process or sequence that will work for us, and to stick with it until and unless we both agree to change it. For example: "We will talk by phone until we disagree, then we will exchange our thinking in writing." OR, "We will never call each other on the phone (except in emergency). We will only communicate face to face three times a year."
3. Each of us agrees to present to the other, as early as possible, any question or future decision to be made—even if it might not occur.
4. Each of us agrees that if we get stuck on a particular mutual decision, we will first find a mediator who will work with us via conference call.
5. Each of us will develop a plan for exchanging news and information. Use the mail, e-mail, fax, audio and video tapes, as well as the telephone.

WHAT IF WE CAN'T AGREE ON A DECISION WE AGREED TO MAKE TOGETHER?

Even in the best of communication processes, it is possible to get stuck. If you agree to mutual decision-making, consider including a paragraph in your agreement about what you will do if you really get stuck on one of your major decisions, after you've tried everything you can think of to get unstuck. The court will be reassured to know that you are not agreeing to mutual decision-making because you do not have the stomach to choose between yourselves, and that you will not come back to court every time you cannot agree on a decision. The more confident your agreement

Communications With the Other Parent

Poor: "Jennifer got a scholarship to Europe, so she won't be coming to visit you."

Better: "Jennifer has a chance at a choir trip to Europe for June and July. Unfortunately, it is during your time with her. What do you think?"

Best: "Jennifer is getting so serious at her music, I wonder if we should explore, with her, options for camp, clinics, performance experience. For instance …."

What We Will Do if We Get Stuck:

Directions: Write here what you agree to do if and when you get stuck on a decision you agreed to mutually.

More Communications with the Other Parent

Poor: "Jennifer is going to Europe in June and July. I put down the first payment last night. It's not refundable."

Better: "Jennifer said she would like to consider the Europe trip for this summer, but she doesn't want to miss seeing you or hurt your feelings. Can you give her a call and discuss some alternatives with her?"

Best: "Here is Jennifer's vacation calendar with the dates of the possible Europe trip penciled in. I will see that she has no other activities scheduled for the summer. She also has nothing scheduled for spring break this year. (Spring break for her is _______ to ________.) By the way, parents are allowed to go on the Europe trip. Would you be able to go for all or some of it? I know Jennifer would be thrilled."

Our Information Exchange List

We agree to share with each other the following information about our children:

1.

2.

3.

4.

5.

6.

7.

8.

sounds about how you are going to go about sharing your mutual decisions, the more likely the court is to approve it without question. If you find yourselves in a stuck place, there are some very workable ways to get past it—the following are some sample ideas.

- Assign a "sphere of influence" to each of you as individual decision-makers for times you cannot reach a decision mutually after trying all your agreed-upon deadlock-breaking techniques. For example, mother makes the medical decisions, father makes the educational decisions. This is the alternative specifically contemplated by the new law in permitting parents to select those decisions most important for them to be in charge of.

- Seek input from a person with special knowledge in the area of the decision you are stuck on. For example, ask the school counselor about whether your child should repeat kindergarten.

- Take the particular issue to mediation. A neutral third-party may help you find your solution.

- Choose a third party to make the decision for you. For example, let your priest or pastor decide a question about religion, your child's teacher make the decision about school.

- Take the particular issue to formal arbitration. You will each have the opportunity to argue for your position, and then the arbitrator decides.

INFORMATION EXCHANGE

Whatever mode of decision-making, in every parenting plan there are matters both parents must stay informed about. An Information Exchange List is very useful not only for mutual decision-making plans, but also for keeping peace within individual decision-making plans. The new law specifically protects the rights of any parent who has been allocated parental responsibility, to information about, but not limited to, medical, dental and school records. Following are some suggestions for your consideration.

- If you cannot arrange for the school, pediatrician or dentist to send a copy of everything concerning your children to both of you, then make arrangements for doing this yourselves. Be very specific about who will copy and send what to whom.

- The parent who first learns of an up-coming activity of a child must agree to notify the other parent (by sending a photocopy, by sending an email or text message, by leaving a voice message, or by putting a note in an agreed upon pocket in the children's backpacks).
- Any minor injury or illness which occurs on your time with the children. This is sometimes hard because you worry that it will reflect badly on your parenting. Sometimes having a promise in your parenting plan will make these most difficult phone calls happen.
- Any change in the normal behavior, sleep, eating pattern of a child. These are also often hard calls to make for fear the other parent will take the opportunity to criticize or worse.
- Let the other parent know about any special award, or accomplishment of a child. Sometimes having the child make this call or write this note is a very positive way of reinforcing your commitment to the importance of the other parent to your children.
- If any child repeatedly complains about something in the other home and/or tells of something you consider dangerous or probably untrue you will then immediately call the other parent to verify (with the child in earshot if appropriate).

INDIVIDUAL DECISION-MAKING RESPONSIBILITIES

The parent who has individual decision-making responsibilities makes decisions without having to consult with the other parent or having to reach agreement. Individual decision-making is appropriate when parents cannot or will not work together. Sometimes individual decision-making is a continuation of the way things were during the marriage in that one parent has historically been the decision-maker. Things may change, however, after you get beyond your initial fear, hurt, and anger. Be open to the possibility of wanting to share decisions about your children at a later date.

As individual decision-maker, you may never get a break. You will never be able to say, "Go ask your father/mother." Some people say single parenting is burdensome and lonely—the hardest job on earth. Even mutual decision-makers have feelings of loneliness and being burdened when they realize their former means of communication and decision-making have to change so radically. The individual decision-maker may have to do without any communication at all with the other parent.

Hurtful Mistakes You Can Avoid.

A helpful resource for separating or separated parents is *The 7 Fatal Mistakes Divorced and Separated Parents Make* by Colorado author Shannon R. Rios, MS, LMFT, available at www.healthychildrenofdivorce.com.

Single Parent Overload?

Family counselors, therapists, and parenting consultants and centers can provide counsel and assistance for single parents. Many of them sponsor groups for single parents to provide insight and mutual support, and even family activities. These resources can be helpful to the individual decision-maker who needs psychological and moral support, as well as to the mutual or joint decision-maker who finds the going rough.

The ability to agree to different modes of decision-making for different decisions in the new law should help parents feel less trapped in an all-or-nothing situation. The combination of individual decision-making is a welcome solution for many parents. For example, when Johnny drives and whose car, or what college and who pays can be designated either individual or mutual decisions. Having some shared decisions can be both an act of self-preservation for the would-be individual decision-maker, and an opportunity for the other parent to be involved in shaping the child's life.

One decision that you might want to consider making mutual, even if no other, is the Big Ticket Item. Some examples might be the school band trip, summer camp, first real bicycle. Most parents can't handle this kind of expense alone, but it is often overlooked in the discussion of more obvious future expenses such as orthodontia or medical crises. Agreeing to discuss any elective major expense ahead of time will go a long way toward making the cost a shared expense. You may include this in either the sample separation agreement in Chapter 12 or in JDF 1113.

Where Will the Children Live?

The question of where your children live is now referred to as the determination of parenting time. The number of overnights the children spend with each of you will affect child support by a) determining which worksheet you will use, and b) becoming a direct calculation if it is over 25 percent per year with both parents. A parent who has the majority of overnights per year with a child has some tax advantages. These are discussed in the next chapter and in Chapter 10. Since most parenting is done while the children are awake, you should probably begin with your day-to-day schedules as they are now.

Parenting time, where your children live and when they will live there, can feel like the most important part of your agreement and you can get hopelessly mired in counting overnights. If you find yourselves getting stuck and angry about this issue, then consider the following information:

- Children change as they grow. The agreement you agonize over today may not work a year from now. One of the most important things that changes is how long a child can be away from the primary parent, or from either parent if you have both been active. Small children have an extremely short separation tolerance, sometimes a matter of less than a day for infants.

- Frequent transfers between parents may become stressful once a child is no longer so much in need of frequent contact.

PARENTING TIME AND THE DEVELOPMENTAL STAGES OF YOUR CHILD

Children have different needs at different stages in their growth and development, meaning that they should learn certain things at certain expected ages. It's vitally important in putting together your parenting plan that the developmental needs of your children be met.

Bear in mind that there is no single right way to allocate parenting time. What's right is what works best for all of you. Every family that succeeds in parenting from two households works out a unique schedule that makes sense for both the children and the parents.

Following is a summary of those stages taken largely from *Sharing the Children* by Robert E. Adler, Ph.D which is out of print and difficult to find. See also *Children of Divorce* by Mitchell Baris, Ph.D., and Carla Garrity, Ph.D, a book that is widely used in this state and may well be the text for the parenting class you are required by the court to take.

Early Infancy – Birth to 6 Months:

The developmental tasks at this earliest of stages are physiological stabilization and bonding to one or more parental figures. The baby needs consistent care and nurturing, which includes feeding, diapering, being talked to, played with, held, and cuddled. This care must be consistent and continuous, with responsive caretakers. The number of caretakers should be small—no more than three—settings stable, and routines smooth and predictable.

The predominate opinion of experts used to be that that small children and infants need one home. They recommended that the majority of parenting time be spent with one parent and that the other parent have short, frequent parenting time (rather than longer contacts farther apart). Many recommended that there be no overnights with the other parent until age 2 or 3, or even later. Many authorities now disagree with this saying that small children and infants can do well with overnights and transfers back and forth between parents when both parents are bonded with the child, actively involved, and motivated to have quality parenting time. You will find adamant expert opinions on both sides of this dilemma. Honor who your children are. If they are attached to both of you, develop a parenting plan where they can have quality parenting time, both work and play, with both parents.

D DEFINITION **Determination of Parenting Time:** The term for where children will live between divorcing parents. Correlates to a former term Physical or Residential Custody.

D DEFINITION **Visitation:** Former word for parenting time of the "non-custodial parent."

Our Infant

Our child ____________________ (name) is in the birth to 6 months age range. He/she fits the description given here in the following ways:

He/she does not fit the description given here in the following ways:

BUNKY **"Children, especially very young ones, must be with their mothers."**

This stereotyping is not borne out by the facts. Children need to be wanted. Research shows that single parents of both sexes struggle with the same problems, and young children fare equally well with parents of either gender.

Our 6-18 Month Old Child

Our child __________________ (name) is in the 6 to 18 months age range. He/she fits the description given here in the following ways:

He/she does not fit the description given here in the following ways:

Baby still nursing?

A nursing baby can still have overnights with the father if the mother can provide breast milk, or an alternative milk or formula that you know the baby can tolerate.

"Children need one home. They can't handle the constant back-and-forth of shared parenting time – young children especially."

The facts indicate otherwise. Long-term research shows that most children desperately want loving relationships with two parents, not just one. Be careful of a parenting time arrangement that views parenting time with the one parent as a disruption of the other household.

Some possible parenting time plans for this age:

- One main home. The other parent spends two or three hours, two or three times per week with the child; becomes primary caretaker one or more alternating days per week including, or not including, one or more overnights.
- One or two homes supplemented by high quality day care (no more than four infants per adult). Other parent spends two or more hours, with or without overnights, two or three times each week with the child.

Later Infancy – 6 to 18 Months

The developmental tasks of this age are the deepening of loving attachments to caretakers, development of basic trust and security, and exploring the environment from a secure base. The baby continues to have the same needs as the previous stage, with emphasis on the addition of predictability, familiarity, and a safe environment to explore.

If the infant is well attached to both parents, then contacts can be longer, spaced no farther than two or three days apart. If the infant is not familiar with one parent, caretaking periods by that parent should be short and frequent, as with a younger infant.

Try to match schedules to the child's temperament. An easy child can handle longer times away from each parent and a more flexible schedule; a slow-to-warm-up child may need to stay with frequent, short contacts until older; a difficult child may require even shorter visits on a very predictable schedule. Overnight stays are still likely to be stressful to the child. An easy and adaptable child with motivated and cooperative parents may handle them well, but other infants in less ideal circumstances will probably do better if overnights are not started this early.

Some possible parenting time plans for this age:

- One primary home. The other parent spends from two hours to a day, two to three times per week with the child.
- Same as above with one or more overnights.
- One or two homes plus high quality day care. Schedule as in the first example above.
- Two homes with two bonded, actively involved, motivated parents sharing parenting time and overnights. This arrangement should be considered only for adjustable children and very cooperative parents.

Toddlers – 18 Months to 3 years

The developmental tasks at this age are becoming an individual, autonomy, and safe separation from parents.

The child needs firm support, meaning that the parents, secure and patient, need to set firm limits while allowing the freedom to explore. During the "terrible two's," parents need to allow the child to resist on unimportant issues, but must stand firm when it comes to safety, self-control, and interacting with others. The parents must be attentive monitors at this time. They must have the patience to provide verbal explanations and reassurance, repeated over and over.

The child needs close, consistent, frequent contact with both parents. Longer stays, entire days or overnights, spaced up to three or even four days apart, can be handled by secure, well-adjusted children towards the end of this age range. Entire weekends away from home base may still be too much for children this age. Less adaptable children, or those still not familiar with a parent, may still need shorter, more frequent contacts.

Some possible parenting time plans for this age:

- One primary home. The other parent has the child during the days up to three times per week, on a predictable schedule.
- One primary home. The other parent has the child as above, but with one overnight per week.
- Two homes, or one primary home, plus good day care. Schedule as in either of the two previous examples, or regularly spaced overnights between homes.
- Two homes, with two, three, or four overnights spaced regularly throughout the week.

Our 18 Month to 3 Year Old Child

Our child ________________ (name) is in the 18 months to 3 years age range. He/she fits the description given here in the following ways:

He/she does not fit the description given here in the following ways:

Preschoolers – 3 through 5 Years

The developmental tasks at this age are development of initiative, impulse management, sex role identification, and peer relationships.

At this age the child needs clear parental roles and values, parental cooperation. Children of this age react strongly to parental conflict. They need frequent and continuing contact with the same-sex parent. A child this age should not be encouraged to feel that he or she has driven away the same-sex parent, and that he or she now has a unique relationship with the opposite-sex parent.

Our 3-5 Year Old Child

Our child ________________ (name) is in the 3 to 5 years age range. He/she fits the description given here in the following ways:

He/she does not fit the description given here in the following ways:

The Case of the Reappearing Parent

The parent who has been absent, physically or otherwise, may reappear. A parent who is not interested in babies may be much better at and more interested in parenting an older child. A parent who is excellent with toddlers may be at a total loss with teenagers. Things change. The best parenting plans give the children access to the best of each parent at any given time.

Our 6-12 Year Old Child

Or child __________________ (name) is in the 6 to 12 years age range. He/she fits the description given here in the following ways:

He/she does not fit the description given here in the following ways:

The child needs frequent and predictable contacts with plenty of reassurance, love, and support. Predictability of schedules is at least as important as frequency or duration. Children this age need to know that the divorce is not their fault, and that they don't have the power to undo it.

The pre-school child needs access to nursery school or other settings for stimulation and socialization.

Even during holiday periods, children this age should not go longer than one week without contact with a parent. Longer separations should be supplemented with phone calls.

Some possible parenting time plans for this age:

- Two or three nights at one home, spaced throughout the week, the remaining time at the other home.
- Same as above, but supplemented by good day care.
- Three consecutive days and nights with one parent, four with the other.
- One week with one parent, the next with the other.

School-age Children – 6 to 12 Years

The developmental tasks at this age are to free energy from family concerns in order to focus on friends, school, learning, self-discipline, and cooperative play; to gain a sense of personal competence and self-esteem; to develop logical thought applied to concrete objects; to develop a sense of fairness.

The school-age child needs enough stability and security at home to allow full involvement outside the home, a reasonably well-structured schedule with some flexibility, exclusion from parents' conflicts, and insulation from their negative views of each other.

These children, especially the older ones, suffer when they feel they have to choose between their parents. They may respond with intense anger or by rejecting one parent completely. They need lots of explanation, discussion, being talked to and listened to. They need geographical proximity to and continuity of school and friends. Both parents continuing to live in the same area is an ideal arrangement for this child.

The child this age also needs flexibility. This becomes important as these children develop strong friendships and activities outside the home. Parental insistence on a planned contact at the expense of a much-desired activity can generate resentment.

Contacts with parents can be spontaneous. A parent dropping in on the child, or the child initiating a contact with a parent, can be valuable as long as such contacts do not stir up parental conflict. Particularly for younger school-age children, two weeks without contact with a parent is too long. Longer separations should be supplemented by brief contacts, spontaneous visits, and phone calls.

If parental conflict is low, school-age children can do well with many different parenting time plans, as long as they provide for relatively frequent and adequate contact with both parents.

"When children reach a certain age, they get to choose which parent they want to live with."

There is no age at which the law in Colorado shifts this decision to the child.

Some possible parenting time plans for this age:

- Friday after school through Sunday evening or Monday morning, every other week, plus one or two overnights during the two-week stay with the other parent.
- Three days with one parent, four days with the other.
- Alternating weeks with each parent.
- Alternate weekends with each parent, two or three days at each home during the week.
- Three and a half days with each parent; weekends are also split.
- Two weeks with each parent, with one or two midweek overnights with the other.
- Older children may be able to handle even longer stays, if these are supplemented by phone calls and some contact with the other parent.
- Some parents find it manageable to have the child spend the school year at one home, and the bulk of vacation time at the other. Supplement contact with frequent and regular calls and visits.

Our Teenager

Our child ________________ (name) is in the 13 to 18 years age range. He/she fits the description given here in the following ways:

He/she does not fit the description given here in the following ways:

"Kids can't make it if they go back and forth between very different parents."

Studies show that children can make these transitions with support and preparation from both parents for every transition.

Some experts say that for two households to work well together, they shouldn't be too terribly far apart in value systems. For example, if one parent lives a "laid-back" lifestyle and the other household uses linen napkins, the child may begin to wonder whether to be like Mom or Dad.

Most children can navigate differences in lifestyle as long as neither parent criticizes the other. "Yes, your Mom/Dad does that different than I do. You get to try things both ways. And when you're an adult, you choose which will work best for you and your family."

Teenagers – 13 to 18 Years

The developmental tasks of teenagers include separation, peer involvement, development of own identity, sexual identity, and independence.

The teenager needs emotional stability and maturity on the part of both parents. He or she needs adequate, but flexible and age-appropriate parental controls, and continuing, meaningful contact with both parents.

Schedules must be flexible enough to respect the teenager's need for involvement with peers and independent activities. The level of parent-parent conflict about scheduling should be low.

Parents should be sensitive to a teenager's need to be consulted, informed, and listened to without giving up the adult/child relationship. The teenager needs to be treated as an individual. Teenagers do not need the same extended time with either parent that they once required.

Some possible parenting time plans for this age:

- Home base with one parent, a mixture of scheduled and spontaneous overnights, shorter visits, and outings with the other parent.
- Children spend school year as above; during summer vacation and other long holidays, the situation is reversed.
- For some teenagers, the more structured plans discussed for younger age groups may continue to work, particularly if the parents are geographically close.
- Some families work out year-by-year arrangements with older children. These plans need to respect the teenager's needs for continuity in friendships and school placement, and should always be supplemented with telephone and other contacts as frequently as possible.

MORE THAN ONE CHILD

Although it usually makes sense for all the children to share the same schedule, be open to the needs of each of your children, even to making different arrangements for each child. Infants have special needs for feeding and holding, teenagers for peer involvement and controlling their own lives. The needs of children of these two ages are significantly different from those from 3 to 12 years of age.

Sometimes it's best for one child to live primarily with the mother and the other to live with the father. It is best to have siblings reside together, but if the children are split, then the schedule should allow for times for the children to be together, especially if siblings are very close. Having an older brother or sister along can be important support for a younger child. The second greatest loss during divorce may be separation from their sibling.

Transfer Carefully

Where tensions still exist between parents, it can be better if the children don't have to go directly from one parent to the other (symbolic of the divorce and being "caught in the middle"). Sometimes it's better if one parent takes them to an activity such as school, church, or Scouts, and the other picks them up afterward. This helps avoid any "drama" (parents arguing, child's separation anxiety, etc.) during the transfer.

TIME SHARING

Some parents want equal time sharing when it may or may not be in the children's best interests. For example, infants and very young children may not be developmentally ready for two homes on a 50-50 basis. Others may be deeply injured if they lose contact with one of their parents for more than one day. Young children may be better served by gradually expanding the overnights with the other parent, with a goal of reaching 50-50, or roughly equal time-sharing by a certain age, such as 5, or 6, or 7. A young child may do quite well in equal time-sharing if his or her connections have been strong with both parents, and/or if there is an older sibling making the same transitions on the same schedule. Teenagers, who can do well with equal time sharing, need to have input about where and how they spend their time. Remember, mellow children, even very young ones, can be transferred back and forth a lot, and would suffer greatly from the loss of either parent. For more hyper children, structure and consistency may be more important than frequent contact with both parents.

Developing Your Parenting Time Schedule

Don't expect to know right away what arrangements are going to be best for your children in the long term. Your first plan may not be your final agreement. If you are just starting to work out your parenting plan, you may want to review Chapter 4 about planning your separation.

4-3-3-4 and Alternating Weeks

Florence and Fred separated, within the same neighborhood, when their two children were in first and third grade. They began with a 4-3-3-4 schedule, splitting the children's time equally between them over a two-week period. After 3 months of this schedule, the children asked if they could alternate weeks, rather than splitting each week. The parents made the change.

BASIC SCHEDULE

Most parents begin a discussion of basic schedules by talking about whether it is in their children's best interest, at the present time, to have one home or two. To some parents this means dividing the children's time between Mom's house and Dad's house nearly equally, and having close to a complete set of clothes, toys, and equipment at each home. To others it means the child's bedroom set, bicycle, and computer are located with one parent, and the child carries a backpack with clothes to the other parent's home, and sleeps on a day bed or in a sleeping bag. For most parents, the distinction between having one home

One Home or Two?

We believe our children would (would not) benefit from having two homes at the present time because:

- ☐ All our children look to both of us for day to day parenting.
- ☐ We will live too far apart to make frequent transportation between two households possible.
- ☐ One or more of our children is/are at a stage which makes frequent shifts from one home to another troublesome for them.
- ☐ Two homes are not possible now, because:

  but we anticipate that it will be appropriate for ______________________ (name) by ______________________ (date/age/stage/circumstance).

or two for the children is not so cut and dried. To decide this for yourselves, consider your children's developmental ages, the geographic distance you will be from each other, and your respective parenting styles. Remember that things change. What works today for your family will, in all probability, not work at some later time, perhaps sooner than you expect.

Sometimes, at divorce, one parent has clearly been the major care-giver for the children, and the other has been more distant. Sometimes divorce brings the more distant parent "out of the woodwork" to become a more interested and active parent. Sometimes the less involved parent just wants to fade away. Sometimes the historical major care-giver resents that the other parent wants now, at the end of the marriage, to become a more active parent. If a parent has been distant from the children, it may be in the children's best interests to phase in the changes gradually. Parenting plans do not need to blindly perpetuate the status quo. Divorce is a time of great change for everyone. Getting away from a difficult or destructive marriage often enables people to become better parents.

Realistically, equal or substantial time sharing usually requires that the parents live near each other, optimally within the same school district. In that situation the children really can enjoy having two homes. This is feasible, usually, if the parents live close together—a few minutes driving or access by bicycle or walking.

Parents who live at least a significant distance apart, but still within driving distance, usually look for a weekend arrangement (every weekend, alternating, one or two a month), during the school year, complemented by some other arrangement during the summer. If you don't live in the same area—a judgment call of the parents who must do the traveling—you will need to look at an arrangement that is more appropriate for a long distance. These ideas reflect what appears to work for most people, not hard and fast rules. You must develop what will work for you, your spouse, and your children.

The two-home concept requires a plan for those times when you will transfer the children between you. Following are some of the questions you will need to consider and discuss. Remember, you may have different responses for each of your children. You may want to photocopy this page so that each of you can make notes.

- Is it important for your children to be in the same house on all school nights?

- How important is it that your children settle in on Sunday night before school?
- Is it important for your children to go to the same church with the same parent every week?
- Can either parent take your child to any given recurring activity (soccer practice, Scouts, doctor's appointment)?
- Can your children go to the same school from either home, and return home from their school to either home?
- Is there a maximum amount of time that any of your children can tolerate being away from either of you?
- How frequently do any of your children need to see each of you?
- Do you live so far apart geographically that your children will probably stay with one parent during school sessions and with the other during non-school time?
- Is this the time to change the day care schedule or provider for one or more of the children?
- Is it important to keep your children's day care schedule the same for the time being, in the face of other changes in their lives right now?

Notes:

Our Basic Schedule

Our initial basic time-sharing plan for our children will be:

☐ Alternating weeks

☐ Alternating two-week periods

☐ Alternating months

☐ Alternating semesters

☐ 4-3-3-4 every two-week period

☐ 5-2-4-3 every two-week period

☐ 6-1 each week

☐ 5-2 each week

☐ 4-3 each week

☐ 2-2-3 each week

☐ One of us works a variable shift. We will arrange the children's schedule around this work schedule as follows:

☐ One of us works 24 hours on, 48 hours off. That parent will have all days off with the children, or:

☐ School sessions with one parent, school breaks with the other.

☐ Other:

SIX-WEEK CALENDAR

Fill in your basic schedule for six weeks. This may be any six weeks, or the next six weeks, whichever is more useful to you. On the following page are questions and suggestions.

This calendar ends the week with Saturday and Sunday together, unlike most published calendars which divide the weekend, a picture which is generally confusing for divorcing parents.

Mon.	Tues.	Wed.	Thurs.	Fri.	Sat.	Sun.

Directions for Six-Week Calendar

Fill in the following information on the calendar on the previous page. Make several photocopies first for your rough drafts. Sometimes it is useful to use different colored pens for each parent, or each member of the family.

1. Parents' fixed schedules. For example: work hours, fixed meetings and appointments.

2. Children's fixed schedules, such as school hours, day care, and planned regular activities such as soccer practice, piano lesson, Scouts, doctor's appointments.

3. If you are planning a specific six weeks, fill in the dates you are planning for, and any holidays or other special days, such as a child's birthday.

4. Sketch in your agreement from "Our Basic Schedule." For example, school nights with one parent, vacation nights with the other, alternating weeks with each parent, etc., dove-tailing with the information in 1-3 above.

5. Indicate on the calendar who will provide the transportation each time. The farther apart you live, the more important the transportation issue will become. If you each agree to bring the children to their other parent, you demonstrate your support and willingness for your children to leave you and relate to the other parent.

7. Make a note about any items which must move back and forth with the children, such as clothing, boots, homework, and musical instruments.

Our Important Days

Directions: Circle any of the following which are important to you, using different colored pens for each parent and each child. Be sure to add to this list any other days or events which are important to you to share with the children, such as Bolder Boulder, Russian Easter, St. Lucy's Day, Ramadan, County Fair, or Stock Show.

New Year's	July 4th
Martin Luther King Day	Labor Day
Super Bowl	Columbus Day
Valentine's Day	Rosh Hashana
Presidents Weekend	Yom Kippur`
St. Patrick's Day	World Series
Passover	Halloween
Easter	Thanksgiving
Mother's Day	Hanukkah
Cinco de Mayo	Christmas
Memorial Day	Kwanzaa
Fathers Day	Mother's Birthday
Children's Birthdays	Father's Birthday
Other	

Does the "Year" Start in January or September?

Your list of days might begin with Labor Day and the start of school, rather than New Year's Day and the start of the calendar year. Experience has shown that most parents and children plan in terms of the school year rather than the calendar year.

HOLIDAYS AND OTHER SPECIAL DAYS

Many parents begin by listing all the holidays recognized by their school, church, or wall calendar. They then alternate each of these by odd-or even-numbered years, or some other mathematical formula. When it comes to writing down your shared holidays, it may be easier to say that Mom will have the children for such-and-such holidays in even-numbered years, and Dad in odd-numbered years.

Typically, arrangements for holidays and special days preempt the regular schedule. Your parenting time plan must include agreement about how and when this happens. You may alternate the days themselves as discussed above, or consider one of the following.

Consider merging federal, state, or school holidays including teacher in-service days, which fall on a Monday or Friday with the weekend next to it. If you are doing an alternating weekend parenting plan, these three-day weekends will even out between you over a period of two or three years. If you can tolerate your sharing of holiday time not being equal within a single year, this can work out well in the long run.

Be sure to include on your list those **days which are special to your children.** For example, children typically care much more about Halloween than they do about New Years. Not all children or families feel the same way about the same holidays. These may change as the make-up of your new families changes. If you have any hesitation about where holidays fit on your children's list, ask them. Be prepared for some surprises. It is possible they will list Mother's and Father's Day or your birthdays, but don't be disappointed if they don't.

Most parents alternate the days special to their children year to year. Others agree that one parent has the children on the day itself, and the other parent celebrates the occasion on their next regular time with the children. If your children are small, and/or your relationship easy, you might consider spending these important days together with your children. For example, give a joint birthday party. If sharing the event is not possible, and if your children are old enough, you might try alternating portions of these days—Christmas morning at Mom's, Christmas afternoon at Dad's. For all but the most stable of children, however, this usually results in emotional overload, an exhausted child trying to be cheerful.

Make a parenting time plan for the **long school breaks,** usually summer, winter, and spring, and sometimes Thanksgiving. Many parents try to equalize the time contained in these school breaks over a calendar year. If you have a long distance parenting time arrangement in which the children spend the school year primarily with one parent, these breaks will constitute the other parent's time.

Summer vacation in most of Colorado starts during the first week in June and ends around the last week in August. Most parents agree that the children need to be where they are going to go to school for a few days to two weeks before school starts.

Some parents reverse primary physical care for the summer. In some long distance situations, the children simply travel to the other home and spend the entire summer there. Others continue their regular pattern (alternating weeks, alternating weekends). Some continue their regular pattern, but agree that either parent has the right to take the children on a 2-week vacation during that time, with a certain amount of notice to the other parent. Some parents agree to meet every April or so to make their summer plans.

Where the children will spend the **winter break** and holiday is of great importance in most families, partly because it contains important holidays, and partly because it is a two to six week period in which the children are out of school. Here are some ideas. For short-distance parenting time, some parents remain with their regular weekly schedule.

If the winter break contains an important holiday to you (Christmas, Hanukkah, Kwanzaa) then your planning will probably focus on that holiday. You may specify that the holiday will be spent with Mother in even-numbered years, with Father in odd-numbered years. You may wish to divide the holiday between the parents. For example, Christmas Eve with mother, Christmas Day with father; first half of Hanukkah or Kwanzaa with father, second half with mother. You can then alternate each year if you wish, but you will have to decide at what time the children travel from one home to the other, and who will provide the transportation.

You may divide the entire break into two parts: one parent for the first half, the other for the second, to be reversed for the next year. The two-week break will usually divide December 26th or 27th.

Three-day Weekends

The holidays which we agree to add to or include in the previous or following weekend, including teacher in-service days, are:

Special Handling

We will handle the following holidays in the following special way:

Summer Vacation

Our plans for summer vacation are:

Winter Break

Our plans for winter break are:

Thanksgiving Break

Our plans for Thanksgiving break are:

Spring Break

Our plans for spring break are:

Transporting Our Children

Our agreement about transporting our children between us is:

Thanksgiving break is usually four days, Thursday through Sunday. **Spring break** is usually nine days, starting and ending with a weekend. Many parents just continue their usual schedule, focusing on the holiday itself (sometimes spring break includes Easter). Some parents take part of their vacation during the school break and travel with the children. This is especially true if that parent works in a field in which summer or Christmas is the busiest time of year. For long distance parents, these can be additional times for travel to the home of the other parent.

If you are long distance parents so that the children spend the school session with one of you and school breaks with the other, you may wish to discuss reserving either Thanksgiving or spring break or both for the school year parent.

TRANSPORTATION

If you are a short distance apart, consider the responsibility for driving to be a shared problem. It's usually difficult for one parent to have to provide it all the time, and can, in itself, put an unfair burden on that parent's relationship with the child. Find a way to divide the picking-up and the dropping-off that creates the maximum convenience—or minimum inconvenience—or each of you. Sharing the transportation is a good way to demonstrate that you support the children's relationships with the other parent. The transportation time can be well used to help the children in their transition to the other home.

If you live far apart, then your parenting plan will have to take into account longer travel time for both you and your children. Look at how much time (how many days) make a long distance visit worthwhile.

Pre-school children must have someone travel with them. Airlines do not allow children to travel alone until age 6. (At age 6 children can fly alone, but the parents must make special arrangements and pay a higher rate.) This means that for very young children the parent may do the traveling rather than the children. Some parents share the additional cost by each accompanying the child in the trips to and from the other parent.

Your parenting plan should be clear about who pays for the transportation of the children between you. Travel tickets are more expensive when purchased at the last minute. Be sure to discuss who will pay the cost if the flight is missed, or if plans have to be changed after tickets are purchased and cannot be modified.

How to Tell the Children

How do you tell your children about your separation and divorce? Have both parents there, if possible, and tell the children not only your decision to separate, but also your plan. Help them understand that you are not separating from or "divorcing" them. Tell them that you will always take care of them, no matter what. Tell them how important it is to both of you that you both stay active in their lives. Be concrete with them about your plans.

When appropriate, share your six-week calendar with your children and ask for their input. Listen to their concerns about the mechanics: "Where will my bicycle live?" "How will my ice skates get from one house to the other?" "I only have one computer, how will I do my homework?"

If you can, discuss in advance the physical plans for your separation with the children. Involve them in the doing—take them with you to see possible new apartments or homes so they can participate in the creation of their second home. They will have their own ideas about which toys and books should be at which place, and how they want their spaces to look. You may have to override some of their choices, but they should be allowed to participate and to express themselves, even to carry out some of their wishes in their own way. The older your children, the more likely they are to have their own ideas about what they want out of your divorce, and the more willing they are to let you know about it. Working toward agreement between the two of you without any input from the children sends them the clear message that you do not care what they think. On the other hand, having them part of the negotiations from the beginning is to give them far too much power over the outcome. They, after all, are the children and you are the adults—a fact which is not always evident when the adults are at their craziest.

So, how do you give your children the chance to tell you what they think will work without deferring decisions to them which you must make as parents? Following are some rules of thumb which may help:

- Do a rough cut of the parenting and support plans by yourselves. Discuss what you each think would be acceptable to the children, but do not ask them yet.
- Invite the children to sit with you and read through the rough cut and react to it. Do this with both of you present. You can do it with the children individually if you think they will speak more freely when the other children are not there, but it is

Our Agreement About Telling Our Children

Our agreement about telling our children is:

CAUTION There are some countries which will not admit children traveling with only one parent, without the signed permission of both parents. Likewise, there are some foreign-based airlines which will not allow children in this situation to board their aircraft. Regardless of the nature of your parenting plan or marital status, a notarized statement signed by both parents authorizing any trip is probably a very good idea.

P PARTNERS Parents are parents, whether partners or married. Partner parents need to be cautious and respectful of their children's needs at this difficult time, and find a responsible way to tell them that their parents are moving apart.

usually the reverse. Many mediators are willing to have you do the sharing of your rough cut in a regular mediation session or in a shorter session just for that purpose.

- Be certain when you share your ideas with the children that you listen carefully to what they have to say. Tell them that their ideas are helpful, but that Mom and Dad will make the ultimate decision. If you don't tell them this, they may get upset and feel misled if you don't do everything they've suggested.

- If any child objects continuously to an aspect of your proposed plan, then you may want to consider having that child speak with a therapist, or even have an attorney or special advocate appointed for your child (see Chapter 2, Parenting Consultants). It is possible to listen to the children but not hear what they are saying due to your own need to have them endorse your options. It is possible for the children to not feel free to speak because they feel any request they might make would sound disloyal to one or both of you.

- If the children have chosen their own confidant who is not one of you (such as a grandparent or babysitter) then you may wish to get the children's permission to have their confidant come to a discussion or mediation session instead of them. Sometimes it is easier for children to express themselves second hand.

- If there is a person with a special relationship to the children in addition to yourselves, you may want that person to attend the session when you present the agreement to the children, or to sit in on your early sessions about parenting so that you can begin being mindful of the children's wishes.

Odds and Ends

As you get close to a working draft of your parenting plan, try to have discussions about the following, even if those discussions never find their way into your written agreement:

- Describe what each of you will do to keep and strengthen your children's connection with the departing parent in his or her new home, to minimize any sense of loss or abandonment they may feel.

- What is the role of grandparents and extended family? Should they have fixed parenting times with the children? Will you count it as part of either parent's time?

- What is the role of your own adult friends, especially a live-in relationship, "significant other," or stepparent. The concern here is to what extent this person may do parenting. May this person discipline your children? May this person transport your children between parents? May this person attend parent-teacher conferences, be Scout leader, coach the soccer team, or be a teacher's aide?
- Do you want to make special commitments about religious upbringing?
- Do you want to put in restrictions about not taking the children out of the state or country, for any reason, without written agreement?
- What happens if the children are too sick to change houses? Go to school? Go to day care? Which parent stays home with the sick child? More otherwise excellent parenting plans have been sunk by the omission of this provision than any other.
- How do you handle make up days? What is the procedure for making a one-time change in the time schedule with the children.
- How do you want the other parent to handle it if the children start complaining about something which is going on at your house.
- What do you do if any child shows consistent signs of changes in behavior, stress?

Teeth

Most people worry, from time to time, that they might not completely fulfill their end of the bargain they are negotiating. If your ex has a new lover, will you be less likely to deliver the children on time, or to tell your ex about the teacher's conference? If you re-marry, will conflict between your loyalties to your new spouse and your former spouse interfere with your parental communications with your ex, so that cooperation would begin to break down? In a money crunch, would you try to increase the children's time with you in order to increase child support? Most people would have to answer yes to at least one of these—or, at least admit that the possibility exists they could be tempted.

If you have any doubts about yourself, or some secret doubts about your soon-to-be-ex, then try putting in some creative incentives to follow through with all your agreements about your children. Some examples are: the parent who delays deciding about

CAUTION

Signing for Emergency Medical Care for Your Children

There are still a few emergency care facilities which will require both parents' signatures in mutual decision-making situations, in order to admit children for care and treatment—unless there is a written court-ordered stipulation which says that either parent may sign. Not only should you have clear agreement about this, but you should carry a copy of this agreement with you and give one to your regular pediatrician, day care provider, and school.

Glad We Asked

Matt and Claire were successful in equally sharing their time with their daughter Bonnie for two years after their divorce. When Bonnie was in second grade, however, Claire remarried and moved about an hour away. The distance made the equal sharing unfeasible. They were stalemated until they asked their mediator to find out what Bonnie thought. Bonnie wanted most not to have to spend the summer in day care. That meant spending summers with her Mom, who was not employed outside the home, and the school year with her Dad who was.

Our Agreement About Anticipated Changes and When We Expect Them to Occur

Write here your agreement about when and under what circumstances you expect to discuss changing your parenting plan.

What happens if I want to move away?

A Colorado law passed in 2001, requires that if your child resides with you a majority of the time, and you want to relocate with the child to a "residence that substantially changes the geographic ties between the child and the other party", that you must give the other parent written notice and a proposed revised parenting plan as soon as possible. The notice must tell the other parent where you intend to reside and the reason for the move.

travel dates for the summer pays the additional cost for plane tickets purchased late. The parent who delivers the children late to the other parent becomes responsible for all transportation for the children for the next week, two weeks, or month. You can design baby teeth for minor misses, molars for larger defaults, and even fangs if you need them—but use these last carefully. Giving notice about problems, and flexibility in dealing with them are frequently the best solutions.

These incentives to right behavior are limited only by your imagination. Try having the person against whom the penalty would act set the penalty. You may be surprised to learn what your former partner fears.

Anticipating Changes

Change happens. Your children's needs and yours will change before your children emancipate. Write down the changes you anticipate in the foreseeable future, and commit to them now. Here are several samples, along with two extra spaces to write in your own:

- "We expect our basic time schedule to change for each child when they begin first grade/begin middle school/high school/reach puberty."
- "We expect to discuss changing physical care if one of us moves so far away that regular transportation is no longer possible."
- "We expect to discuss changing decision-making responsibilities if one of us moves back into close proximity to the other and wants to be included in the important parenting decisions."
- We agree that, with mutual consent, we may deviate from our parenting plan as often as we wish. When not in agreement, we will follow our basic plan.
-
-

Where Do We Go From Here?

You have now finished your first rough look at your parenting plan. It will probably not be your final version. Go on to the next three chapters about the other essential components of your separation agreement. The agreements you reach as a result of each of those chapters may necessitate changes in your parenting plan.

Take heart. Doing your own separation agreement is hard work. Don't expect to get it all done in one sitting. Don't even expect to complete the work of one of the separation agreement chapters in one sitting. Now might be a good time to take a break, relax, and reread Chapter 3, Taking Care of Yourself. Give yourself and each other the time you deserve to make the best decisions for both of you and your children.

Even though it takes work, remember that a well thought out parenting plan that you create *together* will be a better fit for you, your children, and your circumstances. It will reduce conflict and be easier to follow than one imposed upon you by a judge, magistrate or any non-related third party. Your efforts will be worth it, and in the best interests of your children.

You may wish to immediately transfer your agreements about parental responsibilities, as you agree to them to JDF 1113, or draft your own parenting plan using the checklists throughout this chapter and the sample separation agreement provisions concerning parenting in Chapter 12.

Parenting Plan Checklist

Directions: Use this outline to check off each element of your parenting plan as you complete it.

I. Decision Making

- ☐ A. List the mutual decisions.
- ☐ B. List the decisions each of you will make individually.
- ☐ C. Spell out areas for consultation before individual decision making, if any.
- ☐ D. Spell out areas for information exchange.
- ☐ E. Dispute Resolution
  1. Spell out your agreements for communication and process.
  2. Spell out your agreements about what to do to avoid and resolve deadlock, and what you will do when you find yourselves stuck.
  3. State your more formal dispute resolution mechanism (if any) that you wish to have in place as a condition before either of you may take a matter to court.

II. Parenting Time

- ☐ A. State the pattern of parenting times you will start with.
- ☐ B. State your exceptions to A., if any, for holidays and vacations.
- ☐ C. State who will provide and pay for the transportation of the children between parents.

III. Odds and Ends

☐

IV. Teeth

☐

V. Anticipated Changes
State what, if anything, you will look at to determine whether that pattern needs to change in the future.

☐

Notes:

CHAPTER **9**

CHILD SUPPORT SEPARATION AGREEMENT – PART III

Page

CHILD SUPPORT
SEPARATION AGREEMENT – PART III

Before the court can give you a final decree of dissolution of marriage or legal separation, you must resolve and write out all the financial and parental issues remaining from your marriage. This written summary is called the separation agreement, whether you are obtaining a divorce or a legal separation. It must be read and approved by the court.

The introduction to Chapter 7 lists the things you need to do to prepare your separation agreement and directs you to the chapters with information necessary to accomplish this. This chapter discusses child support and its part in your separation agreement.

Chapters 10 and 11 cover ways in which you can save tax dollars by using maintenance to pay some family expenses. Chapter 11 also discusses the tax consequences of a divorce with children. These are consequences which will result with or without your planning for them, so it is wise to understand how to make them work for you.

Chapter 13 covers ways to enforce your child support agreement after your decree, and how to modify or amend your agreement when circumstances of you or your children change, as they undoubtedly will.

The Colorado Child Support Guideline

Child support in Colorado is defined by the *Colorado Child Support Guideline*, an adaptation of the Shared Incomes Model, one of several models suggested by a federal child support task force in 1985. The *Colorado Child Support Guideline* presumes that divorcing parents will share the support of their children in the proportion of their individual gross (before tax) incomes to the family gross income. The Guideline then sets, and therefore presumes, a certain minimum dollar amount which the parents, together, are expected to spend on the basic needs of their children (housing, food, clothing—these are also a presumption). This minimum amount appears in a schedule which is part of the Guideline. All these presumptions are rebuttable, that is, they can be overcome by evidence to the court that the presumption should not apply in this particular family. In practice, however, the presumptions are adhered to in nearly every instance. This does not mean that divorcing parents should cease to bargain about how they will support their children. You will both have to

BUNKY

"Child support is cut and dried. You have to pay whatever the chart says."

Colorado does have a formula-based child support statute, which tells you how much must be paid by parents to cover certain expenses for their children. However, for most couples there is some latitude in how you apply your facts and circumstances to the Guideline as well as questions for some about additional expenses for the children that the Guideline doesn't cover.

D DEFINITION

Retroactive Child Support

While this chapter is about arriving at an agreement about child support to take you into the future, the law also provides that you can reach an agreement about what either of you may owe the other for past child support. You may, if you wish, determine an amount one of you owes the other for past child support, going back to the date of your physical separation or the date of the filing of the petition or service upon the respondent, "whichever is latest," says the statute. You do not need to prepare a child support worksheet for this. Once you have a total for retroactive support that you both agree on, you can pay it now, put it in with all the other items in your property settlement, or decide on an interest rate and an amount for monthly payments. In this last case, it will be shown on the Support Order which accompanies your Decree.

live with the decisions you make here for a long time. The more the decisions are truly yours, the more likely they are to work for you and your children.

This chapter does the following:

- helps you sort your children's expenses into basic, regular additional, and unpredictable additional expenses.
- helps you sort your respective incomes, actual and potential, regular and irregular.
- invites you to make your own agreements about how you want to support your children, both in dollar amounts and in terms of process between you.
- works through the *Colorado Child Support Guideline* showing you how to implement your own plan for supporting your children within the framework and spirit of the law.
- helps you deal with the problem if the Guideline results are too different from your own sense of fairness to your children and yourselves.
- suggests some built-in enforcement techniques to make sure your plan is followed, and discusses the enforcement techniques required by the guideline.

Children's Expenses

In Colorado, divorcing parents are directed by the Guideline to divide between them all the expenses of their children in proportion to their incomes. For example, the parent who has 60% of the family income is to pay 60% of all the costs of rearing the children—regardless of how you have allocated decision-making or parenting time (number of overnights).

There are two categories of expenses of rearing children to which this proportion applies: basic expenses and extraordinary ones. **Basic expenses** include housing, basic food, basic clothing, and may include regular transportation, school lunches, ordinary medical and dental expenses, allowances, and other customary expenses which the parents expressly include. The *Colorado Child Support Guideline* does not leave you any room for choices about the amount you both, together, are presumed to spend on the basic expenses of your children. The Schedule of Basic Child Support Obligations sets this amount. Your choice is how many of your children's expenses you believe are included.

PARTNERS

Partners who put their parenting plan and child support arrangements through the court will need all the information in this chapter. If you have decided not to put the matter through the court, this chapter will help you to discuss and outline the present and future financial needs of your children.

CAUTION

If there is a significant difference between your incomes now, and especially if there will be in the foreseeable future, you should read Chapter 10, Maintenance, and Chapter 11, Taxes before proceeding, to save money as a family with tax planning through maintenance.

BUNKY

"We'll just plug our incomes into the Guideline, and it will tell us what we should do for our children."

You can do it this way if you wish, but the result may be neither payable by one or both of you, nor sufficient for your children's needs. In addition, you are far more likely to carry out a support agreement which you have carefully evolved yourselves, rather than simply obeying a number from a schedule.

DEFINITION

Potential Income: An amount of income attributed to a voluntarily unemployed or underemployed parent for purposes of calculating child support. You can estimate it by "determining that parent's employment potential and probable earnings level based on his or her recent work history, occupational qualifications, and prevailing job opportunities and earnings levels in the community." In other words, what has the parent earned, doing what, can he or she earn it now, here?

The cost of raising children is not limited to those items usually presumed to be covered by the basic child support obligation. **Extraordinary expenses** are those beyond the basic. They are set by the parents, and will vary with each family.

Some typical expenses beyond basic needs are:

- For infants: special clothing, diapers and perhaps diaper service, special foods, well-baby medical visits, and certainly more expensive day care or babysitting as very few services will take infants, and many will not take children who are not yet toilet trained.
- For toddlers and pre-school children: usually full-time day care, immunizations.
- For school-age children: school supplies, school trips and activities, additional school clothing, lessons, activity fees, special clothing and equipment, organization fees and costs.
- For teenagers: car and car insurance, birth control, advanced lessons and clinics, more expensive activity fees, special clothing including shoes and equipment, and graduation expenses.

Gifted and talented children create additional costs. Special-needs children (handicapped, developmentally or educationally delayed, ill, injured, or emotionally troubled) are more expensive still.

Now you are ready to make some decisions for yourselves about how you want to support your children.

You may handle the additional expenses of your children in one of two ways. You may deal with each one as it comes up, or you may estimate them now, arrive at a monthly average, and add this average monthly amount to the basic support. You may choose a different method for different expenses. If you choose to make them part of the regular monthly support payment, you will list them on the appropriate child support worksheet.

The worksheets specifically include four "extraordinary" expenses: work-related child care, education-related child care, health insurance premiums, and extraordinary medical expenses. A space is also provided or additional expenses agreed to by the parents or by court order. Listing an additional expense on the worksheet has three results:

D DEFINITION **Basic expenses:** Those costs of rearing children which the State of Colorado includes in the Basic Support Obligation which it sets for divorcing parents. Usually assumed to include: housing, food, most clothing, and perhaps ordinary medical and other day to day costs.

Our Children's Basic Expenses

Directions: Complete the following sentence using the name of each expense, not the amount.

We agree that the basic expenses for our children are housing, basic food, basic clothing, and:

D DEFINITION **Extraordinary expenses:** Any costs of rearing children which the parents do not define as being included in the Basic Support Obligation from the Schedule. The worksheets name four, and the Guideline lists several more. Parents need to evolve their own list of these to be sure everything is covered.

CAUTION **Expensive Money**

Child support is paid in after-tax dollars. This is expensive money. It can be unnecessarily costly. It is possible to pay some of your children's expenses, especially the extraordinary ones, with pre-tax dollars by having the higher income spouse include these amounts in maintenance (alimony, spousal support, section 71 payments) to the lower income spouse. Therefore, if you are or might be considering maintenance in your separation agreement, read Chapters 10, Maintenance and 11, Taxes before proceeding further with child support.

Our Children's Regular Additional Expenses

We agree that the following expenses for our children are not included in the basic amount on the schedule, are foreseeable and can be quantified monthly:

- ☐ School expenses $______
- ☐ Private school tuition $______
- ☐ Religious training $______
- ☐ Transportation between parents (especially long distance) $______
- ☐ Gifts to and from the children $______
- ☐ Sports: including fees, special clothing, equipment $______
- ☐ Music and art: including lessons and equipment $______
- ☐ Clubs $______
- ☐ Scouts $______
- ☐ Travel $______
- ☐ Tutoring $______
- ☐ Special education $______
- ☐ Automobile: payments, insurance, fuel and maintenance $______
- ☐ Camping $______
- ☐ Family activities $______
- ☐ Summer camp, activities and programs $______
- ☐ Regular babysitting, other than work-related (parent at school, meetings, etc.) $______
- ☐ Chronic medical, dental, mental health (insulin, medication, braces, counseling) $______
- ☐ Infant expenses (shots, well-baby checkup, equipment) $______
- ☐ Other $______

- it fixes that expense, usually an average of this cost over a year or half year. If the expense varies greatly, you will sometimes have too much money and sometimes too little to pay the expense that month. Day care, for instance, varies greatly between school year and summer.

- it requires you to share it proportional to your incomes. There is no opportunity on the worksheet to share something 50/50 even if you believe that is fair, if that is not the proportion of your incomes.

- it makes enforcement easier. The final amount of child support becomes a support order (see Chapter 12) which streamlines collection procedures.

Any extra expense for your children which you do not list on the worksheet:

- can be shared in any proportion you choose;

- can be shared between you as it is incurred instead of estimating it ahead of time, allowing you to adjust for the unexpected and the irregular (such as a broken leg, or summer band camp);

- requires more communication between you on an on-going basis;

- is not as readily enforceable (see Chapter 13).

Sometimes an extra expense is not known at the time of the divorce and can not be included on the child support worksheet. It is therefore a good idea to make some agreement about these future unknown expenses. Most people make an agreement that any extraordinary expense for their children which is not on the worksheet must be agreed to by both parents ahead of time (except emergencies), and paid in a certain percentage. Sometimes parents agree that a certain category of expenses will be paid in one percentage and another category in another percentage. For example, medical expenses may be paid in proportion to the parents' income, but special activities may be paid 50/50.

Joe and Sandy

Joe earns a salary plus commission, plus a performance bonus. Sandy earns a salary plus interest from an investment. The children live with Sandy most of the time. They agree to base their basic support on their salaries, and their regular additional expenses on 70% of Joe's average commissions and 70% of Sandy's interest income. Joe may pay the additional expense amount quarterly in advance, to allow for the fluctuation in his commissions. They agree to put an agreed upon percentage of his remaining bonus and her interest income, when received, into a college and emergency fund for their children. Joe and Sandy are basing regular monthly payments on regular monthly income. They are paying periodic expenses with periodic income, and extraordinary expenses with extraordinary income.

Extraordinary Expenses of Your Children

The Colorado Child Support Guideline specifically anticipates four categories of additional expenses for your children: work-related child care, education-related child care, health insurance premiums, and extraordinary medical expenses. They are referred to as "Adjustments" on the worksheet forms.

WORK/EDUCATION RELATED CHILD CARE

Work/education related child care is defined as care for children which is necessary to enable a parent to go to work, search for a job or (in Colorado) obtain an education. It does not apply to babysitting for a parent's social life or other activities. It does include before and after school care if the parent's work or school day extends beyond the child's school day. Education-related child care is a Colorado tax credit only, is not subject to a Federal tax credit, and is shown separately on the worksheet.

The Child Support Guideline recognizes that the expense of work-related child care is mitigated somewhat by a Federal tax credit which refunds to the "custodial" parent from 20% to 35% of the amount paid, for work-related *(but not education-related)* care of the first two children. It is the after-credit amount of this child care cost which is shared between the parents in proportion to their incomes. The amount which goes on the child support worksheet is the net amount (the amount you actually spend minus the credit). Be sure you read Chapter 11 Taxes, to learn how either of you can qualify for this credit.

There is no child care credit if you pay your children's work-related child care through a cafeteria or flex plan at your work. A cafeteria or flex plan allows the employee to pay child care and family medical expenses with pre-tax dollars that are withheld by the employer and escrowed or held in trust for the benefit and use of the employee and his or her family. The child care credit effectively does the same thing, by returning the tax money already paid on dollars used to pay for work-related child care. You can use one or the other.

Federal Child Care Credit Table

Adjusted Gross Income	Appropriate Percentage	Maximum Allowed Credit for One Child	Maximum Allowed Credit for Two or More Children
Up to $15,000	35%	$1050	$2100
15,001-17,000	34%	1020	2040
17,001-19,000	33%	990	1980
19,001-21,000	32%	960	1920
21,001-23,000	31%	930	1860
23,001-25,000	30%	900	1800
25,001-27,000	29%	870	1740
27,001-29,000	28%	840	1680
29,001-31,000	27%	810	1620
31,001-33,000	26%	780	1560
33,001-35,000	25%	750	1500
35,001-37,000	24%	720	1440
37,001-39,000	23%	690	1380
39,001-41,000	22%	660	1320
41,001-43,000	21%	630	1260
Over, 43,001	20%	600	1200

Directions for calculating your child care credit: Locate your income bracket in the first column. Multiply the percentage next to it times the amount you actually paid for work-related child care. If your result is less than or equal to the amount in the third or fourth column (depending on the number of children you have in child care), then your result is the amount of your credit. If your result is greater than the number in the table, then the number in the table is the amount of your tax credit. IRS Form 2441, which you must include with your tax return in order to take the credit, can also help you calculate the amount of your credit.

Example: Vanessa, whose adjusted gross income is $9,500, has two children in work-related child care, for which she pays $550 per month. $550 × 12 = $6,600 per year. 35% × $6,600 = $2,310 which is more than the maximum allowed at her income level for more than one child. The amount of Vanessa's tax credit is therefore $2,100.

CAUTION

Remember that the Automatic Temporary Restraining Order that went into effect when you filed your case forbids either of you to cancel the existing insurance for your children or each other.

Our Children's Irregular Expenses

We anticipate the following irregular expenses may occur for our children. (List average monthly amount at right.)

One-time major purchases (full-size bed, bicycle, skis,):

Description $

Special events (birth, graduation)

Description $

Other

Description $

HEALTH INSURANCE COVERAGE FOR YOUR CHILDREN

The divorce statute requires you to maintain health insurance for your children, and to bring proof of coverage to your final hearing. You will each list the amount, if any, you pay as premium for the children on the worksheet. On Worksheet A, if the parent who pays child support also pays the insurance premium, his or her child support payment will be reduced by the amount of the premium. If the parent who pays child support is not the parent who also pays the insurance premium, the child support amount will be reduced by his or her percentage share of the premium. Worksheet B proportions the insurance premium between you, regardless of who makes the payment.

Colorado statutes are clear about the importance of health insurance for children. Any company which is covered by E.R.I.S.A. (Employment Retirement Income Security Act of 1974), the same group covered by QDRO'S and COBRA, **must** extend insurance coverage to the child of an insured employee **even** if a) the child does not live with the insured employee, b) the insured does not claim the child as a dependent exemption, or c) a request for payment is made by the other parent (who is not insured). This amendment also requires increased notice and information be provided to the parent who provides physical care, if not the insured, and extends coverage to adopted children, or children placed for adoption, under 18 years of age.

EXTRAORDINARY MEDICAL EXPENSES

The Colorado Child Support Guideline defines "extraordinary medical expenses" as "uninsured expenses, including copayments and deductible amounts, in excess of $250 per child per calendar year." These include, but are not limited to, "such reasonable costs as are reasonably necessary for orthodontia, dental treatment, asthma treatments, physical therapy, vision care, and any uninsured chronic health problem." It may also include "professional counseling or psychiatric therapy for diagnosed mental disorders." You may want to re-define for yourself the meaning of extraordinary medical expenses to include some or all of the following:

- Your insurance deductible—the amount you pay out each fiscal year per person or per family before the insurance starts paying.

- Copayment – the amount you pay up-front on HMO (health maintenance organization) type plans and/or the amount you pay after the insurance has paid for medical expenses—80/20% on many plans—usually 50/50% on mental health and dental, if covered.
- Payment for injuries or illnesses not covered by the insurance or over the limit for that particular kind of illness/ injury.
- Well-child care, inoculations, preventive care—unless you included this in your definition of basic expenses.
- Alternative treatments and healing such as chiropractic, acupuncture, massage, holistic healing.
- Ordinary dental expenses including cleaning—unless you included this in your definition of basic expenses.
- Eye exams and glasses.
- Counseling.

OTHER EXTRAORDINARY EXPENSES

Because the guideline specifically lists only four extraordinary expenses, this suggests to some people that there aren't any additional expenses beyond those named. For most parents, however, there are many others, as you will discover working through this chapter. The worksheets provide a place for you to include other, regular extraordinary expenses for your children. If you have agreed to include additional expenses for your children in the monthly support amount, you will list them on your worksheet.

Your children probably will have extraordinary expenses which are neither regular nor predictable enough to put on a worksheet. You will need your own agreement about how you will pay these. The Child Support Plan Questionnaire on the following page will help you do this.

Organizing Parents' Income and Children's Expenses

Dividing your income and children's expenses into the categories on the following Child Support Plan Questionnaire will help you decide which income will be used to pay which expenses. Being clear about this will help you remember expenses you are apt to forget, and not count on income you may never see.

Colorado Child Care Tax Credit

Colorado has a tax credit for work-related child care, which is a percentage of the amount of your federal tax credit.

Federal Adjusted Gross Income	Appropriate Percentage Of Your Federal Child Care Credit
Up to and including $25,000	50%
$25,001-$35,000	30%
$35,001-$60,000	10%
$60,001 and over	0%

As of this writing, this state income tax credit does not affect the calculation of child support under the Colorado Child Support Guideline.

These percentages may be adjusted if the State has surplus unallocated revenues from the previous year. Watch for the instruction book with your State tax forms to tell you that year's percentages. Or, you can ask your tax preparer.

See Chapter 11, Taxes, for who may claim the child care credit. You may not both claim this credit for the same child.

Maintenance Changes Child Support

Maintenance shifts before-tax (gross) income from one spouse to the other, therefore altering each parent's percentage share of child support. The result is that as you phase in maintenance the child support goes down, and a larger portion of the money being paid between spouses is labeled maintenance. This can be helpful, because paying maintenance instead of child support, where feasible, can reduce your total taxes.

Child Support Plan Questionnaire

Directions: Discuss the numbers/amounts you gathered and summarized on the income section of your Sworn Financial Statements and Budgets in Chapter 6, and the lists of your children's basic and extraordinary expenses in this chapter. Then write down the answers to the following questions:

1. What income for each of you do you want to use in determining the amount of basic child support? All your income from every source (Total Monthly Income on the Financial Statement)? Only income each receives regularly (base pay, retirement benefits, business income minus expenses)? Additional income (overtime, tips, bonuses)? Occasional or uncertain income that may not be long-term (interest and dividends, workers' compensation benefits)? Read the definition of income and potential income from the *Colorado Child Support Guideline* on page 268, the page just before the Schedule of Basic Child Support Obligations, at the end of this chapter. You do not need to include income from additional jobs that result in employment more than 40 hours per week or more than would be otherwise be considered full time employment. Describe the source of these incomes for each of you and estimated amounts:

   The more income you put on the guideline worksheets, the higher your support order for basic expenses.

2. Do you want to estimate all the foreseeable additional expenses for your children, average them monthly, and then apply the guideline formula so that they are pre-paid monthly between you? Which expenses would you include? List those expenses, averaged monthly, which you agree to pay or pre-pay monthly between you, and their estimated amount:

   The more additional expenses you put on the guideline worksheet, the more money is paid by one of you to the other under the support order.

3. Are there any expenses for your children which you cannot estimate monthly, or which you do not want to pre-pay between you monthly?

   a. If so, what are these expenses? List them, and the estimated amounts:

   Any expense you do not list on the worksheets, but which you identify and agree to, may be shared as it arises, in any proportion you feel is fair. It is not included in the support order.

   b. How are you going to handle the occasional expenses in #a (example: proportional to income, 50-50, 60-40, one of you pays all)?

4. Have you set aside some occasional or irregular income sources with which to pay these occasional expenses? (Example: annual performance bonus, sale of stock). If you have an agreement about this, write that agreement here.

Schedule of Basic Child Support Obligations

Having examined together what income you will use to pay which of your children's expenses, you may now use this information to figure your child support arrangement using the Colorado Child Support Guideline.

The centerpiece of the Colorado Child Support Guideline is the Schedule of Basic Child Support Obligations which is printed at the end of this chapter. The schedule contains the percentage of parents' combined gross incomes which the guideline expects them to pay for their children's basic needs.

The amounts in this schedule vary from about 9% to about 22% for one child, and from about 13% to about 32% for two children, in a curve, with the highest percentages reached before $1000 per month combined incomes and decreasing to the highest income. These percentages are based on actual cost-of-living studies of Colorado families.

The studies found that lower income families spend a higher percentage of their family income on the basic expenses of their children than higher income families. In addition, a parent whose income is below a certain level, but does not have primary physical care, has expenses for basic living like housing and food that requires more of that parent's income to be retained and less paid in child support. To address this, the Colorado legislature enacted a low-income adjustment for a paying parent with a monthly adjusted gross income between $850 and $1850.

The basic support amount fixed by the schedule increases with the number of children, but not in strict arithmetical increments. The schedule recognizes that the second child does not cost as much as the first—that there are some basic expenses incurred with one child which are not incurred again with additional children. Therefore, although the amount on the schedule increases with each additional child, it does not double for the second, or triple for the third, etc. This is an important concept to remember as you bargain about changes in support as each child goes to college or emancipates.

If the parents each have the children with them more than 92 overnights per year, the amount on the schedule is multiplied by 1.5, since the same studies show that children are 50% more expensive to maintain in two full homes (in contrast with one primary home and a place to visit).

Incomes Above the Guideline Levels

If your combined monthly adjusted gross income is greater than $20,000 ($240,000 per year), the highest level given in the Guideline, work through this chapter and complete the checklists to assist you in defining the actual costs of your children, as well as your incomes and budgets (Chapter 6), as foundation for coming to agreement about child support. You can skip the sections that relate directly to the Guideline Schedule and the worksheets, because you will not have to prepare a worksheet. Many in this situation do prepare a worksheet, however, by extrapolating (using percentages) from the $20,000 level of the Guideline, to get their child support number. Some then reduce that somewhat, since the cost of rearing children does not necessarily increase at the same rate as the parents' incomes.

When the court decides these cases, the law presumes that the children cannot cost less than the Basic Child Support Obligation given in the Guideline for a combined $20,000 monthly income.

Adjustment for Incomes Under $1850 Per Month

If the parent with the lesser number of overnights per year has a monthly adjusted gross income between $850 and $1850, he or she may be eligible for a Low-income Adjustment on Worksheet A. See the second page of that worksheet to calculate whether this applies to you.

Incomes of $850 or Less

In circumstances where the parents' combined monthly adjusted gross income is $850 or less, the Guideline requires a minimum of $50 in child support from the paying parent, regardless of the number of children. And, if the paying parent's monthly adjusted gross income, by itself, is less than $850, the Guideline will require a $50 monthly child support payment, again regardless of the number of children. One's earnings may be in this range for any number of reasons, including working part time for minimum wage, and going to school.

The Guideline expects parents to be responsible for the amount on the schedule in proportion to their gross incomes. For example, if the father's income is 60% of the family income, and the mother's is 40%, then the father pays 60% of the basic costs of the children, and the mother pays 40%. The Guideline helps you determine potential income if one or both of you is unemployed or underemployed. There are almost no circumstances under which a parent would have no financial responsibility for his or her children.

The guideline requires you to prepare and file at least one worksheet with your separation agreement if you have a minor child, or an unemancipated child. There are two worksheets:

- Worksheet A – Used when one parent has the children living with him or her more than 273 overnights per year.
- Worksheet B – Used when both parents have the children living with them more than 92 overnights per year. The statute refers to this as shared physical care.

When there are different children in different parenting plans, then you may be using more than one worksheet. The statute refers to this situation as split physical care. Here are several illustrations of which worksheet to use for a family with four children.

1. One parent has all the children more than 273 overnights per year. Use one Worksheet A.
2. All the children spend the same amount of parenting time with both parents, which is more than 92 overnights per year with each. Use one Worksheet B.
3. Each parent has more than 273 overnights per year with one or more children. Do two Worksheets A.
4. Each parent has more than 273 overnights per year with one child, and they have shared physical care of the other two. Use two Worksheets A, and one Worksheet B.
5. One parent has two children for more than 273 overnights per year, and they have shared physical care of the other two. Use one Worksheet A and one Worksheet B.

If you are using more than one worksheet because your children are in different parenting arrangements, remember that the Schedule of Basic Child Support Obligations is weighted for the first child in each home, while the increments between the first and second child and on up are all the same.

BUNKY

"The child support schedule will tell us how much we have to spend on our kids."

Not quite. The schedule estimates your children's basic minimal monthly expenses: housing, ordinary clothing, ordinary food, and ordinary medical. As you know, your children cost more than this. You must decide which expenses are not included in the amount on the schedule and how you will share them.

Worksheets A and B will do four things:

a. Establish the Basic Support Obligation from the schedule based on your combined gross incomes. Income may be "potential" as discussed in this chapter.

b. Allocate the duty to pay the Basic Support Obligation between you in proportion to your gross incomes. Worksheet B also takes into account the number of overnights being spent with each parent.

c. Allocate between you, in proportion to your gross incomes, any "extraordinary" (additional) expenses which you choose to list on the worksheet. These are not affected by the number of overnights.

d. Provide a recommended child support amount which will be approved by the court unless you ask for and receive a deviation from that amount.

The following outline frames the approach to support of children taken in this chapter. Read this as a summary, a map, and come back to it if you get lost.

HOW TO MAKE THE *COLORADO CHILD SUPPORT GUIDELINE* WORK FOR YOU

The underlying presumption of the *Colorado Child Support Guideline* is this: divorcing parents should support their children in the proportion each parent's income is to the family income.

A. Determine the gross (before tax) incomes of each parent. See Definition of Income in this chapter.
   1. Use potential income if either parent is unemployed or underemployed, with some exceptions.
   2. Use business gross income minus necessary business expenses for the self-employed.
   3. Decide how you are going to treat irregular or uncertain income.

B. If you pay or receive maintenance for a previous marriage, or have agreed to maintenance for this marriage, you can add/subtract that amount from your gross incomes. If you pay support for a child from another marriage or relationship, you can subtract this from your gross income. See the instructions for the worksheet for restrictions to these adjustments. Adding or subtracting these to your incomes in A will result in an adjusted monthly gross income.

C. If your monthly adjusted gross income is between $850 and $1850, and you have fewer overnights, you may qualify for a low-income adjustment on Worksheet A. Use the Low-income Adjustment worksheet on page 2 of the form to see if this applies.

D. Decide for this family which expenses will be included in the basic support (all clothing? all food? basic medical? transportation? etc.).
   1. If the children live with one parent for 273 overnights or more per year, then assume these expenses are being incurred in that home.
   2. If the parents both have parenting time of more than 93 overnights per year, then assume these expenses are being incurred by both parents in proportion to their time with the child. Verify that this is so. If not, note where this is not true for you for a later discussion of possible deviations from the Guideline. See "Brenda and Bob" example, later in this chapter, for how this works.

E. Agree which expenses for the children in this family are not covered by the basic support obligation from the schedule. Include all such expenses presently incurred by either parent.
   1. Find and write down those expenses which are predictable and regular.
   2. Discuss those expenses which are neither predictable nor regular.

F. Decide how many of the predictable and regular expenses for the children are to be shared between the parents in proportion to their incomes. Average these per month.

G. Decide which, if any, of the predictable and regular expenses for the children are to be shared between the parents in some other proportion. (This is counter to the presumption on which the Guideline is based, so be prepared to explain your reasons.)

H. Discuss how unpredictable and irregular expenses are to be handled and paid. (The presumption is that you will share them in proportion to income at the time of the expense.)

Once your agreements about the items on this page are clearly spelled out between you, the arithmetic on the worksheets will make sense.

☐ District Court ☐ Denver Juvenile Court
______________________________ County, Colorado
Court Address:

☐ **In re the Marriage of:**
1 ☐ **In re the Parental Responsibilities concerning:**
____

Petitioner:

and
Co-Petitioner/Respondent:

Attorney or Party Without Attorney (Name and Address):

Phone Number: E-mail:
FAX Number: Atty. Reg. #:

▲ COURT USE ONLY ▲

Case Number:

Division: Courtroom:

WORKSHEET A—CHILD SUPPORT OBLIGATION: SOLE PHYSICAL CARE

	Children	Date of Birth	Children	Date of Birth
2				

	Check box of parent with 273 or more overnights per year*	☐ Mother	☐ Father	Combined
	1. MONTHLY GROSS INCOME	$	$	
3	a. Plus maintenance received	+	+	
4	b. Minus maintenance paid	–	–	
5	c. Minus ordered child support payments for other children pursuant to §14-10-115(6)(a), C.R.S.	–	–	
6	d. Minus legal responsibility for children not of this marriage/relationship pursuant to §14-10-115(6)(b)(I), C.R.S.	–	–	
7	e. Minus ordered post-secondary education contributions**	–	–	
8	**2. MONTHLY ADJUSTED GROSS INCOME** (If either the paying parent's income or Combined Income is less than $850, enter $50 on line 11 for paying parent.)	$	$	$
9	**3. PERCENTAGE SHARE OF INCOME** (Each parent's income from line 2 divided by Combined Income)	%	%	
10a	**4.** a. **BASIC COMBINED OBLIGATION** (Apply line 2 Combined column to Child Support Schedule)			$
10b	b. Each parent's share of basic support obligation (Each parent's percentage from line 3 times Combined obligation in 4a)	$	$	
11	**5. LOW-INCOME ADJUSTMENT** (If paying parent's income in line 2 is less than $1850, see Low-income Worksheet on page 2)	$	$	
	6. ADJUSTMENTS (Expenses paid directly by each parent)			
12a	a. Work-related Child Care Costs – Actual costs minus Federal Tax Credit pursuant to §14-10-115(9), C.R.S.	$	$	
12b	b. Education-related Child Care Costs [§14-10-115(9), C.R.S.]	$	$	
13	c. Health Insurance premium costs – Children's portion only pursuant to §14-10-115(10), C.R.S. (See page 2 for calculation worksheet)	$	$	
14	d. Extraordinary Medical Expenses – Uninsured only pursuant to §14-10-115(10), C.R.S.	$	$	
15	e. Extraordinary Expenses – Agreed to by parents or by order of the Court pursuant to §14-10-115(11)(a), C.R.S.	$	$	
16	f. Minus Extraordinary Adjustments [§14-10-115(11)(b), C.R.S.]	$	$	

Bradford Publishing 1743 Wazee St., Denver, CO 80202 — (303) 292-2590 — www.bradfordpublishing.com

17	**7. TOTAL ADJUSTMENTS** (For each column, add 6a, 6b, 6c, 6d and 6e. Subtract line 6f. Add two totals for Combined column amount)	$	$	$
18	**8. EACH PARENT'S FAIR SHARE OF ADJUSTMENTS** (Line 7 Combined column times line 3 for each parent)	$	$	
19	**9. EACH PARENT'S SHARE OF TOTAL CHILD SUPPORT OBLIGATION** (Add lines 4b (or line 5 if less) and line 8 for each parent)	$	$	
20	**10. PAYING PARENT'S ADJUSTMENT** (Enter line 7 for parent with less parenting time only)	$	$	
21	**11. RECOMMENDED CHILD SUPPORT ORDER** (Subtract line 10 from line 9 for the paying parent only. Leave receiving parent column blank)	$	$	

22 **COMMENTS:**

* The children reside with one parent for 273 or more overnights per year. If this is not the case, use Worksheet B.

** This adjustment applies only to modification of child support orders entered between 7/1/91 and 7/1/97 that provide for post-secondary education expenses pursuant to §14-10-115(15)(c), C.R.S.

PREPARED BY: | **DATE:**

23 Signature: ______________________ Print Name: ______________________

24 **LOW-INCOME ADJUSTMENT WORKSHEET**

If the parents' combined monthly adjusted gross income is more than $850 and the monthly adjusted gross income of the parent with fewer overnights per year is less than $1850, use this calculation worksheet to determine the adjustment allowed for that parent.

Low-income Adjustment Calculation

Adjusted monthly gross income of parent with fewer overnights (paying parent) from line 2

$ ____________ minus $900 = $ ____________ times 40% (.40) = $ ____________

Plus one of the following, according to number of children

1 child = $75 2 children = $150 3 children = $225

4 children = $275 5 children = $325 6 or more children = $350 + $ ____________

Low-income adjustment amount (#5 on Worksheet) $ ____________

If this amount is less than the amount on line 4b (on page 1) for the parent with fewer overnights per year, this parent qualifies for the Low-income Adjustment. **Enter this amount on line 5 in that parent's column on page 1. If this number is a negative or zero, enter zero.**

25 **HEALTH INSURANCE PREMIUM CALCULATION**

If the actual amount of the health insurance premium that is attributable to the children who are the subject of this order is not available or cannot be verified, the total cost of the premium should be divided by the number of persons covered by the policy to determine a per person cost. This amount is then multiplied by the number of children who are the subject of this order and are covered by the policy. This amount is then entered on line 6c on page 1 of this form.

$ ____________	÷ ____________	= $ ____________	x ____________	= $ ____________
Total Premium	Number of Persons Covered by the Policy	Per Person Cost	Number of Children Who are the Subject of this Order	Children's Portion of Cost of Health Insurance Premium (Enter on line 6c)

No. 1170. Rev. 1-08. WORKSHEET A — CHILD SUPPORT OBLIGATION: SOLE PHYSICAL CARE (JDF 1820) (Page 2 of 2)

Worksheet A – One parent has more than 273 overnights per year.

Complete Worksheet A when one or more of your children spends 75% or more overnights with one parent. A parenting plan which provides for alternate one-overnight weekends, plus half of the holidays and major school vacations with the non-residential parent will usually total less than 25%. Just because you go over 25% of the overnights does not mean that you should use Worksheet B. It is used only if there are two homes for the children, rather than a primary home and a place to visit the other parent.

INSTRUCTIONS FOR FILLING OUT WORKSHEET A

1. Enter the same information here that you entered in these blanks on the petition.
2. List the names and birth dates of only those children for whom you are calculating child support on this worksheet. Check the box of the parent with 273 or more overnights per year.
3. Fill in the Gross Monthly Income (before deductions or taxes) for each of you from your income chart or as you have agreed to use in your Child Support Plan Questionnaire, under the appropriate columns. The definition of income in the Guideline (see excerpt near the end of this chapter) includes not only your regular employment, but any other income as well, such as bonuses, capital gains, severance pay, and monetary gifts. You do not need to include income from additional jobs that result in employment more than 40 hours per week or more than what would otherwise be considered full time employment. In practice, you do not have to include your occasional income on this line of your worksheet if you agree not to do so. The decision of what income to include on this worksheet will affect the amount of money one of you pays to the other. If you used the Child Support Plan Questionnaire earlier in this chapter you have already made this decision.
4. Write any amounts either of you is actually receiving in line 1a, or paying in line 1b for court-ordered maintenance for another marriage or have agreed to for this marriage.

CAUTION If one of you is paying or planning to pay maintenance (spousal support, alimony) to the other, deduct it from the income of the spouse who will pay it, and add it to the income of the spouse who receives it. Do not include it in the gross income of that spouse on line 1. See Chapter 9 Maintenance for more about why you might want to do this.

5. Write any amounts either you or your spouse are actually paying for court-ordered child support for other children not of this marriage.
6. Write any amounts which either of you is legally obligated to pay for children other than of this marriage or relationship, who are born prior to the children of this marriage. The parent wishing to use this adjustment to income must prove that the children in question are living with him or her, or that he or she is actually making such payments. The amount of the adjustment may not exceed the amount of support for that number of children calculated from the Schedule of Basic Support at that parent's income alone. Nor may this adjustment be used to reduce a previously-set child support amount for the children of this marriage.
7. Write any amount either of you is ordered to pay for post-secondary education for another child of this marriage, from an order entered in Colorado between 1/1/91 and 7/1/97. This adjustment is limited to the amount of child support on the Schedule of Basic Support, for that child, based on the paying parent's income.
8. Add lines 1 and 1a and subtract lines 1c, 1d and 1e, for each of you. Then add these two adjusted totals and put that amount under the combined column. If either the paying parent's income or the combined income in line 2 is less than $850, the minimum support for the paying parent is $50. Enter this amount

on line 11 for that parent. If your combined monthly adjusted gross income is more than $20,000, then you may not use the Schedule of Basic Support, but must agree on a fair amount based on the actual cost of rearing your children as set forth in your parenting plan. This amount may not be less than the amount shown in the schedule for $20,000.

9. Divide each of your individual totals by the combined total to get the percentage of the total family income each of you earns. These two percentages should total 100%.

10a. Find the Schedule of Basic Child Support Obligations at the end of this chapter and on the CD (Form 1173). Find your combined monthly gross income in the left-hand column. Read across columns to the number of children you have listed on this worksheet.

If your combined monthly adjusted gross income falls between numbers on the schedule, then you will need to interpolate between the two closest amounts to find the support figure. For example, if you have a combined monthly adjusted gross income of $1960.00 and have three children, on the schedule your income falls between $1950.00 and $2,000.00, and your support obligation falls between $648.00 and $661.00. Your combined monthly adjusted gross income is 1/5 of the way between $1950.00 and $2,000.

$$\begin{array}{r} \$1960.00 \\ \underline{-1950.00} \\ 10.00 \end{array} \qquad \begin{array}{r} \$2000.00 \\ \underline{-1950.00} \\ 50.00 \end{array} \qquad \frac{10.00}{50.00} = \frac{1}{5}$$

The difference between $661.00 and $648.00 is $13.00. To calculate the additional amount, find 1/5 of $13.00 and add that to $648.00

$$\frac{1}{5} \times \frac{13.00}{1} = \frac{13.00}{5} = \$2.60 \qquad \$648 + \$2.60 = \$650.60$$

10b. For each of you, multiply the combined basic obligation in line 4a times your percentage share of income in line 3 and enter that amount in your respective columns.

11. If the amount on line 2 of combined income is more than $850, and the income on line 2 for the parent with less overnights per year is between $850 and $1850, that parent may be eligible for an adjustment to support. To calculate this amount, go to instruction number 24.

12a. Write the amount each of you pays for work-related child care for the children who are listed on this worksheet. The child care to be included on this line refers only to work-related child care, meaning that care necessary for either of you to go to work or search for a job. If that child is your dependent for the purpose of Head of Household tax filing status (see IRS form 2441, and Chapter 10) and if the child care is not paid through a cafeteria or flex plan, then subtract the amount of the child care credit taken from the child care credit table in this supplement (for 2003) from the amount you pay out. If you do not qualify for the child care credit, use the amount you actually spend.

12b. Write the amount each of you pays for education-related child care (while you are in school) for the children who are listed on this worksheet.

You must decide whether child care or babysitting for reasons other than education or work is included in your basic child support obligation from the schedule. If not, and you wish to include it on this form, include that amount in your total for line 6e.

13. Write the actual cost paid by either of you for health insurance premiums for the children listed on this worksheet. In practice, many people also include the premium paid for dental and vision insurance. If your employer does not separate the amount for the employee and the amount for additional persons or family, then use the formula in instruction 25 to calculate the amount for the children on this worksheet.

14. Write any amount in excess of $250 per child, per calendar year, either of you makes for medical expenses (including dental, optical, mental health or copays), for the children listed on this worksheet, which are not paid by insurance, and which you have agreed to include in your child support calculation—unless they are paid by cafeteria or flex plan. If your children's out of pocket medical and dental expenses exceed the deductible on your insurance, you may want to include that amount of that monthly deductible here.
15. Write any additional regular expenses, for the children listed on this worksheet, paid by either of you, which you both agree to include in your child support calculation or which have been ordered by the court.
16. Write any amounts either of you receive or the child receives, as income of, or on behalf of, the children listed on this worksheet, which you agree should offset the children's need for support. Some common examples are child's regular earnings, SSI paid for the child, adoption subsidy for child, income from child's trust. List the amount in the column for the parent in whose home the money is received. Most people do not include on this line occasional income earned by a child that is not being used to defray his or her necessary expenses (money from a weekend job that is being used for dates, gifts, incidental food, entertainment, for instance).
17. Add together any amounts on lines 6a, 6b, 6c, 6d and 6e, and then subtract any amount on line 6f for each of you. Then add the totals for each of you to obtain the combined extraordinary adjustments being paid out by you both and put that amount in the Combined column.
18. Multiply the amount in the combined column in line 7 by the amount in line 3 for each of you and put that amount in your respective columns. This is each parent's share of the adjustments.
19. For each of you, add the amounts in your columns on lines 4b (or line 5 if one parent qualifies for the low-income adjustment) and 8. This is the basic support and adjustments for each parent.
20. Write, in the paying parent's column only, that parent's number from line 7. This number represents those extraordinary expenses which the paying parent disburses directly to third parties for the children.
21. Subtract line 10 from line 9 for the paying parent only and put the result on Line 11, under that column. The recommended child support amount resulting from the use of this worksheet and the guideline should be an amount that makes sense for both of you—meaning that it is payable by the parent who will pay it, and sufficient for the parent who receives it. If this is not so, then read the "Deviations: What if . . ." section of this chapter following the material on Worksheet B.
22. If you wish to ask the court to deviate from the amount on line 11, state your reason here.
23. Whoever prepares this worksheet should sign and date it. If you both prepared it, then you should both sign it. If the preparer is not a parent, that person should also indicate his or her status (CPA, lawyer or one or both, mediator, etc.)
24. Use this worksheet only if the amount on line 2 of combined income is more than $850, and the income on line 2 for the parent with less overnights per year is between $850 and $1850. For example, if the parent who has less overnights has a monthly adjusted gross income of $1600 and 3 children:

    $1600.00 - $900 = $700 x .40 = $280.00.

    $280.00 + $225.00 = $505.00

    If this is less than the amount on line 4b for that parent, this parent qualifies for the low-income adjustment and would write $505.00 on line 5 in that parent's column. If the amount from this worksheet results in a negative or zero number, zero would be entered on line 5.
25. Use this to determine the children's share of the health insurance premium if your policy does not state a particular amount. Enter the total premium, divide it by the total number of persons on the policy, and multiply that amount by the number of children who are covered. Write the result on line 6c.

WORKSHEET B

Use Worksheet B when any of your children spends more than 92 overnights per year with each of you, and you both provide a home for them. Based on the concept of two homes, Worksheet B increases the amount you are jointly expected to spend for the basic expenses of your children by 50%. If your parenting plan is more like one primary home and the other more a place to visit (children do not have their own bedrooms, toys and clothes don't stay there), then you may wish to use Worksheet A even if the children spend more than 92 overnights per year with both parents.

Worksheet B factors the basic child support obligation twice: first by percentage of income, and second by percentage of time the children spend with each parent. It should not be too surprising that when one takes a percentage (ratio of income) of a percentage (ratio of time), the figure one is working with reduces very fast. It is important to remember, therefore, the silent presumption in this worksheet.

Worksheet B contains the silent presumption that parents who share physical care disburse payment for the basic expenses of their children in proportion to parenting time. For example, if the father has 60% of the time and the mother 40%, he is assumed to be disbursing payments for 60% of the cost of shoes, clothing, food, and all other basic expenses. If the parents have 50-50 time, they are each assumed to be disbursing payment for half these costs. If you are developing a parenting plan with shared physical care, it may be wise to begin disbursing payment for these expenses in the ratio of your time, right from the beginning. If you do not, you may find that the child support which results from this worksheet will not be adequate, because it is based on an assumption which is not being met.

You can also resolve the problem by adjusting the recommended support amount for the basic expenses which are in fact being paid by the "wrong" parent. See the later section of this chapter, "Deviations," especially "Brenda and Bob," if the amounts you get when you work through Worksheet B seem to be "off." Especially if they do not match up with the agreements you reached in the Child Support Plan Questionnaire earlier in this chapter.

"If you get more than 92 overnights with your kids, your child support will go down."

This is a widely-held misconception. The payments between the parents may go down, but each parent is still expected to carry his or her income percentage share of the cost of rearing their children. The presumption shifts from expecting only one parent to be disbursing all the children's basic expenses, to expecting the parents to be disbursing them in proportion to their parenting time.

"The parent receiving a child support payment shall be presumed to spend his or her total child support obligation directly on the children." Colorado Revised Statutes 14-10-115(8)(a).

☐ District Court ☐ Denver Juvenile Court
______________________________ County, Colorado
Court Address:

1 ☐ **In re the Marriage of:**
☐ **In re the Parental Responsibilities concerning:**

____

Petitioner:

and
Co-Petitioner/Respondent:

Attorney or Party Without Attorney (Name and Address):

Phone Number: E-mail:
FAX Number: Atty. Reg. #:

▲ COURT USE ONLY ▲

Case Number:

Division: Courtroom:

WORKSHEET B—CHILD SUPPORT OBLIGATION: SHARED PHYSICAL CARE

	Children	Date of Birth	Children	Date of Birth
2				

		Mother	Father	Combined
	1. MONTHLY GROSS INCOME	$	$	
3	a. Plus maintenance received	+	+	
4	b. Minus maintenance paid	–	–	
5	c. Minus ordered child support payments for other children pursuant to §14-10-115(6)(a), C.R.S.	–	–	
6	d. Minus legal responsibility for children not of this marriage/relationship pursuant to §14-10-115(6)(b)(I), C.R.S.	–	–	
7	e. Minus ordered post-secondary education contributions*	–	–	
8	**2. MONTHLY ADJUSTED GROSS INCOME**	$	$	$
9	**3. PERCENTAGE SHARE OF INCOME** (Each parent's income from line 2 divided by Combined Income)	%	%	
10	**4. BASIC COMBINED OBLIGATION** (Apply line 2 Combined column to Child Support Schedule)			$
11	**5. SHARED PHYSICAL CARE SUPPORT OBLIGATION** (Line 4 times 1.5)			$
12	**6. EACH PARENT'S PORTION OF SHARED PHYSICAL CARE SUPPORT OBLIGATION** (Line 3 times line 5 for each parent)	$	$	
13	**7. OVERNIGHTS WITH EACH PARENT** (Must total 365)			= 365
	STOP HERE IF LINE 7 IS LESS THAN 93 FOR EITHER PARENT. IF SO, USE WORKSHEET A.			
14	**8. PERCENTAGE TIME WITH EACH PARENT** (Line 7 ÷ 365)	%	%	
15	**9. SUPPORT OBLIGATION FOR TIME WITH OTHER PARENT** (Line 6 times other parent's line 8)	$	$	
	10. ADJUSTMENTS (Expenses paid directly by each parent)			
16	a. Work-related Child Care Costs – Actual costs minus Federal Tax Credit pursuant to §14-10-115(9), C.R.S.	$	$	
17	b. Education-related Child Care Costs pursuant to §14-10-115(9), C.R.S.	$	$	
18	c. Health Insurance premium costs – Children's portion only pursuant §14-10-115(10), C.R.S. (See page 2 for calculation worksheet)	$	$	

No. 1171. Rev. 1-08. WORKSHEET B — CHILD SUPPORT OBLIGATION: SHARED PHYSICAL CARE (JDF 1821) (Page 1 of 2)

Bradford Publishing 1743 Wazee St., Denver, CO 80202 — (303) 292-2590 — www.bradfordpublishing.com

19	d. Extraordinary Medical Expenses – Uninsured only pursuant to §14-10-115(10), C.R.S.	$	$	
20	e. Extraordinary Expenses – Agreed to by parents or by order of the Court pursuant to §14-10-115(11)(a), C.R.S.	$	$	
21	f. Minus Extraordinary Adjustments [§14-10-115(11)(b), C.R.S.]	$	$	
22	**11. TOTAL ADJUSTMENTS** (For each column, add 10a, 10b, 10c, 10d and 10e. Subtract line 10f. Add two totals for Combined Column amount)	$	$	$
23	**12. EACH PARENT'S SHARE OF ADJUSTMENTS** (Line 11 Combined column times line 3 for each parent)	$	$	
24	**13. ADJUSTMENTS PAID IN EXCESS OF FAIR SHARE** (Line 11 minus line 12. If negative number, enter zero)	$	$	
25	**14. EACH PARENT'S ADJUSTED SUPPORT OBLIGATION** (Line 9 minus line 13)	$	$	
26	**15. RECOMMENDED CHILD SUPPORT ORDER**** (Subtract lesser amount from greater amount in line 14 and enter result under greater amount)	$	$	

27 **COMMENTS:**

* This adjustment applies only to modification of child support orders entered between 7/1/91 and 7/1/97 that provide for post-secondary education expenses pursuant to §14-10-115(15)(c), C.R.S.

** If either the paying parent's monthly adjusted gross income or the combined monthly adjusted gross income is less than $850, see §14-10-115(7)(a)(II)(B) and (C), C.R.S.

PREPARED BY: **DATE:**

28 Signature: ______________________ Print Name: ______________________

The amount of child support ordered for shared physical care should not be more than an order for sole physical care. Complete a Worksheet A for comparison.

29

HEALTH INSURANCE PREMIUM CALCULATION

If the actual amount of the health insurance premium that is attributable to the children who are the subject of this order is not available or cannot be verified, the total cost of the premium should be divided by the number of persons covered by the policy to determine a per person cost. This amount is then multiplied by the number of children who are the subject of this order and are covered by the policy. This amount is then entered on line 10c on page 1 of this form.

$ ________	÷	________	=	$ ________	x	________	=	$ ________
Total Premium		Number of Persons Covered by the Policy		Per Person Cost		Number of Children Who are the Subject of this Order		Children's Portion of Cost of Health Insurance Premium (Enter on line 10c)

Worksheet B

Use this form if both parents have more than 92 overnights per year with the children and both provide a home for them.

INSTRUCTIONS FOR FILLING OUT WORKSHEET B

1. Enter the same information here that you entered in these blanks on the petition.

2. List the names and birth dates of those children who spend at least 93 overnights with each of you.

Steps 3 through 10a are the same as Worksheet A.

11. Multiply the amount on line 4 on the form by 1.5 (150%) and place on line 5.

12. Multiply the Shared Care Support Obligation from line 5 by the percentage of incomes on line 3 for each of you.

13. Write the number of overnights with each of you. If you have 50/50% shared time parenting of more than one child and each wants to be head of household (see "Tax Filing Status," Chapter 11), you might want to fill in this line with the overnights for each child individually, like this:

	Mother	**Father**
Overnights with children	183/182	182/183

This would indicate that Mother has Child A for 183 overnights and child B for 182; Father has child A for 182 overnights and Child B for 183. Mother will have head of household for child A and Father will have head of household for Child B.

14. Divide the number of overnights with each of you by 365. This will result in a percentage (60/40, 57/43, 50/50, etc.).

15. Multiply the amount in the Mother's column on line 6 by the percentage on line 8 in the Father's column and place the result under the Mother's column on line 9. Then multiply the Father's amount on line 6 by the percentage on line 8 in the Mother's column and place the result in the Father's column on line 9. By doing this calculation, each of you is "paying" the other parent your proportional (income-based) share of the basic support obligation for the time the children are with the other parent.

16. Write the amount each of you pays for work-related child care when the children who are listed on this worksheet are with you. The child care to be included on this line refers only to work-related child care, meaning that care necessary for either of you to go to work while the children are with you. If that child is your dependent for the purpose of Head of Household tax filing status (see IRS form 2441, and Chapter 11) and if the child care is not paid through a cafeteria or flex plan, then subtract the amount of the child care credit taken from the Child Care Credit Table on page 247 from the amount you pay out. If you do not qualify for the child care credit, use the amount you actually spend.

    You must decide whether other child care or babysitting is covered in the basic child support obligation from the schedule. If not, and you wish to include it on this form, include that amount in your total for line 10e.

17. Write the amount each of you pays for education-related child care (while you are in school) when the children who are listed on this worksheet. Do not include work-related child care in this total.

18. Write the actual cost paid by either of you for health insurance premiums for the children listed on this worksheet. In practice, many people also include the premium paid for dental and vision insurance. If your employer does not separate the amount for the employee and the amount for additional persons or family, then use the formula on the back of this worksheet to calculate the amount for the children on this worksheet.

19. Write any amount in excess of $250 per child, per calendar year, either of you makes for medical expenses (including dental, optical, mental health or copays), for the children listed on this worksheet, which are not paid by insurance, and which you have agreed to include in your child support calculation—unless they are paid by cafeteria or flex plan. If your children's medical and dental expenses always exceed the deductible on your insurance, you may want to include the amount of that monthly deductible here.

20. Write any additional regular expenses, for the children listed on this worksheet, paid by either of you, which you both agree to include in your child support calculation or which has been ordered by the court.

21. Write any amounts either of you receive or the child receives, as income of, or on behalf of, the children listed on this worksheet, which you agree should offset the children's need for support. Some common examples are child's earnings, SSI paid for the child, adoption subsidy for child, income from child's trust. List the amount in the column for the parent in whose home the money is received. Most people do not include on this line occasional income earned by a child that is not being used to defray his or her necessary expenses (money from a weekend job that is being used for dates, gifts, incidental food, entertainment, for instance).

22. Add any amounts on lines 10a, 10b, 10c, 10d, and 10e then subtract any amount on line 10f for each of you. Add the totals for each of you to obtain the combined extraordinary expenses being paid out by you both and put that amount in the Combined column.

23. For each of you, multiply your total adjustment, line 11, times your percentage share of income, line 3. Place the total in your respective columns. This is your share of the extraordinary expenses for your children based on your relative incomes. These expenses are not factored by your time with your children.

24. For each of you, subtract line 12 from line 11 to find out how much more or less than your income share of extraordinary expenses you are each paying. The differential will be the same—one parent will be underpaying the same amount the other is overpaying—so don't record the underpayment (the minus number).

25. Subtract the overpayment on line 13 from the support obligation, line 10. This number may be a negative for one of you if either of you is overpaying extraordinary expenses by more than your share of the basic support. (Example: Low income parent who is paying large amounts of day care or medical insurance.)

26. Subtract the lower amount of support owing from the higher amount. The difference is the recommended amount of support to be paid. If the lower amount is a negative number, you will ADD it to the higher amount to find the correct amount of support to be paid.

27. If you wish to ask the court to deviate from the amount on line 15, state your reasons here.

28. Whoever prepares this worksheet should sign and date it. That may be both or only one of the parents. If it is neither parent, that person should also indicate his or her status (CPA, lawyer for one or both, mediator, etc.)

29. Use this section to calculate the children's share of your health insurance premium.

Deviations: What if the Recommended Support Is Too High or Too Low for You?

The Child Support Guideline creates a *rebuttable presumption* – something which will happen unless you can convince the court that it should not. This means that the court will expect your agreement to require the payment of the recommended child support amount from your worksheet. In practice, most courts will readily approve a child support amount which is higher than the recommended amount, but deviation is more difficult to obtain when the amount you wish is lower than the recommended support.

Before you consider asking the court to approve a support amount that deviates from the recommended amount on the worksheet, go back to the amounts you agreed to for gross income and your decisions about which extra expenses to include in monthly support on the worksheet as shown on your Child Support Plan Questionnaire earlier in this chapter. See if by changing your agreements about these numbers, you can adjust the recommended amount on the worksheet to a number which will work for you. For example, agree not to use any income except base salary. This may change the shared basic obligation from the schedule, and therefore the support to be paid by support order. Or, agree to not list some or all of the extraordinary or additional expenses on the worksheet. This may also considerably reduce the amount on the support order. You may instead agree to pay these additional expenses as they occur, from irregular or additional income or from a "kitty" account you both contribute to periodically.

You can always pay more money to each other for your children. The issue here is what amounts you wish to make binding on you and enforceable by the court as regular monthly court-ordered child support reflected on the support order and paid automatically.

The Guideline may allow you to deviate from the recommended support amount under some circumstances. If you fit any of the circumstances in the statute, you may be able to convince the court that the recommended child support amount should not apply to you. You must present to the court not only your own suggested amount for support and your reasons for asking for a deviation, but also the appropriate worksheet(s) showing your calculations of the recommended support amount so the court can compare them.

When may we deviate from the amount on the worksheet?

The statute lists factors for which the court may consider deviating from the recommended support amount on your worksheet:

These reasons may include, but are not limited to:

"where its application would be inequitable, unjust, or inappropriate,
"the extraordinary medical expenses incurred for treatment of either parent or a current spouse,
"extraordinary costs associated with parenting time,
"the gross disparity in income between the parents,
"the ownership by a parent of a substantial non-income producing asset,
"consistent overtime not considered in gross income ...
"income from employment that is in addition to a full-time job or that results in the employment of the obligor more than forty hours per week or more than what would otherwise be considered to be full-time employment.
"The existence of a factor enumerated in this section does not require the court to deviate from the guidelines, but is a factor to be considered in the decision to deviate.
"The court may deviate from the guidelines even if no factor enumerated in this section exists."

One of the most frequently encountered situations in which the recommended child support payment may not seem fair occurs when the parents are not spending money on their children in the way the Guideline assumes. Read the following story to see if it explains a difficulty you may have been experiencing.

BRENDA AND BOB

Brenda and Bob have one child, Billy, age 14. Billy is growing four inches a year and is "eating both parents out of house and home." Bob earns $2,000 per month and Brenda earns $1000 per month. The basic child support obligation for them, from the Guideline (shown at the end of this chapter) is $540. This means the State of Colorado expects Billy to cost that much per month for housing, food, clothing, probably daily transportation to school, and possibly ordinary medical expenses like school checkups.

The ratio between Brenda and Bob's incomes is 33%/67%. If Billy lives with Brenda, Bob would pay $540 × .67 = $361.80. If Billy lives with Bob, Brenda would contribute $540 × .33 = $178.20.

Bob has been paying for all of Billy's clothing while they have been living together, and he thinks the clothes alone have been running $150 per month. Billy has been coming to Brenda's home every day after school until Bob picks him up after work. Billy eats a minimum of two peanut butter and jelly sandwiches and drinks a quart of milk every day which Brenda budgets at $50 per month. Both Bob and Brenda think Billy costs more than $540 per month for his basic expenses.

If Brenda and Bob agree that Billy could live most of the time with either of them, they might agree to adjust the amount of support to allow for the parent paying a larger share of one of the basic expenses that the other parent is presumed to cover. In this case, Bob buys all the clothes —if Billy does not live with him he would be presumed to buy none. Brenda buys more groceries than she would be presumed to be buying if Billy lived with Bob.

If Brenda and Bob agree to shared physical care, the problem is more dramatic. If they have 50/50 time with Billy the numbers for child support will look like this.

The basic amount becomes $540 × 1.5 = $810. Brenda's share is $810 × .33 (income %) × .50 (time share) = 133.65. Bob's share is $810 × .67 (income share) × .50 (time share) = 271.35. Bob would pay Brenda the difference, $137.70 in support each month.

But, wait a minute, $133.65 (Brenda's share) + $271.35 (Bob's share) equals $405. That is only half the $651 Billy is supposed to cost for basic support. (Remember, Brenda and Bob think he costs even more than that.) What happened to the other half of Billy's basic support? The answer is that the Guideline assumes the parents are disbursing the cost of Billy in proportion to their time with him. Brenda and Bob are assumed to be spending half of $810 or $405 per month each on housing, food, clothing, daily transportation to school and possibly ordinary medical costs, such as school checkups, and such, in their individual homes.

The purpose of the shared physical care child support paid by Bob to Brenda is to bring Bob's share of Billy's overall expenses back to 67% (his income share). The $405 Bob is assumed to be spending on Billy plus the $137.70 he gives Brenda is indeed 67% of $810. (810 × .67 = $542.70. $405.00 + 137.70 = 542.70. The $405 Brenda is assumed to be spending on Billy minus the $137.70 from Bob equals her 33% share (810 × .33 = 267.30. $405 - 137.70 = 267.30).

As you can see, if Brenda and Bob are not each disbursing half of Billy's expenses then the support paid between them will not be their fair (income) share of Billy's expenses. In this case, Bob is paying for all of Billy's clothes, so Brenda is paying less than half of that component of the basic support amount. Brenda is paying more than half the food cost, since she is feeding Billy all of his after-school "snacks".

Brenda and Bob can figure out the actual cost of the snacks and the clothing and adjust their support accordingly, or they can increase the support overall on the general principle that Billy costs more than what the State thinks. Or they can leave the support amount alone and assume the amount Brenda spends on extra food is equal to her share of the clothing which Bob is paying for.

In many cases no adjustment needs to be made, but the discussion about how the parents are paying out their children's expenses does need to be examined in light of the presumptions the Guideline is making.

Once you have agreed to an amount of child support and how you will pay the extraordinary expenses and health insurance, you may write these provisions into your separation agreement draft, using the sample language at the end of Chapter 12 or JDF 1115.

Post-Secondary Education

The present Colorado law no longer permits the court to consider whether divorcing parents should be required to make provision for higher education expenses for their children. However, if you both agree about these expenses you may ask the court to approve that agreement as part of your settlement. Once the court has done so, it will be a court order and enforceable like any other.

If you want to think about making some provision about college or other education or training after high school, even if your children are very young, then the following suggestions might be useful.

- Consider stating that you acknowledge that your child or children will probably attend higher education, and that you will share this expense when the time comes.

- Consider reserving the choice of school and setting of costs (what you will and will not pay for) as a must-share decision between you regardless of the kind of parental decision-making you have agreed to.

- Consider determining the percentage in which you will carry these expenses, or say it will be according to your incomes at the time.

- Consider setting a ceiling on the amount, either in dollars per year or for the whole cost, or by setting a standard such as in-state costs for the state university that year, as assessed by that college at the time.

- Consider actually starting a fund for your children to be used for higher education or any other purpose you agree on now. You could base the goal for this account on your estimate of the future college costs for which you wish to be responsible, then set a monthly savings amount which you will share in proportion to income. For example, if you feel $40,000 is what you together wish to pledge for a child's higher education, and that child is now two, you would have that amount in savings if you shared an investment of $200 per month beginning now. If the ratio of your incomes were 60/40% now you would put aside $120 and $80, respectively—adjusting these amounts if the ratio of your income changes.

Once you have entered into an agreement about post-secondary expenses, you may include it in your separation agreement draft, if you wish, using the sample provisions at the end of Chapter 12 or using JDF 1115.

Life Insurance and Other Security for Child Support

Both parents may secure the support of their children with insurance on their lives. Even though only one parent may have a monthly child support payment to make, both parents are contributing to the support of the children, as you can see from reading Line 7 of Worksheet A and Line 13 of Worksheet B. Think about whether, if either of you died, your children would be adequately supported without life insurance.

One way to calculate what your anticipated contribution is worth is to take the worksheet lines mentioned above, and multiply.

Post-Secondary Education Checklist

Directions: Complete the following statements:

1. We agree that we want ____________ ____________ (child's name) to attend ____________________ (college or other post-secondary institution). (Repeat for each child.)

2. We agree to be responsible for paying all of the following expenses for post-secondary education for ___________ ______________ (name of child):

   We agree that the upper limit on these expenses is:

   We agree that we will pay these expenses in the following proportion:

3. We agree that we will share the following post-secondary education expenses with the child:

   We agree that we will share these expenses with the child in the following proportion:

4. We agree that we will establish (have established) a bank account at ________________________ (bank) by_____________ (date) to pay the following post secondary education expenses for __________________ ___________ (name of child):

   We agree to contribute to this amount in the following amounts or proportions:

5. We agree that _________________ (name of child) shall be responsible for paying the following post-secondary education expenses himself/herself:

Vanishing Refund

Failure to pay court-ordered child support can result in an interception of any refund on an income tax return for the delinquent parent. At the moment, this can only be done if enforcement is being done through a Child Support Enforcement Unit. See Chapter 13.

Winner is Loser

CAUTION A parent who fails to pay child support as ordered should be prepared to share any large windfall such as lottery winnings or a large court settlement as soon as it becomes public. The Child Support Enforcement Unit can see to it that his or her children are the big winners.

them times 12, for the annual contribution, times the number of years until your child reaches age 19. If you have more than one child, decrease the amount slightly as each child reaches 19, then add your best guess as to your likely share of unexpected extraordinary expenses which you did not put on the worksheet, and your share of post-secondary expenses if you think this is likely.

Agree on the total amount of life insurance you each should carry. You may wish to name each other as trustee for the benefit of the children so long as the children are minors. This can be decreasing term insurance, i.e., the death benefit decreases each year over a certain term—usually the number of years until your last child emancipates or finishes college (age 22 is a good guess). Decreasing term is usually the least expensive life insurance available and is the most common insurance available as a benefit through your employer. Some parents prefer, however, to purchase an annuity which will pay out as life insurance in the event of death, or, be available as a lump sum in time to pay for higher education.

Teeth for Your Child Support Agreement

If your ex gets a new lover, will you be less likely to pay the child support, or make the payments on time? If you lose your job or the bonus does not come through, will you look for a way out of your agreement? Most people would have to answer yes to at least one of these—or, at least admit that the possibility exists they could be tempted.

There are several kinds of internal enforcement which can be used in agreements about child support. What we call "teeth" are voluntary, private, and effective ways of penalizing yourselves with more or less costly consequences if you don't do what you say you will do. What does each of you need to put into your agreement to make sure you keep the promises you make to each other with regard to supporting your children? These incentives to right behavior are limited only by your imagination. Try having the person against whom the penalty would act set the penalty. You may be surprised to learn what motivates each of you.

Here are some examples of teeth in a child support agreement. You can state that the parent who has the tax exemption for the child loses it automatically to the other parent if his or her part of the child support agreement is not kept, or not current as of December 31, or some other date. You can state that if either parent does not disburse his or her share of the expenses included in the basic support obligation as you have agreed, then that parent carries 100% of the extraordinary expenses for the next month.

See the example of "Brenda and Bob." There are sample clauses about internal enforcement included in Chapter 12. You may wish to review them after reading this chapter.

Read Chapter 13 for information about modification of child support.

Conclusion

You have now finished your first rough look at your child support plan. It will probably not be your final version. Go on to the next two chapters about the other essential components of your separation agreement. The agreements you reach as a result of each of those chapters may necessitate changes in your child support.

Take heart. Doing your own separation agreement is hard work. Don't expect to get it all done in one sitting. Don't even expect to complete the work of one of the separation agreement chapters in one sitting. Give yourself and each other the time you deserve to make the best decisions for both of you and your children.

CAUTION

Under Colorado law, failure to pay child support ordered by the court can result in the following enforcement remedies being brought against the non-paying parent:

1. Suspension of driver's license;
2. Denial, suspension or revocation of an occupational or professional license;
3. Income tax refund intercept;
4. Lottery winnings intercept;
5. Liens against real or personal property;
6. Denial or freezing of a passport.

Contact your local child support enforcement office for a list of current remedies, and for more specific information about how each remedy is being used in your county. To find the agency located in your district look in the blue pages under the county department of human services or social services. This works for all counties except Arapahoe, where the Child Support Enforcement Unit is part of the District Attorney's office.

SCHEDULE OF BASIC CHILD SUPPORT OBLIGATIONS

COMBINED MONTHLY ADJUSTED GROSS INCOME	ONE CHILD	TWO CHILDREN	THREE CHILDREN	FOUR CHILDREN	FIVE CHILDREN	MORE THAN FIVE CHILDREN
$ 100	ORDER OF $50 PER MONTH					
200						
300						
400						
500						
600						
700						
800						
850	$ 184	$ 269	$ 319	$ 352	$ 382	$ 409
900	193	282	334	369	400	428
950	202	294	349	386	418	447
1000	211	307	364	402	436	467
1050	220	320	379	419	455	486
1100	228	333	395	436	473	506
1150	237	346	410	453	491	525
1200	246	359	425	470	509	545
1250	255	372	440	487	528	565
1300	264	385	456	504	546	584
1350	273	397	471	520	564	603
1400	281	410	486	537	582	622
1450	290	422	500	553	599	641
1500	298	435	515	569	617	660
1550	307	447	530	586	635	679
1600	315	460	545	602	652	698
1650	324	472	559	618	670	717
1700	333	485	574	634	688	736
1750	341	497	589	651	705	755
1800	350	510	604	667	723	774
1850	358	522	619	683	741	793
1900	367	535	633	700	759	812
1950	375	547	648	716	776	830
2000	383	558	661	730	792	847
2050	391	570	674	745	807	864
2100	399	581	687	759	823	881
2150	407	592	700	774	839	898
2200	415	604	714	789	855	915
2250	423	615	727	803	871	931
2300	431	626	740	818	886	948
2350	439	638	753	832	902	965
2400	447	649	766	847	918	982
2450	455	660	779	861	934	999
2500	462	672	793	876	949	1016
2550	470	683	806	890	965	1033
2600	479	694	819	905	981	1050
2650	487	706	833	920	997	1067
2700	495	718	846	935	1013	1084
2750	503	729	859	950	1029	1101
2800	511	741	873	964	1045	1119
2850	519	752	886	979	1061	1136
2900	527	763	898	993	1076	1151
2950	533	772	910	1005	1089	1166
3000	540	782	921	1017	1103	1180
3050	547	792	932	1030	1116	1194
3100	554	801	943	1042	1130	1209
3150	560	811	954	1054	1143	1223
3200	567	821	965	1067	1156	1237
3250	574	831	977	1080	1171	1253
3300	581	841	989	1093	1185	1268
3350	589	851	1002	1107	1200	1284
3400	596	862	1014	1120	1214	1299
3450	603	872	1026	1133	1229	1315
3500	610	882	1038	1147	1243	1330
3550	617	892	1050	1160	1258	1346
3600	624	903	1062	1173	1272	1361
3650	631	913	1074	1187	1287	1377
3700	638	923	1086	1200	1301	1392

No. 1173. Rev. 1-11. SCHEDULE OF BASIC CHILD SUPPORT OBLIGATIONS

Bradford Publishing, 1743 Wazee St., Denver, CO 80202 — 303-292-2590 — www.bradfordpublishing.com

COMBINED MONTHLY ADJUSTED GROSS INCOME	ONE CHILD	TWO CHILDREN	THREE CHILDREN	FOUR CHILDREN	FIVE CHILDREN	MORE THAN FIVE CHILDREN
3750	645	934	1098	1214	1315	1408
3800	652	944	1110	1227	1330	1423
3850	660	954	1122	1240	1344	1439
3900	667	964	1135	1254	1359	1454
3950	673	973	1145	1266	1372	1468
4000	677	980	1153	1274	1381	1478
4050	682	987	1161	1283	1391	1488
4100	686	993	1169	1292	1400	1498
4150	691	1000	1177	1301	1410	1509
4200	695	1006	1185	1310	1420	1519
4250	700	1013	1193	1318	1429	1529
4300	704	1020	1201	1327	1439	1539
4350	708	1026	1209	1336	1448	1550
4400	713	1033	1217	1345	1458	1560
4450	717	1039	1225	1354	1467	1570
4500	722	1046	1233	1362	1477	1580
4550	726	1053	1241	1371	1486	1590
4600	731	1059	1249	1380	1496	1601
4650	735	1066	1257	1389	1505	1611
4700	739	1071	1262	1395	1512	1618
4750	742	1075	1267	1400	1517	1623
4800	745	1079	1271	1405	1523	1629
4850	748	1083	1276	1410	1528	1635
4900	751	1088	1280	1415	1533	1641
4950	755	1092	1285	1420	1539	1647
5000	758	1096	1289	1425	1544	1652
5050	761	1100	1294	1430	1550	1658
5100	764	1105	1298	1435	1555	1664
5150	768	1109	1303	1440	1560	1670
5200	771	1113	1307	1445	1566	1676
5250	774	1117	1312	1450	1571	1681
5300	777	1122	1316	1455	1577	1687
5350	781	1126	1321	1460	1582	1693
5400	784	1130	1326	1465	1588	1699
5450	787	1135	1331	1470	1594	1705
5500	790	1139	1336	1476	1600	1712
5550	792	1143	1341	1482	1606	1718
5600	795	1147	1346	1487	1612	1725
5650	798	1152	1351	1493	1618	1731
5700	801	1156	1356	1498	1624	1738
5750	804	1160	1361	1504	1630	1744
5800	807	1164	1365	1509	1636	1750
5850	809	1168	1370	1514	1641	1756
5900	812	1172	1375	1520	1647	1762
5950	815	1176	1380	1525	1653	1769
6000	818	1180	1385	1530	1659	1775
6050	820	1184	1390	1536	1664	1781
6100	823	1188	1394	1541	1670	1787
6150	826	1193	1400	1547	1677	1794
6200	831	1199	1407	1555	1686	1804
6250	836	1206	1415	1563	1695	1813
6300	840	1212	1422	1572	1704	1823
6350	845	1219	1430	1580	1713	1833
6400	849	1225	1437	1588	1722	1842
6450	854	1232	1445	1597	1731	1852
6500	858	1238	1452	1605	1740	1861
6550	863	1245	1460	1613	1749	1871
6600	868	1251	1467	1621	1758	1881
6650	872	1258	1475	1630	1767	1890
6700	877	1264	1482	1638	1775	1900
6750	882	1271	1491	1647	1785	1910
6800	887	1278	1499	1656	1795	1921
6850	892	1285	1507	1665	1805	1932
6900	897	1293	1515	1675	1815	1942
6950	902	1300	1524	1684	1825	1953
7000	907	1307	1532	1693	1835	1963
7050	912	1314	1540	1702	1845	1974
7100	917	1321	1549	1711	1855	1985
7150	922	1328	1557	1720	1865	1995
7200	927	1336	1565	1729	1875	2006
7250	932	1343	1573	1738	1884	2016
7300	937	1349	1581	1747	1893	2026

COMBINED MONTHLY ADJUSTED GROSS INCOME	ONE CHILD	TWO CHILDREN	THREE CHILDREN	FOUR CHILDREN	FIVE CHILDREN	MORE THAN FIVE CHILDREN
7350	942	1356	1588	1755	1902	2036
7400	946	1362	1596	1763	1912	2045
7450	951	1369	1603	1772	1921	2055
7500	955	1375	1611	1780	1930	2065
7550	960	1382	1619	1789	1939	2075
7600	965	1389	1626	1797	1948	2084
7650	969	1395	1634	1805	1957	2094
7700	974	1402	1641	1814	1966	2104
7750	979	1408	1649	1822	1975	2113
7800	983	1415	1657	1830	1984	2123
7850	988	1422	1664	1839	1993	2133
7900	993	1428	1672	1847	2002	2143
7950	997	1435	1679	1856	2011	2152
8000	1002	1441	1687	1864	2021	2162
8050	1006	1448	1694	1872	2030	2172
8100	1011	1454	1702	1881	2039	2181
8150	1016	1461	1710	1889	2048	2191
8200	1020	1468	1717	1898	2057	2201
8250	1025	1474	1725	1906	2066	2211
8300	1030	1481	1732	1914	2075	2220
8350	1034	1487	1740	1923	2084	2230
8400	1039	1494	1748	1931	2093	2240
8450	1043	1501	1755	1939	2102	2250
8500	1048	1507	1763	1948	2111	2259
8550	1053	1514	1770	1956	2121	2269
8600	1057	1520	1778	1965	2130	2279
8650	1062	1527	1785	1973	2139	2288
8700	1066	1533	1793	1981	2148	2298
8750	1070	1539	1800	1989	2157	2308
8800	1075	1546	1808	1998	2166	2317
8850	1079	1552	1815	2006	2175	2327
8900	1083	1558	1823	2014	2184	2336
8950	1088	1565	1830	2023	2193	2346
9000	1092	1571	1838	2031	2202	2356
9050	1096	1577	1845	2039	2211	2365
9100	1101	1583	1853	2048	2220	2375
9150	1105	1590	1860	2056	2228	2384
9200	1110	1596	1868	2064	2237	2394
9250	1114	1602	1875	2072	2246	2404
9300	1118	1609	1883	2081	2255	2413
9350	1123	1615	1890	2089	2264	2423
9400	1127	1621	1898	2097	2273	2433
9450	1131	1628	1905	2106	2282	2442
9500	1136	1634	1913	2114	2291	2452
9550	1140	1640	1920	2122	2300	2461
9600	1144	1647	1928	2130	2309	2471
9650	1149	1653	1935	2139	2318	2481
9700	1153	1659	1943	2147	2327	2490
9750	1157	1666	1950	2155	2336	2500
9800	1162	1672	1958	2164	2345	2510
9850	1166	1678	1965	2172	2354	2519
9900	1170	1685	1973	2180	2363	2529
9950	1175	1691	1981	2188	2372	2538
10000	1179	1697	1988	2197	2381	2548
10050	1183	1703	1995	2204	2389	2557
10100	1187	1709	2002	2212	2398	2565
10150	1191	1715	2008	2219	2406	2574
10200	1195	1720	2015	2227	2414	2583
10250	1199	1726	2022	2234	2422	2592
10300	1203	1732	2029	2242	2430	2601
10350	1207	1738	2036	2250	2439	2609
10400	1211	1744	2043	2257	2447	2618
10450	1215	1749	2050	2265	2455	2627
10500	1219	1755	2056	2272	2463	2636
10550	1223	1761	2063	2280	2471	2644
10600	1227	1767	2070	2288	2480	2653
10650	1231	1773	2077	2295	2488	2662
10700	1235	1778	2084	2303	2496	2671
10750	1239	1784	2091	2310	2504	2680
10800	1243	1790	2098	2318	2513	2688
10850	1247	1796	2104	2325	2521	2697
10900	1251	1802	2111	2333	2529	2706

COMBINED MONTHLY ADJUSTED GROSS INCOME	ONE CHILD	TWO CHILDREN	THREE CHILDREN	FOUR CHILDREN	FIVE CHILDREN	MORE THAN FIVE CHILDREN
10950	1255	1808	2118	2341	2537	2715
11000	1259	1813	2125	2348	2545	2724
11050	1263	1819	2132	2356	2554	2732
11100	1267	1825	2139	2363	2562	2741
11150	1271	1831	2146	2371	2570	2750
11200	1275	1837	2152	2378	2578	2759
11250	1279	1842	2159	2386	2586	2768
11300	1283	1848	2166	2394	2595	2776
11350	1287	1854	2173	2401	2603	2785
11400	1291	1860	2180	2409	2611	2794
11450	1295	1866	2187	2417	2619	2803
11500	1299	1871	2194	2424	2628	2812
11550	1303	1877	2201	2432	2636	2821
11600	1307	1883	2208	2440	2644	2830
11650	1311	1889	2215	2447	2653	2838
11700	1315	1895	2222	2455	2661	2847
11750	1319	1900	2229	2463	2669	2856
11800	1322	1906	2235	2470	2678	2865
11850	1326	1912	2242	2478	2686	2874
11900	1330	1918	2249	2486	2694	2883
11950	1334	1923	2256	2493	2703	2892
12000	1338	1929	2263	2501	2711	2901
12050	1342	1935	2270	2508	2719	2909
12100	1346	1940	2276	2515	2726	2917
12150	1349	1945	2283	2522	2734	2925
12200	1353	1951	2289	2529	2742	2934
12250	1357	1956	2295	2536	2749	2942
12300	1360	1961	2302	2543	2757	2950
12350	1364	1967	2308	2551	2765	2958
12400	1367	1972	2315	2558	2772	2966
12450	1371	1977	2321	2565	2780	2975
12500	1375	1983	2327	2572	2788	2983
12550	1378	1988	2334	2579	2795	2991
12600	1382	1993	2340	2586	2803	2999
12650	1386	1998	2347	2593	2811	3007
12700	1389	2004	2353	2600	2818	3016
12750	1393	2009	2359	2607	2826	3024
12800	1397	2014	2366	2614	2834	3032
12850	1400	2020	2373	2622	2842	3041
12900	1405	2026	2380	2630	2851	3050
12950	1409	2032	2387	2638	2859	3059
13000	1413	2038	2394	2646	2868	3069
13050	1417	2044	2402	2654	2877	3078
13100	1421	2050	2409	2662	2885	3087
13150	1425	2056	2416	2670	2894	3096
13200	1429	2062	2423	2678	2902	3106
13250	1433	2068	2430	2685	2911	3115
13300	1437	2074	2437	2693	2920	3124
13350	1441	2080	2445	2701	2928	3133
13400	1445	2086	2452	2709	2937	3142
13450	1449	2092	2459	2717	2945	3152
13500	1453	2098	2466	2725	2954	3161
13550	1457	2104	2473	2733	2963	3170
13600	1461	2110	2481	2741	2971	3179
13650	1465	2116	2488	2749	2980	3189
13700	1469	2122	2495	2757	2989	3198
13750	1473	2128	2502	2765	2997	3207
13800	1477	2134	2509	2773	3006	3216
13850	1481	2140	2517	2781	3014	3225
13900	1485	2146	2524	2789	3023	3235
13950	1489	2152	2531	2797	3032	3244
14000	1493	2158	2538	2805	3040	3253
14050	1497	2164	2545	2813	3049	3262
14100	1501	2170	2553	2821	3058	3272
14150	1505	2176	2560	2829	3066	3281
14200	1509	2181	2567	2836	3075	3290
14250	1514	2187	2574	2844	3083	3299
14300	1518	2193	2581	2852	3092	3308
14350	1522	2199	2589	2860	3101	3318
14400	1526	2205	2596	2868	3109	3327

COMBINED MONTHLY ADJUSTED GROSS INCOME	ONE CHILD	TWO CHILDREN	THREE CHILDREN	FOUR CHILDREN	FIVE CHILDREN	MORE THAN FIVE CHILDREN
14450	1530	2211	2603	2876	3118	3336
14500	1534	2217	2610	2884	3126	3345
14550	1538	2223	2617	2892	3135	3354
14600	1542	2229	2624	2900	3144	3364
14650	1546	2235	2632	2908	3152	3373
14700	1550	2241	2639	2916	3161	3382
14750	1554	2247	2646	2924	3170	3391
14800	1558	2253	2653	2932	3178	3401
14850	1562	2259	2660	2940	3187	3410
14900	1566	2265	2668	2948	3195	3419
14950	1570	2271	2675	2956	3204	3428
15000	1574	2277	2682	2964	3213	3437
15050	1578	2283	2689	2972	3221	3447
15100	1582	2289	2696	2980	3230	3456
15150	1586	2295	2704	2987	3238	3465
15200	1590	2301	2711	2995	3247	3474
15250	1594	2307	2718	3003	3256	3484
15300	1598	2313	2725	3011	3264	3493
15350	1602	2319	2732	3019	3273	3502
15400	1606	2325	2740	3027	3282	3511
15450	1610	2330	2746	3034	3289	3519
15500	1613	2334	2750	3039	3294	3525
15550	1615	2338	2755	3044	3300	3531
15600	1618	2342	2759	3049	3305	3537
15650	1621	2346	2764	3054	3311	3542
15700	1624	2350	2768	3059	3316	3548
15750	1626	2353	2773	3064	3322	3554
15800	1629	2357	2778	3069	3327	3560
15850	1632	2361	2782	3074	3332	3566
15900	1634	2365	2787	3079	3338	3572
15950	1637	2369	2791	3084	3343	3577
16000	1640	2373	2796	3089	3349	3583
16050	1643	2377	2800	3094	3354	3589
16100	1645	2381	2805	3099	3360	3595
16150	1648	2385	2809	3104	3365	3601
16200	1651	2389	2814	3109	3371	3607
16250	1654	2392	2818	3114	3376	3612
16300	1656	2396	2823	3119	3381	3618
16350	1659	2400	2828	3124	3387	3624
16400	1662	2404	2832	3129	3392	3630
16450	1665	2408	2837	3134	3398	3636
16500	1667	2412	2841	3140	3403	3641
16550	1670	2416	2846	3145	3409	3647
16600	1673	2420	2850	3150	3414	3653
16650	1675	2424	2855	3155	3420	3659
16700	1678	2428	2859	3160	3425	3665
16750	1681	2431	2864	3165	3430	3671
16800	1684	2435	2868	3170	3436	3676
16850	1686	2439	2873	3175	3441	3682
16900	1689	2443	2878	3180	3447	3688
16950	1692	2447	2882	3185	3452	3694
17000	1695	2451	2887	3190	3458	3700
17050	1697	2455	2891	3195	3463	3706
17100	1700	2459	2896	3200	3469	3711
17150	1703	2463	2900	3205	3474	3717
17200	1705	2467	2905	3210	3479	3723
17250	1708	2471	2909	3215	3485	3729
17300	1711	2474	2914	3220	3490	3735
17350	1714	2478	2918	3225	3496	3740
17400	1716	2482	2923	3230	3501	3746
17450	1719	2486	2928	3235	3507	3752
17500	1722	2490	2932	3240	3512	3758
17550	1725	2494	2937	3245	3518	3764
17600	1727	2498	2941	3250	3523	3770
17650	1730	2502	2946	3255	3528	3775
17700	1733	2506	2950	3260	3534	3781
17750	1736	2510	2955	3265	3539	3787
17800	1738	2513	2959	3270	3545	3793
17850	1741	2517	2964	3275	3550	3799
17900	1744	2521	2968	3280	3556	3805

COMBINED MONTHLY ADJUSTED GROSS INCOME	ONE CHILD	TWO CHILDREN	THREE CHILDREN	FOUR CHILDREN	FIVE CHILDREN	MORE THAN FIVE CHILDREN
17950	1746	2525	2973	3285	3561	3810
18000	1749	2529	2978	3290	3567	3816
18050	1752	2533	2982	3295	3572	3822
18100	1755	2537	2987	3300	3577	3828
18150	1757	2541	2991	3305	3583	3834
18200	1760	2545	2996	3310	3588	3839
18250	1763	2549	3000	3315	3594	3845
18300	1766	2552	3005	3320	3599	3851
18350	1768	2556	3009	3325	3605	3857
18400	1771	2560	3014	3330	3610	3863
18450	1774	2564	3018	3335	3616	3869
18500	1776	2568	3023	3340	3621	3874
18550	1779	2572	3027	3345	3626	3880
18600	1782	2576	3032	3350	3632	3886
18650	1785	2580	3037	3355	3637	3892
18700	1787	2584	3041	3360	3643	3898
18750	1790	2588	3046	3365	3648	3904
18800	1793	2592	3050	3370	3654	3909
18850	1796	2595	3055	3376	3659	3915
18900	1798	2599	3059	3381	3664	3921
18950	1801	2603	3064	3386	3670	3927
19000	1804	2607	3068	3391	3675	3933
19050	1807	2611	3073	3396	3681	3938
19100	1809	2615	3077	3401	3686	3944
19150	1812	2619	3082	3406	3692	3950
19200	1815	2623	3087	3411	3697	3956
19250	1817	2627	3091	3416	3703	3962
19300	1820	2631	3096	3421	3708	3968
19350	1823	2634	3100	3426	3713	3973
19400	1826	2638	3105	3431	3719	3979
19450	1828	2642	3109	3436	3724	3985
19500	1831	2646	3114	3441	3730	3991
19550	1834	2650	3118	3446	3735	3997
19600	1837	2654	3123	3451	3741	4003
19650	1839	2658	3127	3456	3746	4008
19700	1842	2662	3132	3461	3752	4014
19750	1845	2666	3137	3466	3757	4020
19800	1847	2670	3141	3471	3762	4026
19850	1850	2674	3146	3476	3768	4032
19900	1853	2677	3150	3481	3773	4037
19950	1856	2681	3155	3486	3779	4043
20000	1858	2685	3159	3491	3784	4049

Notes:

CHAPTER **10**

MAINTENANCE
SEPARATION AGREEMENT – PART IV

Page

MAINTENANCE
SEPARATION AGREEMENT – PART IV

Before the court can give you a final decree of dissolution of marriage or legal separation, you must resolve and write out all the financial and parental issues remaining from your marriage. This written summary is called the separation agreement, whether you are obtaining a divorce or a legal separation. It must be read and approved by the court.

The introduction to Chapter 7 lists the things you need to do to prepare your separation agreement and directs you to the chapters with information necessary to accomplish this. This chapter discusses maintenance and how it can be a part of your separation agreement.

Maintenance

Maintenance is a series of payments (or a lump sum payment or payments) made by one spouse to the other, or to some third party (such as the Credit Union for a car loan) on behalf of the receiving spouse. The IRS refers to maintenance as "alimony" or "Section 71 (of the Internal Revenue Code) payments."

Many spouses who would or could pay maintenance shy away from the idea because they don't want to be "on the hook," are angry at the thought of supporting an ex-spouse, or don't want to feel tied to their ex-spouses. Spouses who might receive maintenance may avoid the idea because they must pay tax on it, or because they don't want to be dependent on their ex-spouse through these kinds of payments, even for a short time. For many, if not most, maintenance is an emotional subject.

Allowing your feelings to take over on this issue may prevent you from saving a great deal of money. Maintenance saves money by means of smart tax planning, just at a time when you both need it. We recommend that you read the rest of this chapter so that you understand the potential value this tool has for you before deciding whether or not you wish to use it.

Hot Words

There are certain incendiary words which can turn a healthy discussion of maintenance into an inferno. Some of them are:

"I'm entitled..."

"You've got no right..."

"You owe me..."

"I owe you nothing..."

"It's my right..."

"You don't deserve..."

This Guidebook avoids these hot words by taking a problem-solving, tax-saving approach to the question of maintenance.

Maintenance: Money paid by one separated spouse to or on behalf of the other, also referred to as spousal support. The IRS uses the term alimony.

Tax Significance of Maintenance

The tax significance of a maintenance payment is that it is deductible from income by the person who pays it and taxable as income to the person who receives it.

"If we don't say anything about maintenance in our agreement, then there won't ever be any."

Possibly, but don't count on it. Unless both of you waive (give up your rights to) maintenance, in so many words, in your written agreement, the court can possibly re-open the question in the future if either of you asks. If you do not want the court ever to have the power to consider maintenance, then you both need to expressly waive it.

Spousal support: In some jurisdictions this term means maintenance or alimony.

P PARTNERS Maintenance as an income tax shifting device is not available to partners.

None of the following statements is true:

"Maintenance is always paid to the wife for life."

"Don't ever pay maintenance – you're just opening up the door to more."

"Don't ever accept maintenance, you have to pay taxes on it."

"Maintenance has to be paid monthly."

"You can't use maintenance to pay child support or property division."

"Once you open the door to maintenance, you can't ever close it again."

"The trouble with maintenance is it locks you into a certain payment for life."

None of the following statements is necessarily true:

"Why would I pay maintenance when she's just going to get re-married."

"He/she shouldn't get maintenance, he/she doesn't need it."

"Nobody in this family needs maintenance."

"Why should I pay for her/him to go to school when she/he can work and earn his/her own living?"

"If I agree to maintenance I have to keep paying even if I lose my job."

D DEFINITION **Open ended maintenance:** Maintenance without either an explicit termination or total amount.

D DEFINITION **Fixed term maintenance;** Maintenance in which the total amount is either stated or calculable from its terms.

Sometimes referred to as Contractual Maintenance or Maintenance in Gross.

No Formula for Maintenance

While Colorado now has a formula for calculating temporary maintenance (for the period before your decree) for couples whose combined income is less than $75,000 per year (Chapter 4), there is no such formula for maintenance after the decree, although you may use the same formula if you wish.

SMART MAINTENANCE

Making maintenance work for your unique circumstances is a smart way to save money for your family. There are many ways to do this, some of which are summarized here and discussed in detail in the text that follows. Alongside each discussion is a place for you to initial whether that particular use for maintenance might work for you.

Open-ended maintenance is of unlimited or undetermined duration. It may be used for a variety of purposes including the following:

- To balance income between spouses in two households;
- To provide long term full or supplemental income for a spouse, based on need;
- To meet on-going expenses with tax-deductible dollars;
- To pay spousal support with business income.

Fixed term maintenance is paid for a designated period of time or until a certain amount of money is paid. It is generally for a specific purpose and is often referred to as contractual or in gross. It may be used for a variety of purposes including the following:

- To pay specific marital debts;
- To pay specific expenses for children or spouse;
- To pay for training, education, or therapy of a spouse;
- To supplement while a spouse's income phases in or up;
- To balance property division.

1. OPEN-ENDED MAINTENANCE

Open-ended maintenance is a maintenance plan in which the total amount to be paid in the plan cannot be calculated. Payments of this type of maintenance are usually periodic, and presumed to be modifiable as circumstances change.

a. Maintenance to Balance Income Between Spouses in Two Households

If your goal after divorce is to be able to support your children equally and/or to pay off the remaining marital debt equally, then you may accomplish this with maintenance paid by the higher income spouse to the lower income spouse. In some cases separation will cause a drastic change in lifestyle for one spouse unless some income is shifted. When both spouses are employed full time or have careers, but there is a significant difference in incomes, this kind of "income balancing" can create a foundation for an equal sharing of child support and debt payment after divorce.

Maintenance Checklist 1a

We are interested in maintenance to balance our incomes:

____________	____________
Initials	Initials

Fred and Linda

Fred and Linda are the parents of two children ages 7 and 12. Fred has 70% of the family income, Linda has 30%, and this percentage is likely to continue into the foreseeable future. They have marital debts, freestanding debts not related to any piece of property, which will take three years to pay off if they make minimum payments.

If Fred pays maintenance to Linda of 20% of his gross income, Linda and Fred will then each have 50% of the family gross income. They would continue the income leveling for three years, and each contribute equally to the debt payments during that time.

If they share equal physical care of their children, there will be no child support—each of them is presumed to be paying out 50% of the children's expenses due to the 50/50 time, and that is the same as the ratio of their incomes after maintenance. See Chapter 9, Worksheet B, for how this works. They can each file head of household by agreeing to one more overnight per year of one child to each. See Chapters 9 and 11 for how this works. They can share the dependency exemptions, thus equalizing the tax effects (see Chapter 11).

If you are considering paying substantial maintenance right from the beginning ($1250 per month or $15,000 per year or more) and if you are planning to have it decrease significantly within the first three years, read Chapter 11, Taxes.

Maintenance Checklist 1b

We agree that ___________ needs long term full or supplemental income because:

_____________ Initials   _____________ Initials

An income-leveling maintenance plan can serve to make ex-spouses literally equal partners in supporting their children and paying off the debts remaining from their marriage.

b. Maintenance to Provide Long Term Full or Supplemental Income for a Spouse, Based on Need

Long term spousal support was the original concept of alimony. The divorcing wife in a long marriage, who had dedicated her life to making a home and thus had never worked outside the home, had need of ongoing support for life or until remarriage. The value of the homemaker to the acquisition of property is also affirmed in the current statute. Maintenance of this kind often relates to the length of the marriage and the standard of living established.

Central to planning for long term maintenance is the concept of need, which is reflected in the current statute. Typically, plans of this type begin with the projected living expenses of the spouse who will receive the maintenance. If your circumstances are like any of the following examples, long term spousal support may be an appropriate solution for you.

- One of you has not worked outside the home, or not substantially so, and for reasons of age or mental and/or physical health, cannot look forward to adequate employment. This situation may call for lifetime spousal support.

- One of you is taking care of a child or other dependent whose needs require that you be constantly available, making employment outside the home inappropriate. Perhaps you have an infant you both agree should not yet be in day care, or a disabled or ill child, or an ailing parent. Your individual feelings about this situation may be very different, especially if the dependent is not a child of this marriage.

- One of you is in a line of work that pays significantly less than the other spouse's line of work, sometimes not enough to live on. One of you may be an artist, musician, small rancher or farmer, day-care provider, piece worker, or work in other in-home or "cottage" industries. Even if you both endorsed this career choice while you were together, your feelings about it at this time may be very changed. One of you may feel you are having to pay forever for someone else's career choices. The other of you may be threatened or angry at the difficulties that surround your career choice. It may feel like everyone is saying that you are less valuable or less worthy. Be certain

"If we agree to monthly maintenance, nobody can change it in the future, even the court."

Not true. If maintenance is open ended, then it is presumed to be modifiable by the court on a "showing of a change of circumstances so substantial and continuing" as to render the original order unfair.

your negotiations around the question of maintenance allow plenty of time to air these feelings and to insure that the career choices of each of you are supported by the other.

If lifetime spousal support is payable until the death of the recipient, it may be adjusted upon the retirement of the paying spouse, or when Social Security or other retirement benefits begin for either spouse, so that both parties share in the usual reduction of income experienced at retirement.

If either of you is now struggling with feelings of righteousness, distrust, anger, helplessness, being trapped, dependence, guilt, panic—you are not unusual. Most people feel some of these emotions at different times during this type of long term arrangement. It may be that this is the time for you both to seek professional help—therapists, financial counsel, mediator, medical evaluator, employment evaluator—rather than being weighed down by this emotional baggage long after the divorce is over. See "Divorce and the Legal System," Chapter 2, for resources.

c. Maintenance to Meet Ongoing Expenses With Tax-Deductible Dollars

Maintenance can be used to pay such on-going expenses as a spouse's (or ex-spouse's) life insurance, medical insurance, medical expenses, or to pay all or a part of a mortgage. Some of these costs may be deductible, in whole or in part, by the person who pays them, which can make this alternative particularly attractive. Medical insurance and medical expenses become deductible only after they exceed 7.5% of your adjusted gross income. The interest portion of a home mortgage payment is deductible, but only if the person paying it uses this property as a personal residence.

To investigate the possibility of paying these through maintenance, do the calculations in the following example.

Charlie and Pearl

Charlie and Pearl pay $800 per month in mortgage payments on the family home where Pearl will continue to live. $650 of the $800 is deductible interest and taxes. Pearl's life insurance premium will be $25 per month, and her health insurance premium will be $175 per month after the divorce. The money Charlie could use to pay maintenance would be taxed to him at 25% Federal, 4.63% Colorado totaling 29.63%. Pearl's maintenance income will be taxed at 15% Federal (her earned income will fill the 10% bracket), 4.63% Colorado totaling 19.63%. See Taxes, Chapter 11.

Maintenance Checklist 1c:

We are interested in using maintenance to pay the following expenses:

Expense:_______ Amount:_______

Expense:_______ Amount:_______

Expense:_______ Amount:_______

Expense:_______ Amount:_______

Expense:_______ Amount:_______

_______ Initials _______ Initials

Sometimes It's Maintenance Whether You Like It or Not

The IRS may treat as maintenance any payment made on behalf of a spouse which qualifies as alimony under their definition. Some examples of what you might say in your separation agreement that the husband may pay after the divorce, but that the IRS may treat as maintenance ("alimony"), even if you did not call these maintenance payments are:

- wife's health or life insurance
- wife's mortgage
- upkeep or payments on property that the wife uses but the husband still owns

This would give the husband an after-the-fact tax windfall, and the wife unexpected taxes to pay. Be clear in your agreement whether a payment is or is not taxable maintenance.

Paying Spouse Pays FICA First

The spouse paying maintenance does not save FICA (Social Security or Self Employment Tax) on the maintenance amount, only the Federal and State taxes. The recipient does not pay F.I.C.A. on this money.

Step 1: Add up the amount of the payments which you are considering paying as maintenance. Charlie and Pearl's total is $800 + $25 + $175 = $1,000

Step 2: Subtract Pearl's tax deductions for these payments.

$1,000 – 650 = $350. (If Pearl's medical insurance premium and medical expenses total more than 7.5% of her taxable income, she may be able to deduct some or all of the medical insurance premium. These are not large enough to be deductible in our example.)

Step 3: Subtract Pearl's tax rate from 100% (100% – 19.63% = 80.37%)

Step 4: Calculate Pearl's likely income tax on the remaining maintenance: $350 ÷ 80.37% = $435.49

$435.49 – $350 = $85.49

Step 5: Add together the payments and the remaining tax, to figure the amount to be paid as maintenance. $1,000 + $85.49 = $1085.49.

Step 6: Charlie deducts the full amount as maintenance. Charlie saves the following in taxes: $1085.49 × 29.63% = $321.63

Step 7: Calculate their overall tax savings. $321.63 - $85.49 = $236.14. Charlie and Pearl save $236.14 every month this maintenance agreement is in effect. This total monthly tax savings is money saved from the IRS. The greater the spread between your tax rates, the more you can save in taxes.

The more the amount of maintenance paid exceeds the amount the recipient pays for taxes on the maintenance, the more that spouse shares in the overall savings.

Step 8: Consider increasing the amount of maintenance in order to share the tax savings each month. For example, if Charlie paid $1125 in maintenance, his tax savings would be $333.34. Pearl would pay $93.24 in tax. Their overall savings would be $240.10 per month, of which Pearl would receive $125 and Charlie would keep $115.10.

CAUTION If Charlie and Pearl continued to own the home together, and Charlie paid the entire mortgage payment directly, the IRS might well assume that half the mortgage payment was on Pearl's behalf and therefore maintenance, and unexpectedly deduct it from Charlie's taxable income and tax Pearl on it. Charlie might not be able to deduct all or even half of the mortgage interest and property taxes because the home is no longer his principal residence.

Work with your numbers and these steps until you arrive at an arrangement which is satisfactory to both of you.

Maintenance Checklist 1d:

We are interested in exploring paying maintenance through ________________ business:

____________ Initials ____________ Initials

d. Maintenance Paid From Business Income

You may define your maintenance amount as a percentage of income from the paying spouse's business. This may feel exactly right if the receiving spouse has been part of the business and its development—it satisfies the feeling of getting your share of the family business. This way of defining the amount has a unique tax advantage in that it is not subject to the *recapture* rules (see

Chapter 11 Taxes). Although this isn't a property settlement, it can feel like one, and thereby help with accomplishing what feels like a fair division of your assets.

Since this use of maintenance is unusual, it is wise to utilize the services of an attorney and/or accountant familiar with divorce taxation and this particular use of maintenance before you enter into an agreement of this type.

2. FIXED TERM MAINTENANCE

Fixed term maintenance is a maintenance plan in which the total amount to be paid can be calculated precisely. Payments of this type of maintenance are often short term or lump sum, contractual (sometimes called "in gross"), for a specific purpose, and may be made non-modifiable.

a. Maintenance to Pay Specific Marital Debts

If there is a difference in your incomes—or a significant difference in the tax treatment at the same income level—then you can do some money-saving tax planning as you pay off your marital debts. Have the higher taxed spouse pay to the lower taxed spouse the amount of the debt payments plus the receiving spouse's tax on the payments. Then the lower taxed spouse makes the debt payments. You will save, outright, the difference between the paying spouse's federal income tax rate and the receiving spouse's federal income tax rate. The greater the difference in your tax rates, the larger the savings—often $.13 or more on every dollar.

Sid and Sue

Sid and Sue have some free-standing bills—not tied to, or secured by a piece of property—which will be paid in full over two and a half years if they continue to make the minimum payments. The initial total of these payments is $300 per month.

Assume Sid is in the 28% Federal tax bracket for much of his income, and Sue can absorb a good deal of income before leaving the 15% Federal tax bracket. See Chapter 11, Taxes.

If Sid initially pays $375 in maintenance (including Sue's tax burden), and Sue makes the minimum bill payments, Sid will initially deduct $375 from taxable income instead of paying the debt payment in after-tax dollars. The extra $75 paid for Sue's taxes is less than the savings on Sid's taxes through having $375 per month less in taxable income. The calculations which illustrate are as follows.

To calculate Sue's tax needs if she receives the $300 as income, divide the initial amount of maintenance by the 80.37% (which is the same as diving by .8037).

Maintenance Checklist 2a:

We are interested in using maintenance to pay the following specific debts:

Creditor	Balance	Mo. Pmts.
________	________	________
________	________	________
________	________	________
________	________	________
________	________	________

__________ Initials   __________ Initials

If your maintenance, including the lump sum options, will total more than $15,000 in the first or second post-separation tax year, you may be running into the recapture rules. A solution might be to pay the bulk of the maintenance before your final decree, since temporary maintenance can be exempt from the recapture rules. See Chapter 11, Taxes.

(100% – [15% Fed + 4.63% State]) = 80.37%

$$\frac{300}{.8037} = \$373.27$$

If Sid pays $375 (slightly rounded up), he saves:

(28% Fed + 4.63% State) = 32.63%

$375 x .3263 = $122.36

Sid paid $75 per month more than the debt payments, but saved $47.36 per month beyond that ($122.36 – $75 = 47.36).

If the amount paid to Sue is more than $375, for example $415, then Sue has an extra $25.49, and Sid saves $27.15 overall, thereby sharing the tax savings through doing maintenance between them.

Non-Modifiable Maintenance

CAUTION To make fixed term maintenance non-modifiable, you must state it clearly in the maintenance section of your separation agreement. For example: "We agree that our maintenance plan is contractual in nature and non-modifiable, and request, and intend, that the Court have no further jurisdiction over the matter of maintenance after the entry (date) of our Decree."

- Maintenance to pay off marital debts can stair-step down as the total of the debt payments goes down. Following the example above, the payments could be $375 at first, then $300, then $200, paralleling the total of the minimum payments plus Sue's tax needs, phasing out at the end of the two and a half years when the debts are paid in full.

- Maintenance to pay off marital debts can be paid in a steady amount for a fixed period of time—paying less than the total minimum payments in the first years, and more than the debt payment in the later years. A flat payment plan such as this has the advantage of looking more like traditional alimony to the IRS, as well as being predictable. In the above example, maintenance payments could be $200 per month for 2.5 years, if $200 were the average of debt payments plus Sue's tax needs.

- Maintenance to pay marital debts can also be paid in a lump sum, or several lump sums. In the above example, figure the total amount of debt, add to it the receiving spouse's tax on that amount, and pay it as a lump sum. The receiving spouse then pays off the debts in total. In the above example:

  12 months × 2.5 years = 30 months

  30 months × $150 = $4,500 (assuming the debt payments begin at $300 and decrease steadily to zero over the 2.5 years).

  The lower income spouse's taxes 15% + 4.63% = 19.63%. $4,500 ÷ .8037 = $5,599. (Be sure that such a large amount will not move the lower income spouse from the 15% bracket—see Chapter 11, Taxes for tables which will help you do this).

- Some marital debts are single payment debts—such as joint taxes owing for the last year of the marriage, or from an audit, or a balloon payment on a mortgage, signature loans, short-term loans from friends and family. You can use the same type of planning as on the lump sum example above.

b. Maintenance to Pay Specific Expenses for Children or Spouse

Maintenance can be used to indirectly pay child care. Suppose only one of you qualifies as head of household for tax purposes and therefore is the only one who can use the Child Care Credit—but you both want to share responsibility for paying for work-related child care. In order to maximize the credit, the non-head-of-household parent pays the head-of-household parent his/her portion of the child care as maintenance, and the head-of-household parent pays the child care provider. This enables the head-of-household parent to take the full amount into the formula to figure the credit, while the non-head-of-household parent deducts his/her share of the day care as maintenance. Be sure to add the receiving spouse's tax need on the maintenance to the amount of the payment if the tax rate is larger than the child care credit. See Taxes, Chapter 11, for a complete discussion of head of household status and the child care credit.

If you agree to a fixed amount for a certain number of years for this purpose, then this is contractual or fixed term maintenance, and will be presumed not to change. If your purpose is to lock it in, safe from any change, then this is the way to do it. A different result comes about if you allow the maintenance amount to fluctuate with the costs of child care. An agreement to that affect would be open-ended maintenance, preserving your ability to modify the amount as needed. However, paying child care through maintenance might look to the IRS like child support. See the next section of this chapter, and Chapter 11, Taxes. In practice, whichever kind of maintenance you are designing, don't link the provisions in your agreement about maintenance with the provisions about who pays the child care. These should be in separate sections of your written agreement.

The same kind of planning can be done around medical and dental expenses for a child which are expected to be significant (chronic asthma, braces). These expenses can't be deducted until they reach 7.5% of adjusted gross income. Since the lower income spouse is likely to reach 7.5% sooner than the higher income spouse, have the lower income parent pay the bills and the higher income parent pay his/her share as maintenance. This kind of agreement might also look to the IRS like child support (see the next section of this chapter) and could also fall under the related contingency rule if the children are approaching

Maintenance Checklist 2b:

We are interested in paying the following expenses with maintenance:

Expense:_______ Amount:_______

Expense:_______ Amount:_______

Expense:_______ Amount:_______

Expense:_______ Amount:_______

Expense:_______ Amount:_______

_______ Initials

_______ Initials

If your plan calls for a reduction in maintenance when any child reaches the age of majority (see Chapter 8, Children, for why this is a unique problem in Colorado) and/or you plan reductions in maintenance during the time any two or more of your children are between 18 and 24, see Chapter 11, Taxes about the *related contingency* rule. This rule could undo all your good planning if you do not check.

emancipation. See Chapter 11, Taxes. Be sure both your maintenance and child support agreements will stand on their own.

Whatever your maintenance provision, whether to pay spouse's or children's expenses, you must be absolutely clear in writing about when and under what circumstances you expect it to be modifiable, and when if ever it ends. See Chapter 13, Finishing Up.

c. Maintenance to Pay for a Spouse's Training, Education, or Therapy

Maintenance Checklist 2c: We are interested in maintenance to pay for ____________'s training, education, or therapy as follows:

Item:_______ Cost: $______

Item:_______ Cost: $______

Item:_______ Cost: $______

Item:_______ Cost: $______

Item:_______ Cost: $______

____________ Initials ____________ Initials

Maintenance can be used to provide an opportunity to renew or rejuvenate a career, to obtain the education or training necessary to become self-supporting, or to supplement the new income as it phases in and up. If you are considering maintenance for any of these purposes, the spouse seeking maintenance should gather the following data:

- What will your training or education cost? Direct costs: tuition, books, parking?
- What are the indirect costs: babysitting, loss of income?
- What, if anything, can you earn during your training?
- How long will it take?
- What can you expect to earn once you have completed your plan?

Gathering this information can help assuage some of the feelings which often accompany this situation: anger at paying for someone else's choices; anger at needing someone else to pay for your choices; guilt; fear of poverty, failure, the unknown; concern that your children lose something during this time, and worry about not being able to make ends meet.

State Income Tax on Maintenance Too

Remember in your budget to add in the cost of State income tax on maintenance. The Colorado income tax rate is 4.63% for everybody—there are no tax brackets to play with here.

Tie the maintenance in your agreement directly to your purpose. For example, maintenance is payable only so long as the spouse is in school, in good standing and working toward a degree or certificate. Sometimes it is easier on the family budget if some of this is paid in a lump sum or several lump sums—from a year end bonus or other occasional or irregular income of the paying spouse. Once the recipient spouse's training is completed, the maintenance can stair-step down as the recipient's income increases.

d. Maintenance to Supplement While a Spouse's Income Phases In Or Up

Maintenance Checklist 2d:

We are interested in using maintenance to supplement ____________'s income as follows:

____________ Initials ____________ Initials

If one spouse has recently re-entered the job market or changed careers, that spouse is probably earning entry-level or probationary pay, which is probably less than that person's earning potential. It may take a while for the income to build. This is such a common occurrence that it is even acknowledged in the Child Support Guideline where it says that a parent shall not be treated as under-employed if: "The employment is temporary and is reasonably intended to result in higher income within the foreseeable future;" or "The employment is a good faith career choice. . . ."

Maintenance that stair-steps down can complement nicely a spouse's income that is stair-stepping up. Many people want to make the steps a dollar for dollar reduction: every time the receiving spouse earns a $100 a month more, the maintenance reduces by $100 the next month. Correlating the two this closely, however, can become a disincentive to the lower income spouse (and also makes it open-ended maintenance). Often it is better to agree in advance to regular decreases in maintenance over a fixed period of time, based on your best estimates of the timing of the receiving spouse's future earnings. This way everyone knows what to expect, and not expect.

e. Maintenance to Balance a Property Division

Occasionally spouses will agree to a division of their property which makes sense to them, but which places a larger amount of property with one spouse. If that property does not include liquid assets which can be transferred readily, a compensating amount may need to be paid periodically to make the division feel fair.

Donald and Roxanne

Donald and Roxanne have divided their marital property in a manner which places $20,000 more in value on Roxanne's side of the balance sheet due to a large retirement fund which she cannot touch now. Roxanne can pay $12,000 in maintenance ($10,000 to equalize the property, plus $2,000 to pay Donald's tax on this amount). It can be a lump sum, or periodic (quarterly, monthly), depending on how Roxanne receives income. If she gets quarterly income from stock, or a twice-yearly company performance bonus, these can be a dandy source of funding for this kind of maintenance.

Be sure to disconnect this maintenance provision from the section in your agreement about division of property, since the IRS has historically frowned on paying for property with alimony. Recite in the property division section of your agreement that your division is "fair," even though it is not 50-50. Then put your maintenance agreement in another section. You may wish to state that the receiving spouse needs maintenance so that the maintenance provision stands on its own.

Maintenance Changes Child Support

Maintenance shifts before-tax (gross) income from one spouse to the other, therefore altering each parent's percentage share of child support. The result is that the child support goes down, and a larger portion of the money being paid between spouses is labeled maintenance.

Maintenance Checklist 2e:

There is an imbalance in our property division of $__________ which we are considering using maintenance to offset as follows:

______________ Initials ______________ Initials

Maintenance must not survive the death of the receiving spouse. If it does, it is deemed to be a property payment, and therefore included in the taxable income of the payor. Similarly, maintenance is presumed to end on the re-marriage of the receiving spouse. You can agree that it will not do so—but this might suggest to the IRS that it is actually part of your property division.

Purpose, Amount Needed, and Duration of Our Maintenance Plan

Directions: Fill in any of the following (1-3) uses of maintenance to which you have agreed.

1. (For maintenance use 2a through 2e above.) We will use lump sum maintenance for these specific purposes:

   in this (these) needed amount(s):

   to be paid as follows (dates):

2. (For any use of maintenance.) We will use monthly or periodic maintenance for a specific period of time for the following purposes:

   In this (these) needed amount(s):

   To be paid monthly (or other frequency):

   For the following time frame:

3. (For maintenance use 1a through 1d above.) We will use maintenance with no built-in time limit (lifetime maintenance) for the following purpose:

   In the beginning needed amount of:

IRS MAINTENANCE RULES

Since 1986, the rules about what is and is not permanent maintenance (alimony in IRS language) have simplified. In order to qualify as maintenance which will be deductible by the payor and taxable to the payee, a payment must meet the following requirements:

1. It must be in cash or cash equivalent, like a check, not property (i.e., not in-kind, like a car or horse).
2. It must be received by a spouse or former spouse, or by a third party on behalf of a spouse or former spouse, of the payor.
3. The payments must be made according to a divorce or legal separation instrument (a decree or written separation agreement).
4. You cannot be members of the same household at the time any payments are made either before your Decree (temporary maintenance, Chapter 4) or after the Decree. You must be moved apart and at different addresses within 30 days of the first maintenance payment.
5. The obligation to make the payment cannot continue after the receiving-spouse's death.
6. The payment is not "fixed as child support." See also the related contingency rule in Chapter 11, Taxes.
7. You have not said anywhere in your agreement (see 3. above) that these payments are not to receive maintenance tax treatment.

Before you finish your maintenance agreement, be certain it meets all these criteria.

ORGANIZING YOUR INCOME AND EXPENSES

Since many kinds of maintenance are based on the ability of the paying spouse to pay, as well as on the needs of the receiving spouse, you must be knowledgeable of your incomes and expenses in order to develop a sound maintenance plan. Review the Income Charts and Monthly Budgets you prepared for Chapter 6, and update them as needed. If you prepared Monthly Budgets while designing a temporary agreement (Chapter 4), review and update them now.

PUTTING YOUR MAINTENANCE PLAN TOGETHER

Putting together a smart maintenance plan for your unique circumstances requires that you consider carefully each of the following:

- purpose
- amount needed
- duration
- stair-step, if any;
- circumstances under which it is modifiable, if any;
- tax consequences and amount to be paid;
- circumstances under which it terminates, if any;
- security or teeth.

Following is a discussion of each of these, with examples. Write the elements of your own plan in the sidebar.

Purpose, Amount, and Duration

Review any of the ways to use maintenance at the beginning of this chapter in which either of you indicated interest. How many ways to use maintenance are still of interest to you both? Review and discuss these. Write in detail each purpose for which you both agree to use maintenance. For each purpose, calculate the amount needed based on your Income Charts and Monthly Budgets in Chapter 6.

- If one of your purposes for maintenance is to level incomes or supplement income to the lower income spouse, then use the Budget Analysis Chart in Chapter 4. This chart will compare the incomes and budgets in your two homes.

- If your purpose for maintenance is to supplement income to the lower income spouse for a specific purpose, you will base your analysis on that spouse's Monthly Budget. For example, write down the amount for tuition, books, transportation, parking, and children's day care for a spouse entering college. Estimate the budget needs for the lower income spouse for the immediate future.

- If another purpose for maintenance is to pay specific expenses, be sure you look on both Monthly Budgets. It is possible that a certain expense is now being paid by the "wrong" spouse. Perhaps this expense might be better paid by the other spouse with money received as maintenance.

Stair Steps and Modification

The next step after determining the purpose, amount and duration of your maintenance, is to decide if and under what circumstances the amount should change. You can agree ahead of time

Our Stair Steps

Directions: Complete the following statement as needed to reflect your unique circumstances.

We foresee predictable changes (for example, completion of degree, quitting school, payoff of a debt, child no longer needs day care, receiving spouse's income increases in a predictable amount, specific length of time from decree) in the amount of our maintenance as follows:

Future Changes

Directions: Complete the following statement as needed to reflect your unique circumstances.

We agree that the amount of our maintenance may be re-examined and adjusted by us if the following (for example, unforeseen changes in either income or expenses) happens:

Calculating The Amount To Be Paid

We make the following calculations to determine the tax as well as the amount to be paid for our proposed maintenance:

Therefore our initial maintenance amount to be paid is:

to change the amount on the occurrence of a certain event, or after certain periods of time, or when your incomes change in certain ways, or some other circumstance.

You may want the amount to change when the purpose is satisfied, in whole or in part. You may set the modification amounts now, not to be changed regardless of future occurrences for either spouse. For example, you anticipate that the receiving spouse's income will increase in fairly predictable increments, so you plan for maintenance to phase down at a certain amount per month each year, whether or not either spouse actually earns according to the plan. This is a clear stair-step plan.

If you anticipate future changes for either spouse, instead of stair-stepping the amount as above, you can plan your future changes based on a formula. For example, maintenance will decrease by a percentage of the amount of increase in the receiving spouse's income.

Lastly, you can agree now to review and adjust your maintenance plan in the event circumstances arise later which you cannot foresee now. For example, the paying spouse loses his or her job, illness changes the earning capacity of either of you, or one or several of the assumptions on which you based your maintenance agreement do not prove true, such as your career choices do not produce the income you anticipated.

For more on the question of modifying maintenance after the final decree, see Chapter 13.

Tax Consequences and Amount to be Paid

Now that you know how much maintenance needs to be received, for how long and under what circumstances, you need to calculate how much needs to be paid. To do that you must look at the projected tax status of each of you and the tax effect of your proposed maintenance plan.

Once you have reached agreement about Maintenance you may want to include this agreement in your draft separation agreement using the sample provisions in Chapter 12. The remaining sections of this chapter discuss some important elements of fine tuning.

Termination of Maintenance

Maintenance is presumed to end on the death or re-marriage of the recipient. You are required to state this in your agreement if your state law does not also presume this. Colorado does, but it is good practice to include it anyway.

Can maintenance survive the death of the payor? There is no presumption about this. Many people secure a maintenance obligation with life insurance on the life of the payor. Some people create an annuity tied to the life of the payor, payable to the recipient.

If your agreement to pay maintenance arises from your division of property, you might wish the payments to continue beyond the re-marriage of the recipient. In this case, you must say so in your agreement.

Long term maintenance frequently terminates at the retirement of the paying spouse, especially if the division of property included divisions of retirement or pension monies via QDRO, or if the receiving spouse has sufficient Social Security. See Chapter 7.

Some couples prefer to define their goals for maintenance and set an amount for the first year only. They then meet toward the end of that year to adjust the amount according to their pre-defined criteria.

Non-Taxable Maintenance

It's possible to make an agreement for maintenance which does not shift taxes. It is neither deductible for the payor, nor taxable to the payee, so neither one mentions it on their tax return. Non-taxable maintenance can also be used in conjunction with taxable maintenance to navigate around the recapture rules (see Chapter 11, Taxes). If you want your maintenance plan to be non-taxable, you must say so in your separation agreement. If both spouses are in the same tax bracket, you might not want to shift the taxes at all.

Life Insurance as Security for Maintenance

You may secure the payment of maintenance with insurance on the life of the paying spouse. To figure the amount of insurance to get, take the amount of the payments times the maximum number of months it could be paid. The maximum total amount which could be paid is probably the initial amount of the death benefit. This can be decreasing term insurance, i.e., the death benefit decreases each year over the term of the maintenance.

Cohabitation

When divorcing couples are putting together an agreement about maintenance (spousal support) which will last for some time after

Our Plan for Terminating Maintenance

Directions: Complete the following statement as needed to reflect your unique circumstances.

We agree that our maintenance will end under the following circumstances:

Former Spouse's Medical Insurance – COBRA

Since 1986, every employer of more than 25 employees who is subject to the Federal law called "ERISA", (The Employee Retirement Income Security Act of 1974), has been required to allow divorced spouses of their employees to continued coverage under the same health insurance policy by which they have been covered as the spouse of an employee. The non-employee spouse pays the premium, which may not be more than 105% of the full premium (including the amount the employer may have been paying on behalf of an employee as a benefit). Employers are now required to tell any employee what the cost of this "COBRA" (The Consolidated Omnibus Budget Reconciliation Act of 1985), option would be for their ex-spouse after a divorce. This option is available for thirty-six months from the date of the final decree. Since the ex-spouse does not have to qualify for this insurance, no "pre-existing" conditions will prevent him/her from being insured. Remember, you may use maintenance to pay the premiums.There is usually a time limit within which to activate the COBRA insurance provision for a former spouse. Missing the deadline can be fatal to your agreement. So, be certain to check with the employer and insurer long before you put pen to paper.

Social Security Eligibility in 10-Year Marriage

Once you have been married for 10 years or more, both spouses have the option of having their Social Security benefit at retirement calculated on either their own earnings or on those of their former spouse. If you choose the latter, the benefit is half of that of the former spouse. It is an independent entitlement and does not reduce the benefit to the former spouse. To collect this benefit you must apply for it and be at least 62, and your former spouse must be entitled to or receiving benefits. If you remarry, you generally cannot collect benefits on your former spouse's record unless your later marriage ends (whether by death, divorce, or annulment). For more information contact your local office of the Social Security Administration, or visit www.ssa.gov.

the final decree, they usually end up in a discussion of cohabitation sooner or later. As with many things divorcing couples argue about, the word doesn't convey the real issue. The paying spouse wants the maintenance to end when the receiving spouse is married or living in a marriage-like arrangement. The thinking being that he or she should not pay for a former spouse if that spouse is living in an arrangement which implies that someone else is taking care of or sharing expenses with the former spouse. From the receiving spouse's point of view, a co-habitation provision may feel like the former spouse is trying to tell him or her how to live —or at least trying to dictate the seriousness of his or her new sexual relationship.

The cohabitation label arose in states which do not recognize common law marriage. Therefore, a former spouse could, and did, go on receiving maintenance while in a new relationship which was a marriage in all but the name. Colorado recognizes common law marriage, so many former spouses who live with someone of the opposite sex whom they treat as a spouse may be married by their actions. You could agree that maintenance ceases if the receiving spouse remarries, whether ceremonial or common law.

The real issue is one of economic self-sufficiency, not of sex. For example, you might say that maintenance would cease or decrease within a certain time after the receiving spouse shares the home with an able-bodied adult who is, or is capable of, contributing to basic expenses like housing, utilities, and food. It should not matter what sex this person is, or what the relationship is to the receiving spouse. Such a person could be a relative or a paying boarder. Try to find language for your agreement about when maintenance ceases which focuses on money and not behavior.

TEETH TO MAINTAIN YOUR MAINTENANCE AGREEMENT

If your ex has a new lover, will you be less likely to pay the maintenance? Will you be less likely to pay the debts you agreed to pay through maintenance? If you lose your job, or the bonus does not come through, will you look for a way out of your agreement to pay maintenance? Would any of these be tempting for you?

There are several kinds of internal enforcement which can be used in maintenance agreements. What we call "teeth" are voluntary, private, and effective ways of penalizing yourselves with more or less costly consequences if you don't do what you say you will do. What does each of you need to put into your agreement to make sure you keep the promises you make to each other with regard to maintenance? These incentives to right behavior are limited only by your imagination. Try having the person against whom the penalty would act set the penalty. You may be surprised to learn what motivates each of you.

Agreements you might try: if the maintenance payment is not made on time, the paying spouse loses the tax deduction, and the recipient does not have to declare it as income. Or, if the maintenance is not used for the agreed-upon purpose (paying the house payment), the maintenance will cease, or reduce, and the spouse who was paying maintenance has first option to assume the obligation and receive the property.

It may or may not be appropriate for you to put such strict punishments in your own agreement. That's your decision. But, if you begin right away treating your agreement as a very serious bargain between the two of you, there will be less chance that you will be tempted to take it lightly later on.

Conclusion

You have now finished your first rough look at your maintenance plan. It will probably not be your final version. Go on to the next chapter about taxes if you have not already read it. The agreements you reach as a result of the tax chapter may necessitate changes in your maintenance plan.

Take heart. Doing your own separation agreement is hard work. Don't expect to get it all done in one sitting. Don't even expect to complete the work of one of the separation agreement chapters in one sitting. Give yourself and each other the time you deserve to make the best decisions for your family.

CHAPTER **11**

TAXES
SEPARATION AGREEMENT – PART V

TAXES
SEPARATION AGREEMENT - PART V

Reading this chapter is 90% likely to save you money; not reading it is 100% likely to cost you money.

Before the court can give you a final decree of dissolution of marriage or legal separation, you must resolve and write out all the financial and parental issues remaining from your marriage. This written summary is called the separation agreement, whether you are obtaining a divorce or a legal separation. It must be read and approved by the court.

"The art of taxation consists in so plucking the goose as to obtain the largest possible amount of feathers with the smallest possible amount of hissing." Attributed to Jean Baptiste Colbert. (c. 1665).

The introduction to Chapter 7 lists the things you need to do to prepare your separation agreement and directs you to the chapters with information necessary to accomplish this. This chapter discusses taxes and tax planning as a part of your separation agreement.

The Tax Effects of Divorce

"The wisdom of man never yet contrived a system of taxation that would operate with perfect equality." Andrew Jackson, Proclamation to the People of South Carolina, Dec. 10, 1832.

There are many tax effects of divorce which will happen whether or not you plan for them. There may be a profound change in your incomes; there certainly will be a profound change in their taxability. Dollars which are exempted or deducted from taxable income will change, as will your tax filing status and the tax credits for which you are eligible. Unique to divorce is the concept of maintenance (alimony), the tax rules for which are discussed in this chapter. Property that is transferred between spouses as part of a divorce is not taxed as though it were sold, but any built-in capital gain is a factor to be considered in your bargaining about that property, as you can see in Chapter 7.

"Taxes, after all, are the dues that we pay for the privilege of membership in an organized society." Franklin D. Roosevelt, Worcester, Mass., Oct. 21, 1936.

The four aspects of your taxes which are impacted by your divorce are:

- filing status
- exemptions
- deductions
- credits

Following is a brief discussion of each.

Tax Filing Status

P PARTNERS A partner's tax filing status is either single, or head of household if you have a dependent living with you. That doesn't change when partners move apart. Partners in Colorado who file married filing jointly (or married filing separately) are probably common law married (see Chapter 1).

The IRS taxes income in percentages: the first and lowest portion of your income is taxed at 10%; the second and higher portion, over a certain threshold, at 15%; and above that at 25%, then 28%, then 33%, and then at 35%. Your tax filing status determines how much of your income is taxed at each of these percentages.

There are four statuses: *married filing jointly, married filing separate, single,* and *head of household.* Married filing jointly permits the largest amount of income to be taxed at 10% and 15%. In married filing separately, the smallest amount of income is taxed at 10% and 15% before the percentage changes to 25%. You have probably been filing in one of these statuses. Your current withholding rate at work is probably based on the assumption that you will continue to file in that status, so it is important to begin your tax planning early in your negotiations.

Tax filing status: Category in which your taxes are figured which determines how much of your income is taxed at what percentage. For example: married filing jointly.

Table of Tax Brackets for 2012

Tax Rate	Single Over — But not over	Head of Household Over — But not over
10%	0–$8,700	0–$12,400
15%	$8,701–35,350	$12,401–47,350
25%	$35,351–85,650	$47,351–122,300
28%	$85,651–178,650	$122,301–198,050
33%	$178,651–388,350	$198,051–388,350
35%	$388,351	$388,351
Standard Deduction*	$5,950	$8,700

Tax Rate	Married Filing Joint Over — But not over	Married Filing Separate Over — But not over
10%	0–$17,400	0–$8,700
15%	$17,401–70,700	$8,701–35,350
25%	$70,701–142,700	$35,351–71,350
28%	$142,701–217,450	$71,351–108,725
33%	$217,451–388,350	$108,726–194,175
35%	$388,351	$194,176
Standard Deduction*	$11,900	$5,950

"If we were married for most of the year, then we have to file our taxes as married."

No. You file your tax returns according to your marital status on December 31st. If your divorce was final that day you may not file as married. There may be some tax advantages for you in filing separately because only then can you do planning through maintenance. See Chapter 10.

Initially, your choices for tax filing status are determined by your marital status on December 31st. If your final decree of dissolution (divorce) was signed on or before December 31, then you are single for that tax year, and must file as single or head of household. You no longer have a choice of filing married.

If you remain married through December 31, you may file married filing jointly or married filing separately. If you were still married on December 31st, but you have been separated for more than six months, you have the additional option of filing as head of household if you qualify.

Uneasiness About Tax Returns

You are both legally responsible for any tax return you sign. Separation, when emotions are running high and expenses running even higher, is a time when people are tempted to be unwise on their tax returns (by exaggerating deductible expenses, claiming doubtful deductions, or "forgetting" to list income). If either of you is likely to be less forthcoming than the other, consider filing Married Separate, so you are not legally bound by a tax return you are uncomfortable with. This might cost you some additional tax, but the peace of mind may be worth it.

Finalizing your divorce before or after December 31st may have enormous consequences for this tax year. You can put off finalizing your divorce until after the first of the year if you will save money by filing jointly. You might choose to finalize your divorce before the end of the year if at least one of you will save money by filing as head of household.

Head of household status is the most favorable way to file for divorced or separated persons because it results in the least amount of tax. The head of household income brackets are higher for every tax rate below 35% as compared to those for single filers; so more earnings are allowed to be taxed at the lower rate. The standard deduction is also higher for head of household than for single.

"Filing head of household means that I get the tax exemptions for our children."

This is a frequent misunderstanding. Your filing status and dependent exemptions are different. The dependent exemptions may be taken by either parent, if you agree. The IRS will presume they go to the head of household parent unless you agree otherwise.

A single taxpayer may file as head of household if he or she provides a household for more than half the year for any legal dependent. Still-married persons who have been separated for more than six months may file as head of household if they provide a household for a dependent child.

Tax Exemptions

Tax exemption: Category of income on which you are not taxed. For example, the personal exemption for yourself and members of your family.

A tax exemption is an opportunity to take out, or exempt, a certain amount from your taxable income. The exemption commonly discussed in divorce cases is the *dependent exemption.* This is a fixed amount per person, one for each parent, one for each child. The exemption for any given child cannot be split—one parent gets it for a full tax year. If you have one child you may alternate years, but you must each adjust your withholding every year. If you have more than one child, you may allocate the exemptions between you. The amount of the personal or dependent exemption varies annually and is available by calling the IRS ($3,700 in 2011 and $3,800 in 2012).

The IRS will presume that the parent who has more overnights with a child gets the dependency exemption for that child. But the exemption can be allocated to the other parent, and can be bargained for. Consider whether it will help the family budget or ease a significant tax burden for the non-residential parent to have the exemption this time.

If You Don't Do This, It Won't Happen

Judges do not have to take into account the anticipated tax consequences when they decide divorce cases. Many lawyer-negotiated settlements do not consider this, either. Working together, you have the advantage of being able to do tax planning.

The dependency exemption and the head of household filing status are not the same thing. They are two separate lines on your tax return. To declare head of household status, you must list at least one qualifying person as your dependent, which means that your home was that person's principal place of abode for that tax year. The qualifying person is often a child. You are NOT required to also list that child as your tax exemption. See form 1040 on the next page. Note the difference between line 4 and lines 6 c and d.

If you wish the dependency exemption to be claimed by the parent who does not name that child as the basis for his or her head of household filing status, the head of household parent for that child must sign IRS form 8332. Both parents must file a copy with their tax return. See form 8332 on the next page.

Note that IRS form 8332, shown on the following page, allows you to select whether the exemption will be claimed for one year, or for future years. Since things change, especially where children are concerned, doing this release one year at a time probably makes sense.

Both parents taking the same child's personal exemption, or as a dependent for head of household tax filing status will absolutely cause an audit by the IRS and may trigger a penalty. Be very clear about these arrangements in your agreement.

Form **1040** Department of the Treasury—Internal Revenue Service (99) **U.S. Individual Income Tax Return** **2011** OMB No. 1545-0074 IRS Use Only—Do not write or staple in this space

For the year Jan. 1–Dec. 31, 2011, or other tax year beginning , 2011, ending , 20 | See separate instructions.

Your first name and initial	Last name	**Your social security number**
If a joint return, spouse's first name and initial	Last name	**Spouse's social security number**
Home address (number and street). If you have a P.O. box, see instructions.	Apt. no.	▲ Make sure the SSN(s) above and on line 6c are correct.
City, town or post office, state, and ZIP code. If you have a foreign address, also complete spaces below (see instructions).		**Presidential Election Campaign**
Foreign country name	Foreign province/county / Foreign postal code	Check here if you, or your spouse if filing jointly, want $3 to go to this fund. Checking a box below will not change your tax or refund. ☐ You ☐ Spouse

Filing Status

Check only one box.

1 ☐ Single
2 ☐ Married filing jointly (even if only one had income)
3 ☐ Married filing separately. Enter spouse's SSN above and full name here. ▶
4 ☐ Head of household (with qualifying person). (See instructions.) If the qualifying person is a child but not your dependent, enter this child's name here. ▶
5 ☐ Qualifying widow(er) with dependent child

Exemptions

6a ☐ **Yourself.** If someone can claim you as a dependent, **do not** check box 6a
b ☐ **Spouse**
} **Boxes checked on 6a and 6b**

c **Dependents:** (1) First name Last name	(2) Dependent's social security number	(3) Dependent's relationship to you	(4) ✓ if child under age 17 qualifying for child tax credit (see instructions)
			☐
			☐
			☐
			☐

If more than four dependents, see instructions and check here ▶ ☐

No. of children on 6c who:
• **lived with you**
• **did not live with you due to divorce or separation (see instructions)**
Dependents on 6c not entered above

d Total number of exemptions claimed

Add numbers on lines above ▶

Begin with the assumption that the parent who has a child for more than half the overnights per year will file as head of household, claim the child care credit, and have the dependent exemption for that child. If you want to reverse the last of these—to balance the tax benefits of having children, or as part of your overall bargaining—you may do so by using IRS Form 8332.

Form **8332**
(Rev. January 2010)
Department of the Treasury
Internal Revenue Service

Release/Revocation of Release of Claim to Exemption for Child by Custodial Parent

► **Attach a separate form for each child.**

OMB No. 1545-0074
Attachment Sequence No. **115**

Name of noncustodial parent | **Noncustodial parent's social security number (SSN)** ►

Part I **Release of Claim to Exemption for Current Year**

I agree not to claim an exemption for ____________________
Name of child

for the tax year 20____.

Signature of custodial parent releasing claim to exemption | Custodial parent's SSN | Date

Note. If you choose not to claim an exemption for this child for future tax years, also complete Part II.

Part II **Release of Claim to Exemption for Future Years** (If completed, see **Noncustodial Parent** on page 2.)

I agree not to claim an exemption for ____________________
Name of child

for the tax year(s) ____________________ .
(Specify. See instructions.)

Signature of custodial parent releasing claim to exemption | Custodial parent's SSN | Date

Part III **Revocation of Release of Claim to Exemption for Future Year(s)**

I revoke the release of claim to an exemption for ____________________
Name of child

for the tax year(s) ____________________ .
(Specify. See instructions.)

Signature of custodial parent revoking the release of claim to exemption | Custodial parent's SSN | Date

Tax Deductions

A deduction is an amount you are allowed to subtract from your taxable income before you figure your tax. Some common examples are: interest you paid on your home mortgage, certain taxes and a certain percent of medical and dental costs beyond insurance coverage and medical and dental insurance premiums. These deductions are shown on Schedule A—Form 1040 if you itemize your deductions. Follow Schedule A to estimate your itemized deductions, compare this to the standard deduction in your tax filing status. You will probably want to use the higher of these.

Certain additional expenses, such as tax preparation, tax advice, and certain accounting and other fees, are deductible to the extent they exceed 2% of your adjusted gross income. Some portions of your divorce expenses—for attorney, accountant, mediator—may be deductible in this category. Be sure you seek expert advice on this point as these deductions are not clearly defined in the tax code.

If you have few deductions and choose not to itemize, or are filing the short form tax return (1040 EZ), you may take a "standard deduction." The amount of the standard deduction changes annually and varies with your tax status, the highest one being for head of household. You can learn the amount of the current standard deduction for each filing status by requesting this information from IRS or your payroll department. 2012 amounts are on the Table of Tax Brackets earlier in this chapter.

Tax Credits

A tax credit is just what the name implies. You subtract it (give yourself credit) from the amount of tax you would otherwise pay (bottom line on your income tax return). The child care credit is the most significant one for divorcing or separated parents of young children.

The child care credit is a fixed percentage (varying from 20-35% for up to two children) of the day care amount paid out by single parents while they are at work or seeking work. For divorcing couples the credit is linked to having head of household tax filing status. The qualifying "dependent (child)" is defined the same way. Therefore, even in your very early tax planning you must be careful that the parent who would benefit most from the credit will be able to file as head of household for that child. The parent with head of household filing status for a child must

Tax deduction: Specific expenditures which may be deducted from your income before figuring your tax. For example, the interest portion of your home mortgage is a deduction.

A tax deduction is not the same as a tax exemption.

IRS requires that when one married spouse, filing separately, itemizes his/her deductions, so must the other spouse.

"If I pay the mortgage, I get the deduction."

It's not that simple. In addition to actually making the payments, the home must be your primary residence, and your name must be on the mortgage.

Tax credit: A percentage of certain expenditures which may be subtracted from your tax. For example, a percentage of what one pays for work-related child care is a credit against income tax.

be the one to pay for child care of that child. You can't take credit for something you didn't pay.

> There is no child care credit if you have a flex or cafeteria plan. See Chapter 9.

You can use either the child care credit or a flex (cafeteria) plan, but not both. A cafeteria or flex plan allows the employee to pay for child care and family medical expenses from pre-tax dollars which are withheld by the employer and escrowed or held in trust for the benefit and use of the employee and his or her family. The child care credit effectively does the same thing, by returning to you the tax money already paid on dollars used to pay for work-related child care. A cafeteria plan can, like maintenance, shift the tax benefits of child care to the non-head-of-household parent.

> **"If I pay the day care, I get the child care credit."**
>
> It's not that simple. For divorcing couples, in addition to making the payment to the care giver, you must also qualify and file as head of household—using the same child for whom you are paying the day care as the basis for your head of household filing status.

You will use IRS form 2441 to claim the child care credit. You can calculate the amount of your credit by using the Child Care Credit Table in Chapter 9.

There are other fairly new credits in addition to the child care credit. The child tax credit for 2012 of $1,000 per child under 17 goes to the parent who claims the child's personal exemption. It phases out at higher incomes.

> You can estimate the amount of your child care credit by using the child care credit table in Chapter 9.

There are three education credits. For students in their first and second year of college, graduate school, or vocational training, the Hope scholarship credit refunds to the paying parent or student up to $1800 per year for the first two years for college expenses (tuition, fees, but not books, room and board, or transportation).

The American Opportunity Credit modifies the Hope Credit for 2009 and 2010 and extended through 2011-2012, making it available to a broader range of taxpayers, including many with higher incomes and those who owe no tax, up to a maximum of $2500 per eligible student per year. This credit is available for the first four years of a student's post-secondary education (instead of two). Up to 40% of the credit amount is refundable should the taxpayers liability be insufficient to offset the nonrefundable credit amount.

The Lifetime Learning credit rebates up to 20 percent of the first $10,000 of qualified education expenses for college, graduate school, and job training for children and adults, for any year in which the Hope credit is not claimed. It goes to the person who pays the expense.

All three education credits phase out at higher incomes.

Estimate Your Taxes

Taking into account the tax consequences of your proposed plan is essential to a workable final agreement. As you have seen from the previous sections of this chapter, the tax consequences happen whether you plan for them or not. Misunderstanding or ignoring the tax consequences of your plan can unravel it altogether.

Pre-test your divorce plan to be sure you know your tax result for the next year, or to be sure you have the best overall tax result. Use a current federal income tax form 1040 to estimate taxes for each of you, and be sure you have budgeted for how you will pay them. You may need to revise the W-4 instructions to the employer about withholding from your paycheck or adjust the amounts of your estimated tax payments if you are self-employed. If you can't figure out how to do it yourself, most tax accountants will do an estimated tax calculation for you if you give them your agreement draft and ask them to check for glaring errors or unforeseen traps.

Maintenance Recapture

Your maintenance agreement must meet the IRS rules for what is "alimony". See Chapter 10.

There are some circumstances under which the IRS may void your maintenance arrangement and *recapture* the payments into the income of the paying spouse. This not only voids the tax savings back to the beginning, but, since it is usually discovered later (often in an audit), may incur interest and penalties as well. These circumstances are contained in two *recapture rules:*

1. Maintenance must not decrease more than the rules allow in the first three years if paid from an income source within payor's control; this can be referred to as the "Steep Stair-Step" rule;

2. Maintenance must not reduce on the "happening of a contingency relating to a child" or a "time which can clearly be associated with [such] a contingency;" this can be referred to as the "Related Contingency" rule.

THE STEEP STAIR-STEP RULE

This rule applies to all cases where maintenance is being paid, whether or not there are children. The "steep stair-step" rule was designed to prevent "front-end loading"—a large amount of maintenance being paid in the first year of the divorce, and then reduced rapidly within the first 3 years. Its purpose is to catch divorcing taxpayers who are trying to transfer their property settlement as maintenance in order to gain a tax advantage. Since

CAUTION

Unless you have agreed to 50/50 physical care of more than one child, or you have physical care of at least one child each, only one of you will qualify for the child care credit—the one with more overnights for that child.

D DEFINITION

Alimony: The name the IRS uses for maintenance.

IR$

If you are considering maintenance of $15,000 or more to be paid before December 31st of the year of your separation, **you must read this section**.

Separate Households Required for Maintenance After the Decree

You must actually live in separate households before or within 30 days of your first permanent maintenance payment.

IR$

If you are considering paying substantial maintenance—$1250 per month or $15,000 per year or more—and you are planning to have it decrease significantly during the first 3 years, **you must read this section**.

"First post-separation year:" defined by the IRS as the first calendar year in which payments which the IRS will recognize as "alimony" are paid. This means the first year in which payments are made which fit the rules in Chapter 10. Note the different rules regarding pre-decree temporary maintenance, depending on whether it is part of a court order. See Chapters 4 and 10.

this is some of the tax planning smart couples need do at this time, this is an important rule to be mindful of.

The Internal Revenue Code says that $15,000 per year is the cut-off point, so if you plan to pay less than this amount in maintenance you are in the "safe harbor," as accountants frequently call it. The IRS will examine alimony plans for "front-loading" for three years. So, if you plan maintenance payments over $15,000 a year which will decrease, don't decrease them more than the rules allow during the first three years. There is a significant exception to this rule that is explained in the adjacent sidebar.

Significant Exception to the Steep Stair-Step Rule

If you make your temporary separation agreement into a court order, any maintenance payments that are made DO NOT count in the maintenance considered in the steep stair-step rule. Therefore you can transfer large lump sums as temporary maintenance without recapture (pulled back into the payor's income for taxation).

If you DO NOT make your temporary maintenance agreement into a court order, these payments DO count in the maintenance considered in the steep stair-step rule, and it may be recaptured. Be sure to do the calculation before you decide.

According to this rule, maintenance payments in the first year cannot exceed the average payments for the second and third years by more than $15,000. And payments in the second year cannot exceed payments in the third year by more than $15,000. This rule essentially applies to planned excess payments, but paying late (for whatever reason) can trigger a recapture if the payment is made in the next calendar year.

There is no recapture because of:

death;
remarriage;
temporary payments;
or because the payment is based on a percent payment from income or business profits for at least three years.

If there's any chance your maintenance plan might violate this rule, complete the following worksheet. This is the official form from the IRS's own publication *Divorced or Separated Individuals,* Publication 504.

IRS publishes lots of pamphlets about all aspects of tax law and practice. Two particularly useful publications for separating couples are: *Divorced or Separated Individuals,* Publication 504 and *Selling Your Home,* Publication 523, which contains details on capital gains calculations for many situations too detailed to cover here: Armed Forces personnel, recapture of Federal subsidies, etc.

Worksheet for Recapture of Alimony

Note: Do not enter less than zero on any line.

1. Alimony paid in **2nd year** ...... ________
2. Alimony paid in **3rd year** .... ________
3. Floor $15,000
4. Add lines 2 and 3.................... ________
5. Subtract line 4 from line 1 .... ________
6. Alimony paid in **1st year** .... ________
7. Adjusted alimony paid in **2nd year** (line 1 less line 5) ... ________
8. Alimony paid in **3rd year** .... ________

9. Add lines 7 and 8 .... ________

10. Divide line 9 by 2 .... ________

11. Floor $15,000

12. Add lines 10 and 11 .... ________

13. Subtract line 12 from line 6 .... ________

14. **Recaptured alimony.** Add lines 5 and 13 .... ________

Your result on Line 14 is the amount to be recaptured—taxed to the person who paid it and deducted from the income of the person who received it. Perform this test on your maintenance plan. If your result on Line 14 is zero or negative, there will be no recapture under this rule. If your result is positive, adjust the amounts to be paid under your agreement to avoid recapture.

Any amount paid as temporary maintenance before the decree, so long as it is by court order, does *not* have to be counted in this rule. A solution to the problem of high up-front maintenance is to pay as much as you can before the decree, where there is no recapture. If you want to start the 3-year clock running, begin the payments before the decree, by written agreement, and do not have that agreement made into a court order.

THE RELATED CONTINGENCY RULE

This rule applies to cases with minor children, in which there is a blurring of the distinction between maintenance and child support.

The IRS restricts child-support-as-maintenance by applying two rules to any **reductions** in maintenance which are measured by events that may be tied to your children. (See "Who is a Child?" in Chapter 8 for a discussion of the presumed age of emancipation in Colorado.) The first circumstance under which the IRS will *presume* a relationship between the reduction in maintenance and children is if the reduction occurs when a child reaches a certain income level, leaves the household, becomes employed, dies, marries, or leaves school. Second is if the reduction occurs within six months on either side of the date any child reaches 18, 19, or 21, or if there are two or more children and two or more reductions in maintenance occur when two children reach the same chronological age between 18-24 (or within a year of the same age).

Example: Mary and Tom have two daughters, Sarah (12) and Michele (18). Mary and Tom must make sure that if they reduce maintenance one year either side of when Michele turns 20, that

"We have to write up our temporary agreement and take it to the court in order for the IRS to honor our temporary maintenance."

Not quite. The law does not require that you have your temporary agreement made into a court order. You may do so if you wish. To be temporary maintenance, i.e. to shift taxes, your temporary maintenance plan must be either by court order, or by a written agreement between the two of you that is signed and, to be safe, notarized, *before* your first maintenance payment under the agreement.

If your plan calls for a reduction in maintenance when any child reaches the age of majority and/or you plan reductions in maintenance within one year of when your children reach the same age between 18 and 24, **you must read this section**.

Maintenance Changes Child Support

Maintenance shifts before-tax (gross) income from one spouse to the other, therefore altering each parent's percentage share of child support. The result is that the child support goes down, and a larger portion of the money being paid between spouses is labeled maintenance. This can be helpful, because paying maintenance is tax deductible, and child support is not.

they do not also reduce maintenance one year either side of when Sarah turns 20.

In either of these circumstances the IRS will presume the reductions were contingent on a child reaching a certain age and will disallow the amounts of all reductions as maintenance and treat them, retroactively, as child support. IRS will recapture the amount of all such reductions—all the way back to the beginning. Even including a separate amount of child support is not enough to stop these rules.

Before you throw your hands in the air and give up any hope of an agreement for reducing maintenance when your children are leaving the nest, try making the reductions clearly contingent on something which has nothing whatsoever to do with your children. For example: Make the reductions occur regularly over a long period of time, beginning before any child reaches the "dangerous" age range, and continue the payments past the time the last child could possibly have emancipated. Or, make the contingency which triggers the reduction something related to one of you (for example, 2, 4, 6, 8, and 10 years from the date of the decree, when the recipient remarries, when the paying spouse retires, or when there is a change in income for either of you).

Another way is to state specific dates for reduction of maintenance which are not within 6 months (before or after) of any child's 18th, 19th, or 21st birthday.

But note the downside: if your child or children are emancipated at any unexpectedly early date, the maintenance payments will continue until the date you specify. Decide whether this is too high a price to pay for the tax savings.

It is possible to *rebut* the IRS presumption of relatedness of the reductions in maintenance with a solid, independent reason for the reductions occurring when you agreed to. Then, if the reductions just happen to fall in the danger zone, you can plead coincidence, that you did not plan it that way, and weren't even thinking about how old your children would be and whether they were nearing emancipation. Remember, the IRS will presume the *relatedness* of your planned maintenance reductions and your children's emancipation, if the dates of the reduction(s) fall within a corresponding time. Overcoming any IRS presumption is very hard to do.

Conclusion

You have now finished your first rough look at your tax plan. It will probably not be your final version. Review now Chapters 7-10, the other four separation agreement chapters, and revise or adjust your tentative agreements according to your tax plan, moving toward reaching your final agreement. The sample clauses in Chapter 12 should help you with drafting.

Take heart. Doing your own separation agreement is hard work. Don't expect to get it all done in one sitting. Don't even expect to complete the work of one of the separation agreement chapters in one sitting. Give yourself and each other the time you deserve to make the best decisions for your family.

CHAPTER 12

THE FINAL COURT PAPERS

Decree:

Final order signed by the court granting your dissolution of marriage or legal separation.

Checklist of Our Final Court Papers

Directions: Initial each document you agree to be responsible for preparing, and write in the date you will have it ready.

Person responsible	Date promised	Document
______	_____	Husband's Sworn Financial Statement
______	_____	Wife's Sworn Financial Statement
______	_____	Husband's Certificate of Compliance
______	_____	Wife's Certificate of Compliance
______	_____	Separation Agreement and/or including a Parenting Plan
______	_____	Child Support Worksheet ___
______	_____	Child Support Worksheet ___
______	_____	Certificate of Attendance from parenting-after-divorce class (if ordered)
______	_____	Affidavit for Decree Without Appearance
______	_____	Support Order
______	_____	Decree
______	_____	QDRO and/or other written agreement to divide retirement (as needed)
______	_____	Income Withholding for Support

THE FINAL COURT PAPERS

When you ask the court to sign your final decree of dissolution of marriage or legal separation, you must provide the court with some or all of the forms in this chapter.

Everyone, with or without children, needs the following:

- **Proof of Service,** if the case is not a co-petitioner filing. This will be either a signed Waiver or Certificate of Service from the back of the Summons, or it will be a copy of the Order permitting service by certified mail or publication with proof of certified mail or a copy of the publication with the last date published. See Chapter 5 if any of this is a surprise.

- A **Sworn Financial Statement (No. 253)** The court must receive one of these from each of you. If you have previously filed your financial statement with the court, you do not need to file it again with your other final papers, as long as your financial information has remained the same. If, however, your income, debts, or assets have changed from the original information you provided, or you have remembered something you had forgotten, you must file a new financial statement with the new or updated information.

- A typed or printed **Separation Agreement**, double-spaced, on 8½ x 11" paper, with both of your notarized signatures. Chapters 7-11 of this Guidebook show you how to develop this yourselves. This chapter contains sample clauses to assist you to write your own.

- A **Decree (No. 251)** for the court to sign. See this chapter.

You may need these forms:

- An **Affidavit for Decree without Appearance of Parties (No. 252)** if you qualify. See this chapter.

- A **QDRO**, if applicable, to transfer retirement assets. See Chapter 7.

- **Notice to Set (No. 1195)** Some courts require both the parties to call the clerk to set up a date for a hearing. You will need this form to notify the other party of when to call. Read more about who needs this later in this chapter.

- **Notice of Hearing (No. 1196)** In some cases you will need this to notify the other party of the date of any hearing. Read more about who needs this later in this chapter.

If you have minor children of this marriage, you will need most of these forms.

- **Written Parenting Plan.** You may include the parenting plan in your separation agreement—merely labeling a section "Parenting Plan", do a separate document for this. See Chapter 8.
- The correct **Child Support Worksheet(s) (Nos. 1170 or 1171)** depending on the mode of physical care you have agreed to for your children. See Chapter 9.
- **Certificate of Attendance** by each of you for any court-ordered parenting-after-divorce class. See Chapter 8.
- **Notice to Employer to Deduct for Health Insurance (No. 1162).** If the court orders payment of health insurance for the children, this notifies the employer to withhold and pay the amount ordered to the insurance company. If this arrangement is already in place, you may not need this form. See this chapter.

If one of you will be paying child support and/or maintenance to the other you may need:

- **Support Order (No. 251A).** You will need this if one of you is paying either child support or maintenance to the other. When signed by the court, it then becomes an order. See this chapter.
- **Income Withholding for Support (No. 1155).** Used if one of you will be paying child support and/or maintenance to the other and want to have it paid by an income assignment. See this chapter.

SEPARATION AGREEMENT

If you have hired a mediator, or have worked with some other third party to reach all or some of your agreement, then that person will probably write up the agreements you reached there. If there are still some issues you worked out by yourselves, you will need to write them up. Mediators or other facilitators may title their summary of your agreement(s), "Memorandum of Agreement," or "Memorandum of Understanding." You don't need to re-title it if you are using it as all or part of your separation agreement.

If you have hired attorneys to do the basic paperwork, they will prepare all these papers for you—including the separation agreement. This is true whether they negotiate all the terms of the

D DEFINITION

Caption:

The large box at the top of the first page of forms filed in court which contains specific information that is mandatory according to Colorado Court Rules. This incudes the name and location of the court, the case number, the names of the parties filing the case and the form name.

See page 317 for a sample caption that you can copy onto the top of any forms you create for the court, including your separation agreement.

agreement for you, or you negotiate by yourselves and describe the terms to your attorney.

The decree summarizes the terms from your agreement which have the greatest legal consequences (such as marital status and parenting plan). Once your separation agreement is complete, label it "Exhibit A" and reference it as such in number 5 of the decree.

The court will read your separation agreement to be sure it contains certain minimal provisions (support if there are children, division of property and debts, etc.) and to be certain it is not so bizarre as to be "unconscionable" (i.e. a person of conscience would not have done it). The court will not help you negotiate your agreement. Chapters 7-11 of this Guidebook are designed to help you work out an agreement of which you will both be proud.

If you have only constructive service on your spouse (see Chapter 5), or your spouse has elected not to take part in the divorce, you will not have a written separation agreement. Instead, you may write your own document entitled "Information for the Court". This can be used to tell the court what you would like them to order. You will give testimony in court regarding your requests for child support, parenting plan, and property. See the sample testimony on page 365 to help you write down what you will say.

DECREE

The Decree is the final *order* of the court which grants you a dissolution of marriage or legal separation. Although this is an order to be signed by the court, you fill out the form the way you want it to be signed. If the court is satisfied that your agreement is fair and that you have met all the other requirements for a Decree, then the court will sign it. If you are ever called upon to prove that you are single, this is the one piece of paper you will need. Similarly, if you are ever asked to prove what kind of parental responsibilities you have after the divorce, this piece of paper may be enough.

DECREE WITHOUT A HEARING

If you *do not* have minor children (under 21), then you may avoid a hearing entirely by mailing in an affidavit for decree without appearance of parties, your separation agreement, proposed decree, sworn financial statements, certificates of compliance, and any other order(s) you have agreed the court should sign. Send these in when you are ready to finalize. If you file them within 42 days of filing the petition, you will not have to attend

D DEFINITION **Divorce by affidavit:** Also called Decree Without Appearance of Parties or Decree Without a Hearing; procedure which permits certain parties to a divorce to mail their papers to the court instead of having a hearing.

Sample Cover Letter to the Clerk of the Court for Divorce by Affidavit

(If you file these papers in person, you will not need a cover letter.)

Date

Clerk of the ________ District Court
Address

Re: marriage of _________________
Case # __________

Dear Clerk,

Enclosed please find the final documents for our Dissolution of Marriage. Please return a copy of the conformed decree in (each of) the enclosed stamped self-addressed envelope(s).

Thank you for your assistance.

Sincerely,

____

Enclosures: List all your final documents here, as you have indicated on your Checklists. Send originals with original signatures. Include a photocopy of the decree and a self-addressed, stamped envelope for yourself. Your spouse may do the same.

an initial status conference, but you should notify them of your cancellation.

If you do have minor children, you may also avoid a hearing if EACH of you has a lawyer and they signed your separation agreement, your proposed decree, and support order. Your attorneys will file your papers for you.

To file for divorce by affidavit you will need to take these steps:

a) Complete all of the requirements in your case management order regarding mandatory disclosures, including the Certificates of Compliance (if you haven't filed them earlier), and updated sworn financial statements, if necessary.

b) Sign your Separation Agreement in front of a notary and fill out your proposed Decree. If there are children, fill out the Support Order and the certificate of attendance from your parenting-after-divorce class.

c) Complete and sign the Affidavit for Decree Without Appearance of Parties in front of a notary. Both of you must sign it, if possible.

d) If only you are signing the affidavit, send a copy to your spouse by certified mail—using the best address you have for your spouse if his or her whereabouts are presently unknown. Attach the certified mail receipt to the original Affidavit when you send it to the court. Note: Remember to jot down your case number on the green return card when you get it back with your spouse's signature, so the court will know what file to put it in when you send it to the court to prove your spouse received the Affidavit.

e) File your papers with the court. If you are filing before your initial status conference, ask the clerk if there is any procedure you must follow to "vacate" the order to attend. If you have children, you may still be required to attend.

Once you have provided the Affidavit for Decree Without Appearance and all the other final papers, and the 91 day waiting period is complete, a magistrate or commissioner assigned to non-contested divorces will read your papers at his or her convenience – sometimes on set days of the week.

If you have left something out or done something inadequately (in terms of filling out a form or following a procedure), the court will send you a form telling you what you did not do correctly and offer you a chance to straighten it out. Once you amend your papers to the court's satisfaction, and return them, the court will sign your decree and you will be divorced.

"The Judge will order all the things we want at the final hearing."

It's not that simple.

If you and your spouse have worked out a settlement, then you will appear for a short, non-contested hearing. The court will order exactly what is in your separation agreement, nothing more. The court will make no decisions, just approve or disapprove your settlement.

If you and your spouse have not worked out a complete settlement, you will set your case for a contested hearing concerning anything you have not agreed on. This is a real trial, at which you will each ask for what you want and give your reasons. **No one can guarantee the outcome.**

Only if your spouse can not be personally served, has not been a part of the case and will not appear at the final hearing, will you probably get most of what you ask for. Under these circumstances, however, the court may lack jurisdiction to order some of the things which are most important to you. See Chapter 5 about the problem of jurisdiction.

DECREE WITH A NON-CONTESTED HEARING

In most courts the hearings for non-contested divorces are very low key and short (10-15 minutes). The magistrates who conduct these hearings know you are nervous and usually sad and will try to help you present your documents clearly and with a minimum of discomfort. There is a script for a hearing later in this chapter that you can use to get started. A status conference can sometimes become your final hearing once you have reached agreement on all matters, and your 91 days have run.

DECREE WITH A PARTIALLY-CONTESTED HEARING OR AN ABSENT SPOUSE

Many courts will allow a person filing his or her own divorce action to have a short hearing in front of the magistrate instead of the judge, even if there isn't a complete signed separation agreement, if: a) the spouse is absent and the case was served by constructive service (see Chapter 6), or b) the case was personally served but the spouse has never filed a response or taken part in the case in any way. Lawyers call this a "default". If you are doing such a hearing, you will need to be particularly careful about the Notice to Set and the Notice of Hearing forms.

Notes:

<table>
<tr><td>District Court, ____________________ County, Colorado
Court Address:</td><td rowspan="3">

▲ COURT USE ONLY ▲</td></tr>
<tr><td>In re ____________________________:
Petitioner:

and
Co-Petitioner/Respondent:</td></tr>
<tr><td rowspan="2">Attorney or Party Without Attorney (Name and Address):

Phone Number:
FAX Number:
E-mail:
Atty. Reg. #:</td></tr>
<tr><td>Case Number:

Div.: Ctrm.:</td></tr>
<tr><td colspan="2"></td></tr>
</table>

The Caption

The top portion of the first page any form that gets filed in court is called the "Caption". It includes the information that the court needs to keep track of your case — the name and location of the court, the case number, the names of the parties who are filing and the title of the form.

This book contains most of the forms you will need, but if you decide to create your own Separation Agreement and/or Parenting Plan, or QDRO, you may use the caption shown above. Leave a top margin of 1 1/2" and a left margin of 1". Fill in the title of the form in the blank box across the bottom of the caption, and add your own document below it. Fill out the caption just like you did in the petition, except the title that goes in the blank box at the bottom.

Sample Wording for Your Separation Agreement

The following sample wording is drawn from the material throughout this Guidebook. You may use it as the basis for writing up your own separation agreement. If your spouse has not participated in the case, is not signing a complete separation agreement, or if you served by constructive service, then you may wish to use the JDF forms above as your written requests to the court. To determine if a form is best for you, this might be a good time to go back and read the caution on page 16.

If you and your spouse have been working through this book, you will already have written drafts of most of this material, perhaps even already on these sample paragraphs. If not, gather your notes and all the partial agreements you have made and assemble them, using these paragraphs as a guide to wording and arrangement. The order of topics follows the chapters in this book, and the language is the same as the partial agreements within each chapter. You are referred back to the appropriate chapters so if you have forgotten a topic or agreement you can go back and retrieve it.

It is a good idea to write in these pages in pencil, adding extra paragraphs on a separate piece of paper. When you have finished your first draft, you may wish to flip through the book to be sure your have picked up every agreement and question. Then sit down at your home computer or a friend's and write it up. Copy the caption from the previous page onto the top of your agreement and fill in the information from the caption like all your other papers. Put the document title SEPARATION AGREEMENT in all capital letters and then, using double spacing, start putting in the agreements you have made, as you have written them.

CAUTION These samples are illustrations of some possible agreements. There are many other possibilities. Adapt them to make your written agreement say *exactly* what you agree to. **Do not use these words to tell you what to agree to.** Study the appropriate chapters in this book and talk with each other to be certain you are clear about your agreement, and to be certain that your written words represent it accurately and fully.

A. GENERAL INFORMATION

We, ______________________________ *(full name, and how you will be referred to in this agreement),* and ______________________________ *(full name, how you will be referred to in this agreement (e.g., Karen A. Johnson ("Karen")),* agree to the following:

We were married on ____________________ *(date)* and separated on ____________________ *(date).* Our current addresses are *(as stated in your petition)* ______________________________, and ______________________________, respectively. Our children are: ____________________ *(name),* _____ *(age),* ____________________, _____, and ____________________, _____. They have special needs of ______________________________ ______________________________ ______________________________ *(See Chapter 8).*

____________ is employed at ____________________ and earns __________ per month before taxes. ____________ is employed at ____________________ and earns __________ per month before taxes. (*See Chapter 9)*

OR: We agree that ______________________________ need not seek employment outside the home at this time (in order to be at home with our children) (in order to complete school or training at ________________________________) (due to ____________________ [illness]) (or _________________). *(See Chapter 9)*

We agree our marriage is irretrievably broken, and agree to obtain a decree of dissolution of marriage (legal separation). (*See Chapter 1 and this chapter.)*

We state that we have each provided the other with complete copies of all required disclosures and have each filed a Certificate of Compliance. *(See Chapter 6)*.

We agree that this separation agreement is fair to both of us (and is in the best interest of our children).

We mediated (portions of) this separation agreement with __________________________________ , (during the months of ____________________ , ____________________ , and ____________________) (over a period of _______ hours).

____ *(one spouse)* consulted with ________________________________ *(attorney/accountant/financial planner/therapist)* concerning the terms of this agreement as to him/herself. (*See Chapter 2.)* ____________________________________ *(other spouse)* consulted with ______________________________ *(attorney/ accountant/financial planner/therapist)* concerning the terms of this agreement as to him/herself.

Should either or both of us decide to convert our decree of legal separation to a decree of dissolution of marriage, we agree that the terms of our separation agreement are acceptable as is and should not be modified. *(See Chapters 2 and 13)*

OR

Should either or both of us decide to convert our decree of legal separation to a Decree of Dissolution of Marriage, we agree to renegotiate the following portions of our separation agreement: ____
____
____. *(See Chapters 2 and 13)*

B. ASSETS AND DEBTS *(See Chapter 7)*

1. Family Home or Other Real Estate *(See Chapter 7)*

Our family home is located at ___________________________________ *(address)*. It is titled in our joint names (OR *in* ______________________________ *name)*. We estimate the fair market value of our home to be $____________. The balance on the mortgage is $____________ as of ___________________ *(date)*, and the balance on the second mortgage (OR *home equity line of credit)* is $____________, leaving gross equity of $____________.

We estimate the costs of sale to be $____________, leaving net equity of $____________.

We agree that $____________ of this is ________________________'s separate property.

______________________________ shall quitclaim all his/her title and interest in the property to _________________________, on or before ________________________ *(date or event such as date of our decree, 60 days after the date of our Decree)* to be his/her sole and separate property.

______________________________ *(person getting the property)* shall pay the mortgage(s), property taxes, insurance, and all other expenses of the property starting _________________ *(date or event, often the date of our Decree)*, holding ______________________________ *(person quitclaiming)* harmless from all of these.

____________________ will pay to ____________________ $____________ in payment of his/her interest in the home OR to make our property division equitable, on or before ______________________ *(date or event)*, OR when the home is sold, within _____ days of when ______________________ remarries, when ______________________ occupies the home with an adult (for longer than ___________________), whichever comes first. ______________________ will sign a Promissory Note and a Deed of Trust for this amount to ______________________ *(other spouse)*.

OR

We will retain title to the family home together—converting title to a Tenancy in Common on or before the date of the final decree of ____________________ into a ______% / ______% division, ___________________ having a _____% share and ____________________________ having a ______% share. We will share all expenses for this home in the ratio of our ownership. AND/OR _____________________________ will live in the home and will be solely responsible for payment of: ____ and, we will share the expenses for: ____.

OR

We will sell the family home located at ______________________________ and will share the proceeds, after payment of all mortgages, and expenses of sale as follows: ______% to ___________________________________ , and ______% to ____.

OR

We will rent out the home and will split the proceeds, after payment of _________________________, in the ratio of _____% to ____________________, and _____% to ___________________________. We will share the cost of any capital improvements or repairs not covered by the rent, or the mortgage, utilities and upkeep whenever it is empty. _____________________________ *(one spouse)* will be responsible for keeping it rented and for minor repairs. We will pay for ______________________ *(utilities)* ____________________ *(repairs)*. We will share the benefit of any depreciation ______% to _______________, and ______% to _______________ . When we sell it, we will share the responsibility for any capital gain in the ratio of our share of proceeds, OR ______% to ________________, and ______% to __________________.

OR

Our home is in foreclosure. _____________________ will live there until _____________________ has to leave. We shall share any expenses of the foreclosure ______% for _____________________ and ______% for _____________________.

2. **Personal Property** *(See Chapter 7)*

We have already divided our personal property to our satisfaction. We both agree that this division is fair. We agree that our personal property shall become the separate property of the party who now possesses it. We choose not to place a value on this personal property in our settlement.

OR

_____________________________ will keep the following items of furniture, household goods, and other personal property: ____ , with a total value of $___________________ .

(Repeat for other spouse.)

_________________________ will be responsible for payment to ____________________________ of $_______________ for purchase of ____________________________ or which is secured by ____ .

(Repeat for other spouse.)

OR

_______________________ will maintain possession of the following items of personal property for ____________________ until ____________________________ *(date, has own house, etc.)*: ____

____

____

____

All other items of personal property have been divided to our satisfaction.

3. Cars and Other Motor Vehicles *(See Chapter 7)*

____________________ will retain the ____________________ *(year and make)* automobile, titled ____________________ *(in* ___________________ *name, in our joint names)*, fair market value of $_____________.

There is no loan on this car.

OR

________________________ shall be solely and separately responsible for paying the loan on it, balance of $_____________ as of ____________________________ (date), holding _______________________ (other spouse) harmless from it. _________________________ shall be solely and separately responsible for all of the expenses of this car, including loan payments, taxes, insurance, registration, maintenance, and fuel, starting _______________________ (date or event) *(e.g., date of our decree, within 30 days of signing this agreement, within 60 days of paying off the loan).*

________________________ will refinance the loan into his/her own name on or before _______________________ (date or event).

________________________ will cooperate as needed to sign the title over to _______________________.

(Repeat as needed for each vehicle.

4. Liquid Assets: Cash and Bank Accounts *(See Chapter 7)*

All joint bank accounts have previously been closed.

OR

We shall close our joint checking or savings accounts, or transfer them into the name of one of us as we agree, on or before ____________________ (date or event), and divide the balance on that date between us (______% to ________________ and ______% to ________________; or and the balance shall be ____________________'s sole and separate property).

________________________ will retain his or her checking account at ____________________________, balance of $____________ as of _________________ *(date)*; savings account at ____________________________, balance of $____________ as of _________________ *(date)*; credit union account at ____________________________, balance of $____________ as of _________________ *(date)*; and other account at ____________________________, balance of $____________ as of _________________ *(date)*.

(Repeat for other spouse.)

We will divide the balance in our _________________ account equally between us, OR ______% to _________________ and ______% to _________________, within ______ days of the date of our Decree (OR other date or event).

We will continue to operate the home out of the joint account at ________________________________, AND/OR we will use the joint account at ________________________________ *(for the expenses of this separation and divorce) (until the final decree)* OR *(all the expenses for the home or divorce are paid)* OR the home is sold and the expenses of sale are paid. OR, We will contribute $____________ per ________________ *(week, month, etc.)* each, OR ____________________________ will contribute $____________ and ________________________ will contribute $____________ per ________________ *(week, month, etc.)*, until we agree to close it (OR other date or event).

5. Stocks, Bonds, and Options *(See Chapter 7)*

We will divide the securities and cash in the ________________________ investment account equally between us, including equalizing existing gains and losses, OR ______% to _________________ and ______% to _________________, allocating existing gains and losses between us in the same percentage.

OR

_________________________________ will retain the following stocks OR stock accounts OR investment accounts:

Account at/stock in ____
_____________________ present value of $______________ presently in ___________________________________ name(s). We believe there is/is not a capital gain on this stock/account (of $_________________) at the present time.

(Repeat for all stocks and investment accounts and for both spouses.)

_________________________________ will retain the following bonds:

____

with a face value of $_____________, and a maturity date of _______________, presently in ___________________________ name(s). *(Repeat for each bond for both spouses.)*

We own in_____________'s name, by grant dated _______________, the option to purchase_________shares of___________ stock at $__________. These options are ___________% vested. The pre-tax fair market value of these options, after paying the purchase price, is $_______________ *(state an amount, or 'current zero')*. The expiration date of this grant is __________.

We agree that all of the options in this grant, (vested and unvested), will be _______________'s *(the named spouse)* sole and separate property

OR

We agree that ____________ *(named spouse)* will maintain ____________ of these options for ____________'s *(other spouse)* benefit, and upon exercise will pay the net proceeds from these options after taxes to ____________ *(other spouse)* to be his/her sole and separate property. The remaining options after those held for ____________ *(other spouse)* will be ____________'s *(named spouse)* sole and separate property. *(Consult counsel for further wording about who decides to exercise the options, and when, how to calculate the taxes, and other complexities.)*

6. Life Insurance *(See Chapter 7)*

Be certain that these provisions are consistent with Sections D and E of this Agreement, about security for child support and maintenance, see Chapters 9 and 10.

_______________________ will have the _______________________ *(company)* life insurance policy on his/her life OR on ___________________'s *(the other's)* life, death benefit of $___________ and cash value of $___________ *(with no cash value)*, as his/her sole and separate property, and as of the date of our Decree (or other date) may change the beneficiary at his/her sole option.

___________________ will maintain at least $___________ in life insurance death benefits with ____________________ *(other spouse)* as beneficiary until _________________ (date or event, such as the death of either one of us, until all child support and maintenance obligations are paid in full, until youngest child's _______ birthday).

(Repeat for other spouse, if necessary.)

The owner of the policy will have the option to place it in trust but to provide the same benefits.

We agree that we may lower the amount of these death benefits in the future, but only as we agree in writing and signed by both of us.

We agree to provide proof of coverage and current beneficiary designation to the other in ___________________ of each year, starting in ___________________.

(Annuities are included in Retirement.)

7. Retirement, Pensions, and Profit Sharing *(See Chapter 7)*

IRA's and SEP's

The IRA (SEP) in ________________ 's name, balance of $________________ as of ________________ (date), shall be his/her sole and separate property.

OR

The ________________ IRA (SEP) account in ________________ 's name has a balance of $________________ as of ________________ (date). We agree to transfer $________________ (or ______% as of the date of our Decree) from this account into an IRA in ________________ 's *(the receiving spouse)* name to be ________________ 's *(receiving spouse)* sole and separate property, the balance remaining to be ________________ 's *(paying spouse)* sole and separate property.

For a defined benefit plan under ERISA (401(k), 403(b), etc.), whether you are dividing it or not, obtain the wording you need from your attorney or CPA.

Defined Contribution Plans qualified under ERISA, (401(k), 403(b), etc.)

The ________________ Plan account in ________________ 's name, balance of $______________ as of ________________ (date), shall be his/her sole and separate property.

OR

We agree that $___________ (or ______% as of the date of our Decree) of the balance as of the date of our Decree (or other date) in the ________________ Plan account in ________________'s name shall be transferred to ________________ *(receiving spouse)* by means of a Qualified Domestic Relations Order to be presented to the court for signature at the time of our Decree, to be _________________'s *(receiving spouse)* sole and separate property, the balance remaining in the account to be ___________________'s *(paying spouse)* sole and separate property.

For all other retirements, obtain the wording you need from your attorney or CPA.

8. Business Interests *(See Chapter 7)*

_____________________ *(one spouse)* does business as _____________________ *(name of business)* as a sole proprietor. We agree that this business has a fair market value of $___________ including goodwill, *(OR is of unknown value, or has no market value)*, and that it will be _________________'s sole and separate property. _______________________ *(owner)* will hold _____________________ *(other spouse)* harmless from any and all liabilities and obligations of _____________________ *(name of business)*.

_____________________ *(one spouse)* owns 100% of the shares in _____________________ *(corporation)*, a Colorado *(or other)* corporation, which has a fair market value of $__________ including goodwill. We agree that these shares will be _______________'s *(same spouse)* sole and separate property. ________________ *(owner)* shall hold ___________________ *(other spouse)* harmless from any and all liabilities and obligations of _____________________ *(corporation)*.

_____________________ *(one spouse)* is the sole member and owner of __________________, LLC, a Colorado limited liability company which has a fair market value of $_________ including goodwill. We agree that this membership will be ____________'s *(same spouse)* sole and separate property. _____________________ *(owner)* shall hold _____________________ *(other spouse)* harmless from any and all liabilities and obligations of _____________________, LLC.

Along with ownership of the business _____________________ *(corporation, LLC, sole proprietorship)* _____________________ *(owner spouse)* shall have all the assets of the business as his/her sole and separate property, including _____________________ *(car, truck, bank accounts, computer, copier, cell, any other property which may have been stored at home and/or used by family member other than the business owner)*.

_______________________ will retain all rights to the business ____ , including all stock, membership rights, and/or assets, specifically including: ______________________________________ ____ *(car, computer, any other property which may have been stored at the home and/or used by family member other than the business owner)*.

As between _____________________ (*spouse*) and ______________________ (*other spouse*), _________________ will be solely responsible for all liabilities and debts incurred in the name of the business or in ___________________ name for the benefit of the business, including: ____ ____ *(list any debts which the spouse may have signed, or the proceeds of which may have gone into a joint account or have been used for the family home, car, etc.)*

We believe the present net value of this business to be $ ____________________ , which includes $ ____________________ which we agree is the value of goodwill of this business.

For corporations, partnerships, limited liability companies, and other business entities involving two or more owners, you can obtain the wording you need from your attorney or CPA.

9. Miscellaneous Assets *(See Chapter 7)*

List here any assets that you didn't list in any of the above categories, such as safety deposit box, frequent flyer miles, memberships.

______________________ will have all the frequent flyer miles on the ______________________ account in his/her name.

We will share the remainder of our ______________________ membership until it expires. Any further membership there will be the separate responsibility of each of us.

10. Debts *(See Chapter 7)*

______________________ *(one spouse)* will be solely and separately responsible for paying the following debts, holding ______________________ *(other spouse)* harmless:

______________________ *(creditor, e.g., _____ Credit Union Visa)* in ________________ name *(his/her, our joint names)*, balance of $___________.

Repeat for each debt that spouse will pay.

(Repeat for other spouse.)

We shall close all joint credit accounts on or before ________________ *(date or event)* (or have previously been closed).

We have no debts other than those previously mentioned in this Agreement.

We agree that after ______________ *(date or event)* neither of us will incur any credit, charge, or other obligation in the other's name or in our joint names. Should either of us incur any such obligation, the one of us who incurred it will be solely and separately responsible for paying it, holding the other harmless.

11. Enforcement *(See Chapter 13)*

If _________________________ does not transfer the ______________________ *(property)* as agreed by us, then the court may issue a Commissioner's Deed, and order of transfer of property under Rule 70 of the Colorado Rules of Civil Procedure, for that property on _________ days notice to the court of the failure to transfer.

AND/OR

If _________________________ does not pay the $ ___________ *(debt)* to ______________________ as promised, then he/she will not receive the following property as agreed ____ ____ *(will not get share of home per promissory note, for example, or won't get title to car, boat, stock, etc.)*.

(Repeat for other spouse.)

If either of us files Chapter 7 or 13 bankruptcy on any debt included in this agreement, then we agree that the entire division of property and debts must be re-worked by us. We agree now that if we are unable to work out a new division, and/or if one of us is unwilling to do so, that the court retains jurisdiction over the matter of property and debt division, and may order a different division to compensate for the additional debt for which the spouse not filing bankruptcy is now liable. (*See Chapters 7 and 13.)*

C. PARENTING PLAN *(See Chapter 8)*

(This paragraph, and this type of paragraph, sets a tone. It is not necessary and completely optional.) We agree that the wellbeing of our children is of the utmost importance to both of us. We pledge to each other, as parents, that we will each provide a home where they are cherished, and were they will have the opportunity for full development and to flourish. We will support their relationships with the other parent as well as their sense of home with the other parent. Although we are divorcing, we remain, in ways that involve our children, a family. We agree to deal with our differences out of their presence, to always treat and speak of the other with respect and civility when in their presence, and to not use them for the purpose of carrying messages to or discovering information about the other.

1. Allocation of Decision-Making Responsibilities: Who Will Make the Major Decisions Regarding Our Children

a. We agree to make the following major decisions about our children together;.

____

____

____

____.

__________________________ (one parent) will make the following major decisions about our children:

____

____

____.

__________________________ (other parent) will make the following major decisions about our children:

____

____

____.

b. Emergency Medical Care

We each hereby agree and consent to any emergency care for our children which the other consents to. Any follow-up care, however, will be determined according to our decision-making responsibilities agreement.

c. Day-to-day Decisions

All day-to-day decisions will be made by the parent in whose physical care the child is at the time of the decision and whose exclusive physical care the decision will affect.

d. Communication

We agree that good communication between us is vital to our roles as *(joint decision makers and)* good parents. To that end, we agree to meet monthly *(quarterly, annually)* during the _________ week of each month, in a neutral place away from the children, to discuss exclusively the children's progress, parenting issues, any concerns about the children, any upcoming expenses for the children, as well as to reimburse each other for expenses as agreed, and to plan and conform our calendars.

We agree to inform ourselves and each other, and each of us shall take responsibility to keep ourselves up to date regarding all information about our children's schooling, learning, activities, including but not limited to teacher's reports and comments, medical options and reports, social concerns, parenting issues, activities, performances and the like.

Regardless of the form of parental decision-making we have agreed to, we agree that there are certain facts events, and other matters about which we must exchange information. Therefore, we agree to keep one another continually informed about:

____.

We agree that we will notify the other parent in advance of any major decisions which we wish to discuss at the next regular meeting *(phone call, communications)*.

From time to time we may agree to make a written agreement about matters concerning our children. We agree to "sleep on" *(think on)* any written agreement for 24 hours before signing, then sign it if we still agree.

2. Parenting Time

a. Schedule

We agree to the following schedule of parenting time/physical care with our children *(copy or re-write the schedules, including holidays, which you agreed to in Chapter 8)*: ____
____
____
____.

OR

We agree to the following pattern of parenting time/physical care with our children: *(copy the calendar you have agreed to AND/OR describe this pattern in words).*

We agree to the following arrangements about holidays with our children: ____
____
____.

AND: We agree to the following arrangements about our annual vacation times *(if this is not included in your arrangements about holidays)*: ____
____
____.

The parenting time we have agreed to, described above, results in (approximately) ____________ overnights per calendar year with ______________________________ *(parent) (This may be a percentage, a number, a range or a limitation—not less than ____________ OR not more than ____________).*

b. Transportation of the Children

We agree to the following about transporting the children between us: ____
____
____
____.

OR

We agree to share the transportation of the children between our homes equitably between us.

c. Additional Agreements About Children

We agree that on the occurrence of the following events we will adjust our short-term time schedule with the children:
____
____
____.

We agree to notify each other of the following concerning our children: *(medical and dental exam results, significant events, minor injury or illness, teachers conferences, PTA meetings, recitals, homework or project deadlines)*: ____
____
____.

We agree to the following arrangements about parenting time between our children and *(their grandparents) (other relatives)*: ____
____.

We agree to support our children's relationships with each of our extended families.

d. Attendance at Teacher Conferences, Children's Sports Events and Performances.

We agree that we may both attend events related to the children without interference or harassment from the other, events such as teachers conferences, sporting events, performances, and the like. We agree to be always respectful of the other when in the presence of the children.

e. Future Relationships

We will not introduce any future relationship to the children until it is somewhat serious *(or more than _______ months in duration).*

Each of us agrees to inform the other of any future relationship, and to tell the other before telling the children.

f. Modification

We agree to modify our parenting plan whenever it is in the best interests of our children to do so.

OR

We agree to review our decision-making and/or parenting time arrangements in the event of: ______________________________
____.

(List whatever event(s) you agree will trigger a review.)

We will discuss changes in the decision-making responsibilities of ____________________________ from ___________ to _______________ if ____
____.

We will change decision-making responsibilities at the point in time when ____
____.

We will change our long-term time arrangements *(parenting time/physical care)* from ______________________________
____ when: ______________________________________
if: ____, as follows:
____.

(Repeat each for other children or circumstances.)

g. Moving Away

In the event either of us plans to move a distance away such that our existing parenting plan/parenting time plan is no longer feasible, the moving parent agrees to notify the other as soon as the determination to move is made, and we agree to meet and modify our parenting plan as needed.

OR

In the event either of us plans to move a distance away such that our existing parenting plan/parenting time plan is no longer feasible, the moving parent agrees to notify the other as soon as the determination to move is made, the children will remain with ___________ (which parent).

If we cannot agree we will go to mediation before any hearing in court.

h. Enforcement *(See Chapter 13)*

Should the parent from whom the children are coming not have them ready on the date and times we have agreed to, then ______
____
____.

Should the parent who is picking up the children not arrive on the date and time agreed to, then ________________________
____
____.

D. CHILD SUPPORT *(See Chapter 9)*

1. Worksheet A

__________________ *(paying parent)* will pay child support to ___________________ *(receiving parent)* of $__________ per month, as shown on the attached Worksheet A, starting ______________ *(month and year)*. Payments will be made by _____________________ *(automatic bank transfer, personal check, income assignment, etc.)* and are due to _____________ *(receiving parent)* on or before the _______ day of each month.

AND

We agree that the following expenses for our children are included in the basic support as calculated by us from the Schedule of Basic Child Support Obligations: ____
____
____
(housing, food in the home, basic clothing, possibly medical and dental check-ups, immunizations, transportation, etc.) We acknowledge that these basic expenses are being paid by the parent with physical care.

AND

We agree that the Adjustment Expenses shown on the attached Worksheet will be paid by the parent indicated.

(See below for medical and other expenses not included in the basic amount.)

Child support will continue until each child's 19th birthday, emancipation, or high school graduation if child is already 19.

2. Worksheet B

__________________ *(paying parent)* will pay child support to ___________________ *(receiving parent)* of $__________ per month, as shown on the attached Worksheet B, starting ______________ *(month and year)*. Payments will be made by _____________________ *(automatic bank transfer, personal check, income assignment, etc.)* and are due to _____________ *(receiving parent)* on or before the _______ day of each month.

We acknowledge that the following expenses are included in the basic support as calculated by us from the Schedule of Basic Child Support Obligations as shown on the attached Worksheet B: ______________________________ ______________________________. We acknowledge that we will continue to pay out to third parties these basic expenses in proportion to our time with the children: _______% for __________________ *(one parent)* and ______% for __________________ *(other parent).*

We agree that the Adjustment Expenses shown on the attached Worksheet will be paid by the parent indicated.

3. Medical Insurance and Expenses for Our Child(ren)

__________________ *(paying parent)* will continue to carry the existing medical (dental and vision) insurance coverage for our children, as shown on the attached child support Worksheet A (or B) until each child's 19th birthday, unless we agree otherwise, or longer as we agree. Should __________________'s *(paying parent's)* employment change for any reason, or should we find other preferable coverage, we agree to renegotiate this paragraph (and our child support agreement).

OR

__________________ *(paying parent)* will continue to carry the existing private medical (dental and vision) insurance coverage for our children, as shown on the attached child support worksheet A (or B) until each child's 19th birthday, unless we agree otherwise, or longer as we agree.

We will divide between us all out of pocket medical (dental, vision) expenses for our children, such as co-pays not paid by insurance _______% for __________________ and _______% for __________________ *(OR in the percentage of our incomes as set forth on our then current child support worksheet).*

4. Extra Expenses for Our Children

We agree to split all extra expenses for our children, expenses that are not included in the basic child support amount, that are ongoing or that we agree to prior to incurring, _______% for __________________, and _______% for __________________ (OR in proportion to our incomes as set forth on our then current child support worksheet). We intend that such extra expenses include but are not limited to ______________________________ *(school fees, classes, supplies, books, music lessons and instruments, other lessons and equipment, sports fees and equipment, camp, driving lessons, car expenses and insurance, cell phone, school pictures, prom, ...)*

5. Future Adjustments to Child Support

We understand that upon changed circumstances that would make our existing child support arrangement unfair, either of us may request a modification of child support. We agree to exchange income information with 15 (or 30) days of any such request and to adjust child support accordingly within 30 (or 60) days of the original request.

Any modification of child support may include changing the basic child support amount, the cost and who carries medical/dental/vision insurance coverage for the children, the proportion in which we pay for out of pocket medical expenses and other expenses for our children, and the allocation between us of the children's tax benefits.

We agree to exchange income information in ______________ *(month)* of each year, starting in ________ *(year)*, to determine whether a change in child support is called for. If we agree an adjustment is called for, we will adjust child support accordingly, the new adjusted amount(s) to become effective in ______________ *(next month)* of each year.

We agree that as each of our children emancipates we will recalculate child support for the remaining children on the appropriate worksheet using our then current incomes.

6. Tax Consequences About Children *(See Chapter 11)*

____________________ *(parent)* will have _________________'s *(name of child or children)* personal exemption(s) and tax credit(s) if any, and _____________________ *(other parent)* will have _________________'s *(name of child or children) (if he/she is current in his/her child support payments)(as long as the parenting time of the children remains as written in this agreement, etc.)*

OR

We agree to split any child tax credit between us _______% for _________________ *(one parent)*, and _______% for _________________ *(other parent).*

____________________ *(parent)* will have ____________________ *(name of child or children)* as the basis for his/her head of household tax filing status, and ____________________ *(other parent)* will have ____________ *(name of child or children).*

Since we share parenting time equally between us, ____________________ *(parent)* will have ____________________ *(child)* one extra overnight each year for purposes of head of household tax filing status, and ____________________ *(other parent)* will have ____________________ *(other child)* one extra overnight each year for purposes of head of household tax filing status.

OR

____________________ *(parent)* will have ____________________ *(child)* as his/her dependent for purposes of head of household tax filing status, and ____________________ *(other parent)* will have ____________________ *(other child)* (for as long as we maintain the parenting time plan stated in this agreement).

(Repeat as needed for other parent, and other children.)

The parent who has head of household tax filing status for a particular child will have exclusive right to any Child Care Credit for work-related child care on behalf of that child and will therefore make those payments directly to the care provider, even though we share that cost.

7. Post-Secondary Education Expenses (Optional) *(See Chapter 9)*

________________________________ *(paying parent)* will pay $_______________ per ______________*(month, quarter, semester, year)* to ________________________________ *(other parent, child, institution)* for ______________________ *(tuition, books, fees, room and board on campus, other).*

________________________________ *(paying parent)* will pay $ _________________ per _______________ *(month, quarter, semester, year)* to _______________________________ *(other parent, child)* for _______________ *(off-campus housing, other).*

___________________ *(paying parent)* will pay to ________________ *(other parent)* $ _________ *(per month for the months of* ___________________________*), on or before* ___________ *(date, annually, the occurrence of a particular event)* for board and room during breaks from post-secondary education while the child is residing with ______________ *(other parent).*

We will pay the costs of transportation for _____________ *(child/children)*, to and from school, ___________ times per year, in the following proportion: ___________________________________.

We agree that we will (not) be responsible for re-payment of any student loans obtained by _____________ *(child/children)* (in the following proportion: ___________________________________.

We agree that our children are likely to wish to attend college. We agree now that we will share the parents' portion of the cost as determined by the institution (to the limit of $ ________________ per child) to which we have agreed in the following way: ____.

We have estimated our portion of the cost of post-secondary education for each of our children to be $_________________ . We will set aside the money for this at the rate of $ ___________ per ___________ *(month, quarter, year, other)* which we will share proportional to our incomes as determined on the child support guideline for each year. We will change this proportion if we change the child support due to a change in the percentages of our incomes.

OR

___________________________ *(parent)* will contribute $ __________ per ___________ *(month, quarter, year, other)*, and ___________________________ *(other parent)* will contribute $ ___________ per ___________ *(month, quarter, year, other)*.

We or _________________ *(other person)* have/has established a college fund (trust) for our child (children) which we agree will be sufficient to cover the cost of post-secondary education OR is sufficient that we agree not to contribute further to post-secondary education.

8. Life Insurance as Security for Child Support *(See Chapter 9)*

________________________ *(parent)* will maintain at least $_________ in life insurance with ________________________ *(other parent or other person)* as beneficiary/trustee for the benefit of the children, to secure support for the children in the event of his/her death, until __________________ *(date or event). (Can be youngest child's 19th or later birthday. Some say to age 22-24 to allow for higher education.)*

(Repeat for other parent.)

Each of us agrees to obtain the premarital written waiver of rights to these policies and their proceeds from any future spouse, and to present a true copy of any such agreement to the other before any future marriage.

9. Enforcement of Child Support *(See Chapter 13)*

We agree that all child support (and maintenance) payments will be made by income assignment. ______________________ *(paying spouse)* will sign an Income Withholding for Support form before/on the day of the entry of our decree and deliver it to his/her employer immediately.

OR

We agree that there is good cause not to require the immediate activation of an income assignment for child support (and maintenance) payments because _________________ *(paying parent)* agrees to keep __________________ *(receiving parent)* informed in writing of his/her employer and information on any health insurance coverage to which __________________ *(paying parent)* has access.

If either of us fails to make any child support or any other payment on behalf of a child as agreed to here, the tax benefits related to that payment may be taken by the other parent. (Failure to pay day care will result in the other parent having the child care credit if they qualify; failure to pay basic child support loses the dependency exemption for that parent, etc.)

AND/OR

No money owing to _________________ *(paying parent)* as written in this agreement (promissory note for division of property, repayment of any kind, etc.) will be paid unless all child support obligations have been paid in full at the time the money is due.

AND

Any missed child support payment is a judgment and may be collected by any means, including garnishment and levy on assets.

AND

_______________________ *(paying parent)* will immediately execute an income assignment for payment of the child support agreed to and will amend it each time we change the amount.

OR

If any payment for child support is more than twenty days late, the paying parent will immediately execute an income assignment or other direct transfer for all subsequent child support payments, including any arrears through the date of the first payment made by ________________________________ *(income assignment/direct deposit/electronic transfer/other). (Use this provision if the court has given you permission to opt out of an automatic income assignment at the time of your decree.*

E. MAINTENANCE *(See Chapter 10)*

1. Maintenance Waiver

If one or both of you is not receiving maintenance in your agreement, then you must have the waiver in writing in your separation agreement.

__________________________ *(one spouse)* hereby waives, now and for all time, any right to ask for maintenance from __________________________ *(other spouse)*, arising from this marriage . He/She understands that if he/she does not provide for maintenance now, he/she can not ask for it in the future.

(Repeat for other spouse if both are waiving maintenance.)

2. Maintenance General

___________________ *(paying spouse)* will pay maintenance to ____________________ *(receiving spouse)* of $___________ per month starting ____________________ *(month and year)* and continuing for ________ months/years at which time it will cease *(OR reduce/change to $___________ per month for ________ months/years, at which time it shall cease.) (OR continue continuing on with periodic changes.)*

Payments will be made by ____________________ *(income assignment, personal check, automatic bank transfer, etc.)* and are due to ____________________ *(receiving spouse)* on or before the _________ day of each month.

Maintenance will sooner end on ____________________'s *(receiving spouse's)* death or remarriage.

We intend for all maintenance payments to be included in income for ____________________ *(receiving spouse)* and deductible from income for ____________________ *(paying spouse)* for income tax purposes. *(You need to say this if you want your maintenance payments to shift taxes.)*

3. Maintenance for a Specific Purpose

Each of the following kinds of maintenance may have its own tax rules and consequences, its own rules for modification, and may tie to other parts of your agreement in different ways. The following clauses are suggested in the alternative, but some can be combined and some can be used sequentially. READ CHAPTERS 10 AND 11 BEFORE INCLUDING ANY MAINTENANCE IN YOUR AGREEMENT.

a. ___________________ will pay to ___________________ the sum of $_________ per month as maintenance, starting _________, 20____ *(usually month following your Decree, or whenever you started it)*, in order to equalize our gross incomes. This amount will be adjusted on an annual basis by subtracting the lower of our incomes from the higher of our incomes, and dividing this difference in half. This resulting figure is the new maintenance amount to which we will agree in writing, sign before a notary, and file with the court, asking that it be made into an Order.

We will calculate maintenance this way *(for not less than __________ years/months) (for not more than __________ years/months) (from _____________________ [date] through __________________ [date])*, at which time all maintenance shall cease, OR at which time we shall review our method for calculating maintenance.

OR

b. ______________________ will pay to ____________________ as maintenance the sum of $_____________ per _______________ *(month, quarter, year)*, starting _______________, 20____ (usually month of following your Decree, or whenever you started it). This amount will reduce/increase/change to $____________ per ____________ *(month, quarter, year)* OR an amount to be determined on each of the following occasions: the retirement of ______________ *(the paying spouse)*; receipt by ______________________________ *(the receiving spouse)* retirement or other income. *(You may wish to include here such windfalls as winning Lotto or inheriting a substantial sum.)*

OR

c. _______________________ will pay to ____________________ as maintenance $____________ per month, starting __________________, 20____ *(usually month following your Decree, or whenever you started it)*, in order to assist ________________________ *(receiving spouse)* in the payment of housing. This amount will be adjusted as and when ____________'s *(receiving spouse's)* mortgage payment changes. These payments will end entirely in the month in which _______________'s *(the receiving spouse's)* mortgage is paid off OR when ______________ sells or moves from the property OR when ______________ *(receiving spouse)* no longer pays for his or her own housing OR if receiving spouse loses the house through non-payment.

OR

d. ___________________ *(paying spouse)* will make the necessary arrangements for ___________________ *(paying spouse's business)* to pay directly to __________________ *(receiving spouse)* as maintenance, per ____________ *(month, quarter, year)*, _______% of the business net profits for that period of time as shown on profit and loss statement calculated monthly *(quarterly)* by ______________________ *(accounting service, bookkeeper, etc.—not the paying spouse's calculation). (This use of maintenance may be unfamiliar to your accountant or even your lawyer. Be certain you work with a CPA or attorney with special knowledge of this method. It is beyond the scope of this book.)*

OR

e. _______________________ *(paying spouse)* will pay to ______________________ *(receiving spouse)* the sum of $_____________ per month for _______ months through __________________ *(year) (the term remaining on a certain joint debt which the receiving spouse will make the payments on)*. This amount will not be modifiable, and will terminate only on the death of either party or the sale or payoff of the __________ *(loan for item of property, or house second mortgage)*, except that the receiving spouse will re-finance, pay-off or sell the ______________ *(property)* within 30 days of his or her re-marriage, and pay the remaining balance on this debt, at which time all maintenance will cease.

OR

f. ______________________ will pay to __________________ as maintenance $_____________ per month for a period of _________ years *(months)* unmodified. *(This goes with a clause agreeing to make equal payments on the marital debts.)*

For any kind of maintenance you need to say how long it will last. Maintenance shall continue until _________________'s (receiving spouse) death or remarriage, or _________________ (date), whichever occurs first. *(Omit the date if you are doing lifetime maintenance.)*

4. Life Insurance as Security for Maintenance

_______________________ will maintain __________ years decreasing term of life insurance (or other insurance) in *(initial)* amount of $______________ , and with ______________________ *(receiving spouse)* as irrevocable beneficiary until all maintenance provided for in this agreement has been paid in full. *(This insurance policy can be the same as the policy securing child support, but be sure to add the amounts of coverage together.)*

We agree that we may change the amount of this life insurance death benefit in the future, but only as we agree in writing and signed by both of us.

OR

__________________ *(paying spouse)* will maintain sufficient life insurance on his/her life with ___________________ as irrevocable beneficiary to cover the outstanding balance of his/her maintenance obligation *(Note: only if it can be calculated.)*

5. Medical Insurance

__________________________________ *(non-employee spouse)* will *(not)* exercise the COBRA option available through __________________________________'s *(employee spouse's)* place of employment. We understand the premium will initially be $___________ per ______________ *(month, quarter, year)*. ______________________ *(non-employee spouse)* will be solely responsible for paying this premium, and will hold ___________________ *(employee spouse)* harmless.

____ *(employee spouse)* will pay this premium as maintenance on behalf of ____ *(non-employee spouse)*.

6. Modification of Maintenance

Many of the sample clauses in this Guidebook have built-in modifications. You may use the following in addition, or instead. You MUST specify when and if your maintenance is to be modifiable or to cease.

A maintenance plan is automatically modifiable unless you state that you intend for it to be non-modifiable.

For modifiable, you can say when you intend modify, such as: We agree to exchange income and living expenses information in ________________ *(month)* every year (OR every even-numbered year) and modify maintenance according to the following factors: ____ *(needs, ability to pay, the outcome of a particular investment, other)*.

OR

For non-modifiable: We agree that our maintenance plan is contractual in nature and non-modifiable for any reason, and it is our desire and intent that the court have no further jurisdiction over the matter of maintenance after the entry of our Decree.

We agree that our maintenance provision(s) is/are to be modifiable on the following occurrences: _______________ months/years from the date the signing of our agreement *(from the date of our decree)*; major increase *(decrease)* in *(either of our) (paying spouse's) (recipient spouse's)* incomes; completion by recipient spouse of _________ degree/training; payment of $____________ ; ________________ moving from ______________ ; death or remarriage of recipient spouse in which case maintenance will cease (reduce to $__________); other.

7. Enforcement of Maintenance

We agree that all maintenance payments will be made by income assignment. ______________________ *(paying spouse)* will sign a Income Withholding for Support before/on the date of our Decree, and deliver it to his/her employer immediately.

OR

We agree that there is good cause not to require the immediate activation of an Income Assignment for maintenance because ______________________ *(paying spouse)* has previously made timely payments.

Any maintenance payment required in this agreement which is more than twenty days late will not be tax deductible by the paying spouse or taxable to the receiving spouse.

OR

The maintenance payments required in this agreement are to be secured by a promissory note and a deed of trust against the residence occupied by the paying spouse until the maintenance has been paid in full. *(This is useful only for fixed-term maintenance where the total amount can be calculated.)*

OR

(You may use the following if you are using maintenance to meet certain joint obligations such as mortgage payments on jointly titled property, or payments on marital debts or car loans.) Should ______________ *(receiving spouse)* fall more than forty-five days behind on __________________ *(joint mortgage payment, car or debt payment)* then ______________ *(paying spouse)* is no longer responsible for paying maintenance, and/or has first option to assume the obligation and receive the property.

The Support Order

The Support Order is required in cases where there will be child support, maintenance, or both.

The Support Order makes the child support and maintenance you have agreed to into a separate court order that will become part of your Decree. It specifies how much is to be paid by whom and to whom, as well as when and where the payments are to be made—whether by income assignment (withheld from your paycheck and paid directly by your employer), or some other method. If you write the support check yourself, you can pay it directly to the receiving person, or pay it through the Family Support Registry. Payment through the Registry will cost a small processing fee each month, and may delay the delivery of the payment by up to two weeks.

Lastly, the Support Order spells out specifically which parent shall provide medical insurance for the children, including the name and address of the insurer and the policy number.

1 ☐ District Court ☐ Denver Juvenile Court ____________________ County, Colorado Court Address:	
In re ☐ **The Marriage of:** ☐ **Parental Responsibilities concerning:** 2 ____________________________ **Petitioner:** and **Co-Petitioner/Respondent:**	▲ COURT USE ONLY ▲
	Case Number: Division: Courtroom:

SUPPORT ORDER

3 **Petitioner:** Date of Birth: __________________
Mailing Address: ____
Residential Address: ____
Name of Employer: ____
Employer Address: ____

Co-Petitioner/Respondent: Date of Birth: __________________
Mailing Address: ____
Residential Address: ____
Name of Employer: ____
Employer Address: ____

4 The following are the minor children who are the subject of this Order are:

Full Name of Child	Sex	Date of Birth

5 **The Court orders** the ☐ Petitioner ☐ Co-Petitioner/Respondent to pay ☐ child support and/or ☐ maintenance to ________________________ (name of party).

6 **a.** Payments shall be paid ☐ weekly ☐ bi-weekly ☐ twice a month ☐ monthly
☐ other: ____.

7 **b.** The first payment is due on ________________ (date).

8 **c.** Total arrears owed as of ________________ (date) for Child Support $ ________ and/or Maintenance $ ________.

9 **d.** Total retroactive support as of ________________ (date) that accrued prior to the entry of a support order for the time period of ________________ to ________________ shall be $ ________.

Bradford Publishing, 1743 Wazee St., Denver, CO 80202 — 303-292-2590 — www.bradfordpublishing.com

e. Emancipation occurs when the last or only child reaches the age of 19; unless the child is still in high school, in which case support continues until the end of the month following graduation; or until the child(ren) otherwise emancipate as may be determined by the Court. Child support may be changed or amended upon motion of a party when any of the children reach 19.

The total monthly obligation is as follows:

10 $ ____________ Current Child Support
11 $ ____________ Current Maintenance
12 $ ____________ Payment toward Arrears (child support)
13 $ ____________ Payment toward Arrears (maintenance)
14 $ ____________ Payment toward Retroactive Support

15 **For a total monthly payment of $ ____________**

16 ☐ **Upon payment in full of the Retroactive Support and/or Arrears, the monthly payment is reduced to $ ____________.**

17 ☐ The Court orders the immediate activation of an income assignment against the Obligor, pursuant to §14-14-111.5, C.R.S.

☐ The income assignment must be paid through the Family Support Registry, pursuant to §26-13-114(6)(a), C.R.S.

or

18 ☐ This Order is not subject to the immediate activation of an income assignment because either:

A ☐ Both parties have entered into a written agreement that provides for an alternative arrangement. If a payment is missed, or late, an income assignment shall immediately be activated pursuant to §14-14-111.5, C.R.S.

B ☐ The Court finds there is good cause not to require the immediate activation of an income assignment because:

____

____

19 A ☐ The Court orders the ☐ Petitioner or ☐ Co-Petitioner/Respondent, or ☐ Either party to secure and maintain ☐ medical or ☐ medical and dental and/or ☐ other: ____________________ insurance coverage for the child(ren), when it is provided by his/her employer or acquired individually, at a reasonable cost as defined in §14-10-115(10), C.R.S. Each party shall cooperate and exchange information necessary to provide insurance benefits for the child(ren). If not all children, please identify the names of the children that this party will be providing insurance for:

B ____

C ☐ The Court finds ☐ medical or ☐ medical and dental insurance is not currently available to either party at a reasonable cost and does not order either party to provide coverage for the children at this time, but does order the parties to provide coverage when it becomes available at a reasonable cost.

Payments shall continue until further Order of the Court. Payments shall be:

20 ☐ Mailed to the Family Support Registry **or** ☐ Mailed directly to the appropriate party.
P.O. Box 2171
Denver, CO 80201-2171

21 Date: ____________________ ____________________
☐ Judge ☐ Magistrate

INSTRUCTIONS TO FILL OUT THE SUPPORT ORDER

You will use this form if you have children and child support calculated on Worksheets A or B. (If you do not have children, skip this form.) See Chapter 9 for how to develop a complete and workable child support agreement. You may also use this form for maintenance if there is no child support.

1. Check the box for District Court in the first section and "In re the Marriage of" if you are using this form in a divorce or legal separation action. Check the box for Denver Juvenile Court and "In re the Parental Responsibilities etc., if you are not married and seeking support.
2. Fill in the names of each of you as you would on the Petition.
3. Complete the information about the Petitioner and the Co-Petitioner/Respondent, if either of you is self-employed, note that in the space for the name of employer.
4. List the name, sex, and date of birth of all children for whom this support is being paid.
5. Check the box for the person who will pay support (called the Obligor). Check one or both boxes according to whether this is child support, maintenance, or both. Then fill in the name of the person who receives support (called the Obligee).
6. Check the box for how often payments will be made (twice a month, etc.) and then describe how they will be paid, i.e. on the first and fifteenth day of each month.
7. Fill in the date of the first support payment.
8. If there is any unpaid past due support or maintenance owing, in the first blank fill in the probable date this order will be signed or the date on which you last calculated the arrears. Fill in the total amounts of the unpaid past due child support and/or maintenance that you calculated. If none, put "0".
9. **Retroactive Child Support.** You may, if you wish, determine an amount one of you owes the other for past child support, going back to the date of your physical separation or the date of the filing of the petition or service upon the respondent, "whichever is latest," says the statute. You do not need to prepare a child support worksheet for this. Once you have a total for retroactive support that you both agree on, you can pay it now, put it in with all the other items in your property settlement, or decide on an interest rate and an amount for monthly payments. In this last case, it will be shown on the Support Order which accompanies your Decree.

   In the first blank, enter the date that you think the decree will be signed. In the next two blanks, fill in the beginning and ending dates for which you calculated the amount of support. Put the total retroactive support in the last blank.
10. Fill in the amount of current support you have agreed to.
11. Fill in the amount of current maintenance you have agreed to, if any. If none, put "0" or "none."

    Arrears. In practice, many people make this 1/24 of the whole, plus interest, so it is paid off in 2 years. However, you can also design the payments so that it will be paid off at the end of the tax year, or the annual date on which you have agreed to review the support amount, or any other date which you agree on.
12. Fill in the monthly payment you have agreed to for unpaid past due support listed in step 8 above.

13. Fill in the monthly payment you have agreed to for unpaid past due maintenance that you listed in step 8. (see Caution before step 12).

14. Fill in the monthly amount of any retroactive child support that you calculated in step 9 above.

15. Fill in the total of steps 10 through 14.

16. If you filled in an amount in step 14 for retroactive support, check this box. Subtract the monthly payment that you entered on step 14 from the total in step 15 and enter that new payment in this blank.

17. Check this box if you have agreed to payment by income assignment. (For more information on income assignments see later in this chapter and Chapter 9.) Check the second box if the income assignment must be paid through the Family Support Registry.

18. Check this box if you wish the court to permit you to do without an income assignment, and check A or B to indicate the reason. Check A if you have included a provision in your agreement which ensures the payments, such as a direct transfer (useful when self-employed) or payment by a third party such as a business or trust. Check B and write an explanation of why you expect the court to allow you to do without an income assignment, such as a proven record of direct, timely payments. There is no guarantee that the court will approve either exception. It may be wise to prepare an income assignment form just in case.

19. Check whichever boxes in step 19A or B describes your agreement about health, dental, and vision insurance for the children.

    In step B, if your insurance covers all of your children, leave this blank. If not, list the names of the children it *does* cover.

    In step C., if either health, dental, or vision insurance is not available at this time at a reasonable cost, check the first box and the box for the type of insurance that it applies to.

20. Check the box for whether payments will be mailed to the Family Support Registry or directly to the Obligee.

21. Leave this blank. The court will sign and date this.

Income Withholding for Support and Insurance

Since January 1994, Colorado has required that child support and maintenance with child support, be paid by means of an income assignment in most situations. This means that the court-ordered amount is withheld directly by the employer of the paying spouse and sent directly to the receiving spouse. In cases brought through the Child Support Enforcement Unit, the money is sent to the Colorado Family Support Registry in Denver and then forwarded to the receiving spouse. In some private cases, the money is sent directly to a bank account designated by the receiving spouse. The important aspect of this law is not where the money is sent but how it is obtained. With an income assignment, because the money never goes through the paying spouse's hands, he or she is never tempted to hang onto it or use it for other purposes.

"If the court orders a garnishment I'll get fired."

Your employer is not allowed to fire you because you have a garnishment for child support or maintenance—whether the garnishment is by court order or a voluntary wage assignment.

The court will presume your support, or support plus maintenance, will be paid via income assignment unless: a) you have agreed in writing that it will be paid directly or in some other manner, or b) the paying spouse is self-employed or working for a number of employers so that an income assignment is not possible or is cumbersome.

In addition to an income assignment for support, a more recent amendment to the law permits an income assignment for health insurance premiums for minor children.

"I don't have to do a wage assignment if I don't want to."

This is true only if you and your soon-to-be-ex agree to an alternate method of payment. Otherwise, the law requires an income assignment where possible.

An even newer wrinkle permits the court to order the employer to cover the minor children, even if the paying spouse had failed or refused to do so. There has long been some question among employers and insurance companies whether they could or should insure children who do not live with their employee or, more often, when their employee did not, or could not, claim the child as a dependent exemption. Now it is clear that the employer and insurer can and should, and must if the company is covered by ERISA. See Chapter 7 about ERISA companies and Chapter 11 about dependency exemptions.

The forms include a lengthy advisement to the employer about how much he must withhold and how much income is protected as to his employee. This information makes collection that much more likely and hassle-free.

Select from these forms to fit your facts. Do use them if you need to protect your children from the all-too-human potential frailties and temptations of their parents. No receiving parent need feel they are being mean by asking that the payments for their children be paid in this reliable manner. No paying parent need feel punished by being asked to see that payments for the benefit of their children are secure.

1

☐ District Court ☐ Juvenile Court _________________ County, Colorado Court Address:	
☐ **In re the Marriage of:** ☐ **In re the Parental Responsibilities concerning:** __________________________________ **Petitioner:** and **Co-Petitioner/Respondent:**	▲ COURT USE ONLY ▲
Attorney or Party Without Attorney (Name and Address): Phone Number: E-mail: FAX Number: Atty. Reg. #:	Case Number: Document Tracking Identifier: Division: Courtroom:

INCOME WITHHOLDING FOR SUPPORT

2 ☐ **ORIGINAL INCOME WITHHOLDING ORDER/NOTICE FOR SUPPORT (IWO)** ☐ **AMENDED IWO**
☐ **ONE-TIME ORDER/NOTICE - LUMP SUM PAYMENT** ☐ **TERMINATION of IWO**

3 ☐ Child Support Enforcement (CSE) Agency ☐ Court ☐ Attorney ☐ Private Individual/Entity **(Check One)**

NOTE: This IWO must be regular on its face. Under certain circumstances you must reject this IWO and return it to the sender (see IWO instructions http://www.acf.hhs.gov/programs/cse/newhire/employer/publication/publication.htm#forms). If you receive this document from someone other than a State or Tribal CSE agency or a Court, a copy of the underlying order must be attached.

State/Tribe/Territory: ____ 4 ____ Case Identifier: ____ 7 ____
City/County/Dist./Tribe: ____ 5 ____ Order Identifier: ____ 7 ____
Private Individual/Entity: ____ 6 ____

8 ________________ RE: 10 ________________
Employer/Income Withholder's Name — Employee/Obligor's Name (Last, First, Middle)

9 ________________ 11 ________________
Employer/Income Withholder's Address — Employee/Obligor's Social Security Number (if known)

12 ________________
Custodial Party/Obligee's Name (Last, First, Middle)

Employer/Income Withholder's FEIN ____ 13 ____

Child(ren)'s Name(s) (Last, First, Middle) — Child(ren)'s Birth Date(s)
14 ________________

ORDER INFORMATION: This document is based on the support or withholding order from __________ 15 ______________________ (State/Tribe). You are required by law to deduct these amounts from the employee/obligor's income until further notice.

$__16__ Per __________ current child support
$__________ Per __________ past-due child support – **Arrears greater than 12 weeks?** ☐ Yes ☐ No
$__________ Per __________ current cash medical support
$__________ Per __________ past-due cash medical support
$__17__ Per __________ current spousal support
$__________ Per __________ past-due spousal support
$__________ Per __________ other (must specify) ______________________________
for a **Total Amount to Withhold** of $__________ per __________.

18 ***AMOUNTS TO WITHHOLD:*** You do not have to vary your pay cycle to be in compliance with the Order Information. If your pay cycle does not match the ordered payment cycle, withhold one of the following amounts:

$__________ per weekly pay period.
$__________ per biweekly pay period (every two weeks).
$__________ per semimonthly pay period (twice a month).
$__________ per monthly pay period.
$__________ **Lump Sum Payment:** Do not stop any existing IWO unless you receive a termination order.

REMITTANCE INFORMATION: If the employee/obligor's principal place of employment is __________ 19 ______________________ (State/Tribe), you must begin withholding no later than the first pay period that occurs ______ 20 days after the date of __________ 21 __________. Send payment within ______ 22 working days of the pay date. If you cannot withhold the full amount of support for any or all orders for this employee/obligor, withhold up to __23__% of disposable income for all orders. If the employee/obligor's principal place of employment is not __________ 24 ______________ (State/Tribe), obtain withholding limitations, time requirements, and any allowable employer fees at http://www.acf.hhs.gov/programs/cse/newhire/employer/contacts/contact_map.htm for the employee/obligor's principal place of employment.

For electronic payment requirements and centralized payment collection and disbursement facility information (State Disbursement Unit [SDU]), see http://www.acf.hhs.gov/programs/cse/newhire/employer/contacts/contact_map.htm.

Include the ***Remittance Identifier*** **with the payment** and if necessary this FIPS code: ______ 25 ______.

Remit payment to ____Family Support Registry____ (SDU/Tribal Order Payee)
at ____P.O. Box 2171, Denver, CO 80201-2172____ (SDU/Tribal Payee Address)

26 ☐ **Return to Sender [Completed by Employer/Income Withholder].** Payment must be directed to an SDU in accordance with 42 USC §666(b)(5) and (b)(6) or Tribal Payee (see Payments to SDU below). If payment is not directed to an SDU/Tribal Payee or this IWO is not regular on its face, you must check this box and return the IWO to the sender.

Signature of Judge/Issuing Official (if required by State or Tribal law): ______________________
Print Name of Judge/Issuing Official: ______________________
Title of Judge/Issuing Official: ______________________
Date of Signature: ______________________

If the employee/obligor works in a State or for a Tribe that is different from the State or Tribe that issued this order, a copy of this IWO must be provided to the employee/obligor.
☐ If checked, the employer/income withholder must provide a copy of this form to the employee/obligor.

No. 1155. Rev. 5-12. NOTICE TO WITHHOLD INCOME FOR SUPPORT (JDF 1804) (Page 2 of 5)

ADDITIONAL INFORMATION FOR EMPLOYERS/INCOME WITHHOLDERS

State-specific contact and withholding information can be found on the Federal Employer Services website located at: http://www.acf.hhs.gov/programs/cse/newhire/employer/contacts/contact_map.htm

Priority: Withholding for support has priority over any other legal process under State law against the same income (USC 42 §666(b)(7)). If a Federal tax levy is in effect, please notify the sender.

27 **Combining Payments:** When remitting payments to an SDU or Tribal CSE agency, you may combine withheld amounts from more than one employee/obligor's income in a single payment. You must, however, separately identify each employee/obligor's portion of the payment.

Payments To SDU: You must send child support payments payable by income withholding to the appropriate SDU or to a Tribal CSE agency. If this IWO instructs you to send a payment to an entity other than an SDU (e.g., payable to the custodial party, court, or attorney), you must check the box above and return this notice to the sender. Exception: If this IWO was sent by a Court, Attorney, or Private Individual/Entity and the initial order was entered before January 1, 1994 or the order was issued by a Tribal CSE agency, you must follow the "Remit payment to" instructions on this form.

Reporting the Pay Date: You must report the pay date when sending the payment. The pay date is the date on which the amount was withheld from the employee/obligor's wages. You must comply with the law of the State (or Tribal law if applicable) of the employee/obligor's principal place of employment regarding time periods within which you must implement the withholding and forward the support payments.

Multiple IWOs: If there is more than one IWO against this employee/obligor and you are unable to fully honor all IWOs due to Federal, State, or Tribal withholding limits, you must honor all IWOs to the greatest extent possible, giving priority to current support before payment of any past-due support. Follow the State or Tribal law/procedure of the employee/obligor's principal place of employment to determine the appropriate allocation method.

Lump Sum Payments: You may be required to notify a State or Tribal CSE agency of upcoming lump sum payments to this employee/obligor such as bonuses, commissions, or severance pay. Contact the sender to determine if you are required to report and/or withhold lump sum payments.

Liability: If you have any doubts about the validity of this IWO, contact the sender. If you fail to withhold income from the employee/obligor's income as the IWO directs, you are liable for both the accumulated amount you should have withheld and any penalties set by State or Tribal law/procedure.

Anti-discrimination: You are subject to a fine determined under State or Tribal law for discharging an employee/ obligor from employment, refusing to employ, or taking disciplinary action against an employee/ obligor because of this IWO.

Withholding Limits: You may not withhold more than the lesser of: 1) the amounts allowed by the Federal Consumer Credit Protection Act (CCPA) (15 U.S.C. 1673(b)); or 2) the amounts allowed by the State or Tribe of the employee/obligor's principal place of employment (see *REMITTANCE INFORMATION*). Disposable income is the net income left after making mandatory deductions such as: State, Federal, local taxes; Social Security taxes; statutory pension contributions; and Medicare taxes. The Federal limit is 50% of the disposable income if the obligor is supporting another family and 60% of the disposable income if the obligor is not supporting another family. However, those limits increase 5% – to 55% and 65% – if the arrears are greater than 12 weeks. If permitted by the State or Tribe, you may deduct a fee for administrative costs. The combined support amount and fee may not exceed the limit indicated in this section.

For Tribal orders, you may not withhold more than the amounts allowed under the law of the issuing Tribe. For Tribal employers/income withholders who receive a State IWO, you may not withhold more than the lesser of the limit set by the law of the jurisdiction in which the employer/income withholder is located or the maximum amount permitted under section 303(d) of the CCPA (15 U.S.C. 1673 (b)).

Depending upon applicable State or Tribal law, you may need to also consider the amounts paid for health care premiums in determining disposable income and applying appropriate withholding limits.

No. 1155. Rev. 5-12. NOTICE TO WITHHOLD INCOME FOR SUPPORT (JDF 1804) (Page 3 of 5)

Arrears greater than 12 weeks? If the *Order Information* does not indicate that the arrears are greater than 12 weeks, then the Employer should calculate the CCPA limit using the lower percentage.

Additional Information: NOTICE: 1) Pursuant to 14-14-111.5(4)(d) C.R.S., each disbursement shall be identified by the case number, the name and social security number of each obligor, the date the deduction was made, the amount of the payment, and the family support registry account number. 2) Pursuant to 14-14-111.5(4)(n) C.R.S., a fraudulent submission of a Notice to Withhold Income For Support shall subject the person submitting the notice to an employer, trustee, or other payor of funds to a fine of not less than one thousand dollars and court costs and attorney fees.

NOTIFICATION OF EMPLOYMENT TERMINATION OR INCOME STATUS: If this employee/obligor never worked for you or you are no longer withholding income for this employee/obligor, an employer must promptly notify the CSE agency and/or the sender by returning this form to the address listed in the Contact Information below:

☐ This person has never worked for this employer nor received periodic income.

28 ☐ This person no longer works for this employer nor receives periodic income.

Please provide the following information for the employee/obligor:

Termination date: ______________________ Last known phone number: ____________________

Last known address: ____

Final payment date to SDU/Tribal Payee: __________________ Final payment amount: __________

New employer's name: ____

New employer's address: ____

29 **CONTACT INFORMATION**

To Employer/Income Withholder: If you have any questions, contact ____________________ by phone at ______________, by fax at ______________, by email or website at: ______________ ______________________. Send termination/income status notice and other correspondence to: ____ (Issuer address).

30 **To Employee/Obligor:** If the employee/obligor has questions, contact ____________________ by phone at ______________, by fax at ______________, by email or website at: ______________ ______________________.

______________________________________ 31 ______________________________

Signature of Attorney, if applicable Date ☐ Petitioner or ☐ Co-Petitioner/Respondent

____

Address

____

City, State, Zip Code

____

(Area Code) Telephone Number (home)

____

(Area Code) Telephone Number (work)

____

Email

No. 1155. Rev. 5-12. NOTICE TO WITHHOLD INCOME FOR SUPPORT (JDF 1804) (Page 4 of 5)

CERTIFICATE OF SERVICE

32 I certify that on _________________________ (date) a true and accurate copy of the **Income Withholding for Support** was served on the other party by:
☐ Hand Delivery **or** ☐ by placing it in the United States mail, postage pre-paid, and addressed to the following:

To: ____________________________________
____
____

and

33 I certify that on _________________________ (date), I sent the original Income Withholding for Support and a certified copy of the Support Order to the Obligor's employer by United States Mail, first class postage prepaid, addressed as follows:

To: ____________________________________
____
____

Date: ____________________________________ ____________________________________
Signature

Income Withholding for Support

This form is used to inform an employer or other withholder what amount is required to be withheld from the paying spouse's income for child support or maintenance. Self-employed persons, people doing subcontracting for several companies, or others who do not have a steady paycheck from a single payroll office probably won't be able to do an income assignment. These persons can usually set up some kind of automatic transfer from an account of one spouse to an account of the other, or simply mail or deliver a personal check on a regular and timely basis.

INSTRUCTIONS TO FILL OUT THE INCOME WITHHOLDING FOR SUPPORT

1. Check the box for District Court and fill in the county and case number as on your petition. Check the box "In re the Marriage of" and fill in the rest of the caption as on your petition
2. Check the first box for ORIGINAL INCOME WITHHOLDING ORDER/NOTICE FOR SUPPORT (IWO)
3. Check "Court".
4. Fill in "State of Colorado".
5. Fill in the name of your court, such as "Jefferson County District Court".
6. Fill in the name the spouse requesting the income assignment.
7. Leave these spaces blank.
8. Fill in the name of the employer.
9. Fill in the address of the employer.
10. Fill in the name spouse whose income is to be assigned.
11. Fill in the Social Security number of the spouse whose income is to be assigned.
12. Fill in the full name of the person the assignment is to be paid to.
13. Leave blank. Employer will fill this out.
14. Write the name(s) of the children the support is for, and their birth dates.
15. Fill in Colorado
16. Put the amount of child support to be paid, followed by the time frame for it to be paid, usually $xxx.xx per month. Leave blank if none.
17. Put the amount of maintenance (alimony) to be paid, followed by the time frame for it to be paid, usually $xxx.xx per month. Leave blank if none.
18. Leave this blank. Employer will fill this out.
19. Write "Colorado".
20. Fill in 14 days
21. Fill in the date on the Income Withholding for Support form.

22. Fill in 7 days.
23. Put 65%.
24. Write "Colorado".
25. Leave this blank.
26. Check this box only if you want the employer to provide a copy of this document to the employee.
27. Nothing needs to be filled in on this page.
28. Leave this entire box blank.
29. Fill in contact information for the person who prepared this document.
30. If the employee/obligor prepared this document, leave this blank. If the non-employee spouse prepared this document, write your contact information.
31. Check the box for which one of you is requesting the assignment, add your signature, address, and phone numbers.
32. Fill out the Certificate of Service to state the date and method you provided a copy to the other spouse.
33. Staple a copy of the Support Order to the original of this document. Then fill in the date you mailed it, with the Support Order, to the employer, and the address to which you mailed it.

The original of this form goes to the paying spouse's employer. Make additional copies for the court, for yourself, and for the receiving spouse.

If you wish to formally serve it, you may adapt the Return of Service (see page 4 of the Summons in Chapter 6).

Note: If you are the paying spouse, you must keep the receiving spouse informed of your current employer and any health insurance that you have access to.

1 ☐ District Court ☐ Juvenile Court ______________________ County, Colorado Court Address:	
☐ **In Re the Marriage of:** ☐ **In Re Parental Responsibilities concerning:** ______________________ **Petitioner:** and **Co-Petitioner/Respondent:**	▲ COURT USE ONLY ▲
Attorney or Party Without Attorney (Name and Address): Phone Number: E-mail: FAX Number: Atty. Reg. #:	Case Number: Division: Courtroom:

NOTICE TO EMPLOYER TO DEDUCT FOR HEALTH INSURANCE

2 TO: Name of Employer: ______________________
Address of Employer: ______________________

3 Pursuant to §14-14-112, C.R.S., you are required to enroll the child(ren) of the Obligor who are listed below (and the Obligor, if required by the plan) in the following checked health insurance plan(s) (☐ medical ☐ dental ☐ vision) offered by you for the Obligor's benefit. Any reference herein to health insurance shall apply to the types of insurance checked above.

4 Name of Obligor: ______________________ Social Security Number: ____________
Address: ______________________

5

Full Name of Child	Date of Birth	Social Security Number

You are required to deduct from the wages due the Obligor an amount sufficient to provide for premiums for health insurance for the Obligor and his/her child(ren). **Premium payments are to be made directly to the insurance carrier.** Please deduct for health insurance premiums before you deduct any amounts for child support pursuant to §13-54-104, C.R.S.

If the Obligor is no longer employed by you, you shall promptly notify the Court in writing of the Obligor's last known address, social security number, and the name of the Obligor's new employer, if known.

The Obligor's child(ren) shall be enrolled in the health insurance plan in which the Obligor is enrolled if the child(ren) can be covered under the plan. If the Obligor is not enrolled in a plan, the

Bradford Publishing, 1743 Wazee St., Denver, CO 80202 — 303-292-2590 — www.bradfordpublishing.com

child(ren) shall be enrolled in the least costly plan otherwise available to the child(ren) regardless of whether the child(ren) was/were born out of wedlock, is/are claimed as a dependent(s) on the Obligor's federal or state income tax return, live(s) with the Obligor, or live(s) within the insurer's service area, notwithstanding any other provision of law restricting enrollment to persons who reside in an insurer's service area.

This withholding shall take effect no later than the first pay period after 14 days from the date on which this Notice is mailed to you or from the date on which the Obligor submits an oral or written request to you, whichever occurs sooner. The deduction for health insurance is treated as a significant life change under open enrollment requirements.

It is your responsibility to ensure that the child(ren) of the Obligor is/are enrolled in a health insurance plan and that premium payments are withheld and forwarded to the insurer. If you wrongfully fail to deduct health insurance premiums, you, the employer, may be liable for the amount of accumulated premiums that should have been withheld from the Obligor's wages. You shall not discharge, refuse to hire, or take disciplinary action against an employee because of the entry or service of this Notice. If you do, you may be found in contempt of court and the Obligor may bring a civil action against you for reinstatement, lost wages, costs, and attorney's fees. Compliance with this Notice shall not subject you to liability to the Obligor for wrongful withholding. As long as the Obligor is employed by you, this Notice shall not be terminated or modified, except upon one of the following:

1. Written notice by the Court, Obligee, or the Delegate Child Support Enforcement Unit.
2. Written verification, provided by the Obligor to the employer, the employer determines that the child(ren) is/are enrolled in a comparable health insurance plan that takes effect no later than the effective date on which the child(ren) is/are no longer enrolled under your plan.
3. Elimination of family health insurance coverage for all employees.

When enrollment is terminated for any of the above reasons, within 14 days, you shall send, to the location described on the premium notice, a written notice of cancellation of enrollment or a copy of the verification provided by the Obligor to the employer that the child(ren) is/are enrolled in a comparable plan.

If the Obligor terminates employment, you must notify the Court, Obligee, or Delegate Child Support Enforcement Unit in writing within 14 days after termination, and provide, if known, the name of the Obligor's new employer.

The Obligor may file an objection to this Notice with the Court or Delegate Child Support Enforcement Unit if the premium amount does not meet the definition of reasonable cost as provided in §14-10-115(10)(g), C.R.S. A premium that results in a child support order of $50.00 or less or that is 20% or more of the Obligor's gross income shall not be considered reasonable.

6

CERTIFICATE OF MAILING

I certify that on ______________________ (date), I sent the original Notice to Employer to Deduct for Health Insurance to the Obligor's employer by United States Mail, first class postage prepaid, addressed as follows:

____
____
____

and

I certify that I sent a copy of the Notice to Employer to Deduct for Health Insurance to the Obligor by United States Mail, first class postage prepaid, addressed as follows:

____
____
____

and

I certify that I filed a copy of the Notice to Employer to Deduct for Health Insurance with the Court.

Date: _________________________________ ______________________________________
Signature (Obligee or Obligee's Representative)

Notice to Employer to Deduct for Health Insurance

You will use this form if you have children and child support and either parent has agreed or been ordered to provide health insurance for the children through his or her employment.

INSTRUCTIONS TO FILL OUT THE NOTICE TO DEDUCT FOR HEALTH INSURANCE

1. Fill out these lines the same as on your Petition.
2. Fill in the name and address of the employer who provides the insurance for the children.
3. Fill in the name and address of the parent working for the employer in #2 who is providing insurance for the children, and that parent's social security number.
4. Check the boxes for the types of insurance you are requesting.
5. Fill in the name, birth date, and social security number of each of the children who are to be covered by this insurance.
6. Fill out and sign the Certificate of Mailing showing that you sent the original Notice to the employer, one copy to the Obligor, and filed one copy with the court

NOTICE: If child support has been ordered in this case, an income assignment will be activated in the event of default in child support.

1 District Court, ______________________ County, Colorado Court Address:	
In re the Marriage of: **Petitioner:** and **Co-Petitioner/Respondent:**	▲ COURT USE ONLY ▲
	Case Number: Division: Courtroom:

2 **DECREE OF ☐ DISSOLUTION OF MARRIAGE ☐ LEGAL SEPARATION**

This matter was reviewed by the Court on 3 ______________________ (date).

4 Petitioner
☐ Appeared in person
☐ Signed the non-appearance affidavit
☐ Was represented by ______________________
____

5 ☐ Co-Petitioner ☐ Respondent
☐ Appeared in Person ☐ Did not appear
☐ Signed the non-appearance affidavit
☐ Was represented by ______________________
____

6 ☐ The Court has read the Non-Appearance Affidavit.
☐ The Court has heard the evidence and testimony of ______________________________________.
☐ The Court has considered any Financial Statements filed and makes the following findings and orders: ______________________________________

The Court has examined the record and makes the following findings:

7 A 1. The Court has jurisdiction over both parties based on:
B ☐ The parties filing jointly on ______________________ (date).
C ☐ Respondent ☐ Respondent's Attorney signed the waiver of service on ______________ (date).
D ☐ Service on the Respondent on ______________________ (date) at ______________________
______________________________ (place).
E ☐ The Court has jurisdiction over in-state property based on publication in accordance with C.R.C.P. 4(g)(2).
F ☐ The Court has subject-matter jurisdiction based on publication by consolidated notice, or certified mail.

8 2. The ______________________ was domiciled in Colorado for 91 days before this case was filed.

3. At least 91 days have passed since filing, service or completion of publication, whichever is later.

4. The marriage between the parties is irretrievably broken.

9 5. ☐ The separation agreement between the parties
☐ which is attached as Exhibit ________ and is incorporated into this Decree,

Bradford Publishing 1743 Wazee St., Denver, CO 80202 — 303-292-2590 — www.bradfordpublishing.com

☐ which has been read into the record and will be filed by the parties on or before _____________, has been considered by the Court and is found not to be unconscionable as to support, maintenance, and division of property.

10 6. ☐ The Court has entered permanent orders that will be filed by ______________________ (date).
☐ The Court finds it is in the best interest of the parties that a decree be entered even though there are no permanent orders on this date.

11 7. ☐ All provisions of the parenting plan, including residence and allocation of parental responsibilities (including parenting time and decision-making responsibilities), are in the best interests of the children.
☐ The parenting plan is attached as Exhibit _______ and is incorporated into this Decree.

12 8. ☐ The Support Order, when entered, will become a part of this Decree.

13 9. ☐ The name change request is not detrimental to the interest of any person.

14 The Court therefore ORDERS:

A ☐ The marriage is dissolved and a Decree of Dissolution of Marriage is entered.
B ☐ A Decree of Legal Separation is entered. The parties are advised that either may, six (6) months from this date, apply for entry of a Decree of Dissolution of Marriage, which will be granted upon proof of notice to the other party.
C ☐ Each parent shall perform the applicable provisions of the parenting plan.
D ☐ A Protection/Restraining Order was issued on ____________________________ (date) and is:
☐ Vacated.
☐ Continued to ____________________________ (date) pursuant to § 13-14-102(9)(c), C.R.S.
☐ No changes have been made to the existing Protection/Restraining Order.
☐ Changes have been made to the existing Protection/Restraining Order, as follows:
____.

If the Protection Order has been modified, the party requesting the modification must serve a copy of the modified Temporary or Permanent Protection Order, as applicable, on the other party.

E ☐ The _______________ is granted a restoration of name to _________________________.

Each party shall perform the applicable provisions of the separation agreement, permanent orders, or non-appearance affidavit.

15 THE COURT FURTHER ORDERS:

16

________________________________		________________________________	
Attorney for Petitioner	Date	Attorney for Co-Petitioner/Respondent	Date

17

________________________________	________________________________
Date	☐ Judge ☐ Magistrate

No. 251. Rev. 7-12. DECREE OF DISSOLUTION OF MARRIAGE OR LEGAL SEPARATION (Page 2 of 2)

Instructions For Decree of Dissolution of Marriage or Legal Separation

Although the decree reads as though the court wrote it, the court does not, in practice, fill it out. You must fill out the decree form as you wish the court to sign it.

1. Fill out these lines the same as you did on your Petition.

2. Check the appropriate box depending on whether you are asking for a dissolution of marriage or a legal separation.

   You may now be requesting something different from what you asked for in the petition. For example, you may have decided during the 91-day waiting period that you really do want to get divorced after all, even though your petition asks for a legal separation. Or, you might have asked for a dissolution in your petition and now prefer a legal separation in order to continue some benefit or to give yourselves a chance at preserving your relationship. (See Chapter 1 for a discussion of these considerations.)

   It is perfectly okay to "waffle" throughout the waiting period about whether you want a divorce or legal separation. Just be clear in your decree and separation agreement which marital status you both want now. If this is a change from what you asked for in your petition, it is a good idea, in either your separation agreement or your testimony at the final hearing—or both—to point out to the court that this is a change and why you want it. Once the decree is signed by the judge, you become that marital status, divorced or legally separated, so it is important to be certain you agree on which one you want in the final order of court.

3. If you are asking for a decree by affidavit (without hearing) leave this blank—the judge will write in this date. If you are expecting to have a hearing, fill in the date of the hearing.

4. As to the Petitioner: Check the box next to "Signed the Non-Appearance affidavit" if you are asking for a decree without a hearing. If you are going to the hearing, check the "Appeared in person" box. Check the appropriate box if the Petitioner is represented by an attorney, and write his/her name. (If you are represented, your attorney will probably prepare this form for you.)

5. As to the Co-Petitioner/Respondent: Check the same box you checked in step 3. In the boxes below, check the appropriate space for you, the Co-Petitioner, or your spouse, the Respondent, depending on whether he or she also signed the Non-Appearance Affidavit, will personally appear in court, is represented by an attorney, or will not appear. Check the appropriate box if the Co-Petitioner/Respondent is represented by an attorney, and write his/her name. (If you are represented, your attorney will probably prepare this form for you.)

6. Check the box next to "heard the evidence and statements of" only if you or your spouse plan to appear in court. Indicate which of you will appear at the hearing by writing "Petitioner," "Respondent," or "Co-Petitioner,"—or "the parties" if you will both appear—in the space that follows. Check the box next to "read the affidavit of" if no one is appearing and you are filing the Affidavit for Decree Without Hearing. Check the third box.

7. Check the appropriate box according to whether you filed as co-petitioners, whether there was service, or waiver of service. (See Chapter 6 for a discussion of service of process.)
   - Check boxes A and B if you are co-petitioners. Show the date you filed the petition with the clerk of the district court and paid your filing fee.
   - Check boxes A and C if the respondent, or the respondent's attorney, signed a waiver and acceptance of service. Show the date he or she signed the waiver.

- Check boxes A and D if the respondent was personally served with copies of the petition and summons. Show the date, city and state where he/she was served.
- Check box E only if the respondent was served by individual publication (See chapter 5).
- Check box F if you published by consolidated notice or served by certified mail.

8. Indicate which or both of you was domiciled in Colorado for ninety-one days prior to filing your petition by filling in "Petitioner," "Co-Petitioner" or "Respondent, or "Petitioner and Co-Petitioner" or "Petitioner and Respondent", as appropriate.

9. Check the appropriate box depending on whether:
   - You are making your separation agreement a part of your decree, in which case this will read, "attached as Exhibit A;" (Be sure to write "Exhibit A" on page 1 of your separation agreement.)
   - You have told the court the terms of your agreement and will write it up later (you run the risk of the court withholding approval of your decree until the written agreement is received). Fill in the date of your deadline for filing the written agreement, if you know it.

10. Leave these boxes blank. These situations won't arise if you are doing your own divorce.

11. Check the first box if there are minor children. Check the second box if you are making a separate parenting plan, and it will be a part of your decree, insert "B" in the blank after "Exhibit", and write Exhibit B on page 1 of your parenting plan. If your parenting plan is included in your Exhibit A, write "A" in the blank.

12. Check this box if you have completed a Support Order.

13. Check this box only if either of you is asking for a former name back.

14. Check box A if you are asking for a dissolution of marriage.

    Check box B if you are asking for a legal separation.

    Check box C if you have completed a parenting plan.

    Check box D if a Protection or Restraining Order has been issued against either of you, and the specifics about its status.

    Check box E if you or your spouse are asking for a former name back, indicate this by writing whether the Petitioner or Co-Petitioner or Respondent—or both—wants the change, and then write in the complete new name(s). (Remember, you can only return to one of your names before the marriage through your divorce action, not change to a completely new name.)

15. Leave this blank.

16. You may both sign the Decree on the lines provided for attorneys. Delete "Attorney for" beneath both signature lines.

17. Leave these blank.

[1] District Court, ______________________ County, Colorado Court Address:	
In re the Marriage of: **Petitioner:** and **Co-Petitioner/Respondent:**	
[2] Attorney or Party Without Attorney (Name and Address): Phone Number: E-mail: FAX Number: Atty. Reg. #:	▲ COURT USE ONLY ▲ Case Number: Division: Courtroom:
AFFIDAVIT FOR DECREE WITHOUT APPEARANCE OF PARTIES	

Please complete the appropriate information in Numbers 1 – 6 prior to filing with the Court.

[3] The ☐ Petitioner and/or ☐ Co-Petitioner/Respondent files this Affidavit in support of a request for issuance of a Decree of Dissolution of Marriage or a Decree of Legal Separation without appearance of the parties.

1. The Petition for Dissolution of Marriage/Petition for Legal Separation was filed on ____[4]____ (date). On that date, the ☐ Petitioner and/or ☐ Co-Petitioner/Respondent ______[5]______ (name) had been domiciled in Colorado for more than 91 days immediately before the Petition for Dissolution of Marriage was filed.

[6] **2.** The Petition and Summons were served by: **(check one)**

[A] ☐ A Co-Petitioner filing (when both parties sign the Petition).
[B] ☐ Personal service (service by Return of Service/Affidavit of Service) on ____________________ (date).
[C] ☐ Waiver of service (Respondent signs Waiver to accept service) signed on ____________________ (date).
[D] ☐ Publication/Certified Mail. (**Note:** Service by either of these methods is only allowed by Court Order.) The publication occurred on ____________________ (date) **OR** the return receipt for Certified Mail was signed by the Respondent on ____________________ (date).

[7] **3.** ☐ **There are no minor child(ren) and wife is not pregnant.**

Or

☐ **There are minor child(ren) <u>and each party</u> is represented by counsel.** The parties have completed a Parenting Plan that provides for the allocation of parental responsibilities (decision-making responsibilities and parenting time) and have reached an agreement with respect to child support, and medical/dental insurance of the child(ren) of the marriage. The Parenting Plan is in the best interests of the child(ren). **(*The Parenting Plan must be filed with the Court.*)**

[8] **4.** **Check only one.**

☐ **The parties have signed a written Separation Agreement.** The parties have completed a Separation Agreement that provides for the division of all marital property and marital debts, and addresses spousal support/maintenance. The parties agree that the Separation Agreement is fair and not unconscionable. **(*The Separation Agreement must be filed with the Court.*)**

Or

Bradford Publishing, 1743 Wazee St., Denver, CO 80202 — 303-292-2590 — www.bradfordpublishing.com

9 ☐ **There is no marital property to be divided and there are no marital debts and neither party requests spousal support/maintenance.**

5. ☐ There are no genuine issues of material fact and the marriage is irretrievably broken.

10 **6.** The ☐ Petitioner ☐ Co-Petitioner/Respondent wishes to have the prior name of ____________________ restored. The restoration of the prior name will not defraud any creditors or injure third parties.

11 **7.** Other:

____

____

____

12 The ☐ Petitioner and/or ☐ Co-Petitioner/Respondent request that the attached Decree of Dissolution of Marriage/ Decree of Legal Separation be entered after the statutory waiting period has elapsed.

Petitioner:	☐ Co-Petitioner ☐ Respondent (check one):
13 ______________________ Signature Date	______________________ Signature Date
______________________ Address	______________________ Address
______________________ City State Zip Code	______________________ City State Zip Code
______________________ Home Phone # Cell #	______________________ Home Phone # Cell #
14 ______________________ Attorney Signature, if any	______________________ Attorney Signature, if any

15 Subscribed and affirmed, or sworn to before me in the County of ____________, State of ____________, this ______ day of ______________, 20____.

My Commission expires: ____________________

____
Notary Public/Clerk

Subscribed and affirmed, or sworn to before me in the County of ____________, State of ____________, this ______ day of ______________, 20____.

My Commission expires: ____________________

____
Notary Public/Clerk

16

CERTIFICATE OF SERVICE

(If only one party signs this Affidavit, complete the Certificate of Service below.)

I certify that on ______________________ (date) a true and accurate copy of the ***AFFIDAVIT FOR DECREE WITHOUT APPEARANCE OF PARTIES*** was served on the other party by:
☐ Hand Delivery, ☐ E-filed, ☐ Faxed to this number ________________, **or** ☐ by placing it in the United States mail, postage pre-paid, addressed to the following:

TO: ______________________________

____

____

____
Your signature

No. 252. Rev. 7-12. AFFIDAVIT FOR DECREE WITHOUT APPEARANCE OF PARTIES (Page 2 of 2)

Divorce or Legal Separation By Affidavit: Affidavit for Decree Without Appearance of Parties

If you have no minor children or you are both represented by different lawyers, and you are requesting a decree of dissolution of marriage or legal separation, then you do not need to present your agreement at a hearing in order for the court to grant a final decree. You may mail in your final papers. If you have lawyers, they will probably prepare and mail the final papers for you.

If you are preparing your own papers and doing your divorce by affidavit, see the Checklist of Our Final Court Papers at the beginning of this chapter.

INSTRUCTIONS TO FILL OUT THE AFFIDAVIT FOR DECREE WITHOUT APPEARANCE OF PARTIES

1-2. Complete these lines the same as you did on your petition and all the other papers. Be sure to include the case number and the division or courtroom number.

3. Check the appropriate box or boxes to tell the court who is signing this affidavit, one of you or both of you.

   CAUTION: If only one of you signs this Affidavit, you must prove that the other party received a copy. See step 17.

4. Write the date the Petition was filed.

5. If you both were domiciled in Colorado for ninety-one (91) days prior to filing your petition, write "the parties" here. If only one of you was domiciled for 91 days, write "Petitioner," "Co-Petitioner," or "Respondent," whichever is true.

6. Check the box according to your situation:

   A. If you filed as co-petitioners, check this box.

   B. If you personally served the respondent, check this box and fill in the date that the process server filled in on the Return of Service on your summons.

   C. If your spouse signed the Waiver of Service, check this box and fill in the date from the Waiver (see page 3 of your Summons).

   D. Check this box if your spouse was served by certified mail or publication. Write in the date your spouse either received the certified mail (from the post office receipt), or the last date of publication if served by publication.

7. Check the appropriate boxes.

8. Check either the first or second box. If you have property but no minor children, check only the first box. If you have no property or children and you are not filing a separation agreement, do not check either box.

9. Check this box if all outstanding matters regarding your divorce or legal separation have been resolved between you.

10. If one or both of you plans to return to a former name, write "Petitioner," "Co-Petitioner," or "Respondent" here and fill in the name to be restored. Otherwise, leave it blank.

11. Add here any other requests you would like the court to order.

12. Check the appropriate boxes the same as you did for step 3.

13. One party must sign in the presence of a notary. If the other party is joining in this affidavit, he or she should also sign in front of a notary.

    NOTE: If you are not both signing this form, the signing spouse must notify the other (see step 16).

14. If you are represented by attorneys, they will sign here. If you are doing this yourselves, write "none."

15. Leave these spaces blank for the notary to use.

16. If only one of you signs this form, that person must send a copy by certified mail to the other spouse. Fill in the date you mailed the copy, the name and address of the other spouse, and sign the certificate of mailing on the back of the affidavit. In practice, allow reasonable time for your spouse to object to not having a hearing, such as 20 or 30 days. You must allow for at least five working days from the date in this step to the date the court is likely to receive this affidavit. If the other spouse's address is not known, mail a copy of this form to his or her last known address. When you receive them back, file with the court the green receipt card from the Postal Service, or the entire envelope marked that delivery was not possible. In either case, be sure to put your case number on it.

Getting Your Case Set for a Hearing

In most situations, you will have a final non-contested court hearing, separate from a status conference, often called a Permanent Orders hearing. Courts differ about how they set the date and time for it. The court may give you a date for a non-contested final hearing at the time you filed your Petition, while at a status conference, or afterward according to other procedures of your particular court. If the procedure for setting your final hearing is not explained in your Case Management Order or other written instructions from the court, you will have to ask.

Some courts require some paperwork, a Notice to Set, just to set the date and time for your final hearing. This is to coordinate the hearing date with both of you and the court's calendar.

NOTICE TO SET

The purpose of a Notice to Set is to let the other party know that the case is being set for a hearing. You are telling your spouse that on a certain date and time you will call or drop by the court and ask them to find a date on the magistrate's calendar for hearing your case.

Fill out the Notice to Set form that is shown on the next page. Fill in the date you are to contact the court and the Certificate of Mailing section that shows you sent it to your spouse. If there is the slightest chance that your spouse will want to come to the hearing, but has a particularly rigid schedule (fireman, long distance truck driver, out-of-town salesperson) then it is best to send it by certified mail. This shows the court that you did your best to help your spouse find the most convenient date. Send an original form to the court.

If You Are Concerned About Privacy

In practice, the only document you are required to leave in your court file at the time of your final hearing is the decree, plus the child support worksheet(s) if you have children.

You must show your sworn financial statements, and your separation agreement to the judge at your hearing, in order for the judge to "find" your agreement to be "fair and not unconscionable" with regard to property, debts, and maintenance, and to be "in the best interest of the children" with regard to child support and your parenting plan. You may then ask that these documents be returned to you if you do not wish to have the separation agreement incorporated into the decree. Or, you may ask that all or some of your documentation be "sealed," which means that they may not be read without a judge's approval. See Chapter 2 for a more complete discussion of privacy in your divorce.

☐ District Court ☐ Denver Juvenile Court ______________________ County, Colorado Court address: **In re** __________________________________**:** **Petitioner:** and **Co-Petitioner/Respondent:**	▲ COURT USE ONLY ▲
Attorney or Party Without Attorney (Name and Address): Phone Number: E-mail: FAX Number: Atty. Reg. #:	Case Number: Division: Courtroom:
NOTICE TO SET HEARING	

☐ Petitioner ☐ Co-Petitioner/Respondent will contact the Court on _______________ (date) at _________ (time) to set a date and time for a hearing in the District Court or Juvenile Court _____________ (Division/Courtroom) at this telephone number: ______________. The hearing will take approximately __________ ☐ hours ☐ minutes and will address the following:

- ☐ Temporary Orders Hearing
- ☐ Final Hearing on Dissolution of Marriage
- ☐ Motion to Modify Child Support
- ☐ Other ____

Notice to the Other Party: If you wish to participate in the setting of the hearing, you must telephone the Division Clerk at the above number at the stated date and time.

Date: ________________________________ ___________________________________
Signature

CERTIFICATE OF SERVICE

I certify that on ________________ (date) a true and accurate copy of the **NOTICE TO SET HEARING** was served on the other party by:
☐ Hand Delivery, ☐ E-Filed, or ☐ Faxed to this number _______________, or
☐ by placing it in the United States mail, postage prepaid, and addressed to the following:

To: _______________________________
_______________________________ ___________________________________
_______________________________ Signature

NOTICE OF HEARING

This is the form you will send your spouse that states the day and time of your final hearing. Fill in the top of this form just like the petition. Fill in the date and time once you have that information. Put the address for your spouse in the Certificate of Mailing section at the bottom.

Mail a copy to your spouse by certified mail with sufficient time to allow the signed receipt or the whole envelope to come back to you before the hearing. You will take whichever it is to the hearing with you to show the court that you did, indeed, try to notify your spouse of the hearing date.

It is best if you both attend the hearing. This reassures the court that you do, indeed, agree. It also provides the court with a chance to ask any questions it might have of either of you.

<table>
<tr><td>☐ District Court ☐ Denver Juvenile Court
_____________________ County, Colorado
Court address:</td><td rowspan="2">

▲ COURT USE ONLY ▲</td></tr>
<tr><td>In re _________________________________:
Petitioner:

and
Co-Petitioner/Respondent:</td></tr>
<tr><td>Attorney or Party Without Attorney (Name and Address):

Phone Number: E-mail:
FAX Number: Atty. Reg. #:</td><td>Case Number:

Division: Courtroom:</td></tr>
<tr><td colspan="2">NOTICE OF HEARING</td></tr>
</table>

To: ____
☐ Petitioner or ☐ Respondent/Co-Petitioner and attorney of record:

You are hereby notified that a hearing has been set on ______________________ (date) at ____________ (time), in courtroom _________, located at the above address.

The hearing will take approximately ______ ☐ hours ☐ minutes and will address the following issues:

☐ Temporary Orders
☐ Final Hearing on Dissolution of Marriage
☐ Motion to Modify Child Support
☐ Other ____

If you fail to appear at that hearing, the Court may enter Orders against you. Please do not bring children to the hearing. If you do bring children, your hearing may be vacated and you will have to re-schedule.

Date: ______________________________ ________________________________
Signature

CERTIFICATE OF SERVICE

I certify that on ______________________ (date) a true and accurate copy of the **NOTICE OF HEARING** was served on the other party by:
☐ Hand Delivery, ☐ E-Filed, or ☐ Faxed to this number __________________ or
☐ by placing it in the United States mail, postage pre-paid, and addressed to the following:

To: ______________________________
______________________________ ________________________________
______________________________ Signature

No. 1196. Rev. 4-12. NOTICE OF HEARING © 1997 (Page 1 of 2)

Bradford Publishing, 1743 Wazee St., Denver, CO 80202 — (303) 292-2590 — www.bradfordpublishing.com

Checklist of Our Papers Ready to Send to Court, or to Bring to Court for Our Final Hearing

Directions: Initial and date each item when it is ready for court.

Initials	Date Done	
____	_____	Affidavit for Decree Without Appearance (if doing decree without a hearing, divorce by affidavit)
		OR
____	_____	Notice of Hearing Date and Receipt (if only one of you is attending)
____	_____	Separation Agreement and/ or including a Parenting Plan
____	_____	Wife's Sworn Financial Statement
____	_____	Husband's Sworn Financial Statement
____	_____	Wife's Certificate of Compliance
____	_____	Husband's Certificate of Compliance
____	_____	Decree
____	_____	QDRO (if applicable)
____	_____	Agreement to Divide Retirement Plan (if applicable)
		If we have children:
____	_____	Child Support Worksheet(s) (usually attached to the separation agreement)
____	_____	Support Order
____	_____	Income Withholding for Support
____	_____	Notice to Employer to Deduct for Health Insurance
____	_____	Parenting-after-Divorce class attendance certificate

D DEFINITION

Non-contested hearing: Appearance by one or both spouses before a magistrate to present their final separation agreement, and request that a final decree be signed by the court.

APPEARANCE BY TELEPHONE

Some courts allow the appearance by telephone for one of the parties in non-contested hearings. This is especially useful when one spouse has already moved to another state. You must arrange the telephone call procedure in advance with the clerk of your particular courtroom. Some may require a written request of the judge. Make clear arrangements including the exact time of the call, who will place the call, and of course the phone number. This information should be included on your Notice of Hearing.

WHAT TO BRING TO THE FINAL HEARING

Many courts require that all your final papers be filed with the court two or more weeks before your hearing date, while some courts ask you to *bring* them to the final hearing. Some require the originals plus one photocopy of every document. Be sure to keep copies of everything for each of you, not only for your own records, but to refer to at the hearing if there are questions. Make two copies of the Decree and clip them to the original, along with two stamped envelopes—one addressed to each of you.

AT THE HEARING

Make sure you are on time for your hearing. You should dress nicely, because it shows respect for yourself and for the legal process. Avoid jeans, shorts, undershirts or tank tops, halter tops, or play clothes.

Unless you have previously filed all your final papers, hand them to the magistrate, clerk, or court reporter, as you are directed. In some counties, the clerk and court reporter are the same person. The magistrate, clerk, or court reporter will swear you in. Everything you say will be taken down either by a court reporter or tape recording.

Preparing your sample testimony ahead of time will help you stay organized during the hearing. Sometimes, the magistrate will ask you questions, usually the same ones that you have prepared, so you can look at your notes. The magistrate has the right to ask you what you are reading from and even to ask to see it. If the magistrate does not ask questions, he or she may tell you to "state your case." If this happens, begin reading your sample testimony out loud.

SAMPLE TESTIMONY

Most magistrates and other court officials who hear non-contested divorces are accustomed to working with laypersons. They will help you present your agreement or arguments and will direct how you are to file your papers. Just in case you encounter a magistrate who is as new at this as you are, here are the things you must not forget to say and do:

1. State your name and address (both mailing and physical address if you have both).

2. Tell the court whether you are the Petitioner, Co-Petitioner or Respondent in the case.

3. Give the original of all your final papers to the magistrate, court clerk or reporter—whichever the court directs you to do. If you are not certain, ask.

4. Read the statistical information in your Petition, pointing out any corrections which have come to light during your case. Have a copy of your Petition in front of you, so you can read down it in order. The magistrate will be following along on the court original.

You must state:

a) names of the parties; names and birth dates of the children, if any;
b) whether the wife is pregnant and, if so, if this is a child of the marriage;
c) date of the marriage and date of the separation;
d) date the case was filed, and which of you lived in the state for at least 91 days before that date. Point out if this is a Co-Petitioner filing.

5. If your case is not a Co-Petitioner filing, turn to the second page of the Summons and read the information there about the manner in which the case was served (waiver and acceptance of service or personal service) and, most important, the date of this service. Remember, this began your 91 days.

6. If you served by certified mail or publication, draw the court's attention to the Order giving you permission to do so, and either the certified mail receipt or the proof of publication. These must have been completed at least 91 days before the hearing.

7. State that you believe the marriage to be irretrievably broken, with no hope of a reconciliation. These are very precise phrases which enable the court to make the correct "finding" which in turn enables the court to issue the Decree, so be sure you state them exactly this way.

8. Draw the court's attention to your separation agreement, partial agreement or written request for permanent orders. Tell the court the major points in this document, in the order they appear. Be certain you cover:

a) Parenting Plan for your children, if any, especially your decision-making and physical care provisions.
b) The amount of child support and maintenance, if any, and whether this is being paid by income assignment. Remember, if you are asking for a deviation from the recommended support or to pay directly instead of by assignment, you must have the court's permission. See Chapter 9 if this is news.
c) The way in which you are dividing your assets and paying your debts. Be certain to draw the court's attention to the fact that you made the mandatory exchange of documents and have each filed sworn financial statements so the court is reassured that you each had full knowledge of your assets and liabilities. Review Chapter 6 if you skipped this step.

If your spouse is not participating, remind the court of this by explaining why there is only one sworn financial statement and perhaps incomplete disclosure. If you served by publication, this is absolutely the time to tell the court that you want title to certain in-state assets. Review Chapter 5 for when this is possible.

d) Any agreement about division of retirement accounts which requires the court to sign a separate document, such as a QDRO.

e) Whether either of you wishes to be restored to a former name.

f) Any other peculiarities of your agreement or requests which you think are important to place on the record.

g) State that you believe the separation agreement is fair to you and your spouse, and that it is in the best interest of your children, if any. These are more of the phrases which you must say exactly this way so the court can make the correct findings and issue the orders you need.

9. Ask the court to approve your separation agreement, and to sign the Decree, Support Order, Income Withholding for Support, and QDRO if any.

10. Introduce your spouse if he or she is present. The court will ask if your spouse wishes to testify also, and will almost certainly ask if he or she agrees the marriage is irretrievably broken with no hope of reconciliation and if he or she feels the separation agreement is fair and if the parenting plan is in the best interest of the children.

Once you have both given your testimony, the magistrate will spend a moment or so reviewing the papers you have filed, may ask another question or two to clarify things, and then will sign the Decree, Support Order, Income Withholding for Support, and QDRO, if any. You are divorced the moment the court signs the Decree, a fact which the court will undoubtedly announce as he or she does so.

You will probably not be able to go home with a signed copy of the Decree in your pocket, however. In most courts, the magistrate will return your court file to the clerk's office and they will "conform" the copy(s) of the Decree you left with the court and mail them to you in the self-addressed envelope(s) you provided. Some smaller jurisdictions do this for free without you having to supply either the Decree copy or the envelopes. You should ask in court if this is so, if the clerk of your court has not given you this information in writing or conversation.

What to Do if the Court Does Not Sign Your Decree

If the magistrate does not sign your decree, or another order you have asked for, he or she will tell you why, in person if you are there, or by mail if you apply for your decree by affidavit. It might be that you left out one of the necessary forms, or did not wait the full 91 days, or did not sign one of the papers. It may be that the court did not think some provision(s) of your separation agreement was fair or complete. You may:

- supply the missing form
- provide the missing signature
- wait the correct number of days
- amend or complete your separation agreement to conform to the court's concerns

If the court is questioning your separation agreement and you are present in court, you may ask for a continuance to a later date to give you time to deal with the objection. If you applied for your decree by affidavit and your written response from the court does not tell you the reasons, you may request a hearing or a meeting with the judge or magistrate to discuss the problem.

If the court does not approve your agreement even after you have had a chance to explain, don't give up. This would be a good time to consult with a lawyer or lawyer-mediator, with expertise in family law, to find out either how to change your agreement to make it acceptable to the court, or how best to go about persuading the court to approve your agreement as is.

Copies of Your Decree

To prove you are divorced or legally separated, a copy of your final decree showing the court's signature and the date signed is usually sufficient. However, some insurance companies or other institutions may require a *certified copy.* Since the ORIGINAL which the court signs stays in the court file, you may ask the court clerk to certify your copies.

CERTIFIED COPIES

In some courts, the magistrate will sign the extra copies of your decree during your hearing or just afterwards. If this is done, you can take them to the clerk of the district court to be certified the same day. The clerk certifies that it is an accurate copy of the decree which the judge or magistrate signed that day, by signing and applying the court seal.

If the judge or magistrate does not sign the copies at the time of the hearing, then you may have all of your copies certified and returned to you by mail. You must give the court as many copies as you would like certified, a fee for each (usually about $20.00), and stamped envelopes addressed to where you want them sent. Payment must be made by cash, credit or debit card, cashier's check, or money order. The clerk will certify the copies by stamping them with a facsimile of the judge's signature, or a stamp that says "Original signed by ________________ ," date it the day the original was signed, apply the court's seal, and mail it back to you in the envelope(s) you provide.

D DEFINITION **Certified copy:** A copy of any order of court on which the clerk has signed under seal that it is a true copy of an actual order of court.

CONFORMED COPIES

If you do not need a certified copy, but just a copy showing the date the judge signed it, then follow the above procedure, but ask for *conformed* rather than certified copies, and omit the payment. This means the clerk uses the court's signature stamp and dates the copies to "conform" to the original decree, without the certification. If you supply the photocopies, this service is usually free.

SEND SPOUSE A COPY

If your spouse does not come to the hearing, you are responsible for sending him or her a signed copy of your final decree, and any other orders signed at the final hearing. If you know where your spouse lives, it is good practice to send it by certified mail, with return receipt requested, and then send the returned receipt to the court to be put in your file. Be sure to put your case name and number on the receipt so it will find its way into the correct case file.

D DEFINITION **Conformed copy:** a copy of any order signed by the court, showing the date signed by the judge or magistrate and his or her facsimile signature (sometimes a stamped statement saying, "Original signed by ....").

CHAPTER 13

FINISHING UP

Page

FINISHING UP

This chapter is about carrying out all the terms of your separation agreement, including transferring titles to real estate, motor vehicles, stocks, bank accounts, retirements, and other assets. Finishing up also requires paying debts as agreed, which may include a payment by one of you to the other, or signing a promissory note and deed of trust. Notices of changes in either names or addresses are a must.

Once your separation agreement has been incorporated into your decree, whether of dissolution of marriage or legal separation, it becomes an order of the court (in addition to being a contract). As a court order, certain enforcement measures are readily available. Since this guidebook is for the friendly divorce or legal separation, how to carry out enforcement measures is not discussed in detail.

Transfers of Title

Your agreement may have been silent about when certain transfers were to take place, or it may have specified that some transfers are to take place later. Now is the time to take care of all of these. Make a checklist, or calendar them, if you need to, so you don't overlook anything. Be certain every item which may have value is specifically transferred. For transfers which we have not described in this book, you may wish to ask the appropriate entity (the company in which you own stock, the breed organization in which your livestock or pet is registered), how to carry out the transfer.

For many items, such as household goods and furniture, transferring ownership is a matter of transferring possession. Information about simple transfers of real estate, and promissory notes secured by real estate is provided next, followed by information about how to transfer motor vehicles, stocks and stock accounts, insurance policies, and business interests.

REAL ESTATE

Quitclaim Deed

A quitclaim deed is used to transfer title to real estate from both spouses to one spouse. There is no warranty of title with this type of transfer—whatever interest is owned by one spouse is simply "quitted" to the other. For transferring real estate outside of Colorado, contact a real estate attorney in that state.

"We don't need to do all this paperwork about our house. We trust each other."

Trust is not enough to cover the possibilities your future may hold. Should either of you become disabled or die, or feel pressure from future relationships, things could get very difficult indeed without this paperwork.

This is an area partners frequently overlook, perhaps because of the rush to get away from a painful situation, as well as the absence of a court or other process that requires you to look at it all. Not taking timely action to wind things up can lead to much frustration later on, trying to find your ex to sign off on something. Be sure to make your own checklist of all items to be split or titles transferred, including joint obligations or debts, and then get it done. Consult an attorney or CPA about any tax effects you need to plan for.

Where to Find the Forms I Need

There are a number of forms mentioned in this chapter and throughout this book that you will need to accomplish your divorce or separation. The forms in this chapter that you need to transfer property, enforce your agreement if things don't go as expected, or modify your support in the future, can be found at Bradford Publishing Company, the publisher of this book. Bradford, where most attorneys go for their forms, has been the provider of Colorado legal forms since 1881. Printed forms are available from their Denver store below or can be filled out and printed from their website at www.bradfordpublishing.com.

Bradford Publishing
1743 Wazee Street
Denver, CO 80202
303-292-2590

Checklist of Titles We Need to Transfer

Directions: With your separation agreement in hand, review it paragraph by paragraph to check each item on the following list which has not yet been transferred according to your agreement. Once the transfer is completed, write the date on the line next to the item.

Real Estate

Check if needed — Date Done

____ Quitclaim Deed ____________

____ Promissory Note ____________

____ Deed of Trust ____________

Motor Vehicles

____ Title ____________

____ Title ____________

____ Power of Attorney ____________

____ Power of Attorney ____________

Other

____ Stock ____________

____ Stock ____________

____ Bond ____________

____ Bond ____________

____ Bank account ____________

____ Bank account ____________

____ Investment account ____________

____ Investment account ____________

____ IRA ____________

____ IRA ____________

____ Registered/ pedigreed pet ____________

____ Membership ____________

____ Ticket Priorities ____________

____ Other ____________

____ ____________

____ ____________

Take the signed, notarized quitclaim deed to the Clerk and Recorder in the county where the real estate is located, and pay the fee (per page). The transfer is not complete until recording. The Clerk will mail the original back to you usually within about two weeks.

Promissory Notes

Use a promissory note to ensure any payment of money to each other that is part of your property settlement other than child support or maintenance. Payments may be regular and frequent, variable in amount, or in one lump sum. There are many different published forms for promissory notes.

When the promissory note is signed by the person promising to pay, the original should be kept by the person who will receive the payments. When the note is paid in full, the recipient should write "Paid in full" across the face of the original note, then sign it, and return the original to the person who paid it, keeping a photocopy for records. The Deed of Trust or other security should then be released.

Deed of Trust

A Deed of Trust is the document that spells out the terms of your mortgage and, when recorded, creates a lien against your real estate. The real estate thus becomes *security* for the payment. The real estate must be owned by the person who signs the promissory note. If there is already a mortgage on the real estate, the deed of trust becomes a second mortgage. If there is already a second mortgage on the property, the deed of trust becomes a third, etc.

There are many forms of Deed of Trust, each with different enforcement provisions. Whichever one you use, record it, along with the Quitclaim Deed, and ask that the Quitclaim Deed be recorded first. This insures that the person who signs the Deed of Trust has full power to *convey the security interest.* The recording fee, which is subject to change, is currently $6.00 for the first page and $5.00 for each additional page of an 8½ x 11" document, and $10.00 per page for larger documents. Record it with the Public Trustee in the office of the Clerk and Recorder in the county where the real estate is located.

When the Promissory Note is paid in full, the person to whom the money is paid and who holds the Deed of Trust will fill out a Release of Deed of Trust and send it to the Clerk and Recorder.

PERSONAL PROPERTY

Items of personal property are not usually titled. Once your decree is entered, your separation agreement controls ownership. Your personal property should either be divided by the time of the decree, or at the time stated in your separation agreement. If one of you will care for some pieces of personal property for the other, that arrangement should be clearly stated in your separation agreement.

Art and other creative works can frequently prove a problem if they come into vogue and therefore increase in value after the divorce. If the item does not have a paper title now, you can create one by drafting a bill of sale which describes the item in detail. For example, "12 x 24 water color of boat and dock in shades of blue, with 6-line original poem in calligraphy on bottom right corner." Create a paper trail of the disposition of your important things now and you won't have to find one another later in order to sell or transfer them.

MOTOR VEHICLES

Titles to motor vehicles are easily transferred. The person who keeps the vehicle should obtain the spouse's signature on the title. You may then take the signed title to the motor vehicle registration office and request that a new title be issued in your name.

If there is a loan in both names on the vehicle, the lender probably holds the title. Typically, lenders do not allow either party to sign off the title until the loan is paid in full.

LIQUID ASSETS: CASH AND BANK ACCOUNTS

Cash is, of course, easily divided. Just count it out. If you have significant amounts, prepare and sign a receipt.

Transferring ownership of bank accounts usually requires one or both of you to prepare a new signature card, or to sign other transfer documents provided by the bank. Be sure that the bank has the correct Social Security number on each account after the transfer.

STOCKS, BONDS, AND OTHER SECURITIES

If your stocks and bonds are owned through a broker account, it is sufficient to simply change the name on the account, or, if you are dividing the contents of the account, to open a second

Directions: Complete the following checklists as they relate to your situations. Do on separate piece of paper as necessary.

Personal Property Transfer Checklist: We have the following artworks, antiques and collectibles which have been transferred in writing and in fact as follows:

Item	To Whom	Date Transferred
________	________	________
________	________	________
________	________	________

Motor Vehicle Transfer Checklist: Wife (or husband and wife) has/have transferred title or signed power of attorney to husband of:

Vehicle Description	Date Transferred
______________	__________

Husband (or husband and wife) has/have transferred title or signed power of attorney to wife of:

Vehicle Description	Date Transferred
______________	__________

Bank Account Transfer Checklist: Only husband's name appears on the following bank accounts:

Bank	Type of Account	Date Transferred
________	________	________

Only wife's name appears on the following bank accounts:

Bank	Type of Account	Date Transferred
________	________	________

account with the same broker and ask that shares be allocated between the two accounts. If the original account is in your joint names, be sure to close it, or remove one of the names. As long as you don't sell any of your securities, you will not incur any taxes transferring these securities between you. See section about capital gains in Chapter 7.

If you have the actual stock certificates, you will find a form on the back of the certificate for transferring ownership. Be sure, after you have filled it out, that you sign it in front of the proper authority indicated on the certificate. The new owner must present the signed certificate to the company so that a new certificate may be prepared by the company, and ownership of the shares transferred on the books of the company.

A bond should be transferred according to the procedures which accompanied the bond when you received it. If it is not being held for you as part of an investment account and you do not know how it should be transferred, contact the entity which issued the bond (U.S., municipality, Power Company, etc.).

LIFE INSURANCE

Transferring ownership of life insurance is handled by completing forms provided by the insurance company. Contact your agent or the company directly to obtain the appropriate forms.

Be sure to make any necessary changes in your beneficiary designation required by your agreement. Your designation must be absolutely accurate. You may obtain a copy of your existing beneficiary designation from the insurance company. If you have agreed to continue designating each other, for the benefit of the children, or to insure a maintenance obligation, be sure your designation does not refer to the other as "wife" or "husband" or "spouse." This will create a serious ambiguity if you re-marry.

MEDICAL INSURANCE; COBRA

Make certain that if the non-employee spouse will take the COBRA option to continue his/her medical insurance you have prepared all the necessary paperwork before the final decree. Most insurance is paid to the end of the month or a month in advance, so there may be a grace period within which a former spouse is covered.

MOTOR VEHICLE INSURANCE

Contact your agent to separate your motor vehicle insurance. You will likely separate one of your cars from the family policy. Your

Stocks, Bonds and Securities Transfer Checklist:

Stock/Bond	To Whom/Date
__________	__________
__________	__________
__________	__________
__________	__________
__________	__________

Insurance Transfer Checklist

Directions: Complete the following as you accomplish each one.

Husband has changed his insurance policies as follows:

Life insurance at __________ (company) now benefits ______________.

Life insurance at __________ (company) now benefits ______________.

Health insurance at ________________ (company) now covers ______________.

Car insurance on ____________________ (vehicles) is in his name only.

Wife has changed her insurance policies as follows:

Life insurance at __________ (company) now benefits ______________.

Life insurance at __________ (company) now benefits ______________.

Health insurance at ________________ (company) now covers ______________.

Car insurance on ____________________ (vehicles) is in her name only.

Non-employee spouse has elected _______ years of COBRA option through ____________________ and completed the paper work, so that coverage for ____________ will begin on ______date.

agent will do this for you. If there are only two cars, you will both lose the multi-car discount and each pay more than half the previous joint premium. Be very clear about who will insure your children's cars.

RETIREMENT, PENSIONS, AND PROFIT SHARING

Tax deferred savings plans and IRA's may be divided by directly transferring all or some of the balance to a similar account in the name of the other spouse. As long as such a transfer is done by one trustee to another, and the money in no way comes directly into your hands, you will avoid withholding, tax, and penalty. See Chapter 7.

To transfer all or a part of a military retirement, contact the accounting office for the service in question for their forms and procedures. Similarly, for Civil Service Retirement System, Federal Employees Retirement System, and TIAA-CREF, contact the Plan Administrator for their forms and procedures for transfers. You must have all this lined up before you finalize your separation agreement because the terms you put in your agreement about these assets controls what you can do after your Decree.

For those plans which are covered by E.R.I.S.A. and are therefore divisible or transferable by Qualified Domestic Relations Order (QDRO), send a certified copy of the QDRO, previously signed by the judge, to the Plan Administrator who will carry out the transfer as described in the Order. For greater security, you can request a signed receipt for it, or send it by Certified Mail. However, NOTE that it is important to have obtained the Plan Administrator's approval of the QDRO or agreement *before* giving it to the court to Order. In most cases, it will go to the Plan administrator twice, once to approve (or tell you why he or she won't so you can amend it and resubmit) and then again to carry out. See Chapter 7 for more on this.

For a defined contribution plan QDRO, the plan administrator will then contact the receiving spouse to determine how he/she wants the transfer to occur (rollover to an IRA, cash with withholding for income taxes, other, a combination of these). The actual transfer is usually completed within six weeks of the Decree. For a defined benefit plan QDRO, ask your attorney, CPA, or plan administrator for what to expect.

BUSINESS INTERESTS

If your business interest is a corporation, the transaction may be simply a transfer of stock from one spouse to the other, or from both spouses to one spouse.

Retirement Transfer Checklist:

Directions: Complete the following as it relates to your situation. Do on separate piece of paper if necessary:

Retirement	To Whom/Date
__________	__________
__________	__________
__________	__________

Have your QDRO, or other agreement that divides or transfers the retirement plan, approved by the Plan Administrator before the final decree.

Business Interests Transfer Checklist:

Directions: Complete the following as it relates to your situation. Do on separate piece of paper if necessary:

Business Interest	To Whom/Date
__________	__________
__________	__________
__________	__________

Notice of Change of Name Checklist

Check off each of the following, as you send or show them a conformed copy of your signed decree.

Husband Wife

_____ _____ Employers

_____ _____ Dept. of Motor Vehicles Drivers License Office

_____ _____ Social Security office (name on your Social Security card)

_____ _____ bank

_____ _____ credit union

_____ _____ life insurance

_____ _____ auto insurance

_____ _____ homeowner's insurance

_____ _____ other insurance

_____ _____ mortgage company

_____ _____ credit card companies

_____ _____ doctor

_____ _____ dentist

_____ _____ children's school

_____ _____ day care

_____ _____ pediatrician

The persons relating to your children are especially important if your last name will now be different from your children's.

_____ _____ other

_____ _____

You probably do not need to supply a copy of the signed decree to most of these, but do not forget to notify them.

_____ _____ newspaper and magazine subscriptions

_____ _____ membership organizations

_____ _____ personal correspondents

_____ _____ other

_____ _____

For either a partnership or a sole proprietorship, usually no other transfer of ownership is necessary beyond the statement in your separation agreement. If the business has a trade name, however, notice of the change in ownership must be given to the office of the Secretary of State.

OTHER ASSETS

For other assets, contact the related institution or organization to find out what they require. For pedigreed animals, for example, contact the breed organization. For Avalanche or symphony ticket priorities contact the ticket office. For frequent flyer miles, contact the airline to see how and if they can be transferred.

DEBTS

As a rule, creditors don't need to be notified that you have divorced and that one of you is now responsible for paying the debt, rather than both of you. It's very important, however, to be sure each creditor has the address of the person responsible for paying. If it was a joint debt, you may ask the creditor to remove the non-paying spouse's name from the debt, but the remaining spouse must have sufficient income alone to manage the debt. Remember that the creditor has no obligation to do this. See "Dealing with Debt" in Chapter 7.

Changing Your Name

If one of you asked that a former name be restored as part of your divorce, you will need to follow up to make this a reality. Make many photocopies of your conformed final decree and give or send one to anyone who needs official notice of your new name. Be sure to change this name as a beneficiary on any life insurance or other assets.

Changing Your Address

You probably agreed fairly early in your separation how to divide the mail. You each did, or should now do, a change of address for any mail to each of you individually. But, what about mail, magazines, etc., which come addressed to Mr. and Mrs.? Holiday cards will prove particularly difficult if you are not clear about this. Usually, it is best to agree that one of you will receive the joint mail, sort it, and promptly send or deliver it to the other spouse. If, and only if, it is ok with your children, you might consider sending mail with them. However, the most innocuous mail can sometimes prove explosive—the catalogue from which you disagreed about a large purchase, for example. If you have even the slightest doubt about the volatility of exchanging mail in person, don't. Send it in a large envelope—after leaving a telephone message telling the other spouse that it is coming.

Calendaring Later Events

You may have agreed to some transfers of title or payments, or changes and stair-steps in your parenting, support or maintenance plans, which are to take place on a date or event in the future. For example, you may have agreed to sell the home when the last child emancipates and pay the other spouse his or her interest in the home. You may have anticipated changes in your parenting plan, in the support of your children or each other. Be sure to calendar all of these now and have a system to remind you of the date. If the payout or transfer is tied to the sale of the home, put a note to yourself on the Deed, or Deed of Trust, in the house file or safety deposit box. If an event is tied to the tax year, put a note to yourself in your tax file. If an event is related to a child's age, put a note in that child's file.

Checking Your Credit Ratings

Whether or not you requested your credit ratings during the early stages of your negotiations, you should do this now. Finishing your divorce with an adequate credit rating is a major step toward financial health in the years to come. Make certain that any corrections to your credit reports that you both agreed to have been made, and that your new names are reflected on your current rating along with your correct addresses. See Chapter 4 for more about credit.

Converting from Legal Separation to Dissolution of Marriage

Six months after the court has signed a Decree of Legal Separation, either spouse may ask that it be converted to a Decree of Dissolution of Marriage; or you may do it together. The forms you will need to prepare, the Motion to Convert, JDF 1321 and Order to Convert, JDF 1322 are available from Bradford Publishing. If only one of you is doing the conversion you must notify your spouse when you do this, and prove that you have done so by filling out the Certificate of Service at the bottom of the Motion form. This is another time when it is a good idea to use certified mail. The court will grant the conversion automatically, if there are not other requests with it.

Notice of Change of Address Checklist

Directions: fill in according to your agreement:

Husband will notify the following of his change of address, if any:

Wife will notify the following of her change of address, if any:

We will handle the joint mail as follows:

It is assumed that you will continue the terms of the Separation Agreement which the court approved when you were granted the Decree of Legal Separation. If you want to amend some of these terms, then it is a good idea to treat the changes as a modification, and file a separate Motion to Modify or to specifically include the requested changes in the Motion to Convert. You should file new Sworn Financial Statements and child support worksheets if the changes concern money or children. These modifications may require a hearing unless you have both agreed to them in writing, a stipulation. Any motion filed more than 60 days after your decree will require payment of a motion filing fee to the court.

Making Things Happen: Enforcement

One or both of you may be less than reliable about making promised payments, or find yourself unable or unwilling to follow through with transfers of property or children. You may need to invoke the teeth you included in your agreement or may need to seek outside help in getting things back on track. For example, you may need to change payments to an income assignment. You may need a court order transferring property to you, either to effect your agreement or to make up for something your agreement called for which did not happen.

"Figuratively if not literally, the participants shall come to see themselves as working side by side, attacking the problem, not each other." Roger Fisher and William Ury, *Getting To Yes.*

INTERNAL ENFORCEMENT

If some element of your agreement does not work as planned, look first to the agreement itself. Did you anticipate this event and provide for what was to happen? For example, did you agree that a missed (late) payment of maintenance means a loss of the tax deductibility? Does a mortgage default mean the other spouse may take back the home? Does unpaid support mean the receiving spouse gets access to a bank account? Each of the separation agreement chapters (7-11) contains ideas for teeth and security. Chapter 12 contains sample wordings.

"If it ain't broke, don't fix it."

If you find that your agreement did not anticipate the present malfunction, try to find the least expensive, least damaging means of fixing it. The more of your agreement you leave intact, the more chance there is that the erring spouse will feel able to honor the rest of the provisions, once the immediate difficulty is resolved. As difficult as it may be, try to focus only on the thing which has gone wrong. If you allow your frustrations at the current breakdown to lead you back into all the old resentments, you are apt to forget the harmony you found when you worked together.

Security

If you fear that one of you might not be able to keep the promises made, especially about large ticket items, see if there is some way to "secure" the action. For example, agree to withhold the transfer of title to an asset until the debt against it is paid. Record a Deed of Trust or Promissory Note against a future-paying asset, savings account, or the family home. Sometimes you can sign over title to the person who should receive an asset on the payment of certain money, but hold the signed paperwork in the file with the attorney or mediator until the money is paid.

Income Assignment

An income assignment is a formal arrangement between the employee and his or her employer to withhold a regular amount of money each payday and forward it to the other spouse. This removes the danger of memory lapse, as well as all temptation to spend the money other than in the way you agreed, by effectively making someone else responsible for making the payments for you. Income assignment for child support, or maintenance when combined with child support, was mandatory as of January 1, 1994, with some significant exceptions. You may also, now, do an income assignment for health insurance premiums for children. The forms and procedures for doing this at the time of the decree are in Chapter 12.

Some people set up their own private income assignment by creating an automatic transfer from the bank or credit union account of the paying spouse to an account of the receiving spouse. Check the cost of this beforehand.

If you did not do an income assignment at the time of the decree, because it was not possible then, or you did not think it was necessary, you may start one at any time. You may use the forms and instructions in the previous chapter.

ENFORCEMENT THROUGH THE COURT

The court may stand in the place of the non-cooperative spouse and transfer the property for him or her. The court can open the door for you to collect money owed directly from your spouse's assets and can punish the spouse for non-compliance, in order to make him or her comply.

"Commissioner's Deed" Enforcement of Property Transfers

This procedure contained in Rule 70 of the Colorado Rules of Civil Procedure gives the court the power to act in the place of a defaulting spouse to transfer the title of property that is presently in his or her name. This procedure may be used when you have a signed separation agreement incorporated into your Decree that spells out the agreement for the transfer of property and the spouse with title is unable or unwilling to transfer it.

This procedure is also the only way to transfer property which is in the name of an absent spouse. To set up this procedure, you must have specifically described the titled property in your summons and again in your final order of court. See Chapters 5 and 7 about how and why to do this. If you did not specifically name and request the property you are now seeking title to, in your first papers, you may now find that the court will find it lacks jurisdiction and will not issue this order for you. For this procedure, use JDF 1814 and 1815 available from Bradford Publishing.

Reduction to Judgment

D DEFINITION **Judgment:** A court order which acknowledges and fixes the amount past due, or action not completed, so that the person to whom the money is owed or for whose benefit the activity was to be done, can go directly after the income or assets of the person who failed to pay or act.

When the court incorporates your separation agreement into your decree, it makes your agreement an order of the court. Everything you promised to do in the agreement is now ordered by the court and therefore more than a private contract. If one of you fails to keep any agreement about the payment of money, the court may simply *enter judgment* against you for the unpaid amount. This allows the *moving party* to collect by any means available for collection of judgments, including garnishment and remedies against property.

Any amounts in a judgment can be collected later if the person failing to pay has a positive change of fortune.

Contempt Citation

Every unpaid installment of child support automatically becomes a judgment enforceable by the spouse who was to receive the payment, or by the child being supported.

A contempt citation is based on the premise that anyone who does not comply with a court order *offends the dignity of the Court.* If your separation agreement has been made an order of the court *(incorporated into the decree),* this form of enforcement is available to you. The *aggrieved* person swears in an affidavit that the other has not done what the court said they should do. The court then orders the *offending* party to appear in court to "show cause" why they should not be *held in contempt.* In other words, the affidavit creates a presumption that the non-compliance happened, and the burden of proof is on the person who allegedly did not comply to prove that he or she either did comply or was unable to do so. This is one of the few times in law in which innocence is not presumed. It is a quasi-criminal matter and if the aggrieved party is seeking punitive damages (jail/fine) as well as remedial damages (payment of what is owing), then the accused has a right to an attorney and a hearing.

If the court finds that the accused person did have the ability to keep the court order and did offend the court, then the court can enter fines and/or a jail sentence. In most cases, the court will suspend the jail time, and sometimes the fine, for a period of time to give the non-complying party a chance to comply. Contempt citations can thus come up for review after review, waiting for a promising party to come through with money or action. A contempt citation almost always requires a lawyer to prepare, argue, and defend. They are expensive and not always satisfactory.

Unless you have agreed to, and the court orders, party-to-party payment, all child support and/or maintenance payments are made to the Family Support Registry, which in turn sends the payment on to the other parent. The records of this registry will be all the evidence necessary to establish failure to pay in a contempt action.

If the court finds, at the hearing on contempt, that the person was unable to pay, you can no longer collect the amounts described in the motion for contempt citation by any means, including judgment.

Title IV D Federal Law Enforcement of Child Support and Maintenance, by the County Child Support Enforcement Unit (CSE)

Each County in Colorado has an office of Child Support Enforcement, whose job it is to enforce child support and maintenance when combined with child support orders, within the judicial district as well as between counties, states, and even countries. There is a small fee. This remedy is not swift, due to the volume of cases and the necessity of finding and personally serving the person who is not paying. If despite the friendly manner in which you worked out the child support and/or maintenance, it is not being paid, this is the least expensive means of collecting, especially across state lines. Like contempt citations and garnishments, the technical instructions for this kind of enforcement are beyond the scope of this book. If you need this kind of help, call your County Child Support Enforcement Office.

"The best laid schemes o' mice and men Gang aft a-gley." Robert Burns

CSE actions to collect child support and maintenance result in a judgment and a lien "by operation of law" against any real or personal property of the defaulting spouse. The CSE unit may use these liens to get to income tax refunds and lottery winnings.

CAUTION Collecting unpaid child support is enforceable by the child in question, even after the child emancipates.

Federal Law Enforcement of Parenting Plans: PKPA and UCCJA

There are two Federal laws that help enforce "custody" and "visitation" orders state to state. The Parental Kidnapping Prevention Act (PKPA) makes it a crime to violate a "custody" order, and permits the FBI and other Federal agencies to enforce them.

The Uniform Child Custody Jurisdiction Act (UCCJA) sets guidelines about which state is the best one to make decisions about a given child's "custody". This question comes up if the parents at the time of the divorce live in different states, or if one parent moved to another state after the divorce decree. This law helps prevent *forum shopping* in which a parent moves with the children from state to state until he/she can find one which will give him or her "custody" or will change an old custody order.

These federal laws do refer throughout to "custody". They may be used to enforce orders about children that use alternate words, as the Colorado law does now. Both laws are beyond the scope of this book. If you need enforcement under one of these laws, you should consult an attorney.

Can We Change Our Agreement After the Court Approves It?

Modification: Formally changing a court order.

This section concerns your ability to change your agreement after the court has entered it as an order. The legal term for this is *modification.* If you are agreeing to the changes, you and your ex-spouse have only to write them up and sign them. If you want to have them filed with the court so they become a new court order, you can follow the procedure in Chapter 4 for making an agreement into a court order—but delete the word "temporary" from that example.

If only one of you is asking the court to change the order, there are certain rules—burdens of proof—which you must follow in order for the court to do what you want. These rules differ from one area to another, i.e., from property to parental responsibilities, from child support to maintenance. Reading them now, as you settle the matters involved in your divorce, may help you phrase your agreement for the long run.

MODIFYING YOUR PROPERTY AND DEBT DIVISION

The court cannot change your agreement as to property and debts without the agreement of you and your former spouse. In practice, the only *grounds* for changing a property settlement without agreement is showing that the original separation agreement was obtained by fraud or duress. This is very hard to prove. The court will not modify or set aside your final division of property and debts even if you made mistakes in your interpretation of the tax consequences or made honest mistakes about the value of things or the balances due. It is therefore a good idea to approach the property and debts portion of your agreement as though it will be chiseled in stone.

The court may, if requested by any party or on its own, order all parties to mediate requests for modification of parenting time, child support or maintenance.

MODIFYING PARENTAL RESPONSIBILITIES

The court keeps jurisdiction over children, parenting plans and child support arrangements until your children are emancipated. You always have the right to ask the court to modify your parental responsibilities arrangements. You must, however, have sufficient grounds, unless you both agree in writing to the change.

If you are asking the court to change your parenting plan in a way that substantially changes physical care between the parents, then the statute says the court shall not do so unless a) the parties agree to the change, b) the child has been integrated into the new home with the consent of the other parent, c) the parent with primary physical care substantially relocates or d) the child would be endangered if the present plan continued. Win or lose, once such a request has been made, no other such request may be brought for two years.

If you share physical care and decision-making and ask the court to change your parenting plan, then you only need to show that such a change is in the best interest of the children.

If the "primary" physical care parent wishes to substantially relocate with the children, and the other parent is opposed, then recent law allows the court to consider many things (see sidebar). If you have shared physical care and decision-making, then it takes much more proof that such a change would be in the best interest of the children.

In troublesome parenting situations after the divorce, the court may appoint a *parenting coordinator* to work as a neutral person to assist parents in resolving conflicts in parental responsibilities, including the implementation of court ordered parenting plans. This person has no decision making authority. The court may also, but only with the consent of the parents, appoint a *decision maker* with binding authority to resolve disputes between the parents concerning their minor children, such as parenting time, specific parental decisions, and child support, "in a manner consistent with the substantive intent" of the court order that is being implemented.

MODIFYING CHILD SUPPORT

The Child Support Guideline strongly suggests an annual review of the support amount based on an exchange between the parents of their previous year's tax returns, current income information, and verification of the children's medical insurance coverage and its costs. If you do not want to do this annually, you may say in your agreement that you will review incomes for the purpose of

What if I Wish to Move Away

Colorado courts must consider several things if the parent with primary physical care is seeking to relocate with the child to a residence that "substantially changes the geographical ties between the child and the other party."

1. The reasons for relocation.
2. The reasons for opposition.
3. The history and quality of each parent's relationship with the child.
4. Educational opportunities of both locations.
5. Extended family at both locations.
6. Advantages of remaining with the present primary caregiver.
7. The impact of the move on the child.
8. A new, reasonable parenting time schedule is possible.
9. Any other factors in the best interest of the child.

Another Note About Privacy

If you agree to exchange income tax returns annually to re-evaluate child support, then you will be likely to know a great deal more about your former spouse's new spouse's income than you or that spouse may be comfortable with. You might want to agree instead that if either of you re-marries, you will exchange W-2's, 1099's, Schedule C's (business profit & loss), K-1's, rental profit and loss statements, and Corporate tax returns, all concerning income and businesses of your former spouse only.

adjusting child support at the request of either one of you. This means you will always cooperate; neither of you can say no.

Fill in your new incomes on a new child support worksheet. If the bottom line amount (final *suggested support amount*) changes by more than 10%, either direction, then you *must* make the change. The easiest way is to file the new worksheet with the court, along with current financial affidavits and your signed agreement to pay and accept the new amount.

If you need a modification of your child support agreement, and have not worked out the terms ahead of time, you will need *grounds* to ask the court to change your agreement. The grounds for changing the support amount are "a change of circumstance so substantial and continuing" as to make the original agreement "unfair." The fact that the change(s) which have occurred change the bottom line on the same child support worksheet by more than 10% (up or down) is sufficient grounds.

If you change the physical care parenting plan for your children you will almost always need to change the child support accordingly—sometimes changing which worksheet you use. You can still do the kind of calculations suggested in Chapter 7 to avoid having the Child Support Guideline force you into an unworkable amount for either the paying or receiving parent.

MODIFYING MAINTENANCE

Modifying or changing maintenance generates more horror stories among lawyers and divorcing people than probably any other aspect of divorce. The misunderstandings are many, and the consequences sometimes unforeseen and unpleasant. It is vital that you review the chapters on maintenance and taxes if you are thinking of modifying your maintenance plan, or the terms of an old maintenance order.

The grounds for modifying maintenance in front of a court are that there have been "changed circumstances that are substantial and continuing" such that the original agreement or order as to maintenance is now "unfair." Case law has tightened that criteria further to require that the change not be voluntary or in the control of the person seeking the change (quit job, for example). The ability to modify a maintenance order is usually defined by the type of maintenance. See Chapter 10 for a complete discussion.

If maintenance is for a fixed amount for a fixed period of time, or a lump sum amount—any plan in which the total amount to be paid can be calculated in advance—then that maintenance is said to be *contractual* or *in gross* and is presumed to be not modifiable. If you want your fixed-term maintenance plan to be modifiable under certain circumstances, you must say so clearly in your agreement.

If you and your spouse waived your right to maintenance in your original agreement, then there is probably no hope of doing it now—even if you both agree. The IRS definition of maintenance requires that it be *under* or *incident to a divorce or separation instrument.* That is generally accepted to mean that it must be agreed to or at least contemplated at the time of the decree. If you want to leave the door open for maintenance at a later date (for a spouse with a chronic illness in remission or an injury which is not completely healed, for example) then that spouse must not waive maintenance at the final decree, and you should state in your agreement the condition which you agree might give rise to the need for maintenance in the future.

"Don't let yesterday use up too much of today." Cherokee proverb

Notes:

ONWARD

If you have used this Guidebook well, you have brought yourself and your family through a difficult transition, and saved a significant amount of money. If you have children, you have learned, or are learning, how to work together as parents without having to relate to each other as spouses.

You can take pride in how you have done your divorce or separation, and be pleased that you have completed the process without accumulating more baggage than you already had, and perhaps even gotten rid of some.

May your near and distant futures be better for your choices about how to complete a friendly divorce.

We welcome your comments. Please send them to:

Bradford Publishing Company
1743 Wazee Street
Denver, Colorado 80202
(303) 292-2590
www.bradfordpublishing.com

✧

M. Arden Hauer
Center for Non-Adversarial Divorce
603 Point Park Drive
Suite 120
Golden, CO 80401
(303) 526-7749
www.friendlydivorce.com

✧

BIBLIOGRAPHY

I. Books About the Divorce Process

BETWEEN LOVE AND HATE: A Guide to Civilized Divorce. Lois Gold. Plenum Publishing, 1992. A "road map for sane and civilized divorce" by a therapist/mediator. How to negotiate with your ex even in the difficult times after the final decree.

THE CASE AGAINST DIVORCE. Diane Medved. Ivy Books, 1990. Things to consider and reconsider before giving up on your marriage.

DANCING WITH LAWYERS: How to Take Charge and Get Results. Nicholas Carroll. Royce Baker Publishing, 1992, Guide to hiring a lawyer without giving up control of your life.

THE DIVORCE BOOK. Matthew McKay, Peter D. Rogers, Joan Blades, and Richard Gosse. MJF Books, 2001. Overview of the divorce process, including the emotional, legal and relationship divorces. Written by a lawyer and several mental health experts.

GETTING APART TOGETHER: The Couple's Guide to a Fair Divorce or Separation. Martin A. Kranitz. Impact Publishers, 2000. How to use mediation and other non-adversarial routes.

GETTING DIVORCED WITHOUT RUINING YOUR LIFE. Sam Margulies. Fireside Books, Simon and Schuster, 2001. Advice to divorcing spouses about negotiating a wise and workable settlement.

THE GOOD DIVORCE: Keeping Your Family Together When Your Marriage Comes Apart, Constance R. Ahrons, PhD. Quill, 1998. Advocates and anticipates a cultural shift from thinking of divorce as a failure, to thinking of divorce as a natural change of life. Think not of divorced or separated families, but of whole families with two nucleii – the bi-nuclear family. Shows how such a change in thinking can help children, especially, to heal.

A GUIDE TO DIVORCE MEDIATION: How to Reach a Fair, Legal Settlement at a Fraction of the Cost. Gary J. Friedman. Workman Publishing, 1993. Story-filled guide to optimum use of mediation.

SECOND CHANCES: Men, Women and Children a Decade After Divorce. Judith Wallerstein and Sandra Blakeslee. Mariner Books, 1996. Results of 10 and 15 year studies of California families following divorce, showing long-term effect of divorce on the children.

WOMAN'S GUIDE TO DIVORCE AND DECISION-MAKING: A Supportive Workbook for Women Facing the Process of Divorce. Christina Robertson. Fireside Books, Simon and Schuster, 1989. Workbook which teaches the decision-making process through examples of decisions which are encountered at divorce.

YOUR DIVORCE ADVISOR: A Lawyer and a Psychologist Guide You Through the Legal and Emotional Landscape of Divorce. Diana Mercer, JD and Marsha Kline Pruett, PhD, MSL. Simon & Schuster, Inc. (Fireside), 2001. A book about legal strategy to protect your assets without destroying your family, including anticipating the emotional repercussions of your decisions.

COLORADO REVISED STATUTES

10-16-104	Health insurance for children
14-2-101 – 113	Uniform Marriage Act
14-2-201 – 210	Rights of married women
14-4-101 – 107	Domestic abuse
14-5-101 – 1007	Uniform Interstate Family Support Act
14-6-101 – 113	Non-support in this state
14-7-101 – 105	Support of children in custody of State
14-10-101 – 133	Dissolution of Marriage
14-10-115	Child Support Guidelines and Schedule
14-10.5-101 – 104	Parenting time enforcement
14-11-101	Out-of-state divorces, how handled
14-12-101 – 106	Marriage counseling through Court
14-13-101 – 403	Uniform Child Custody Jurisdiction Act: State to state custody jurisdiction
14-14-101 – 113	Child support enforcement procedures – income assignments, garnishment, and other remedies

II. Books About Your Other Divorces — Communication and Relationships

CONSCIOUS DIVORCE: Ending a Marriage with Integrity. Susan Allison. Three Rivers Press/Random House, 2001. A practical and spiritual guide for moving on.

DANCE OF ANGER. Harriet Lerner. Quill, 1997. Helpful guide to understanding anger and other emotions in close relationships.

THE DANCE OF INTIMACY: A Woman's Guide to Courageous Acts of Change in Key Relationships. Harriet Lerner. Perennial, 1990. A significant writing about "making responsible and lasting changes that enhance our capacity for genuine closeness *over the long haul.*"

FIGHTING FOR YOUR MARRIAGE: Positive Steps for Preventing Divorce And Preserving a Lasting Love. Howard Markman, Scott Stanley and Susan L. Blumberg. Jossey-Bass, 2001. Blueprint for how to celebrate and use differences between spouses to enable problem-solving and working communication. Since these are often the marriage-busting problems, this book and *We Can Work It Out* may well save many, many marriages.

FOR BETTER OR WORSE: Divorce Reconsidered. E. Mavis Hetherington and John Kelly. W. W. Norton, 2003. A comprehensive study of the impact of divorce on the life span of each family member, showing positive results and that the pathway out of divorce can be one of healing and fulfillment.

FROM CONFLICT TO RESOLUTION: Skills and Strategies for Individual, Couple, and Family Therapy. Susan M. Heitler. Norton, 1993. Negotiation and dispute resolution and how to do them. Written for professionals.

GETTING THE LOVE YOU WANT: A Guide for Couples. Harville Hendrix. Owl Books, 2001. Practical, encouraging advice about how to help yourself find fulfillment within a relationship.

GROWING THROUGH DIVORCE. Jim Smoke. Harvest House Publishers, 1995. Examples of how to learn from the ending of this relationship.

HOW TO SURVIVE THE LOSS OF A LOVE. Melba Colgrove, Ph.D., Harold H. Bloomfield, M.D., and Peter McWilliams. Prelude Press, 1993. Tips for negotiating through the grief process.

LEARNING FROM DIVORCE; How to Take Responsibility, Stop the Blame, and Move On! Christina A. Coates, JD, and E. Robert LaCrosse, PhD. Jossey-Bass, 2003. A practical book to help you rid yourself of negative feelings of guilt and worry and replace them with positive feelings of growth and hope.

LEARNING TO LEAVE: A Woman's Guide. Lynette Triere and Richard Peacock. Warner Books, 1993. All about leaving: making the decision, your emotions, timing, crisis planning, developing a backup system, money, jobs, children, and more.

(THE) MAGIC OF CONFLICT: Turning a Life of Work Into a Work of Art. Thomas F. Crum. Touchstone, 1998. Wise, how-to book about how to use conflict – physical, emotional, or intellectual – to progress and grow.

REBUILDING: WHEN YOUR RELATIONSHIP ENDS: The Divorce Process Rebuilding Blocks. Bruce Fisher. Impact Publishers, 1999. Book and workbook from the Fisher Divorce Seminar. For the spouse who is ready to begin looking past the end of this relationship.

SURVIVING THE BREAKUP: How Children and Parents Cope With Divorce. Judith S. Wallerstein and Joan Berlin Kelly. Basic Books, 1996. An authoritative study about how children and parents cope with divorce.

TOO GOOD TO LEAVE, TOO BAD TO STAY: A Step-by-Step Guide to Helping You Decide Whether to Stay In or Get Out of Your Relationship. Mira Kirshenbaum. Penguin (Plume) 1997. How to diagnose your unique situation with self-analysis and questions that help you gain insight into the heart of your problems.

YOU JUST DON'T UNDERSTAND: Women and Men in Conversation. Deborah Tannen. Perennial, 2001. Witty and pungent illustrations of how gender differences in communication styles may affect the success of relationships.

III. Books About Children and Divorce

101 WAYS TO BE A LONG-DISTANCE SUPER-DAD... OR MOM, TOO! George Newman. R & E Publishers, 1996. Handy, helpful, creative ideas for maintaining a close relationship with your children from miles away.

CAUGHT IN THE MIDDLE: Protecting the Children of High-Conflict Divorce. Carla B. Garrity and Mitchell A. Baris. Jossey-Bass, 1997. Readable discussion of the on-going effect of high-conflict divorce on children. Suggests the role of a Parenting Coordinator to help the family after the decree.

THE CO-PARENTING SURVIVAL GUIDE: Letting go of Conflict after a Divorce. Elizabeth S. Thayer, Ph.D., and Jeffrey Zimmerman, Ph.D. New Harbinger, 2001. Tips for navigating hostility and conflict ion communication, visitation (parenting time), children's activities, holidays, and new partners.

CUSTODY CHAOS, PERSONAL PEACE: Sharing Custody With an Ex Who Drives You Crazy. Jeffrey P. Wittman, Ph.D. Penguin Putnam Inc. (Perigree), 2001. A common-sense guide for reclaiming your life, relating to a difficult ex while raising children from two homes, and helping your children deal with it.

DIVORCED DAD'S SURVIVAL BOOK: How to Stay Connected With Your Kids. David Knox, PhD, with Kermit Leggett. Perseus Books Group, 2000. Offers guidance and plant to help fathers remain positive, involved parents, and honestly evaluate their own capabilities as fathers and ex-spouses.

EX-ETIQUETTE FOR PARENTS: Good Behavior After a Divorce or Separation. Jann Blackstone-Ford, M.A., and Sharyl Jupe. Chicago Review Press, 2004. Offers "Basic," "Intermediate," and "Advanced" ex-etiquette with good advice and helpful ideas for getting along and raising your family after divorce.

GROWING UP WITH DIVORCE: Helping Your Child Avoid Immediate and Later Emotional Problems. Neil Kalter. Ballantine Books, 1991. Compassionate and helpful discussion of the states of the divorce process for children at each developmental age.

WHAT ABOUT THE KIDS? RAISING YOUR CHILDREN BEFORE, DURING, AND AFTER DIVORCE, 2004. Judith S. Wallerstein, PhD. Comprehensive guide to easing the impact of divorce on your children.

HELPING YOUR KIDS COPE WITH DIVORCE THE SANDCASTLES WAY. M. Gary Neuman, LMHC with Patricia Romanowski. Random House (Times Books) 1998. A warm, empathetic guide to help you help your children grow and strengthen through the divorce process, including hundreds of pieces of artwork from children of divorce to help you appreciate how children perceive the experience.

JOINT CUSTODY WITH A JERK: Raising a Child With an Uncooperative Ex. Julie A. Ross, MA, and Judy Corcoran. St. Martin's Press, 1996. Describes examples of common problems and offers communication techniques to help deal with your ex, and teaches you to see your role in these sticky situations.

MOM'S HOUSE, DAD'S HOUSE: Making Shared Custody Work. Isolina Ricci. Fireside, 1997. Self-help guide for crafting a shared parenting plan, with sample language, examples and practical hints.

PARENTING AFTER DIVORCE: A Guide to Resolving Conflicts and Meeting Your Children's Needs. Philip M. Stahl, Ph.D. Impact Publishers.

TALKING ABOUT DIVORCE AND SEPARATION: A Dialogue Between Parent and Child. Earl A. Grollman. Children of Separation and Divorce Center, Inc., 1999. Family activity book based on pictures to which participants may react. Adult guide to what children's reactions mean.

THE TRUTH ABOUT CHILDREN AND DIVORCE: Dealing With the Emotions so You and Your Children Can Thrive. Robert E. Emery, Ph.D. New and helpful research and down to earth advice on putting your children first, setting new relationship boundaries with your spouse, and the extraordinary benefits to your family of mediation over going through the court.

IV. Books for Children

AT DADDY'S ON SATURDAYS. Linda W. Girard. Albert, Whitman and Company, 1991. Picture book about a young child with visitation in father's home.

BOYS AND GIRLS BOOK ABOUT DIVORCE. Richard Gardner. Bantam Books, 1985. Classic discussions of traditional custody with mother and father visiting. Helpful. See also Dr. Gardner's other books in this series: *PARENTS BOOK ABOUT DIVORCE, 1977. BOYS AND GIRLS BOOK ABOUT ONE-PARENT FAMILIES. BOYS AND GIRLS BOOK ABOUT STEP-FAMILIES.*

DADDY'S ROOMMATE. Michael Wilhoite. Alyson Publications, 1991. Story of school age boy visiting with father and father's gay lover.

DINOSAUR'S DIVORCE: A Guide for Changing Families. Laurence Krasney Brown and Marc Tolon Brown. Little Brown and Co., 1986. THE book for young children facing divorce. Picture book of likely situations, most of those encountered after the divorce.

DIVORCE IS NOT THE END OF THE WORLD: Zoe's and Evan's Coping Guide for Kids. Zoe and Evan Stern, with a little help from their mom Ellen Sue Stern. Tricycle Press, 1997. A teenage brother and sister whose parents are divorced discuss topics relating to this situation, respond to letters from other children, and offer tips based on their experience. Includes insights from their mother. Ages 9-12.

HEATHER HAS TWO MOMMIES. Leslea Newman. Alyson Publications, 2009. Story of school age girl who lives with her mother and mother's lesbian lover.

HOW IT FEELS WHEN PARENTS DIVORCE. Jill Krementz. Alfred A. Knopf, 1988. Collection of their own stories by kids 4-6 describing their parents' divorces. Some happy, some difficult. All enlightening.

I DON'T WANT TO TALK ABOUT IT. Jeanie Franz Ransom, illustrated by Kathryn Kunz Finney. Uses delightful animal metaphors and beautiful illustrations to assure that lives may change, but the love of families will persist. Ages 4-8.

IT'S NOT THE END OF THE WORLD. Judy Blume. Yearling, 1986. Young adult novel about early adolescent girl who tries to cope with and prevent her parents' divorce. Re-printed recently due to popular demand.

IT'S NOT YOUR FAULT, KOKO BEAR, A Read-Together Book for Parents and Young Children during Divorce. Vicki Lansky, illustrated by Jane Prince. Book Peddlers, 1998. Koko Bear can help both children and parents during divorce. Ages 4-8.

TWO HOMES. Claire Masurel and Kady Macdonald Denton. Candlewick Press, 2001. A comforting story that reassures that even in the face of divorce there can be warmth and love.

WHAT IN THE WORLD DO YOU DO WHEN YOUR PARENTS DIVORCE?: A Survival guide for Kids. Kent Winchester and Roberta Beyer, Free Spirit Publishing, 2001. A question and answer book for kids of all ages, with wisdom and sound explanations.

WHY ARE WE GETTING A DIVORCE? Peter Mayle, illustrated by Arthur Robins. This book tackles such topics as "Why Your Parents Got Married", "Parents Need All the Help They Can Get", and "At Last the Good News" with insight and humor.

V. Books About Financial Considerations and Tax at Divorce

BUYING AND SELLING A BUSINESS: A Step by Step Guide. Robert F. Klueger. John Wiley and Sons, Inc., 1988. Steps for buying a business and one good chapter on preparing a business for sale.

DIVORCE AND MONEY: How to Make the Best Financial Decisions During Divorce. Violet Woodhouse and Victoria Felton-Collins, with M.C. Blakeman. Nolo Press, 1992, revised edition Dec. 1993. Workbook about all the financial issues in divorce. Updated regularly.

SURVIVAL MANUAL FOR WOMEN IN DIVORCE, 2000. *SURVIVAL MANUAL FOR MEN IN DIVORCE,* 1994. Edwin Schilling III and Carol Ann Wilson. Kendall Hunt Publishing. Answers to the most-asked, or should-be- most-asked, questions about financial issues at divorce.

THE WALL STREET JOURNAL GUIDE TO UNDERSTANDING PERSONAL FINANCE. Kenneth M. Morris and Alan M. Siegel. Fireside, 2000. Visually rich illustrated guide to all the financial terms you never understood, such as what is a mortgage, how does credit work, and how to read a credit report.

IRS Publications, updated annually, which you may find at your public library, or order directly from the IRS for free:

#504: Tax information for Divorced or Separated Individuals
#523: Tax information on selling your home.
#551: Basis of assets
#590: Individual Retirement Arrangements (IRA's)

Internal Revenue CODE, selected sections

Sec. 2 Definition of tax rates (head of household, married or single)
Sec. 21 Child care credit defined
Sec. 71 Alimony defined
Sec. 121 One-time capital gains exclusions at 55
Sec. 125 Cafeteria plans
Sec. 151 Personal exemptions defined
Sec. 152 Dependent defined
Sec. 1034 Roll over of gain on sale of principal residence
Sec. 1041 Transfers of property in divorce not taxes
Sec. 1221–1223 Capital Gain defined
Sec. 7703 Determination of marital status for filing

Your public library will have copies of the Internal Revenue Code, many with explanatory text and interpretive cases.

There are many tax workbooks published each year which highlight any changes in the Code during the previous year, for both consumers and tax professionals.

V. Online Subscription

BRADFORMS ONLINE, FAMILY LAW GROUP ONLINE SUBSCRIPTION. Bradford Publishing Company, 2012 Denver, CO. This online subscription contains the forms for dissolution of marriage, legal separation, child support and modification in Word® and WordPerfect®. The financial statements include the ability to calculate totals. The child support worksheets utilize Excel® and QuattroPro® spreadsheets to automatically calculate child support and create the appropriate Worksheet. Licensed annually and designed for attorneys.

APPENDIX A: FORMS SHOWN IN THE BOOK

APPENDIX B: CHECKLISTS

APPENDIX C: EXAMPLES

APPENDIX D: COLORADO DISTRICT COURTS

APPENDIX E: DESIGNATED BENEFICIARY FORMS

County	Court	St Address	PO Box	City	CO	Zip
Adams	Adams County Justice Center	1100 Judicial Center Dr		Brighton	CO	80601
Alamosa	Alamosa County Courthouse	702 4th St		Alamosa	CO	81101
Arapahoe	Arapahoe County Justice Center	7325 South Potomac St		Centennial	CO	80112
Arapahoe	Arapahoe County Center	1790 West Littleton Blvd		Littleton	CO	80120
Archuleta	Archuleta County Court	449 San Juan St	P.O. Box 148	Pagosa Springs	CO	81147
Baca	Baca Combined Court	741 Main St		Springfield	CO	81073
Bent	Bent Combined Court	725 Bent Ave		Las Animas	CO	81054
Boulder Combined	Boulder Combined	1035 Kimbark		Longmont	CO	80501
Boulder	Boulder County Justice Center	1777 Sixth St	P.O. Box 4249	Boulder	CO	80306
Broomfield	Broomfield Combined Court	17 Des Combes Dr		Broomfield	CO	80020
Chaffee	Chaffee Combined Court	142 Crestone	P.O. Box 279	Salida	CO	81201
Cheyenne	Cheyenne County Combined Court	51 S 1st St, 2nd Fl	P.O. Box 696	Cheyenne Wells	CO	80810
Clear Creek	Clear Creek Combined Court	405 Argentine	P.O. Box 367	Georgetown	CO	80444
Conejos	Conejos County Courthouse	6683 County Rd 13	P.O. Box 128	Conejos	CO	81129
Costilla	Costilla County Court Complex	304 Main St	P.O. Box 301	San Luis	CO	81152
Crowley	Crowley Combined Court	110 East 6th St, Rm 303		Ordway	CO	81063
Custer	Custer Combined Court	205 S. 6th St	P.O. Box 60	Westcliffe	CO	81252
Delta	Delta Combined Court	501 Palmer, Rm 338		Delta	CO	81416
Denver District	Denver City & County Building	1437 Bannock St		Denver	CO	80202
Denver Probate	Denver City & County Building	1437 Bannock St		Denver	CO	80202
Delores Combined	Delores Combined Court	409 N. Main		Dove Creek	CO	81324
Douglas	Douglas County Justice Center	4000 Justice Way Rm 2009		Castle Rock	CO	80109
Eagle	Eagle Combined Court	885 Chambers Ave	P.O. Box 597	Eagle	CO	81631
El Paso	El Paso County Judicial Building	270 South Tejon		Colorado Springs	CO	80901
Elbert	Elbert Combined Court	751 Ute St	P.O. Box 232	Kiowa	CO	80117
Fremont	Fremont Combined Court	136 Justice Center Rd, Rm 103		Canon City	CO	81212
Garfield	Garfield Combined Court	109 8th St, Ste 104		Glenwood Springs	CO	81601
Gilpin	Gilpin Combined Court	2960 Dory Hill Rd, Ste 200		Blackhawk	CO	80422
Grand	Grand Combined Court	307 Moffat Ave	P.O. Box 192	Hot Sulphur Springs	CO	80451
Gunnison	Gunnison Combined Court	200 E. Virginia Ave		Gunnison	CO	81230
Hinsdale	Hinsdale Combined Court	317 Henson St	P.O. Box 245	Lake City	CO	81235
Huerfano	Huerfano County Courthouse	401 Main St, Ste 304		Walsenburg	CO	81089
Jackson	Jackson Combined Court	396 Lafover St	P.O. Box 308	Walden	CO	80480
Jefferson	Jefferson Combined Court	100 Jefferson County Pkwy		Golden	CO	80401
Kiowa	Kiowa Combined Court	1305 Goff St	P.O. Box 353	Eads	CO	81036
Kit Carson	Kit Carson Combined Court	251 16th St		Burlington	CO	80807
La Plata	La Plata Combined Court	1060 Second Ave		Durango	CO	81301
Lake	Lake Combined Court	505 Harrison Ave	P.O. Box 55	Leadville	CO	81461
Larimer	Larimer County Justice Center	201 La Porte Ave, Ste 100		Fort Collins	CO	80521
Las Animas	Las Animas County Courthouse	200 East First St, Rm 304		Trinidad	CO	81082
Lincoln	Lincoln Combined Court	103 Third Ave	P.O. Box 128	Hugo	CO	80821
Logan	Logan County Justice Center	110 N Riverview Rd	P.O. Box 71	Sterling	CO	80751
Mesa	Mesa County Justice Center	125 N Spruce	P.O. Box 20,000	Grand Junction	CO	81501
Mineral	Mineral County Courthouse	1201 N Main St	P.O. Box 337	Creede	CO	81130
Moffat	Moffat Combined Court	221 West Victory Wy, Ste 300		Craig	CO	81625
Montezuma	Montezuma District Court	109 W. Main, Rm 210		Cortez	CO	81321
Montrose	Montrose Combined Court	1200 N. Grand Ave		Montrose	CO	81401
Morgan	Morgan County Justice Center	400 Warner	P.O. Box 695	Fort Morgan	CO	80701
Otero	Otero Combined Court	13 West Third St		La Junta	CO	81050
Ouray	Ouray Combined Court	541 S. 4th St		Ouray	CO	81427
Park	Park Combined Court	300 Fourth St	P.O. Box 190	Fairplay	CO	80440
Phillips	Phillips Combined Court	221 South Interocean Ave		Holyoke	CO	80734
Pitkin	Pitkin Combined Court	506 E. Main, Ste 300		Aspen	CO	81611
Prowers	Prowers Combined Court	301 South Main, Ste 300		Lamar	CO	81052
Pueblo	Pueblo County Judicial Building	320 West 10th St		Pueblo	CO	81003
Rio Blanco	Rio Blanco Combined Court	555 Main St		Meeker	CO	81641
Rio Grande	Rio Grande County Courthouse	925 6th St, Rm 204		Del Norte	CO	81132
Routt	Routt Combined Court	1955 Shield Dr	P.O. Box 773117	Steamboat Springs	CO	80477
Saguache	Saguache County Courthouse	501 Christy Ave	P.O. Box 197	Saguache	CO	81149
San Juan	San Juan County Court	1557 Greene St	P.O. Box 900	Silverton	CO	81433
San Miguel	San Miguel Combined Court	305 W. Colorado Ave	P.O. Box 919	Telluride	CO	81435
Sedgwick	Sedgwick Combined Court	Third and Pine		Julesburg	CO	80737
Summit	Summit Combined Court	501 N. Park Ave	P.O. Box 269	Breckenridge	CO	80424
Teller	County Courthouse	101 West Bennett Ave	P.O. Box 997	Cripple Creek	CO	80813
Washington	Washington County Justice Center	26861 Highway 34		Akron	CO	80720
Weld	Weld County Combined Court	901 9th Ave	P.O. Box 2038	Greeley	CO	80632
Yuma	Yuma Combined Court	310 Ash St	P.O. Box 347	Wray	CO	80758

DESIGNATED BENEFICIARY AGREEMENT

DISCLAIMER

Warning: While this document may indicate your wishes, certain additional documents may be needed to protect these rights.

This designated beneficiary agreement is operative in the absence of other estate planning documents and will be superseded and set aside to the extent it conflicts with valid instruments such as a will, power of attorney, or beneficiary designation on an insurance policy or pension plan. This designated beneficiary agreement is superseded by such other documents and does not cause any changes to be made to those documents or designations. The parties understand that executing and signing this agreement is not sufficient to designate the other party for purposes of any insurance policy, pension plan, payable upon death designation or manner in which title to property is held and that additional action will be required to make or change such designations. The parties understand that this designated beneficiary agreement may be one component of estate planning instructions and that they are encouraged to consult an attorney to ensure their estate planning wishes are accomplished.

We, ____

______________________________, (insert full name and address) referred to as Party A,

and ____

______________________________, (insert full name and address) referred to as Party B,

hereby designate each other as the other's designated beneficiary with the following rights and protections, granted or withheld as indicated by our initials:

TO GRANT ONE OR MORE OF THE RIGHTS OR PROTECTIONS SPECIFIED IN THIS FORM, INITIAL THE LINE TO THE LEFT OF EACH RIGHT OR PROTECTION YOU ARE GRANTING. TO WITHHOLD A RIGHT OR PROTECTION, INITIAL THE LINE TO THE RIGHT OF EACH RIGHT OR PROTECTION YOU ARE WITHHOLDING.

TO GRANT A RIGHT OR PROTECTION INITIAL			TO WITHHOLD A RIGHT OR PROTECTION INITIAL	
Party A	Party B		Party A	Party B
________	________	The right to acquire, hold title to, own jointly, or transfer inter vivos or at death real or personal property as a joint tenant with me with right of survivorship or as a tenant in common with me;	________	________

TO GRANT A RIGHT OR PROTECTION INITIAL			TO WITHHOLD A RIGHT OR PROTECTION INITIAL	
Party A	Party B		Party A	Party B
________	________	The right to be designated by me as a beneficiary, payee, or owner as a trustee named in an inter vivos or testamentary trust for the purposes of a nonprobate transfer on death;	________	________
________	________	The right to be designated by me as a beneficiary and recognized as a dependent in an insurance policy for life insurance;	________	________
________	________	The right to be designated by me as a beneficiary and recognized as a dependent in a health insurance policy if my employer elects to provide health insurance coverage for designated beneficiaries;	________	________
________	________	The right to be designated by me as a beneficiary in a retirement or pension plan;	________	________
________	________	The right to petition for and have priority for appointment as a conservator, guardian, or personal representative for me;	________	________
________	________	The right to visit me in a hospital, nursing home, hospice, or similar health care facility in which a party to a designated beneficiary agreement resides or is receiving care;	________	________
________	________	The right to initiate a formal complaint regarding alleged violations of my rights as a nursing home patient as provided in Section 25-1-120, Colorado Revised Statutes;	________	________
________	________	The right to act as a proxy decision-maker or surrogate decision-maker to make medical care decisions for me pursuant to Section 15-18.5-103 or 15-18.5-104, Colorado Revised Statutes;	________	________
________	________	The right to notice of the withholding or withdrawal of life-sustaining procedures for me pursuant to Section 15-18-107, Colorado Revised Statutes;	________	________
________	________	The right to challenge the validity of a declaration as to medical or surgical treatment of me pursuant to Section 15-18-108, Colorado Revised Statutes;	________	________
________	________	The right to act as my agent to make, revoke, or object to anatomical gifts involving my person pursuant to the "Revised Uniform Anatomical Gift Act", Part 1 of Article 34 of Title 12, Colorado Revised Statutes;	________	________

TO GRANT A RIGHT OR PROTECTION INITIAL			TO WITHHOLD A RIGHT OR PROTECTION INITIAL	
Party A	Party B		Party A	Party B
________	________	The right to inherit real or personal property from me through intestate succession;	________	________
________	________	The right to have standing to receive benefits pursuant to the "Workers' Compensation Act of Colorado", Article 40 of Title 8, Colorado Revised Statutes, in the event of my death on the job;	________	________
________	________	The right to have standing to sue for wrongful death in the event of my death; and	________	________
________	________	The right to direct the disposition of my last remains pursuant to Article 19 of Title 15, Colorado Revised Statutes.	________	________

THIS DESIGNATED BENEFICIARY AGREEMENT IS EFFECTIVE WHEN RECEIVED FOR RECORDING BY THE COUNTY CLERK AND RECORDER OF THE COUNTY IN WHICH ONE OF THE DESIGNATED BENEFICIARIES RESIDES. THIS DESIGNATED BENEFICIARY AGREEMENT WILL CONTINUE IN EFFECT UNTIL ONE OF THE DESIGNATED BENEFICIARIES REVOKES THIS AGREEMENT BY RECORDING A REVOCATION OF DESIGNATED BENEFICIARY FORM WITH THE COUNTY CLERK AND RECORDER OF THE COUNTY IN WHICH THIS AGREEMENT WAS RECORDED OR UNTIL THIS AGREEMENT IS SUPERSEDED IN PART OR IN WHOLE BY A SUPERSEDING LEGAL DOCUMENT.

________________________________ ________________________________

Signature of Designated Beneficiary Signature of Designated Beneficiary

State of Colorado

County of ________________

This document was acknowledged before me on __________________________ (date) by _________

____.

My commission expires ________________

[seal]

____

Notary Public

REVOCATION OF DESIGNATED BENEFICIARY AGREEMENT

I ______________________________ (insert your full name), reside at ______________________________ (insert your current address) and I entered into a designated beneficiary agreement on ______________ (insert the date) with the following person ______________________________ (insert the other person's name) whose last known address is ______________________________ in which I designated such person as a designated beneficiary. This designated beneficiary agreement was recorded on ______________ (insert the date) in the County of ______________. The indexing file number of the designated beneficiary agreement is ______________. I hereby revoke that designated beneficiary agreement, effective on the date and time that this revocation is received for recording by the clerk and recorder of ______________ County.

______________________ Date

______________________ Name

State of Colorado
County of ______________

This document was subscribed, sworn to, and acknowledged before me on ______________ (date) by ______________________________.

My commission expires ______________

[seal]

____
Notary Public

This revocation of beneficiary agreement was recorded in my office on ______________, ______, at ________ o'clock, and, pursuant to Section 15-22-111, Colorado Revised Statutes, I mailed a copy of this revocation of beneficiary agreement to ______________________________ at the address contained in this revocation of beneficiary agreement.

Clerk and Recorder of ______________ County

By: ______________________

No. 450R. REVOCATION OF DESIGNATED BENEFICIARY AGREEMENT

Bradford Publishing, 1743 Wazee St., Denver, CO 80202 — (303) 292-2590 — www.bradfordpublishing.com

INDEX

D

E

M

N